Fundamentals of
Management

SELECTED READINGS

Fundamentals of Management
SELECTED READINGS

Edited by

JAMES H. DONNELLY, JR.

Professor
Department of Business Administration
University of Kentucky

JAMES L. GIBSON

Professor
Department of Business Administration
University of Kentucky

JOHN M. IVANCEVICH

Professor
Department of Organizational Behavior
and Management
University of Houston

Revised Edition   1975

BUSINESS PUBLICATIONS, INC.   Dallas, Texas   75231
Irwin-Dorsey International, London, England   WC2H 9NJ
Irwin-Dorsey Limited, Georgetown, Ontario   L7G 4B3

© BUSINESS PUBLICATIONS, INC., 1971 and 1975

Revised Edition

First Printing, March 1975

ISBN 0-256-01706-9
Library of Congress Catalog Card No. 74-25811
Printed in the United States of America

Preface

Each year the field of management is becoming more mature and influential in organizations. This increased maturity is a result of more research and of more communication between practitioners, researchers, and scholars. The greater influence in organizations has occurred because of the need to improve effectiveness. Practitioners continue to search the literature for better techniques and guidelines for managing individuals, groups, and total organizational systems. As a result of the increased maturity and influence of the field of management the literature covers a wide range of topics and is found in journals, books, and magazines, and in speeches.

The early management writers were practitioners who attempted to describe their experiences in case analysis format, from which they generalized to broad management principles. These writers were guided by pragmatic considerations, focusing on improving overall employee efficiency. Recently many writers have attempted to concentrate on scientifically validating management principles, processes, and models. These writers, by using scientific methods, attempt to make no value judgments concerning managerial practice.

The early and contemporary writings are often placed in a specific category for students, practitioners, and scholars. Some writers are considered pragmatic, others mathematically oriented, and still others scientific. The editors of this revised edition believe that order can be brought to the field of management and its existing literature by employing a three-way classification framework. The framework identifies three schools of management: the *Classical School,* the *Behavioral School,* and the *Management Science School.* We believe that to accept any one of these schools as providing the complete set of answers and guidelines to real-life management problems is incomplete. The ideas, concepts, and approaches of each of the schools contribute positively to the total body of knowledge that comprises modern management practice.

The purpose of this revised edition is to bring together a balanced coverage of the three schools. By integrating balanced writings it is hoped that the reader will see that the three schools are mutually supportive; each one makes a contribution to the field of management. The dynamic and complex environment in which managers must reach decisions and lead people requires the knowledge found in each of the schools.

Even a cursory review of the growing volume of management literature indicates that numerous articles could be categorized in terms of the schools.

Thus, relevant articles were subjected to a number of selection criteria. The criteria used to develop this revised edition were: (1) the acceptance of articles included in the first edition by students and adopters, (2) the clarity and readability as expressed by students, (3) the relevance of the content to practitititioners, (4) the professional quality of the article, and (5) the recency of the publication date of the article.

The book can be used in undergraduate, graduate, and training courses. The total book or selected articles can be used to supplement appropriate course materials. It is assumed that practitioners and college students will use the book or parts of it to update and improve their knowledge of management.

The book is divided into five major parts. Each of the parts is preceded by comments and discussion by the editors. A brief summary of each article in the particular part is presented in the discussion. Thus, the reader can obtain a flavor of what each article covers by reviewing the article summaries.

Part One is titled "Introduction to Management" and sets the overall tone of the field of management. Two excellent articles deal with management theory. Part Two presents the *Classical* school of management. Articles that deal with principles and functions of management are included. In Part Three the *Behavioral* school of management is discussed. Articles that cover such areas as the behavioral sciences, motivation, management development, work groups, and organizational change are presented. Part Four covers the *Management Science* school. Six articles are presented which review some management science concepts. The final set of articles, Part Five, concentrates on the future of management. Articles on such topics as multinational management, pollution control, and changing organization structures are included.

Without the cooperation of the authors of the articles and publishers this revised edition would not be possible. These people deserve a special thank you for permission to use their material.

We are particularly appreciative of the contributions of Mr. John Burnett who reviewed and organized a large quantity of materials. In addition a number of typists are due a special thank you for doing excellent work—Teresa D'Arcy, Mary Heintze, and Patricia Scott.

February 1975

JAMES H. DONNELLY, JR.
JAMES L. GIBSON
JOHN M. IVANCEVICH

Contributors

Robert C. Albrook
Glenn A. Bassett
David G. Bowers
Rex V. Brown
Stephen Carroll
Frank H. Cassell
Leslie M. Dawson
Allan T. Demaree
John S. Fielden
Robert N. Ford
Wendell French
Robert T. Golembiewski
Douglas T. Hall
Harold Koontz
Donald G. Malcolm
William H. Newman
William F. Pounds
Daniel D. Roman
William A. Ruch
Stanley E. Seashore
Dennis Slevin
Harold Stieglitz
Stewart Thompson
Henry L. Tosi
Lyndall F. Urwick
William J. Vatter
V. Seymour Wilson
M. Y. Yoshino

Contents

Part Four
Management Science School of Management

Part Five
Contemporary Management in a Dynamic Environment

CROSS-REFERENCE TABLE

For Relating These Readings to the Authors' *Fundamentals of Management: Functions, Behavior, Models* rev. ed., 1975, and Other Management Textbooks

Parts in *Fundamentals of Management: Selected Readings*

Selected Management Textbooks	Part One: Intro- duction	Part Two: Classical School of Manage- ment	Part Three: Behavioral School of Manage- ment	Part Four: Management Science School of Management	Part Five: The Manager in a Dynamic Environment
Dale, Ernest. *Management: Theory and Practice* (New York: McGraw-Hill Book Co., 1973).	Chaps. 1, 2, 3	Chaps. 5, 7, 8, 9, 10, 13, 14, 17, 19	Chaps. 6, 8, 11, 12, 15, 16	Chaps. 20, 26, 27, 28	Chaps. 4, 18, 21, 22, 23, 29
Donnelly, James H.; James L. Gibson; and John M. Ivancevich. *Fundamentals of Management: Functions, Behavior, Models* (Dallas, Texas: Business Publications, Inc., 1975).	Chap. 1	Chaps. 2, 3, 4, 5	Chaps. 6, 7, 8, 9, 10, 11	Chaps. 12, 13, 14, 15, 16	Chap. 17
Filley, Allan C., and Robert J. House. *Managerial Process and Organizational Behavior* (Glenview, Ill.: Scott, Foresman and Co., 1969).	Chap. 1	Chaps. 4, 8, 9, 10, 11	Chaps. 2, 3, 4, 12, 13, 15, 16, 17	Chap. 5	Chaps. 3, 4, 27, 28, 29
Haiman, Theo, and William C. Scott. *Management in the Modern Organization* (Boston: Houghton, Mifflin Co., 1974).	Chaps. 1, 4	Chaps. 2, 6, 7, 8, 9, 10, 11, 12, 13, 17, 18	Chaps. 14, 19, 20, 21, 22, 23, 24, 25, 26, 27	Chaps. 28, 29, 30, 31	Chaps. 3, 5
Haynes, W. Warren, Joseph L. Massie, and Marc J. Wallace. *Management: Analysis, Concepts and Cases* (Englewood Cliffs, N.J.: Prentice-Hall, Inc., 1975).	Chap. 1	Chaps. 3, 9, 11, 19, 21, 23	Chaps. 5, 7	Chaps. 13, 15, 17, 21	Chaps. 25 27, 29
Hicks, Herbert G. *The Management of Organizations* (New York: McGraw-Hill Book Co., 1972).	Chaps. 1, 2, 3, 4, 5, 6, 24	Chaps. 12, 16, 17, 18, 19, 23, 25, 26, 28	Chaps. 7, 8, 9, 10, 11, 13, 14, 15 20, 21, 22	Chaps. 29, 30	Chaps. 31, 32
Hodge, Billy J., and Herbert J. Johnson. *Management and Organizational Behavior* (New York: John Wiley & Sons, Inc., 1970).	Chap. 2	Chaps. 7, 16	Chaps. 6, 9, 10, 12, 18, 19, 20	Chaps. 11, 13, 14, 15, 16	Chaps. 1, 3, 4, 5
Kast, Fremont E., and James E. Rosenzweig. *Organization and Management* (New York: McGraw-Hill Book Co., 1974).	Chaps. 1, 2	Chaps. 3, 7, 9, 17, 18	Chaps. 4, 8, 9, 10, 11, 12, 13, 16, 19, 20, 21, 23	Chaps. 4, 14, 15	Chaps. 6, 23

Cross-Reference Table—*Continued*

Selected Management Textbooks	Part One: Introduction	Part Two: Classical School of Management	Part Three: Behavioral School of Management	Part Four: Management Science School of Management	Part Five: The Manager in a Dynamic Environment
Koontz, Harold, and Cyril O'Donnell. *Principles of Management* (New York: McGraw-Hill Book Co., 1972).	Chaps. 1, 2	Chaps. 3, 6, 7, 8, 9, 10, 12, 14, 15, 21, 22, 23, 24, 29	Chaps. 13, 16, 17, 18, 19, 20, 25 26, 27, 28	Chaps. 30, 31, 32	Chaps. 4, 5
Longenecker, Justin G. *Principles of Management and Organizational Behavior* (Columbus, Ohio: Charles E. Merrill Publishing Co., 1969).	Chap. 1	Chaps. 2, 4, 6, 8, 9, 10, 24, 25, 26	Chaps. 12, 13, 15, 17, 18, 19, 20, 22, 23	Chap. 7	Chaps. 2, 3, 16, 27
Lundgren, Earl F. *Organizational Management* (San Francisco: Canfield Press, 1974).	Chap. 1	Chaps. 2, 6, 7, 8, 9	Chaps. 3, 8, 9, 10, 11, 12, 13, 15	Chaps. 4, 5, 14	Chap. 16
McFarland, Dalton E. *Management: Principles and Practices* (New York: Macmillan Publishing Co., 1974).	Chaps. 1, 2	Chaps. 4, 5, 6, 12, 14, 16, 17, 25	Chaps. 7, 8, 9, 10, 11, 15, 18, 19, 20, 21, 22, 23, 24	Chap. 13	Chaps. 3, 26, 27
Newman, William H.; Charles E. Summer; and E. Kirby Warren. *The Process of Management* (Englewood Cliffs, N.J.: Prentice-Hall, Inc., 1972).	Chap. 1	Chaps. 2, 3, 4, 5, 6, 10, 15, 16, 17, 18, 24	Chaps. 7, 8, 9, 20, 21, 22, 23, 26	Chaps. 11, 12, 13, 14, 19, 25, 27	Chaps. 28, 29
Richards, Max D., and Paul S. Greenlaw. *Management Decision Making* (Homewood, Ill.: Richard D. Irwin, Inc., 1972).	Chap. 1	Chaps. 8, 9, 12, 13	Chaps. 5, 6, 7, 10, 11	Chaps. 2, 3, 4, 14, 15, 16, 17, 18, 19	Chap. 20
Sisk, Henry L. *Principles of Management: A Systems Approach to the Management Process* (Cincinnati: South-Western Publishing Co., 1973).	Chaps. 1, 2, 3	Chaps. 4, 5, 6, 9, 10, 11, 20	Chaps. 12, 13, 14, 15, 16, 17, 18, 19	Chaps. 7, 8, 21, 22	Chap. 23
Terry, George R. *Principles of Management* (Homewood, Ill.: Richard D. Irwin, Inc., 1972).	Chaps. 1, 2	Chaps. 3, 4, 5, 6, 7, 8, 10, 11, 12, 13, 14, 15, 17, 23	Chaps. 9, 16, 18, 19, 20, 21, 22	Chaps. 24, 25, 26	Chap. 27
Voich, Dan, Jr., and Daniel A. Wren. *Principles of Management* (New York: The Ronald Press Co., 1968).	Chap. 1	Chaps. 4, 5, 7, 9	Chaps. 8, 10, 19	Chaps. 2, 6, 10, 11, 12, 13, 18	Chaps. 3, 20

part ONE
An Introduction to Management

The field of study termed "management" is concerned with the *process* by which resources including machines, money, materials, and people are coordinated to achieve predetermined goals. The literature which comprises the field of management includes many different viewpoints of the most fruitful manner in which to study management. Each viewpoint proposes a particular definition which emphasizes one or more aspects of management. For example, one definition, or viewpoint, places emphasis on the process of achieving goals through the efforts of *people*. Another viewpoint emphasizes management as only one aspect of *group behavior*. A third definition emphasizes the technical aspects of coordinating and focuses on the elements of coordination, or the *functions* of management. Other definitions could be mentioned, but the point to be made here is that the field is far from settled.

The unsettled nature of the field reflects not only the complexity of managing but also the relative recency of scholarly interest in management. The complexity of the management process is well understood by even the most casual observer and practitioner. Management is a fundamental human activity and, similar to other such activities (parenthood, citizenship, and the like), it defies easy analysis. Serious efforts to analyze the process are primarily the product of the 20th century; in comparison with other fields of study, management is a newcomer still struggling with the basic issues. In fact, there now exists no *general theory* of management which serves to consolidate and direct the efforts of researchers and practitioners. Such a theory must be developed if the field is to take its place alongside of other scientific disciplines.

The first article in this section, "The Management Theory Jungle," is Professor Harold Koontz's now-famous discussion of six of the various viewpoints, or schools. They are:

1. The Management Process School.
2. The Empirical School.
3. The Human Behavior School.
4. The Social System School.
5. The Decision Theory School.
6. The Mathematical School.

1

Koontz's discussion of each of these schools provides considerable insight into the content and issues of modern management thought. Of course, there can be disagreement with the author's classification scheme. For example, the editors of this readings book use a three-way classification scheme: we combine (1) the Management Process and Empirical Schools into the *Classical School,* (2) the Human Behavior and Social System Schools into the *Behavioral School* and (3) the Decision Theory and Mathematical Schools into the *Management Science School.*

The appropriateness of any particular classification of management literature is not our central concern. Rather we should focus upon the issues which Koontz raises in the last section of his article. The key issue concerns the disentanglement of management theory and the creation of a foundation for building a general theory. The basic issue of any field is the definition of content; this issue along with others which Koontz raises must be resolved, at least tentatively, before the field of management can consider a general theory.

The second article, "EDP Leads the Thirteen 'Most Popular' Management Techniques," reports the results of an attempt to determine the relative popularity of certain management techniques. The study consisted of a national sample of firms of all sizes in various industries. The results reflect considerable variation in the popularity of such techniques as electronic data processing (EDP), management information systems (MIS), management by objectives (MBO), organizational development (OD), and direct costing. The survey found that the use of all techniques is on the increase, but that variations in degree of satisfaction are to be found. In addition to introducing the reader to a variety of management techniques, this article also reinforces the idea that the practice of management is itself as diverse as the literature of management.

The third article, "The Qualifications of a Manager" by Glenn A. Bassett, focuses on managers as distinct from managing. In particular, the author writes about the importance and difficulty of selecting and developing managers. He notes that managers have different styles, personalities, skills, and talents and though we might personally prefer one type, each is suitable at some time and place depending upon needs of the business. Basset suggests one basis for classifying the many styles of managers along both qualitative and quantitative dimensions. The reader should critically examine Bassett's conclusions about the way to select managers; but equally important the reader should recognize that the diversity of *managers* accounts for much of the diversity in the field of management.

The final article, "Potential for Career Growth" by Douglas T. Hall, introduces yet another factor which contributes to the complexity of management. Specifically he deals with the impact of changing values and orientations among young people. The present generation includes not only the managers of the future, but also the consumers of the future. What they want for themselves within organizations and what they want from organizations are critical factors for contemporary managers to consider. This specific concern is the focus of the article, yet it is part of a larger concern—the certainty of change. Simply said, management is complex because it is part of a complex environment.

1

The Management Theory Jungle*

HAROLD KOONTZ

Although students of management would readily agree that there have been problems of management since the dawn of organized life, most would also agree that systematic examination of management, with few exceptions, is the product of the present century and more especially of the past two decades. Moreover, until recent years almost all of those who have attempted to analyze the management process and look for some theoretical underpinnings to help improve research, teaching, and practice were alert and perceptive practitioners of the art who reflected on many years of experience. Thus, at least in looking at *general* management as an intellectually based art, the earliest meaningful writing came from such experienced practitioners as Fayol, Mooney, Alvin Brown, Sheldon, Barnard, and Urwick. Certainly not even the most academic worshipper of empical research can overlook the empiricism involved in distilling fundamentals from decades of experience by such discerning practitioners as these. Admittedly done without questionnaires, controlled interviews, or mathematics, observations by such men can hardly be accurately regarded as *a priori* or "armchair."

The noteworthy absence of academic writing and research in the formative years of modern management theory is now more than atoned for by a deluge of research and writing from the academic halls. What is interesting and perhaps nothing more than a sign of the unsophisticated adolescence of management theory is how the current flood has brought with it a wave of great differences and apparent confusion. From the orderly analysis of management at the shop-room level by Frederick Taylor and the reflective distillation of experience from the general management point of view of Henri Fayol, we now see these and other early beginnings overgrown and entangled by a jungle of approaches and approachers to management theory.

There are the behavioralists, born of the Hawthorne experiments and the awakened interest in human relations during the 1930's and 1940's, who see management as a complex of interpersonal relationships and the basis of management theory the tentative tenets of the new and undeveloped science of psychology. There are also those who see management theory as simply a

*Source: Reprinted by permission from *Academy of Management Journal* (December 1961), 174-78.

3

manifestation of the institutional and cultural aspects of sociology. Still others, observing that the central core of management is decision-making, branch in all directions from this core to encompass everything in organization life. Then, there are mathematicians who think of management primarily as an exercise in logical relationships expressed in symbols and the omnipresent and ever revered model. But the entanglement of growth reaches its ultimate when the study of management is regarded as a study of one of a number of systems and sub-systems, with an understandable tendency for the researcher to be dissatisfied until he has encompassed the entire physical and cultural universe as a management system.

With the recent discovery of an ages-old problem area by social, physical, and biological scientists, and with the supersonic increase in interest by all types of enterprise managers, the apparent impenetrability of the present thicket which we call management theory is not difficult to comprehend. One can hardly be surprised that psychologists, sociologists, anthropologists, sociometricists, economists, mathematicians, physicists, biologists, political scientists, business administration scholars, and even practicing managers, should hop on this interesting, challenging, and profitable bandwagon.

This welling of interest from every academic and practicing corner should not upset anyone concerned with seeing the frontiers of knowledge pushed back and the intellectual base of practice broadened. But what is rather upsetting to the practitioner and the observer, who sees great social potential from improved management, is that the variety of approaches to management theory has led to a kind of confused and destructive jungle warfare. Particularly among academic disciplines and their disciples, the primary interests of many would-be cult leaders seem to be to carve out a distinct (and hence "original") approach to management. And to defend this originality, and thereby gain a place in posterity (or at least to gain a publication which will justify academic status or promotion), it seems to have become too much the current style to downgrade, and sometimes misrepresent, what anyone else has said, or thought, or done.

In order to cut through this jungle and bring to light some of the issues and problems involved in the present management theory area so that the tremendous interest, intelligence, and research results may become more meaningful, it is my purpose here to classify the various "schools" of management theory, to identify briefly what I believe to be the major source of differences, and to offer some suggestions for disentangling the jungle. It is hoped that a movement for clarification can be started so at least we in the field will not be a group of blind men identifying the same elephant with our widely varying and sometimes viciously argumentative theses.

THE MAJOR "SCHOOLS" OF MANAGEMENT THEORY

In attempting to classify the major schools of management theory into six main groups, I am aware that I may overlook certain approaches and cannot deal with all the nuances of each approach. But it does seem that most of the approaches to management theory can be classified in one of these so-called "schools."

The Management Process School

This approach to management theory perceives management as a process of getting things done through and with people operating in organized groups. It aims to analyze the process, to establish a conceptual framework for it, to identify principles underlying it, and to build up a theory of management from them. It regards management as a universal process, regardless of the type of enterprise, or the level in a given enterprise, although recognizing, obviously, that the environment of management differs widely between enterprises and levels. It looks upon management theory as a way of organizing experience so that practice can be improved through research, empirical testing of principles, and teaching of fundamentals involved in the management process.[1]

Often referred to, especially by its critics, as the "traditional" or "universalist" school, this school can be said to have been fathered by Henri Fayol, although many of his offspring did not know of their parent, since Fayol's work was eclipsed by the bright light of his contemporary, Frederick Taylor, and clouded by the lack of a widely available English translation until 1949. Other than Fayol, most of the early contributors to this school dealt only with the organization portion of the management process, largely because of their greater experience with this facet of management and the simple fact that planning and control, as well as the function of staffing, were given little attention by managers before 1940.

This school bases its approach to management theory on several fundamental beliefs:

1. that managing is a process and can best be dissected intellectually by analyzing the functions of the manager;
2. that long experience with management in a variety of enterprise situations can be grounds for distillation of certain fundamental truths or generalizations—usually referred to as principles—which have a clarifying and predictive value in the understanding and improvement of managing;
3. that these fundamental truths can become focal points for useful research

1/It is interesting that one of the scholars strongly oriented to human relations and behavioral approaches to management has recently noted that "theory can be viewed as a way of organizing experience" and that "once initial sense is made out of experienced environment, the way is cleared for an even more adequate organization of this experience." See Robert Dubin in "Psyche, Sensitivity, and Social Structure," critical comment in Robert Tannenbaum, I. R. Weschler, and Fred Massarik, *Leadership and Organization: A Behavioral Science Approach* (New York: McGraw-Hill Book Company, 1961), p. 401.

both to ascertain their validity and to improve their meaning and applicability in practice;

4. that such truths can furnish elements, at least until disproved, and certainly until sharpened, of a useful theory of management;
5. that managing is an art, but one like medicine or engineering, which can be improved by reliance on the light and understanding of principles;
6. that principles in management, like principles in the biological and physical sciences, are nonetheless true even if a prescribed treatment or design by a practitioner in a given case situation chooses to ignore a principle and the costs involved, or attempts to do something else to offset the costs incurred (this is, of course, not new in medicine, engineering, or any other art, for art is the creative task of compromising fundamentals to attain a desired result); and
7. that, while the totality of culture and of the physical and biological universe has varying effects on the manager's environment and subjects, as indeed they do in every other field of science and art, the theory of management does not need to encompass the field of all knowledge in order for it to serve as a scientific or theoretical foundation.

The basic approach of this school, then, is to look, first, to the functions of managers. As a second step in this approach, many of us have taken the functions of managers and further dissected them by distilling what we see as fundamental truths in the understandably complicated practice of management. I have found it useful to classify my analysis of these functions around the essentials involved in the following questions:

1. What is the nature of the function?
2. What is the purpose of the function?
3. What explains the structure of the function?
4. What explains the process of the function?

Perhaps there are other more useful approaches, but I have found that I can place everything pertaining to management (even some of the rather remote research and concepts) in this framework.

Also, purely to make the area of management theory intellectually manageable, those who subscribe to this school do not usually attempt to include in the theory the entire areas of sociology, economics, biology, psychology, physics, chemistry, or others. This is done not because these other areas of knowledge are unimportant and have no bearing on management, but merely because no real progress has ever been made in science or art without significant partitioning of knowledge. Yet, anyone would be foolish not to realize that a function which deals with people in their various activities of producing and marketing anything from money to religion and education is completely independent of the physical, biological, and cultural universe in which we live. And, are there not such relationships in other "compartments" of knowledge and theory?

The Empirical School

A second approach to management I refer to as the "empirical" school. In this, I include those scholars who identify management as a study of experience, sometimes with intent to draw generalizations but usually merely as a means of teaching experience and transferring it to the practitioner or student. Typical of this school are those who see management or "policy" as the study and analysis of cases and those with such approaches as Ernest Dale's "comparative approach."[2]

This approach seems to be based upon the premise that, if we study the experience of successful managers, or the mistakes made in management, or if we attempt to solve management problems, we will somehow understand and learn to apply the most effective kinds of management techniques. This approach, as often applied, assumes that, by finding out what worked or did not work in individual circumstances, the student or the practitioner will be able to do the same in comparable situations.

No one can deny the importance of studying experience through such study, or of analyzing the "how-it-was-done" of management. But management, unlike law, is not a science based on precedent, and situations in the future exactly comparable to the past are exceedingly unlikely to occur. Indeed, there is a positive danger of relying too much on past experience and on undistilled history of managerial problem-solving for the simple reason that a technique or approach found "right" in the past may not fit a situation of the future.

Those advocating the empirical approach are likely to say that what they really do in analyzing cases or history is to draw from certain generalizations which can be applied as useful guides to thought or action in future case situations. As a matter of fact, Ernest Dale, after claiming to find "so little practical value" from the principles enunciated by the "universalists," curiously drew certain "generalizations" or "criteria" from his valuable study of a number of great practitioners of management.[3] There is some question as to whether Dale's "comparative" approach is not really the same as the "universalist" approach he decries, except with a different distiller of basic truths.

By the emphasis of the empirical school on study of experience, it does appear that the research and thought so engendered may assist in hastening the day for verification of principles. It is also possible that the proponents of this school may come up with a more useful framework of principles than that of the management process school. But, to the extent that the empirical school draws generalizations from its research, and it would seem to be a necessity to do so unless its members are satisfied to exchange meaningless and structureless experience, this approach tends to be and do the same as the management process school.

2/Ernest Dale, *The Great Organizers: Theory and Practice of Organization* (New York: McGraw-Hill Book Company, 1960), pp. 11-28.
3/Ibid., pp. 11, 26-28, 62-66.

The Human Behavior School

This approach to the analysis of management is based on the central thesis that, since managing involves getting things done with and through people, the study of management must be centered on interpersonal relations. Variously called the "human relations," "leadership," or "behavioral sciences" approach, this school brings to bear "existing and newly developed theories, methods, and techniques of the relevant social sciences upon the study of inter- and intrapersonal phenomena, ranging fully from the personality dynamics of individuals at one extreme to the relations of cultures at the other."[4] In other words, this school concentrates on the "people" part of management and rests on the principle that, where people work together as groups in order to accomplish objectives, "people should understand people."

The scholars in this school have a heavy orientation to psychology and social psychology. Their primary focus is the individual as a socio-psychological being and what motivates him. The members of this school vary from those who see it as a portion of the manager's job, a tool to help him understand and get the best from people by meeting their needs and responding to their motivations, to those who see the psychological behavior of individuals and groups as the total of management.

In this school are those who emphasize human relations as an art that the manager should advantageously understand and practice. There are those who focus attention on the manager as a leader and sometimes equate management to leadership, thus, in effect, tending to treat all group activities as "managed" situations. There are those who see the study of group dynamics and interpersonal relationships as simply a study of socio-psychological relationships and seem, therefore, merely to be attaching the term "management" to the field of social psychology.

That management must deal with human behavior can hardly be denied. That the study of human interactions, whether in the environment of management or in unmanaged situations, is important and useful one could not dispute. And it would be a serious mistake to regard good leadership as unimportant to good managership. But whether the field of human behavior is the equivalent of the field of management is quite another thing. Perhaps it is like calling the study of the human body the field of cardiology.

The Social System School

Closely related to the human behavior school and often confused or intertwined with it is one which might be labeled the social system school. This includes those researchers who look upon management as a social system, that is, a system of cultural interrelationships. Sometimes, as in the case of March

4/Tannenbaum, Weschler, and Massarik, op. cit., p. 9.

and Simon,[5] the system is limited to formal organizations, using the term "organization" as equivalent to enterprise, rather than the authority-activity concept used most often in management. In other cases, the approach is not to distinguish the formal organization, but rather to encompass any kind of system of human relationships.

Heavily sociological in flavor, this approach to management does essentially what any study of sociology does. It identifies the nature of the cultural relationships of various social groups and attempts to show these as a related, and usually an integrated, system.

Perhaps the spiritual father of this ardent and vocal school of management theorists is Chester Barnard.[6] In searching for an answer to fundamental explanations underlying the managing process, this thoughtful business executive developed a theory of cooperation grounded in the needs of the individual to solve, through cooperation, the biological, physical, and social limitations of himself and his environment. Barnard then carved from the total of cooperative systems so engendered one set of interrelationships which he defines as "formal organization." His formal organization concept, quite unlike that usually held by management practitioners, is any cooperative system in which there are persons able to communicate with each other and who are willing to contribute action toward a conscious common purpose.

The Barnard concept of cooperative systems pervades the work of many contributors to the social system school of management. For example, Herbert Simon at one time defined the subject of organization theory and the nature of human organizations as "systems of interdependent activity, encompassing at least several primary groups and usually characterized, at the level of con-sciousness of participants, by a high degree of rational direction of behavior toward ends that are objects of common knowledge."[7] Simon and others have subsequently seemed to have expanded this concept of social systems to include any cooperative and purposeful group interrelationship or behavior.

This school has made many noteworthy contributions to management. The recognition of organized enterprise as a social organism, subject to all the pressures and conflicts of the cultural environment, has been helpful to the management theorist and the practitioner alike. Among some of the more helpful aspects are the awareness of the institutional foundations of organization authority, the influence of informal organization, and such social factors as those Wight Bakke has called the "bonds of organization."[8] Likewise, many of

5/J. G. March and H. A. Simon, *Organizations* (New York: John Wiley & Sons, Inc., 1958).

6/Chester Barnard, *The Functions of the Executive* (Cambridge, Mass.: Harvard University Press, 1938).

7/"Comments on the Theory of Organizations," *American Political Science Review*, vol. 46, no. 4, p. 1130, December 1952.

8/Wight Bakke, *Bonds of Organization* (New York: Harper & Row, Publishers, Incorporated, 1950). These "bonds" or "devices" of organization are identified by Bakke as (1) the functional specifications system (a system of teamwork arising from job

Barnard's helpful insights, such as his economy of incentives and his theory of opportunism, have brought the power of sociological understanding into the realm of management practice.

Basic sociology, analysis of concepts of social behavior, and the study of group behavior in the framework of social systems do have great value in the field of management. But one may well ask the question whether this *is* management. Is the field of management coterminous with the field of sociology? Or is sociology an important underpinning like language, psychology, physiology, mathematics, and other fields of knowledge? Must management be defined in terms of the universe of knowledge?

The Decision Theory School

Another approach to management theory, undertaken by a growing and scholarly group, might be referred to as the decision theory school. This group concentrates on rational approach to decision—the selection from among possible alternatives of a course of action or of an idea. The approach of this school may be to deal with the decision itself, or to the persons or organizational group making the decision, or to an analysis of the decision process. Some limit themselves fairly much to the economic rationale of the decision, while others regard anything which happens in an enterprise the subject of their analysis, and still others expand decision theory to cover the psychological and sociological aspect and environment of decisions and decision-makers.

The decision-making school is apparently an outgrowth of the theory of consumer's choice with which economists have been concerned since the days of Jeremy Bentham early in the nineteenth century. It has arisen out of such economic problems and analyses as utility maximization, indifference curves, marginal utility, and economic behavior under risks and uncertainties. It is, therefore, no surprise that one finds most of the members of this school to be economic theorists. It is likewise no surprise to find the content of this school to be heavily oriented to model construction and mathematics.

The decision theory school has tended to expand its horizon considerably beyond the process of evaluating alternatives. That point has become for many only a springboard for examination of the entire sphere of human activity, including the nature of the organization structure, psychological and social reactions of individuals and groups, the development of basic information for decisions, an analysis of values and particularly value considerations with respect to goals, communications networks, and incentives. As one would expect, when the decision theorists study the small, but central, area of decision *making,* they are led by this keyhole look at management to consider the entire field of

---

specifications and arrangements for association); (2) the status system (a vertical hierarchy of authority); (3) the communications system; (4) the reward and penalty system; and (5) the organization charter (ideas and means which give character and individuality to the organization, or enterprise).

enterprise operation and its environment. The result is that decision theory becomes no longer a neat and narrow concentration on decision, but rather a broad view of the enterprise as a social system.

There are those who believe that, since management is characterized by its concentration on decisions, the future development of management theory will tend to use the decision as its central focus and the rest of management theory will be hung on this structural center. This may occur and certainly the study of the decision, the decision process, and the decision maker can be extended to cover the entire field of management as anyone might conceive it. Nevertheless, one wonders whether this focus cannot also be used to build around it the entire area of human knowledge. For, as most decision theorists recognize, the problem of choice is individual, as well as organizational, and most of what has been said that is pure decision theory can be applied to the existence and thinking of a Robinson Crusoe.

The Mathematical School

Although mathematical methods can be used by any school of management theory, and have been, I have chosen to group under a school those theorists who see management as a system of mathematical models and processes. Perhaps the most widely known group I arbitrarily so lump are the operations researchers or operations analysts, who have sometimes anointed themselves with the rather pretentious name of "management scientists." The abiding belief of this group is that, if management, or organization, or planning, or decision making is a logical process, it can be expressed in terms of mathematical symbols and relationships. The central approach of this school is the model, for it is through these devices that the problem is expressed in its basic relationships and in terms of selected goals or objectives.

There can be no doubt of the great usefulness of mathematical approaches to any field of inquiry. It forces upon the researcher the definition of a problem or problem area, it conveniently allows the insertion of symbols for unknown data, and its logical methodology, developed by years of scientific application and abstraction, furnishes a powerful tool for solving or simplifying complex phenomena.

But it is hard to see mathematics as a truly separate school of management theory, any more than it is a separate "school" in physics, chemistry, engineering, or medicine. I only deal with it here as such because there has appeared to have developed a kind of cult around mathematical analysts who have subsumed to themselves the area of management.

In pointing out that mathematics is a tool, rather than a school, it is not my intention to underestimate the impact of mathematics on the science and practice of management. By bringing to this immensely important and complex field the tools and techniques of the physical sciences, the mathematicians have already made an immense contribution to orderly thinking. They have forced on people in management the means and desirability of seeing many problems more clearly, they have pressed on scholars and practitioners the need for establishing goals and measures of effectiveness, they have been extremely helpful in getting the management area seen as a logical system of relationships, and they have caused people in management to review and occasionally reorganize information sources and systems so that mathematics can be given sensible quantitative meaning. But with all this meaningful contribution and the greater sharpness and sophistication of planning which is resulting, I cannot see that mathematics is management theory any more than it is astronomy.

THE MAJOR SOURCES OF MENTAL ENTANGLEMENT IN THE JUNGLE

In outlining the various schools, or approaches, of management theory, it becomes clear that these intellectual cults are not drawing greatly different inferences from the physical and cultural environment surrounding us. Why, then, have there been so many differences between them and why such a struggle, particularly among our academic brethren to obtain a place in the sun by denying the approaches of others? Like the widely differing and often contentious denominations of the Christian religion, all have essentially the same goals and deal with essentially the same world.

While there are many sources of the mental entanglement in the management theory jungle, the major ones are the following:

The Semantics Jungle

As is so often true when intelligent men argue about basic problems, some of the trouble lies in the meaning of key words. The semantics problem is particularly severe in the field of management. There is even a difference in the meaning of the word "management." Most people would agree that it means getting things done through and with people, but is it people in formal organizations, or in all group activities? Is it governing, leading, or teaching?

Perhaps the greatest single semantics confusion lies in the word "organization." Most members of the management process school use it to define the activity-authority structure of an enterprise and certainly most practitioners believe that they are "organizing" when they establish a framework of activity groupings and authority relationships. In this case, organization represents the formal framework within an enterprise that furnishes the environment in which people perform. Yet a large number of "organization" theorists conceive of organization as the sum total of human relationships in any group activity; they thus seem to make it equivalent to *social* structure. And some use "organization" to mean "enterprise."

If the meaning of organization cannot be clarified and a standard use of the term adopted by management theorists, understanding and criticism should not be based on this difference. It hardly seems to me to be accurate for March and Simon, for example, to criticize the organization theories of the management process, or "universalist," school for not considering the management planning function as part of organizing, when they have chosen to treat it separately. Nor should those who choose to treat the training, selecting, guiding or leading of people under staffing and direction be criticized for a tendency to "view the employee as an inert instrument" or a "given rather than a variable."[9] Such accusations, proceeding from false premises, are clearly erroneous.

Other semantic entanglements might be mentioned. By some, decision-making is regarded as a process of choosing from among alternatives; by others, the total managerial task and environment. Leadership is often made synonymous with managership and is analytically separated by others. Communications may mean everything from a written or oral report to a vast network of formal and informal relationships. Human relations to some implies a psychiatric manipulation of people, but to others the study and art of understanding people and interpersonal relationships.

Differences in Definition of Management as a Body of Knowledge

As was indicated in the discussion of semantics, "management" has far from a standard meaning, although most agree that it at least involves getting things done through and with people. But, does it mean the dealing with all human relationships? Is a street peddler a manager? Is a parent a manager? Is a leader of a disorganized mob a manager? Does the field of management equal the fields of sociology and social psychology combined? Is it the equivalent of the entire system of social relationships?

While I recognize that sharp lines cannot be drawn in management any more than they are in medicine or engineering, there surely can be a sharper distinction drawn than at present. With the plethora of management writing and experts, calling almost everything under the sun "management," can one expect management theory to be regarded as very useful or scientific to the practitioner?

The a priori Assumption

Confusion in management theory has also been heightened by the tendency for many newcomers in the field to cast aside significant observations and analyses of the past on the grounds that they are *a priori* in nature. This is an often-met accusation made by those who wish to cast aside the work of Fayol, Mooney, Brown, Urwick, Gulick, and others who are branded as "universalists." To make the assumption that the distilled experiences of men such as these

9/March and Simon, op. cit., pp. 29-33.

represent *a priori* reasoning is to forget that experience in and with managing *is* empirical. While the conclusions that perceptive and experienced practitioners of the art of management are not infallible, they represent an experience which is certainly real and not "armchair." No one could deny, I feel sure, that the ultimate test of accuracy of management theory must be practice and management theory and science must be developed from reality.

The Misunderstanding of Principles

Those who feel that they gain caste or a clean slate for advancing a particular notion or approach often delight in casting away anything which smacks of management principles. Some have referred to them as platitudes, forgetting that a platitude is still a truism and a truth does not become worthless because it is familiar. (As Robert Frost has written, "Most of the changes we think we see in life are merely truths going in or out of favor.") Others cast away principles of Fayol and other practitioners, only to draw apparently different generalizations from their study of management; but many of the generalizations so discovered are often the same fundamental truths in different words that certain criticized "universalists" have discovered.

One of the favorite tricks of the managerial theory trade is to disprove a whole framework of principles by reference to one principle which the observer sees disregarded in practice. Thus, many critics of the universalists point to the well-known cases of dual subordination in organized enterprise, coming to the erroneous conclusion that there is no substance to the principle of unity of command. But this does not prove that there is no cost to the enterprise by designing around, or disregarding, the principle of unity of command; nor does it prove that there were not other advantages which offset the costs, as there often are in cases of establishing functional authorities in organization.

Perhaps the almost hackneyed stand-by for those who would disprove the validity of all principles by referring to a single one is the misunderstanding around the principle of span of management (or span of control). The usual source of authority quoted by those who criticize is Sir Ian Hamilton, who never intended to state a universal principle, but rather to make a personal observation in a book of reflections on his Army experience, and who did say, offhand, that he found it wise to limit his span to 3 to 6 subordinates. No modern universalist relies on this single observation, and, indeed, few can or will state an absolute or universal numerical ceiling. Since Sir Ian was not a management theorist and did not intend to be, let us hope that the ghost of his innocent remark may be laid to deserved rest!

What concerns those who feel that a recognition of fundamental truths, or generalizations, may help in the diagnosis and study of management, and who know from managerial experience that such truths or principles do serve an extremely valuable use, is the tendency for some researchers to prove the wrong things through either misstatement or misapplication of principles. A classic case of such misunderstanding and misapplication is in Chris Argyris' interesting book on *Personality and Organization*.[10] This author, who in this book and his other works has made many noteworthy contributions to management, concludes that "formal organization principles make demands on relatively healthy individuals that are incongruent with their needs," and that "frustration, conflict, failure, and short-time perspective are predicted as results of this basic incongruency."[11] This startling conclusion—the exact opposite of what "good" formal organization based on "sound" organization principles should cause, is explained when one notes that, of four "principles" Argyris quotes, one is not an organization principle at all but the economic principle of specialization and three other "principles" are quoted incorrectly.[12] With such a postulate, and with no attempt to recognize, correctly or incorrectly, any other organization and management principles, Argyris has simply proved that wrong principles badly applied will lead to frustration; and every management practitioner knows this to be true!

The Inability or Unwillingness of Management Theorists to Understand Each Other

What has been said above leads one to the conclusion that much of the management theory jungle is caused by the unwillingness or inability of the management theorists to understand each other. Doubting that it is inability, because one must assume that a person interested in management theory is able to comprehend, at least in concept and framework, the approaches of the various "schools," I can only come to the conclusion that the roadblock to understanding is unwillingness.

Perhaps this unwillingness comes from the professional "walls" developed by learned disciplines. Perhaps the unwillingness stems from a fear that someone or some new discovery will encroach on professional and academic status. Perhaps it is fear of professional or intellectual obsolescence. But whatever the cause, it seems that these walls will not be torn down until it is realized that they exist, until all cultists are willing to look at the approach and content of other schools, and until, through exchange and understanding of ideas some order may be brought from the present chaos.

DISENTANGLING THE MANAGEMENT THEORY JUNGLE

It is important that steps be taken to disentangle the management theory jungle. Perhaps, it is too soon and we must expect more years of wandering through a thicket of approaches, semantics, thrusts, and counterthrusts. But in

10/Chris Argyris, *Personality and Organization* (New York: Harper & Row, Publishers, Incorporated, 1957).
11/Ibid., p. 74.
12/Ibid., pp. 58-66.

any field as important to society where the many blunders of an unscientifically based managerial art can be so costly, I hope that this will not be long.

There do appear to be some things that can be done. Clearly, meeting what I see to be the major sources of the entanglement should remove much of it. The following considerations are important:

1. *The Need for Definition of a Body of Knowledge.* Certainly, if a field of knowledge is not to get bogged down in a quagmire of misunderstandings, the first need is for definition of the field. Not that it need be defined in sharp, detailed, and inflexible lines, but rather along lines which will give it fairly specific content. Because management is reality, life, practice, my suggestion would be that it be defined in the light of the able and discerning practitioner's frame of reference. A science unrelated to the art for which it is to serve is not likely to be a very productive one.

Although the study of managements in various enterprises, in various countries, and at various levels made by many persons, including myself, may neither be representative nor adequate, I have come to the conclusion that management is the art of getting things done through and with people in *formally organized groups,* the art of creating an environment in such an organized group where people can perform as individuals and yet cooperate toward attainment of group goals, the art of removing blocks to such performance, the art of optimizing efficiency in effectively reaching goals. If this kind of definition of the field is unsatisfactory, I suggest at least an agreement that the area should be defined to reflect the field of the practitioner and that further research and study of practice be done to this end.

In defining the field, too, it seems to me imperative to draw some limits for purposes of analysis and research. If we are to call the entire cultural, biological, and physical universe the field of management, we can no more make progress than could have been done if chemistry or geology had not carved out a fairly specific area and had, instead studied all knowledge.

In defining the body of knowledge, too, care must be taken to distinguish between tools and content. Thus mathematics, operations research, accounting, economic theory, sociometry, and psychology, to mention a few, are significant *tools* of management but are not, in themselves, a part of the *content* of the field. This is not to mean that they are unimportant or that the practicing manager should not have them available to him, nor does it mean that they may not be the means of pushing back the frontiers of knowledge of management. But they should not be confused with the basic content of the field.

This is not to say that fruitful study should not continue on the underlying disciplines affecting management. Certainly knowledge of sociology, social systems, psychology, economics, political science, mathematics, and other areas, pointed toward contributing to the field of management, should be continued and encouraged. And significant findings in these and other fields of knowledge might well cast important light on, or change concepts in, the field of management. This has certainly happened in other sciences and in every other art based upon significant science.

2. *Integration of Management and Other Disciplines.* If recognition of the proper content of the field were made, I believe that the present crossfire of misunderstanding might tend to disappear. Management would be regarded as a specific discipline and other disciplines would be looked upon as important bases of the field. Under these circumstances, the allied and underlying disciplines would be welcomed by the business and public administration schools, as well as by practitioners, as loyal and helpful associates. Integration of management and other disciplines would then not be difficult.

3. *The Clarification of Management Semantics.* While I would expect the need for clarification and uniformity of management semantics would largely be satisfied by definition of the field as a body of knowledge, semantics problems might require more special attention. There are not too many places where semantics are important enough to cause difficulty. Here again, I would suggest the adoption of the semantics of the intelligent practitioners, unless words are used by them so inexactly as to require special clarification. At least, we should not complicate an already complex field by developing a scientific or academic jargon which would build a language barrier between the theorist and the practitioner.

Perhaps the most expeditious way out of this problem is to establish a commission representing academic societies immediately concerned and associations of practicing managers. This would not seem to be difficult to do. And even if it were, the results would be worth the efforts.

4. *Willingness to Distill and Test Fundamentals.* Certainly, the test of maturity and usefulness of a science is the sharpness and validity of the principles underlying it. No science, now regarded as mature, started out with a complete statement of incontrovertibly valid principles. Even the oldest sciences, such as physics, keep revising their underlying laws and discovering new principles. Yet any science has proceeded, and more than that has been useful, for centuries on the basis of generalizations, some laws, some principles, and some hypotheses.

One of the understandable sources of inferiority of the social sciences is the recognition that they are inexact sciences. On the other hand, even the so-called exact sciences are subject to a great deal of inexactness, have principles which are not completely proved, and use art in the design of practical systems and components. The often-encountered defeatist attitude of the social sciences, of which management is one, overlooks the fact that management may be explained, practice may be improved, and the goals of research may be more meaningful if we encourage attempts at perceptive distillation of experience by stating principles (or generalizations) and placing them in a logical framework. As two scientists recently said on this subject:

> The reason for this defeatist point of view regarding the social sciences may be traceable to a basic misunderstanding of the nature of scientific endeavor. What matters is not whether or to what extent inexactitudes in procedures and predictive capability can eventually be removed . . . : rather it is *objectivity*, i.e., the intersubjectivity of findings independent

of any one person's intuitive judgment, which distinguishes science from intuitive guesswork however brilliant. . . . But once a new fact or a new idea has been conjectured, no matter how intuitive a foundation, it must be capable of objective test and confirmation by anyone. And it is this crucial standard of scientific objectivity rather than any purported criterion of exactitude to which the social sciences must conform.[13]

In approaching the clarification of management theory, then, we should not forget a few criteria:

1. The theory should deal with an area of knowledge and inquiry that is "manageable"; no great advances in knowledge were made so long as man contemplated the whole universe;
2. The theory should be *useful* in improving practice and the task and person of the practitioner should not be overlooked;
3. The theory should not be lost in semantics, especially useless jargon not understandable to the practitioner;
4. The theory should give direction and efficiency to research and teaching; and
5. The theory must recognize that it is a part of a larger universe of knowledge and theory.

13/O. Helmer and N. Rescher, "On the Epistemology of the Inexact Sciences," The Rand Corporation, P-1513, Santa Monica, Calif., pp. 4-5.

2

EDP Leads the Thirteen "Most Popular" Management Techniques*

While it should come as no surprise that electronic data processing and MIS, or management information systems, are among today's most powerful administrative tools, a recent study shows them also to be the most popular management techniques of the past quarter-century. Both are currently used by more than nine out of ten major companies.

The study, based on a national sampling of firms of all sizes in various industries, found five management tools in widespread use—EDP, MIS, management by objectives (MBO), organizational development (OD), and direct costing. Sponsored jointly by four independent consulting firms, each the largest dealing in general management in its region, the survey not only identifies major trends, but for the first time quantifies the relative impact of many management theories currently in vogue.

Among the key findings:

A wide cross-section of management is dissatisfied with many of today's administrative tools. For example, 12 percent of the 147 corporate presidents queried are disappointed with their data processing systems; 15 percent are dissatisfied with MBO.

Large companies—those with over $50-million in sales—tend to use twice as many modern management techniques as smaller companies. At least ten of the 13 management techniques included in the study are used by more than half of the large companies.

Most smaller companies use only the five "most popular" management tools.

There is an increasing interest in human resource development. Three out of four companies now use OD techniques. More than two out of five have introduced job enrichment programs.

Utilities, insurance companies, banks, and basic chemical and petroleum companies are among industries reporting the widest use of modern management tools.

Companies on the West Coast—on the average—report using more management tools than companies in other parts of the country.

*Source: Republished with permission from *Administrative Management* (June 1973), 26-9, 64-5, copyright 1973 by Geyer-McAllister Publications, Inc., New York.

Conglomerates report using the greatest number of sophisticated management tools.

In general, business management is using a greater variety of modern management tools than was generally suspected.

Two very new techniques that have received wide attention are beginning to gain management supporters, the study shows. They are the "cafeteria" approach to executive compensation, and social accounting—an effort by business to assign dollar values to socially relevant activities. Although these are the least popular management tools found in the survey, they are being used by an increasing number of progressive companies.

The four firms that joined to sponsor the study are Lawrence-Leiter & Co., Kansas City, Mo.; Lifson, Wilson, Ferguson & Winick Inc., Dallas; Rath & Strong, Inc., Boston, and Theodore Barry & Associates, Los Angeles. All are members of ACME, the Association of Consulting Management Engineers. The study is said to be the first of its kind conducted as a joint project by competing management consultants.

Each firm surveyed company presidents within its own geographic region. Each president was asked to report whether his company currently uses any of 13 modern management processes introduced within the last 25 years, or had used any in the past. For processes in use, the presidents were asked to report whether "results have been disappointing or less than expected," or if the tools' "impact on management results has been significant," or if the results are not in yet and the presidents "don't know what the impact will be."

"Management tools, by their definition, imply a centralized style of management," comments H. Warren Lang Jr., vice-president of Lawrence-Leiter. "Therefore, industries and segments of the country that employ centralized approaches would naturally have a higher incidence of use of management tools."

The results indicate to Thomas Lawrence, also of Lawrence-Leiter, that "company presidents and corporate management in general are highly oriented to the technical, economic, and operational tools of management, but they still have a long way to go in visualizing, projecting and applying the 'human tools' of management—job enrichment, for example."

A factor at least partially determining the extent to which certain tools are used is simply how long they've been around. "It would be unrealistic to expect some of the newest management techniques to be as widespread as EDP," says Lawrence. "EDP has been around for almost 25 years and generally available to management for over 15 years. EDP should, therefore, be expected to be far more widespread than, say, social accounting which dates back only to 1970. Every manager has had some experience with EDP. Very few have had a chance to come in contact with social accounting."

To summarize how widely used the five most popular tools are: nine out of ten companies use EDP and MIS; MBO programs are used in over eight out of ten companies, and slightly less than eight out of ten are using or testing OD. Over six out of ten companies currently make use of direct costing (DC).

According to Duane Kromm, controller at Theodore Barry, "Direct costing, when well conceived and tailored to an individual company's needs, can be a useful system. However, direct costing in many cases can lead to oversophistication. Costs can be allocated and tracked with such precision and in such detail that maintenance of the system becomes burdensome, and data often lose some of their potential usefulness. When this happens the system can lead to disenchantment among managers."

To Charles Ferguson of Lifson, Wilson, Ferguson & Winick, the finding that eight of ten companies use MBO seems "surprisingly high." The number of companies using OD also was higher than he expected.

Looking at the other tools, almost half the companies are using discounted cash flow analysis and systems approach/systems engineering to view their organization. SA/SE has been used as a management system for only about six years. Job enrichment and indirect work measurement are in use in four out of ten firms. More than one-third are using modeling to simulate business situations.

Arnold Putnam, president of Rath & Strong, focused on the finding that only half as many companies use job enrichment as report using OD. "The use of OD at some time encompasses the employment of job enrichment," Putnam points out. "I would expect a closer correlation. Perhaps the failure to use job enrichment more extensively is because its installation and use have not been handled as a part of a larger organizational development program."

"Management sometimes tends to view specific management techniques as independent from each other," concurs Carlton P. McNamara, manager of the Management Services Group at Theodore Barry. "Unfortunately, this tendency has the effect of obscuring many real, significant, and often subtle interrelationships among various tools. The progressive manager tends to integrate, as an

Some Techniques Dissatisfy

Technique	Rate of Dissatisfaction (percent)	Total No. of Companies Using	No. of Companies Dissatisfied
Indirect work measurement	25	61	15
Cafeteria approach to compensation	22	18	4
Operations research	20	46	9
Job enrichment	16	63	10
Management by objective	15	122	19
Discounted cash flow analysis	14	70	10
Modeling	13	52	7
Social accounting	13	23	3
Electronic data processing	12	137	17
Management information systems	12	137	16
Direct costing	12	92	11
Systems approach	10	69	7
Organizational development	07	115	8

example, a computer-based information system with ongoing job enrichment and OD programs by considering the potential conflicts and the potential synergies of the combined systems."

Why the "Disappointment"?

The fact that tools generating the lowest rate of dissatisfaction are the ones most frequently used may indicate that at least some companies do not develop a detailed plan for their systems prior to installation. "There is a high probability that the widespread disappointment should be focused on the design and implementation of the tool used," says LeRoy Malouf of Rath & Strong, "rather than on the tools themselves."

"In many companies systems often 'growed like Topsy'," adds Rath & Strong's Romeyn Everdell. "We often find very cumbersome and expensive EDP systems held together as if by baling wire. The company then faces large costs to integrate the system and make it sufficiently flexible to meet new needs. The same lack of proper planning often exists with other management techniques."

For example, a medium size textile products firm on the West Coast reports it is now using four modern management techniques—EDP, DC, MIS, and SA/SE. The last was recently installed and the president says "we don't know what its impact will be." But the results he obtained from the other three systems are below expectations.

There are a variety of reasons for a company getting poor results from a management system. Perhaps management installed the systems without sufficient understanding of the kinds of techniques appropriate for the business. Or "they may have inadequate transaction discipline to control data accuracy," according to Everdell.

Some Gain in Popularity

Technique	No. of Companies Recently Adding Technique	Total No. of Companies Using Technique
Organizational development	44	115
Management by objective	34	122
Job enrichment	31	63
Systems approach/systems engineering	28	69
Indirect work measurement	23	61
Modeling	22	52
Direct costing	21	92
Operations research	17	46
Discounted cash flow	15	70
Management information systems	14	137
"Cafeteria" approach to compensation	12	18
Electronic data processing	10	137
Social accounting	6	23

The textile company was not alone in its disenchantment. A small manufacturer in the South was disappointed with its EDP and MIS results and had already discontinued the use of OD at the time of the study. But still seeking useful tools, the president had recently begun to use DC. A bank president reported that he was displeased with the results from seven systems including EDP. His only favorable results were being obtained from an indirect work measurement system.

"The low dissatisfaction rate with OD may be due in part to the fact that the technique is riding a wave of popularity approaching faddism," cautions James Morrison, a vice president of Lawrence-Leiter. "Also, it is difficult to set measurable objectives. Where OD consists mainly of a collection of sensitivity training programs, a high percentage of dissatisfaction can be predicted."

The highest frequency of dissatisfaction reported involved indirect work measurement. One-fourth of the companies were negative. A reason may be that companies have been applying this technique too widely.

Indirect work measurement (IWM) is a technique for assessing the volume and nature of nonproduction jobs to establish efficient staffing levels and control productivity costs.

"Applications of IWM can run the gamut from office clerical to maintenance crafts," explains Raymond J. Arris of Rath & Strong. The more complex indirect areas such as maintenance crafts are costly and difficult to measure and control. Office clerical presents fewer measurement problems.

"Because maintenance and similar complex indirect functions require greater sophisticated measurement and control tools," Arris says, "companies undertaking measurement in these areas are more likely to encounter frustrations. Companies, such as banks, whose major indirect functions are clerical, and manufacturing concerns which measure clerical operations, can have highly rewarding programs that are easy to install and administer. Companies would be wise, at least at the start, to undertake IWM of less complex areas."

The "cafeteria" approach to compensation, which ranked last in total usage, was the second most disappointing technique among the companies actually using it. "Of course," points out Charles Ferguson, "'cafeteria' compensation is one of the newest of management tools. Its light frequency may be simply a function of the length of time management has been exposed to it."

One of the older techniques in the survey, operations research, also a lightly used management tool—only 31 percent of the company presidents reported using the tool—produced the third highest rate of dissatisfaction. OR covers a wide variety of mathematical techniques, including modeling with an analytical approach to business problems. The survey found it little used except in banks and the largest companies. This low usage level does not project a wide range of support in the future, says Arnold Putnam of Rath & Strong. In fact, OR Operations Research reached its peak of popularity over 10 years ago.

Job enrichment, a program for changing the nature or structure of jobs to make them more meaningful, has been increasing in recent years. Forty-three percent of the companies studied used it, but it was the fourth most disappointing tool. Sixteen percent of the users were disappointed with the results.

"Job enrichment is very difficult to measure in terms of results, and unless the programs were carefully defined when they were originated, management may never be certain as to the results they are getting from the techniques," says Charles Ferguson of Lifson, Wilson, Ferguson & Winick. "Job enrichment particularly has a way of providing results that were not expected nor in line with corporate results."

The fifth most disappointing tool is MBO, used by 83 percent of the companies.

Lawrence-Leiter's James Morrison, who has taught MBO basics to executives here and overseas, suggests a reason: "Too many managers think of MBO as a 'program.' Actually, it is a 'process.' We advise clients considering MBO to look forward to two or three years of intensive individual and group effort to get it operational. Those who believe it can be installed in a few months through two or three training sessions are bound to be disappointed."

How Use Varies with Size

Large companies, the survey results indicate, are more willing—or able—to introduce modern management techniques than smaller companies. But Romeyn Everdell questions whether large companies do in fact have an advantage over smaller companies in this regard. One critical factor is how many people have to be involved in a program to make it work. "Most modern techniques require closer relationships among people, and large organizations find this harder to achieve than small ones," Everdell says.

Nonetheless, one of the clearest patterns developed by the survey results is that large companies tend to introduce twice as many modern management techniques as small or medium-size ones.

Heavy industrial firms, utilities, and financially oriented companies such as banks and insurance companies apparently use a wider range of the management tools than do other industries. In general, the study finds that highly technical firms—those requiring large capital resources or generating records and a heavy paper flow—are using the most such tools.

Banks make broad use of eight of the management techniques under study, as do insurance companies. Perhaps as could be expected, the greatest concentration of management tool installations is found among conglomerates. Since conglomerates are among the largest firms in the study, their experience is parallel to large companies as a group. Even so, conglomerates' use of management tools is even more intense.

Comparatively low on the scale of usage are light consumer manufacturers and distributors. As a group these companies—which include apparel, jewelry, and housewares manufacturers and distributors—report the least frequent use of any group in the study. Only four techniques are in use by at least half of these companies: EDP, MIS, MO, and OD.

While the effect of geography on management may be nonexistent or at least unknown, the survey did find that Western-based firms are using modern management tools with a much higher rate of frequency than companies located in other areas of the country. The reasons for this are unclear, but may be due in part to the relative youthfulness of West Coast firms.

Organizational development is one technique that, survey results indicate, recently has grown in popularity. Eight out of ten companies use the process. Other tools that are coming on strong, the ones to watch in the near future, are job enrichment, indirect measurement (a tool available for some 20 years), and systems approach. While these three are used by less than half of the companies surveyed, they are gaining in popularity. Half of the companies currently using job enrichment have only recently added the technique. Systems approach is a new tool for 40 percent of the company presidents using it. IMW is new at 38 percent of the companies reporting it.

Modeling may also be picking up new adherents. While it is currently reported in use at about one-third of the companies surveyed, over 40 percent of these companies firms have only recently begun to put it into use.

3

The Qualifications of a Manager*

GLENN A. BASSETT

As the Industrial Revolution has proceeded on its course and as technology has changed the face of the entire industrial landscape, one thing has become clear: there is a great deal the modern business organization can do without, but one thing it cannot do without is an adequate number of skilled and effective managers. As *Forbes* magazine put it recently, "The one clear lesson after study of fifty years of U.S. business is: If a company has nothing going for it except one thing—good management—it will make the grade. If it has everything going for it except good management, it will flop."[1] But the managerial talent to manage increasingly complex organizations and technology is itself becoming a scarcer and more critical commodity. In large part, this scarcity derives from an inevitable increase in the level of skill and expertise demanded of an effective manager by expanding markets and technology, but it is no less a scarcity.

Undoubtedly, *Forbes* refers to the management team at or near the top of an organization which sets the policies and value climate of the operation, but this select population is only the top of the iceberg. The basic level of drive, experience, and systematic advance preparation (usually through formal education), already accepted as indices of potential for selection as a manager, is constantly being raised. Upgrading of managerial qualifications is being forced at every level of the operation, and even those managers appointed to positions designed to test, develop, and season them for future assignments must now be a higher quality of entrant. It is no longer sufficient to rely on trial and error as the principal method for developing future managers; managerial resources are increasingly scarce, and the selection and development process itself must be managed.

However, we must first develop a useful understanding of the process of selecting and developing managers. How to determine what the business requires in the way of managerial resources and how we are to go about meeting those needs, once specified, must be established. We must, in a phrase, have a workable theory of what managerial selection and development is all about.

The Popular Point of View. The myths and folklore relating to the manner in which progression takes place through the executive ranks and into top manage-

*Source: Copyright 1969 by The Regents of the University of California. Reprinted from *California Management Review,* vol. 12, no. 2, 35-44, by permission of The Regents.
1/*Forbes,* Fiftieth Anniversary Issue, September 15, 1967.

ment and the executive chambers are rich and fascinating. As the popular fiction of executive succession would have it, getting ahead as a manager is mostly a matter of being the toughest, smartest, and politically most astute of all those in competition for the job.

This perspective is at least partially right. A certain amount of basically amoral jockeying for position, stabbing in the back, and survival-of-the-fittest tactics do take place, but probably to a lesser extent than is popularly assumed. Rather, judgments about the qualifications of the man promoted to high office are, for the most part, pretty sound ones. To begin with, the man promoted has probably been around for quite a while and has been observed at close range by the people who make the selection decision. His will and ability to get results in his field of specialization have been demonstrated to the full. His capabilities and qualities, his strengths and his weaknesses are reliably known. Indeed, he has probably adopted something in the way of a characteristic style which, given a particular set of business needs and circumstances, makes him a predictable quantity as far as managerial performance is concerned.

For instance, Manager Doe is seen as a do-it type of manager who rams through programs and drives himself and his organization toward achievement of the objectives which have been set for him. Manager Roe has a reputation as a man of great depth of knowledge and intellectual capacity who can be relied upon to solve the seemingly unsolvable problem. Manager Ecks is a compromiser, forever arguing the question on both sides, inconsistent and contradictory in his actions, but striving constantly (and often successfully) to persuade, seduce, or trap people into doing things his way. Manager Zee experiments with his style, continually altering and expanding it to fit the situation, but doing so with a consistent sense of ethics and an insistence upon maintaining his own personal integrity while all the while seeking results.

Each of these four managers is a distinctly different person with a distinctly different style of operation. And, although we might prefer one or another of the styles, it is only good management practice to assume that each is suitable for application at some time in some place, *depending upon the needs of the business.* That is, managerial style is itself a resource which should be skillfully and differentially applied in terms of the availability of various styles and the demands of the business environment. Personal preferences for one or another style should never blind us to the fact that every managerial style can and does have a place in a results-oriented business world.

To be well managed, a business should have in its manpower stable a variety of managers representing a cross section of managerial styles. Somewhat in the fashion of the baseball manager who carefully assures a balance of right- and left-handed pitchers so that he may apply the pitching talent appropriately in the face of the hitting talent he must deal with, the business manager must develop a balanced assortment of managerial styles within his organization in order to be assured that the best man for the job is available when the opening comes along.

The Habitual/Intellectual Dimension. Certainly, in the art of managing there are more varieties and shades of style than just these several I have chosen to illustrate for openers.[2] The styles illustrated, however, arise from a fundamental polarity in human behavior. Human beings deal with their environment on either or both of two relatively distinct levels: the habitual and the intellectual. On the habitual level, we learn directly through experience how to react to a wide variety of situations. In behaving from habit, it makes no difference whether we are aware of our behavior or of the bases of that behavior. Indeed, there is typically a heavy element of unawareness or subconsciousness to habitual behavior.

On the intellectual level, by contrast, we consciously manipulate systems of symbols such as language or mathematics. (Systems include both the symbols, themselves, and the rules for their use.) With symbol systems, we are no longer limited to our own experiences as the basis of our behavior but, rather, can now draw upon the experiences of others. In addition, our symbol systems may be employed to understand and deal with experiences which are unique, or even inaccessible to us, if we become skilled enough in their use and application.

Most human beings operate on both these levels. Each level has its own advantages, and, depending upon which level of behavior is the more appropriate under a given set of circumstances, one may be emphasized in its development in preference to the other. For instance, in public speaking, in driving a car, in learning to play a musical instrument or operate a machine, the best and sometimes the only route to success is through intensively practiced habits. Decisions (choices) related to such activities are best based on one's practical "feel" for them. When time is too brief to work out the situation intellectually, a habitual reaction may be the only behavior acceptable. On the other hand, when errors are potentially too serious to tolerate and we must plan carefully to avoid them or when we are faced with a problem for which we have no applicable experience to draw upon, we are most likely to find that only rational, intellectual solutions will do.

Man, then, has two separate and relatively distinct cognitive resources or faculties with which he may know and cope with his environment: the habitual/reactive and the rational/symbolic. To a certain extent, these two faculties are mutually exclusive; in large part they overlap. They supplement and complement one another. Too often, however, the success and competence enjoyed at one level creates a sense of complacency which results in studied ignorance or even rejection of the other level. We *polarize on the reactive level or the intellectual level.* In a business context, these polarities are often accentuated through the creation of staff functions such as finance, legal counsel, or engineering, which emphasize the systematic, intellectual approach to problem solution, and line functions such as production or sales, where habitual, reactive behavior domi-

2/See my *Management Styles in Transition* (New York: American Management Association, 1966), for a considerably more detailed discussion of the elements of both managerial style and skill.

nates. And, because managers tend to come up through the ranks of their functions before being considered for middle and higher management positions, they also tend to polarize in their style of operation and in the way they employ their habitual versus their intellectual resources toward the solution of business problems.

Generally, managers may be found either to cluster around the poles of habitual or intellectual preferences, or to struggle to find some suitable middle ground between them. Therein, indeed, lies the basis of the four illustrations cited in the opening of this discussion.

Managers who differ distinctly in style of operation tend to differ in the way they employ their reactive and their intellectual resources toward the solution of managerial problems. At one pole is the subjective decision maker (Manager Doe) who uses his experiences as a basis from which to arrive at artful, intuitive decisions. This type of manager tunes his senses and reactions fully to the world around him. His keen senses, indeed, are his principal operating tools. Objectivity to him is a simple matter of facing facts.

At the other pole is Manager Roe, who cultivates his intellect for the purpose of processing information systematically and arriving at decisions logically. He typically avoids opinion and intuition in favor of seeking out the truth, using all the tools of intellect at his command. He holds his emotions in check and uses them predominantly for imagining potential new methods, new techniques, and new systems of symbols with which to solve his problems. To him, objectivity is scientific method.

The former of these two managers relies heavily upon an intimate association with all aspects of reality as his basis of operation, whereas the latter depends principally upon intellect and the realm of ideas. The one is *reality-oriented* and might best be thought of as a realist, whereas the other is *idea-oriented* and might most accurately be labeled an idealist.[3]

The Integrative Dimension. Two additional styles can be identified by

3/I recognize that the terms "realist" and "idealist" are widely abused in common use, and their use in this context may cause some confusion at first. William James in his *Essays on Pragmatism* (New York: Washington Square Press, 1963), to which this conceptualization owes much, calls these polarities "tough-minded" and "tender-minded." The current fad of tough-mindedness in business, however, has resulted in an artificial polarizing of preference toward tough-mindedness which obscures the importance of having both these polarities of managerial temperament represented in a business organization. And, while the terms "idealism" and "realism" are themselves charged with a certain amount of emotion and personal preference, they are a little nearer to equality in preference across our culture. The fact that they are strong words may even work in our favor by making them useful as long as they are defined and used with care. We could, of course, have used other terms slightly less charged, such as "theoretical" vs. "practical," but such a substitute would only have made the discussion calmer and more academic in quality. The existence of an emotional charge—that is, personal preference—is what makes these managerial styles problematic when it comes to developing and selecting a manager, but it also assures that they have vitality and relevance to today's problems. The reader's forbearance must therefore be asked, even though the terms "realism" and "idealism" are used in ways which may seem at first to be wrong-headed.

looking at the manner in which the middle ground between idealism and realism is used. On the one hand is Manager Ecks, who has no firm base in either idealism or realism and who vacillates back and forth, ignoring or even denying any inconsistencies in his behavior. On the other is Manager Zee, who accepts the validity of both the idealistic and the realistic points of view and finds himself struggling constantly to integrate and reconcile the basic contradictions he finds between them. The managers who use these styles we might call opportunists and reconcilers, respectively. These styles are distinguished by the *level of integrity* each man brings to the job of managing.

Differential styles of using habitual and intellectual resources are clearly attractive and potentially useful bases from which to describe and manage managerial resources. The dimensions along which managerial style may be developed are highly varied, and we should be aware that the polarities discussed here are only one pair among the many which may be relevant. The habitual/intellectual dimension, as well as the way it is integrated by the individual, however, appears to have more power for explaining managerial behavior and permitting sensible differential selection and development of managers than any other approach.

Figure 1 illustrates the qualities which describe the realistic and idealistic styles of operation and the relationship of these polarities to reconciliatory and opportunistic styles of operation. Realism/idealism represents the dimension of manner of use of habitual/intellectual resources, and opportunism/reconciliation represents the degree to which any attempted combining of realistic/idealistic polarities is integrated.

Practical and Policy Implications of the Theory. What does all this mean from a practical and policy point of view? The mere recognition of the polarity of realists and idealists in managing immediately points to several implications. For one, it is quite possible to build a business organization that is oriented to realism or idealism by emphasizing one pole or the other in the selection, training, and rewarding of personnel. Any preference in selection which emphasizes formal education or technical proficiency, for instance, tends to breed idealism, while a bias against eggheads and fuzzy-minded theorists favors realism. Criticism of snap, seat-of-the-pants decision makers for failing to think the problem through sufficiently downgrades the realistic style and implies advantage in an idealistic approach. With respect to formal training, exercises such as T-Groups, sensitivity training,[4] and timed in-basket tests[5] strictly favor realism by going directly to the problem of tuning one's senses to recognize the situation and respond automatically to it.[6] Rational training techniques of

---

[4]/See Chris Argyris, "T-Groups for Organizational Effectiveness," *Harvard Business Review*, March-April 1964, p. 60.

[5]/See Felix M. Lopez, Jr., *Evaluating Executive Decision Making: The In-Basket Technique* (New York: American Management Association, 1966).

[6]/One of the earliest cues which pointed me toward this conceptualization of management development came out of the use of a timed in-basket test as a predictor of managerial potential. It was discovered that a strong technical background in engineering or the sciences

FIGURE 1
Polarities of Managerial Temperament

THE OPPORTUNIST
Vacillates between idealism
and realism in operating
style.
Ignores or denies inconsistencies or hypocrisies in his
behavior.
Compromises conflict which
should be resolved.
Has no strong affinity to either
idealism or realism as the
base of his behavior.
Seeks to reduce pressures.

Style of Use of Cognitive

← ——— Resources ——— →

Integrity of
Combined Style

THE RECONCILER
Accepts and works to integrate the contradictory
traits of idealism and realism.
Can apply idealistic, realistic,
or combined perspectives as
the problem demands with-
out gross inconsistencies.
Chooses subordinates in terms
of the need for realistic or
idealistic temperament
based on the business situation.
Seeks balanced short- and
long-range results.
Is the rarest managerial temperament of all.

THE REALIST
Reacts to the problem.
Is an autocrat; relies on the
authority of power.
Yields to expedience.
Is an artful practitoner of his
specialty.
Is priority-oriented.
Is intuitive in his judgments.
Strives for optimal perfor-
mance.
Employs resources.
Cuts the problem down to
manageable size.
Is practical.
Reaches decisions quickly re-
gardless of the information
available.
Assumes the fact of resource
scarcity and works around it.
Pursues attainable, tangible
goals.
Seeks immediate results.

THE IDEALIST
Reflects on the problem.
Is a technocrat; relies on the
authority of fact.
Sticks to principles.
Is a skilled technician.
Is process- and method-
oriented.
Is systematic and rational in
his judgments.
Strives for professional perfor-
mance.
Creates resources.
Attacks the total problem.
Is theoretical.
Defers decisions until the in-
formation available is suffi-
cient to support them.
Assumes that critical or
scarce resources should be
made plentiful and works to
create them.
Sets the ideal as his goal.
Seeks high quality results.

the Kepner-Tregoe type,[7] on the other hand, emphasize method and logic as the most suitable way in which to solve business problems and thereby lend support to any existing idealistic bias.

was a detriment to effective performance of an in-basket test, whereas practical experience in a shop or production environment, regardless of educational background, was associated with relatively effective handling of the in-basket task. Out of this finding, the old bias favoring a man of practical experience over the theorist for production jobs began to take on meaning.

7/See C. H. Kepner and B. B. Tregoe, *The Rational Manager* (New York: McGraw-Hill, 1965).

These approaches and practices can serve to increase or decrease the amount of realism or idealism practiced in a business organization. Where competitive business conditions demand increased realism or where the market demand for product innovation requires increased idealism, one or the other of each of these pairs of alternatives might well be applied as appropriate. It should be noted, however, that tactics which increase one at the expense of the other and methods which ignore the opportunity and need to integrate realism and idealism may serve merely to defer problems into the future. Integrity of style is also needed—preferably a flexible integrity which encompasses both idealism and realism.

Obviously, one way of avoiding the frustrations and hazards of trying to maintain strict personal integrity of style would be to polarize one's style single-mindedly on either the pure realistic or the idealistic ends of the scale. Thus, the theory suggests that, if top management values integrity more highly than flexibility, we should predict a tendency among subordinate managers toward sharper polarization of operating style in both directions, along with a general rejection of opportunism (and perhaps reconciliation, too) as an acceptable style of managing. Conversely, heavy emphasis on flexibility to the exclusion of integrity might be expected to reduce sharpness of polarization and increase the use of opportunistic and reconciliatory tactics.

Approximately equal emphasis on flexibility and integrity should force styles toward reconciliation but could also serve to drive good, effective realists and idealists out of the operation because they can not tolerate the stress of having such demands put on them.

Using this theory, management should be able to influence the mix of available managerial talent in the direction needed by changing business conditions merely by re-emphasizing the value of integrity versus flexibility of operating style. This theory of managerial selection and development tells us, in effect, that *integrity and flexibility are key values:* Depending upon how they are stressed (rewarded and penalized) management can determine the pattern of managerial style development in the organization.

Something to Build On. To back up for a moment, style is only the *qualitative* aspect of managerial resources. Whether the job to be done should be assigned to an idealist, a realist, an opportunist, or a reconciler is a highly relevant consideration when it comes to utilizing existing managerial resources in the most effective manner. We must presume, though, that every applicant has an adequate fund of relevant skill, experience, courage, motivation, and personal commitment to the risky, arduous journey which progressing through the managerial ranks involves. These are the *quantitative* prerequisites of managerial selection and promotion.

There are *two quantitative prerequisites to selecting capable managers:*

First, a manager must have a history of striving for personal betterment and a high level of energy/drive/motivation for application to the problems he faces. There is not enough time in a lifetime, much less in a manager's day, to deal with all the information that must be dealt with and to solve all the problems that have to be solved unless a high order of energy and drive characterizes the individual's mode of behavior. The manager's job is to deal with problems and preside over change in his organization. The complexity of technology and society makes it impossible for the dull, lethargic individual to achieve even the minimum of personal skill which is essential to meeting the management challenges of the twentieth century. A manager without a zest for living, without imagination, without a need for fresh challenges on which to whet his intellect and emotions can do little more than preside over an established routine.

Second, an effective manager must have a rich fund of experience. He must have seen life and business from a variety of perspectives. The range of experience possessed, of course, will often be rather closely correlated to the level of energy and drive applied in the individual's life style, and it is reasonable to expect that a high level of applied energy and drive will have resulted in a rich variety of experiences.

The need for a broad range of experience stems from the fact that, in the pressure of the moment, many of a manager's decisions are fabricated largely out of his immediate knowledge and experience. A narrow basis of experience results in narrow managerial decisions and limited courses of action. The most energetic of managers, if he has not been exposed outside a narrow field of specialization, may be seriously handicapped in dealing with the rough problems of our times. The manager who has several college degrees, who has served in a variety of functions and a variety of different kinds of business, and/or who has lived life under a wide variety of circumstances and statuses is the manager most likely to have the greatest fund of information that can be applied directly to the solution of business problems.

These are, indeed, the very qualities which are demanded of candidates for succession through the managerial hierarchy. It is the bright, well-educated, highly motivated, committed self-starter who is the odds-on favorite as the future manager, and the more of these qualities he possesses in abundance, the more likely he is to advance.

This should come as no surprise to anyone. These are the qualities which educators and business theorists have for most of the past century been touting as essential. They are directly observable, measurable in a relatively reliable and objective fashion, widely accepted, and evident in the selection of most managerial appointees. But they are only the *prerequisites for admittance* to the manpower pool from which critical appointments will eventually be made. Once the prerequisites have been met, the actual selection and appointment to high managerial positions is more likely to turn on *style of operation*.

It is important for everyone in the candidate pool to recognize the place of style in selection decisions. To the extent that the importance and relevance of operating style is not appreciated, candidates for promotion may perceive appointments to be based on political considerations and may even perceive (correctly on occasion) admission to top management spots to be based on favoritism. Where the importance of style is realized, on the other hand, and the relevance of appointments based on operating style is recognized as essential to the best utilization of managerial talent, such charges and the resultant personal demoralization that accompanies them should greatly diminish.

Awareness of the prerequisite status of motivation and experience can permit sensible variation in the level of entry requirements in order to expand or diminish the pool of available managerial candidates as business needs demand. To the extent that a wide range of motivation and experience is applicable to the job at hand and a broader range of operating styles is needed, the promotable pool can be opened up. Or to the extent that the promotable pool is unavoidably restricted, a better allocation of available styles of operation may be sought to meet existing needs. This approach to managerial qualifications makes explicit the points at which something can be done about managerial development.

What Is Business All about to Begin with? A key assumption is inherent here and, for that matter, in the formulation of economic laws and the operation of businesses which should now be articulated: *Managing involves at its core the ability to allocate resources of variable scarcity/abundance in satisfying to the full needs of the business, its shareholders, its customers, its employees, and society as a whole.*

That is to say, management is the arrangement, use, creation, and preservation of all the resources at hand in satisfying the total variety of demands and pressures that are placed upon the business in the total environment in which it operates. The skill with which abundance is exploited and scarcity is overcome will, in the long run, determine the effectiveness of a manager. Two critical resources which must be employed skillfully in effecting satisfactory allocation of these resources are *time and human creativity.*

Time is an often overlooked resource. It is often overlooked because the two fundamental polarities of managerial style tend to trap people into one or another of two time orientations: the realistic style of managing emphasizes the short term, the intermediate, the here and now, and it severely downgrades the future as a problem-solving resource. The idealistic style, on the other hand, tends to treat time in much the same way that other resources are treated; it is something to spend and use to one's own purposes.

Creativity is likewise biased by a tendency to a realist/idealist polarity. For instance, the problem is to meet the competition by shipping a product to a customer faster, and the problem of delay stems from errors and time lag in shipping from the warehouse because of the heavy backlog of work. To solve this, one of several things might be done: Hire more clerks and spread the heavy work load thinner, or create a better system for handling incoming orders and shipments so that the available clerks can, with proper training, handle their jobs more expeditiously. The first tactic would emphasize exploiting clerical labor in solution of the problem; the second would address itself to the creation of a new resource—the improved system—to do the job. If clerical help is more abundant or less expensive than the talent needed to innovate a better system, the first solution would be the better. If, on the other hand, clerical help is in short supply or is more expensive than innovative talent, the latter solution would be the superior one. The manner in which scarcity/abundance of resources arrays itself should point to the most appropriate solution. But the existence of either an idealistic or realistic bias will probably itself determine the solution chosen.

The manner in which these resources of time and creativity are utilized is related to and typically limited by the existence of tendencies toward either a realistic or an idealistic style of managing. Too often, the fullest use of the resource of time is not achieved because of a realistic orientation, or, conversely, the idealist fails to recognize time constraints which, if not met, could destroy the effectiveness of all other efforts. Similarly, opportunities to create new resources to overcome severe scarcities are ignored by the realist, while opportunities to exploit abundant resources are missed by the idealistic managerial temperament. Our theory of manager development now begins to point to ways in which managerial resources should be allocated to meet the demands of the marketplace.

What Does a Business Environment Demand? The determination of the most appropriate approach—realistic or idealistic—can now be based upon an evaluation by top management of the business environment as it exists at any given point in time. At one point in time, a realistic style may be critical; at another, only idealism will turn the tide in meeting the market. The considerations for determining who should be appointed as between a realist and an idealist in the managerial talent pool might well be the following:

1. What are the primary time constraints and options?

   What is the competition doing?

   What are the advantages of quick entry into the market as against taking the time to deliver a product of unquestioned quality, utility, and reliability?

   How hungry are higher managers, stockholders, or financiers for quick success?

2. Where does the greater opportunity lie?

   With innovation?

   With exploitation of existing resources and technology?

Depending upon how top management answers these questions, the direction in which it should go in choosing a realistic or idealistic managerial style could largely be decided.

Why Not All Reconcilers? It is perhaps obvious at this point that the ideal manager genuinely integrates all the elements of realism and idealism within one skull. He appreciates the need for flexibility of style sufficiently to vary his own style between realism and idealism as the demands of the business environment make it appropriate. Why worry about idealists or realists at all? Why not pick only reconcilers for managers? The answer is that reconcilers are in short supply. Strictly speaking, they probably do not exist at all except in the ideal, and we are a long way from the ideal with respect to managerial resources in industry today. Beyond this, reconciliation demands the very fullest development of skills and an exceptional level of drive/energy/motivation which in itself is extremely rare. The motivation and opportunity to learn how to become a reconciler come dearly, and few people are fortunate to luck into both.

At the same time, reconciliation is the most difficult of all managerial styles to identify. This is because the operating reconciler may, in different circumstances and at different times, appear to be either highly realistic or highly idealistic. Furthermore, it is particularly difficult to determine whether the opposite polarity exists if circumstances demand that a given style be predominant at one time and place. Identifying a reconciler can require extensive observation of performance over a long period of time. But the real key to the reconciler's temperament is his ability to accept seeming contradictions of style without compromising his integrity.

The highly polarized realist, for instance, typically feels the need to reject the soft-headedness of the theoretician, while the committed researcher working from a strictly idealistic point of view typically finds it necessary to criticize the crudeness, expedience, and even amorality of the realist. The realist who cannot get along with idealists and the idealist who finds it necessary to exclude realists from his circle of intimates clearly are not reconciliatory managers. The manager who can accept opposites of polarity, reconcile them, and apply them appropriately in the face of varying circumstances without resorting to opportunism or hypocrisy may very well be a reconciler. With such limited cues to go on, close observation and intimate knowledge of the individual's style of operation are called for to reliably determine whether he is the kind of resource who could be described as a reconciliatory manager.

Certainly it is desirable that reconcilers themselves be involved as fully as possible in the selection of other managers. The rationale for this is a basic one: The man who has this scarcest of all managerial resources can most surely be relied upon to test the needs and demands of the market objectively and select an idealist or a realist—or even an opportunist, perhaps—to meet those needs. Lacking a reconciliatory manager at the point of selection, the realist will tend to value subordinates with a realistic outlook, idealists will favor candidates with idealistic tendencies, and the opportunist will tend to seek the company of his own kind as well. As a result, changes in the environment which require adaptation on the part of the organization and its management may be neither perceived nor appropriately met.

Many modern corporations have at one time or another been forced to face the fact that, when a segment of the business has gone sour, it is not the manager who has failed. Rather, a market has changed and now demands a style of managing which the incumbent lacks. The manager himself may be as good as he ever was—given his particular style of operation. If, however, corporate management fails to recognize and act on the changing situation and permits such a man to be tarred with the brush of failure, a perfectly good managerial resource may be lost to the organization or even destroyed. In today's explosive economy, the right to fail without stigma, to make mistakes and learn from them, may be the most important single element of a successful manager development program. Higher management which fails to appreciate this fact is not preserving its managerial resources and using them wisely. The existence of realism or idealism in energetic, richly experienced managers makes for superb managerial resources, but, if these resources cannot be diagnosed and applied appropriately to the problems of the business, or if they cannot be salvaged in the face of a changing market, they are lost as surely as if they had never been developed or identified at all.

Measures and Indicators of Managerial Potential. The key to success in allocating scarce managerial resources, as in allocating any other resources, is in developing useful measures and indicators which will tell when a needed potential exists. An important strength of this theory of managerial temperament lies in the fact that it suggests a variety of objective measures which may be used at a number of levels for screening managers and appointing them to open position. On the level of motivation and breadth of experience, some of these measures would be:

Salary progress within age group.

High level of general involvement and activity (agitators and troublemakers should be screened in, not out).

A record as a self-made individual who has achieved results and a reputation far exceeding the norm for his background and level of education.

Multiple degrees.

Postgraduate work or an advanced degree in a field different from the first degree.

Patentable inventions.

Published material.

An unusually wide range of interests and general activities.

Leadership activities off the job.

Higher rate of salary growth than comparable employees.

The particular advantage of measures and indicators of this sort is that they are relatively objective in quality. Certainly they can be defined as to be very nearly factual and can thereby make potential managerial talent more visible to managers and staff personnel throughout the organization. In addition, tightening or loosening of screening standards for the managerial talent pool is entirely feasible based upon some kind of objective summary system covering all these indicators and measures. Experience and observation will point up additional useful indicators to any experienced businessman.

Measures and indicators of the idealistic and realistic styles of managerial operation are also available, though they are somewhat less objective. The only certain way to pin down style of operation is to observe and investigate performance closely over a period of time, using a variety of sources. The following indicators should be useful in identifying managerial styles:

The range of time in which plans are made.

The reliability with which tough deadlines are met, depending upon whether they are long term or short term.

Specificity/objectivity versus generality/breadth of personal and business goals and objectives.

The measures used to measure the performance of subordinates.

The methods used to analyze problems.

Decision-making style.

The extent to which a manager's manner is cool and calculated versus emotional and spontaneous.

The traits a manager looks for in a good or poor subordinate manager.

The kinds of people a manager works with best. The kinds he works with least well.

Personal theory of economics. (Be careful with this one. "Safe" answers in the area of economics tend to emphasize realism for the simple reason that such answers have been systematically inculcated by our culture.)

A number of sources of information are available for filling out the picture; depth evaluative interviews, skilled reference interviews, inquiries with the current manager, interviews with other managers who have had opportunity to observe style of operation, contacts with fellow managers, and even interviews with subordinates can yield information on management style. Any sources or techniques which need to be exploited should be exploited in so sensitive and important a matter as the selection and promotion of a new manager.

Summary and Conclusions. Managers who are fully qualified for the job to which they are appointed are a rarity. For the most part, we must manage our managerial resources with at least as much creativity, artfulness, and skill as we apply to handling our physical, financial, and other business resources. The overall level of energy/drive/motivation and the richness of background and experience—the quantitative elements—are the foundations of managerial selection which can to a substantial degree be identified objectively and defined factually. Such traits can further be confirmed and examined by skilled use of an interview with those candidates identified as having managerial potential.

For appointments further up the managerial ladder, the actual selection turns more and more on qualitative elements such as style of operation rather than upon absolute qualifications for the job. This is not to say that style is anything less than a qualification in its own right. If a managerial appointee must, for instance, be able to create resources in working out problems, his style must include the skill and disposition to be creative. By and large, the style that best fits the market situation in the judgment of the appointing manager is the style that should get the nod for the appointment. Small differences in operating style can be crucial to managerial success. The use of style as a criterion of selection is not only appropriate but necessary as well.

The rarest of all managers is the reconciler; this is the manager who can at least in some degree combine the diverse and contradictory traits of idealism and realism into a single integrated style of operation flexible enough to cope with the dynamics of the marketplace. The reconciler is also best suited to mediating between and coordinating the team activity of those realist and idealist managers who so often fail to appreciate one another's style of operation.

Finally, the theory of managerial qualifications proposed here suggests useful measures and indicators which can become the foundation of an effective program of managerial development and selection, and it further specifies the points of leverage for managing manager development.

If, as the initial quote from *Forbes* suggests, good management is the difference between business success and failure, the quality of a managerial selection and promotion program may be *a key point of leverage* in determining the future of a business, and the implementation of an effective program may be *the most important investment* the business ever makes. The theory of managerial qualifications which has been outlined here may help in conceptualizing a management operating philosophy upon which and within which such a program can be created and managed.

4

Potential for Career Growth*

DOUGLAS T. HALL

Most recent discussion of the generation gap has focused on its negative aspects—the conflicts and destructiveness which receive so much attention from the mass media. This paper will examine the impressive potential of energy, ideas, and other resources which lies in the differences between young people in organizations and their older colleagues.

The careers of young people, recent graduates, in organizational settings, will be examined.

We will review what seem to be the desires and the values of new graduates, how they affect the organization, and how the organization in turn affects the new graduates. Despite some strong feelings that managers may have about the way new people are shaking up organizations, the reverse process is still stronger.

We will examine research and theory on careers and identify factors which facilitate success in career development.

We will try to translate the research findings into suggestions for changing organizations to improve the ways careers are managed.

Gap in Values

The concerns of present youth differ from those of previous generations in the following important areas:

1. There is now more concern about basic values, not just different values, but values *per se.*
2. Action is more important. Not only are values more salient, but there is strong emphasis on behaving in accord with one's values. Merely talking about one's values tends to be suspect; values are not trusted unless they are backed by action. The cry is, "Do it!"
3. Personal integrity, honesty, openness, and realness are more important. After the revolution, hypocrisy may be a capital offense!
4. Many of the "new culture" (Slater, 1970) values are humanistic. Today's students are more concerned about personal development, their own intel-

*Source: Reprinted from *Personnel Administration* (May-June 1971), 18-30, by permission of the International Personnel Management Association.

lectual and especially emotional growth, than students were previously. This reflects a movement away from concerns for occupational success and security, away from a vocationally-oriented education form, and toward a greater awareness and pursuit of their own personal definition of a meaningful life and life's work. As Jerry Rubin has put it, "We're not in school to learn how to make a living; we're here to learn how to live!" In terms of Maslow's (1954) need hierarchy, the change is a shift away from security and toward growth. Maslow's theory would explain this shift by saying that since security needs have been largely satisfied for today's youth (by their present affluence and lack of experience of an economic depression), they are not concerned about the determinants of future career security—organizational promotions, professional recognition, or a high income. The satisfied security needs are no longer a source of motivation. Present day youth are free to pursue personal growth and meaning more fully.[1]

5. Related to the humanistic and value orientation is a concern for the ultimate social value of one's work. Not only is the intrinsic meaning and challenge of a job important, but also the *consequences* of one's work are more important to youth (as recruiters for large chemical companies realize). Similarly, work involving social service is becoming increasingly important.

6. The definition of legitimate authority is changing. Authority based on age or position is less highly regarded. The authority of one's expertise, personal style, personal convictions, or accomplishments carries much more weight with today's youth. Greater mutual influence is also valued in young people's relationships with authority (Ondrack, 1971). In career terms, this means that young people want more personal control over decisions affecting their lives.

If there is a gap in our society it is probably more accurate to call it a value gap rather than a generation gap. There is probably just as much of a gap in attitudes within the population of college students or people in their twenties as there is between the mode of young people and people twenty years older. And, of course, many "over-30's" hold the values described above. We have to be more specific and talk about values as well as age.

What Young People Want in Work

When one translates these new values into a work situation, what do people look for in their work? Most important, perhaps, recent graduates want challenging work—work that is meaningful and ability-stretching to them. Basically they want to have more of a sense of feeling competent in the work they do.

1/This need hierarchy also explains the differences between the goals of Black and White activists. The above reasoning applies mainly to White middle class youth. Generally, Black youths have not grown up in such affluence. As a result, White activists tend to repudiate their affluence and focus on humanizing society and facilitating greater personal growth and "internal freedom." Blacks, on the other hand, tend to focus on the specific economic and political forces that are still depriving Black people of basic security.

Competence, the need to have an impact on one's personal environment, is a critically important human need (White, 1959). This seems especially strong in the present generation of young people.

Another valued feature is a more collaborative relationship with their superiors: they want a lowering of the authority distance between them and the next man up, more opportunities to make their own personal choices, and an organizational climate that is more open and flexible. They also want an opportunity to get more psychologically involved in the work they are doing; they place increasing stress on intrinsic rather than extrinsic rewards for their work. Dissatisfaction about intrinsic work challenge is especially strong in the first year of work (Schein, 1968). There are many complaints about job rotation training programs, in which people are given special projects and are asked to do research on a limited problem. Very often they feel they are unable to get deeply enough into that one project to get a sense of being competent and a feeling that they are really learning something new; it may be a standard project that all new people are assigned to for two or three months, a training assignment that the company does not really take seriously. The new employees may also feel frustrated because they cannot go to the next step and be responsible for action that may grow out of their recommendations.

Difficulties Encountered

Often, however, the talk of wanting challenge and competence seems to be more rhetoric than reality. When one looks at what happens, what the new people actually do, they often seem to avoid precisely what they say they most desire.

There is a tendency to avoid sustained effort on one activity, even though there is much talk about wanting to get really involved in something. If the opportunity exists young people often do not take advantage of it. Related to this, although they talk of personal involvement and growth, one senses that they really do not push themselves to their limits. This is especially frustrating when one knows that these are impressively bright people. Perhaps one reason athletes tend to do well in business is that they are used to developing themselves—setting goals for themselves and getting into the disciplined process of pushing themselves to their limits. Unfortunately, many new recruits are so bright that they can perform fairly well on a minimum amount of effort. Then they tend to become apathetic because they rarely experience success by their own high standards.

Another frequent problem is a difficulty in committing oneself for too long to any one system. Very often, when young people talk about personal searching and discovering themselves, one gets the impression that they are actually avoiding committing themselves to anything permanent. They move from one job to another and from one system to another—whether the system is an organization, a group, or a family relationship.

In spite of their concern for challenge, new people often avoid some of what I see as the true challenges in work—facing up to authoritarian supervisors and trying to work with them, confronting differences, and resolving those differences. As Ondrack (1970) says, among people who score low on authoritarianism there is a tendency to give up on those who score high and say, "Okay, he's rigid, that's his bag. I can't fight it."

There is a tendency to avoid interpersonal conflicts, which is surprising because a lot of students are committed to the idea that there are very strong conflicts and problems existing in society, and that there is a need to use power and confrontation to produce social change. I had one of Yale's Students for a Democratic Society leaders in one of my T-groups, and I wondered what would happen when he became active in the group. "He's really going to blow the lid off," I thought. He was the meekest person in the group. What we, and he, learned was that his way of coping with interpersonal conflicts was to raise them to an institutional level and say, "I can face aggression, I can face conflict, but not a one-to-one basis. I can't face it myself. I've got to be part of some organization like Students for a Democratic Society that gives me the sense of power to confront other organizations."

However, conflict can be one of the most important determinants of challenge in a job. Indeed, some returned Peace Corps volunteers have indicated that business—or work in other types of large organizations—is more challenging than anything they faced in the Peace Corps, because in business there is greater conflict and resistance to their ideas. It is relatively easy, they say, to go to a foreign country where everybody sees them as experts. However, when a person goes to work in business, people resist his ideas; he has to compete and sell his ideas to superiors skeptical of (and perhaps threatened by) the efforts of the young.

Another characteristic of recent graduates is a sense of impatience and confidence often based on moral imperatives that create an appearance of arrogance. These are people who are critical and concerned. They look as if they have all the answers, and this creates a sense of threat for older people in an organization. Unfortunately, it may be an impression that is quite a bit stronger than the young people themselves want to communicate.

A Syndrome of Unused Career Potential

One unfortunate overall result of these differences between young graduates and older members of organizations is the creation of a syndrome of unused potential, a syndrome which shows up in several different self-reinforcing effects.

Results from a number of different studies (Berlew and Hall, 1966; Schein, 1967; Hall and Lawler, 1969; Campbell, 1968) show clearly that challenge is very important to the way a person's career develops. In a way it is unfortunate that the word *challenge* has become a part of the rhetoric both for students criticizing organizations and for recruiters praising their organizations, because people tend to lose track of just how important it really is. A study of young managers (Berlew and Hall, 1966) followed people at American Telephone & Telegraph for five years and in another company for seven years. Performance was evaluated by their salary scale and ratings from their supervisors and other people, mainly in personnel, who were in a position to evaluate them.

The more challenging a man's job was in his first year with the organization, the more effective and successful he was even five or seven years later.

Unfortunately, the amount of challenge in initial jobs in most organizations is invariably low, despite the fact that it is very important. In a study of R & D organizations, there were only two companies out of twenty-two interviewed in which people described their first jobs as being moderately high or high on challenge (Hall and Lawler, 1969). There was only one company that had a conscious policy of making the first assignments difficult. Most companies felt that they should bring the person along slowly, starting him off on an easy project and cautiously adding more challenge only as the recruit proved his ability at each stage of escalation. This is a strategy to *measure* the person's ability by approaching it from below rather than by *stretching* it through high work goals and high standards of excellence!

A traditional problem is the expensive training which is invested in new employees before they can earn their pay. Increased challenge and less formal training would increase the utilization of new people from the very beginning, benefiting both the individual and the organization.

Another factor found to be related to performance was pressure on the person to do high quality work and to assume a degree of financial responsibility in his work (Hall and Lawler, 1970). In the R & D setting this pressure was often associated with accepting responsibility, getting new projects for the organization, and obtaining outside funding for the work. This may have required direct contact with customers rather than through the supervisor. Organizations in which people felt personal pressure for quality work and attaining the financial goals of the organization were found to be highly effective. But again, we rarely found evidence of quality pressure or evidence of professional people being given financial responsibility in their work.

Self-Actualization Satisfied Least

A further problem was that the most important need for the researchers—self-actualization—was the least satisfied (Hall and Lawler, 1969). Further, we found that the longer researchers worked for an organization, the less important self-fulfillment was to them and the more important security was. Increasing tenure was also related to three significant changes in self-image: the people reported themselves as being less active, less strong, and less independent as tenure increased. The intriguing idea here was that there is theory (Argyris, 1957) that predicts just this kind of human decay with increasing length of service in organizations. Because of the conflict between the needs of growing individuals and the requirements for organizations for tight control and uniformity, people become less concerned about their own growth, and they become less independent, less strong, and less active as they spend more time in the organization.

Another finding (Hall and Lawler, 1969) that surprised the R & D managers in our feedback session with them concerned a communications gap—a disagreement between what the managers were doing and what their subordinates said the managers were doing. We asked everyone if the organization had a regular performance appraisal system and, if so, were the results discussed with the man appraised. In most of the organizations, the directors said, "Sure, we do it every six months."

We talked to the researchers. Not only did they generally report that the appraisals did not take place, but for some we had to explain what a performance appraisal system was!

Because the appraisal system seemed to be there when we talked to the directors and it was not there when we talked to the professionals, we called it the "vanishing performance appraisal." There was little feedback on how people were performing. We know that feedback is important for the learning and self-correction of any kind of system, and this resource was being lost to these R & D systems.

High Aspirations

Another aspect of the syndrome was a great sense on the part of the recent graduates that their important skills and abilities were not being used. New graduates possess high levels of training when they begin work. Indeed, the definition of education is to bring students to the frontiers of knowledge, the very latest techniques and theories. One purpose of a college or university is to perform the change function in society, and one way it does this is through the people they send out. In this sense, new graduates are societal change agents. They come into the organization with new techniques, and they want to apply them. They find this difficult first because they lack the skills of applying what they know and second, because the organization tends to resist innovation. This difficulty is compounded by the fact that people coming out of college build up a falsely high aspiration level about the extent to which they are going to be using their new skills.

One example of the unrealistic aspiration problem is a man I knew who had just finished his first year at the Harvard Business School. He was seriously hoping to begin as a vice president of finance for a respectably-sized organization. He was convinced that he had the ability to perform the job, and he was going to find it. Although he did not find it, he still felt that he *ought* to be a vice president in charge of finance. That attitude shows through; on the one hand it creates anger on the part of his superiors, and on the other hand it creates a certain amount of threat. In fact, developing this degree of confidence in students is one of the main socializing functions of many business schools.

Creating Challenge

Another problem is that the new recruit really does not know how to create his own challenge in a job. This is the fault of educational institutions. Very often people are accustomed to being *given* projects and *given* challenging work. They do not know how to take an unstructured and undefined situation and find something important in it, thereby defining the job for themselves. There is a contradiction: they want challenge, and independence, but they don't want to find challenge independently. They want it given to them by someone else. Research has shown that people tend to be rather passive about even major career decisions: the type of organizations they work for, whether they change jobs, and the type of jobs they accept (Roe and Baruch, 1967). Very often they respond to external challenge, demands, or changes more than they do to their own career blueprint. A person does not tend to chart a course for himself and decide that this is the time to make this move, and this is the time to make this other move, and this is how to get from point A to point B. Career choice is not really as much a conscious strategy as one might expect.

Sources of Threat

Young graduates often threaten their superiors (Schein, 1968) and this threat is probably a major contributor to the syndrome of unused potential. There are different reasons why superiors may be threatened by a new man. For one, training programs are often defined so that the new man is seen as someone special, a "bright young man," or a "crown prince." However, his supervisor may be in a terminal position. He may have worked all his life to reach his position, and now is confronted with a "young kid," who within a year, may be promoted above the position which the supervisor had taken his whole career to attain.

Another cause for threat is that new men are coming in right out of college and may know more about a special area than the superior does. This threat may apply more in technical work than in general management. This threat is compounded when the superior has had to spend a great deal of time doing administrative work which kept him from upgrading his technical knowledge.

High starting salaries cause problems, too. The young man today makes far more than the boss did when he started his career; in fact, the new man's salary probably comes painfully close to what the boss is making right now. Personal styles are also different—the young man is probably more likely to rock the boat, make waves, and create pressure for change. All of these personal threats created by young people can reinforce the syndrome of unused potential and actually make their later experiences less satisfying.

Negative Effect

The overall result of this syndrome is that in the early career years one finds great changes in the man's self-image, attitudes, aspirations and motivation—all generally in a negative direction. He is less optimistic about how he is going to succeed with the organization (Campbell, 1968). He sees himself as having less impact on the organization, and his values tend to conform more to those of the organization (Schein, 1967). Schein's research shows how the values of business students tend to move toward those of authority figures in whatever system they join. Among students in an MBA program, values tend to move toward the values of the faculty and, interestingly, away from those of businessmen. But when the MBA's start working, they move back again toward the managers' values and away from the faculty's values. Thus, as they become more integrated into their organization, a certain amount of change toward organizational values tends to occur, but one would hope that the new man would not also lose whatever creativity he might bring into the system.

Model for Career Growth

If there is some sort of self-perpetuating syndrome causing decay in the new man's self-image and career motivation, it is possible to reverse that process and find a way to increase his motivation and self-image.

One way of thinking about career growth is in terms of analogies with child development. It is generally agreed that the first year of a child's life is a critical period (Bowlby, 1951), and that the first year of a person's work experience seems equally critical (Berlew & Hall, 1966). We also know that there tend to be more changes in attitude and motivation in the career than in specific skills and ability (Campbell, 1968); i.e., post-college career development seems to be more a process of socialization and attitude change than a process of acquiring skill and competence.

If the first year is the critical period in developing attitudes, why not begin by giving the new person the kind of challenging job experience which will have a lasting effect?[2]

Every challenge can establish a self-motivated cycle of behavior. Hall and Nougaim (1968) found that young managers who were successful in their organization experienced greater satisfaction of their achievement and self-

---

2/Some companies have found that upgrading initial jobs has the unintended consequences of making subsequent jobs seem less exciting and stimulating. However, if the impact of the first job is more enduring than that of later work, the gains of initial challenge will outweigh the problems. What these companies' experiences have shown, however, is the systematic and interactive nature of jobs with careers and organizations: changing a person's job affects his attitude toward his subsequent jobs. To maintain the positive gains from improved initial jobs, the organization should also improve later jobs. Changing such a wide range of jobs, though, very quickly evolves into a full-blown program of organization development. The last section of this paper describes in more detail the connection between career development and organization development.

esteem needs than people who were less successful; also, in all managers there was a marked increase in the need for achievement over time, which seems appropriate for business managers.[3] Achievement is important in a business career, but achievement satisfaction increased only for successful people; it decreased for less successful people. The more successful men also became more involved in their work—they saw work as playing a more important role in their total lives at the end of five years in the organization than they did in their first. It is interesting that the people who were less successful did not become less involved; they stayed about equally involved. This is encouraging, because it may mean that if there is some sort of cycle, it may work more in the positive direction than in the negative. The encouraging thing for the people who are less successful is that they do not seem to decrease their involvement or to "drop out." At some later point they may move into more challenging jobs, experience some sort of success, and then become more involved. Therefore, the problems of unused potential may not be irreversible.

Conditions for Psychological Success

When one puts these ideas of success cycles together, one comes close to a concept developed by Kurt Lewin (1936) and applied by Chris Argyris (1964) to organizations, called *psychological success*. In experimental studies where people were working on attaining very specific tasks, a person would be asked to set a target or goal for himself and try to achieve it. Lewin measured their aspiration levels and then looked at what happened to the aspiration levels and self-esteem after either success or failure. After people were successful they generally tended to raise their level of aspiration and to experience greater self-esteem. The response to failure varied. If the person had an initially high sense of self-esteem, he tended to persist, not to lower his aspirations. The reaction to success also varied. If a person had a history of failure and had succeeded once, he often stopped while he was ahead.

The relationship between a career and the experiment seems clear; the difference is that with the career the time span is the person's entire life rather than a two-hour experimental session. But the similarities seem quite strong. One can get some clues to career growth by looking at the conditions that Lewin found were important to psychological success.

1. The person had to choose a challenging goal for himself, one that represented a challenging level of aspiration to him.
2. He had to set his goals independently; it had to be his own goal, not one imposed by somebody else.

3/A business career is probably one of the best arenas for satisfying a person's achievement needs. Businesses have very concrete goals and one can easily measure his performance. Despite all the negative stereotypes about business careers, one cannot overlook how useful a setting they create for satisfying achievement needs.

3. The goal must be meaningful to him, central to his image of himself, so that if he succeeded he would see himself in a different light as a more competent person.

4. He had to attain the goal he sought.

In terms of the psychological success model, then, if people set challenging goals for themselves related to their careers, and if they work independently and attain them, they should experience a sense of success, and they should see themselves in a different light. This success would then lead to self-identity growth. The experience of increased self-esteem may also generalize to their career identity, so that they would be more committed to their careers and be more likely to set additional career goals again at a later time.

This model is shown in Figure 1.

The success model is also similar to McGregor's (1960) description of management by objectives and target setting. McGregor was not talking specifically about a man's career, but it is easy to relate the two. Challenging goals, as used here, are similar to what McGregor talks about as an objective, a concrete measurable target that a man can work for and either attain or not attain over a particular time period. Then later to the extent that the person attains the goal, he becomes more involved in his career and also becomes a more effective member of his organization.

FIGURE 1
A Model of Career Growth Through Psychological Success

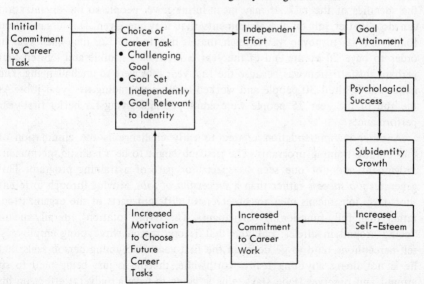

Source: From Douglas T. Hall, "A theoretical model of career subidentity development in organizational settings," *Organizational Behavior and Human Performance,* in press.

CHANGES NEEDED TO FACILITATE GROWTH

What kind of changes in the organization might be made to facilitate career development? Probably the very first would be changes in jobs. How does one change jobs to get people into a positive success cycle?

The First Assignment

The first step would be to analyze the initial jobs that new people are given in the organization. What happens to a young person when he walks in the door? If that first year is a critical period, when he is especially susceptible to learning new attitudes, what is happening to him during that important time? Is he just absorbing information and not really accomplishing important objectives? Is that time sort of an investment that the company feels required to make in him? Or is the first year a time when the company really expects to challenge him? Does the company have some concrete goals for him to reach?

The ironic fact seems to be that organizations look at the first year as a necessary evil: an investment they have to make in the person, until they can assign him an important project where he can make a valuable contribution. At the same time, the man is impatient for something that has meaning and challenge.

Both the organization and the individual want and need the new person to have challenge and good performance, but for understandable reasons both are frustrated. It is not easy to make jobs more challenging when one gets down to the specifics of the task. It may mean hiring fewer people so the organization can do a better job on the assignments that they are given. One organization found that its turnover was so high that it had to hire 120 men each year in order to have 20 at the end of the year. So it took a gamble and figured that perhaps this attrition was because the first-year jobs were so unchallenging. The next year it hired 30 people and worked hard on upgrading first-year jobs. At the end of the year 25 people were employed and giving far better first-year performances.

Another recommendation related to early challenge is the elimination of job-rotating training programs. The first job ought to be a realistic, permanent assignment and not one seen as special or part of a training program. This generates *job success* rather than a *succession of jobs*. Moving through different short-term jobs means men are observers of different parts of the organization, rather than fully-functioning participants. The term "rotation" literally means "going around in circles." Maybe that is one reason why young employees' self-perceptions tend to go down in the first year. The young person feels that he is not doing anything really worthwhile, that he is just being paid to sit around and observe. If he stays, this is going to have an adverse effect on his self-image—he is being paid a lot for doing little.

The Supervisor

Another consideration is the superior to whom a new man is assigned. Probably the boss has more impact on the definition of the job than any other factor. Therefore, if management is going to redesign jobs, it must also redesign bosses or train them to deal with a new man.

This was another realization of the previously-mentioned company that tried upgrading first-year jobs. It learned in the first year that it had to work with the bosses as well as new recruits. In the second year it put the supervisors through a long training program before new people came into the organization. Then, as part of the training program for the new people, the company also involved the superiors, so that each recruit and his boss went through the program as a team.

This type of learning helps a superior develop a sense of what we call "supportive autonomy" (Hall and Schneider, 1969), so he can tread the fine line between allowing a man independence (i.e., "sink or swim") on the one hand, and providing assistance with excessive control, on the other hand. The combination of autonomy and the supervisors' availability and willingness to work as a coach when the young person wants help may be the best combination for learning (Hall and Schneider, 1969; Pelz and Andrews, 1966).

Performance Review

Supervisors should also learn how to provide performance reviews. This very specific kind of skill is one that supervisors ought to be able to do quite well. If the new employee is left on his own to determine his performance, his conclusion may be based on highly distorted information. It is far better to have the feedback come through formal channels and get it straight rather than have the person get it through indirect and unreliable means, such as the supervisor's manner of saying hello on a certain morning.

An important need for supervisors in this area is to develop skills in confronting interpersonal problems. If the new person is given autonomy, and if the supervisor sees himself as a bit more of a helper than he may have originally, this suggests that some new problems may arise. The new man is going to make mistakes, and he and his supervisor are going to have to learn how to get through these problems and conflicts as a pair. Also, the supervisor has to learn to put on pressure at the appropriate times, when to exercise authority, and when to get tough. It is not only a matter of learning new values and attitudes about supervisory style, it is also a matter of translating these into specific interpersonal skills and knowing how to apply them at various times.

One way of achieving some of the necessary confrontation and problem-solving skills would be through a planned, structured exercise. A group of new employees could meet and draw up a statement describing their attitudes toward the organization, toward their supervisors, and toward their careers. Their supervisors would also meet as a group and draft a similar statement covering their attitudes toward the new men and their ideas of what the views of the new recruit are. These statements would then be used in diagnosing important career and organizational problems. The structured process and the group-level focus may make it less threatening to confront the problems and to work through to solutions than unstructured or one-to-one encounters may be.

The Recruit and His Goals

A third area of change concerns the organization's long-term plans for the new recruit. Perhaps most important would be the creation of a semi-annual work planning and review program, designed after the work of McGregor (1960) and the General Electric Company.

The purpose of such a program would be to establish collaborative goal-settings and more self-directed careers. However, the organization and the individual must be aware of and avoid the tendency for such programs to "vanish." Such a program should allow for individual differences in administrative and interpersonal skills, which have been found to be related to career success (Campbell, 1968). Its focus should be on developing these skills in terms of specific day-to-day behaviors which can be measured and changed by the person and his supervisor.

Another useful exercise would be for the new recruit and his supervisor to examine the company's goals (or the department's or work group's goals) in relation to the recruit's personal goals and desires. One issue would be the valence of the organization's goals to the recruit: can he identify with them? Are they important to him and how can they be made more important? The other issue is their instrumentality: does he see his efforts toward the organization's goals as also leading to his own satisfactions? If not, how could this connection be better established?

The organization must be aware of the emotional development taking place in the recruit in his early career years. Organizations, like universities, have tended to see personal growth as being independent of or irrelevant to the "really important" career development changes—new skills, abilities, and knowledge. The bulk of a man's career changes, however, are in the motivational and attitudinal area (Campbell, 1968). Since motivation and attitudes are related to performance and success (Hall, 1971), it is clear that organizations should see these personal changes as relevant to their interests. In particular, one never knows when, how, and what attitudes may be acquired by a new man. The change may result as much from the climate of the organization as from the work itself. Much personal stress may result from the need to achieve, and the relative lack of security in the first year with a new organization. It would also be useful to be alert for turning points which may help mark important career transitions—the first performance appraisal, the first completed project, or a particular transfer or promotion. Certain events may have symbolic value which make them far more important to the recruit than the organization or the supervisor may realize, and it is important to attempt to see the recruit's career as it appears to him.

Family Changes

Along with recognizing the career as emotional change and identity development, it is also important to recognize the impact of another important contributor to these changes—the family. Family changes, such as marriage, children, relocation, or the death of a relative often have profound effects on a person's identity, attitudes, and motivation. If these family changes happen to be congruent with career changes, the mutually reinforcing effects could be far more potent than the sum of the separate influences. An example of congruent family and career effects might be the way marriage and a significant promotion could both contribute to increased career involvement and personal responsibility. On the other hand, a problem in a critical family transition could greatly disrupt a person's adjustment to an equally important career change. An example here might be in-law problems in the new marriage and problems with the supervisor in the recent promotion which might both center on the issue of competence in relationships with older people or authority figures. The combination of similar problems around the same issues in two central areas of one's life could greatly compound any feeling of incompetence or low esteem which might result from either problem separately. This interaction of family and career issues is discussed in White (1952), Levinson (1968), and Cox (1970).

The Organization Reward Structure

The fourth arena for facilitating career development concerns characteristics of the organization itself. One important activity would be the examination of the organization's reward structure in relation to the new recruit's path-goal profiles. Is the company using rewards that are valued by the new recruit? Also, does the recruit know what kind of behavior leads to these rewards? An example of a mismatch here occurred in R & D labs, where the most common rewards were money (pay raises); however, the scientists did not really understand what they had to do to get a pay raise, and furthermore, there was evidence that intrinsic satisfactions, such as greater challenge or autonomy, meant more to them than money. As a result the companies were trapped in an upward spiral of salaries with little apparent change in employee satisfaction (Hall and Lawler, 1969). Therefore companies should: 1) attempt to design jobs so that efforts toward company goals also contribute to satisfying employees' needs, and 2) clarify the organization's reward structure so that executives and lower-level employees are in agreement about the kind of performance that is expected and rewarded. Again, an examination of these issues through a structured exercise involving senior managers and recent graduates would probably be fruitful.

Even before the recruit is hired these organizational expectations should be communicated to him, clearly and realistically. College students have become surprisingly accurate at diagnosing inflated or distorted recruiting information, and it usually backfires. This is especially important in view of the great sensitivity and value for openness found in today's students. Indeed, according to Schein (1969), students report that the areas companies stress the most in their recruiting literature are often those about which they are most defensive; therefore, what are promoted as their strongest points often betray their weakest. In the insurance industry, an experiment revealed that recruitment literature stressing both the pros and cons of selling life insurance attracted just as many new agents and resulted in lower turnover among the new employees and the concomitant high costs of training (LIAMA, 1966). Therefore to get and retain good people, "Tell it like it is."

Impact of Peer Group

Another part of the individual's organizational environment with high potential for career impact is his employee peer group. Most of the new member's informal learning is communicated by the peer group (Becker, Geer, Hughes and Strauss, 1961; Becker, Geer, and Strauss, 1969; Hall, 1969). The peer group can also provide important emotional support, coaching, and identification models to help the new recruit manage identity changes, difficult problems, and critical turning points (Hall, 1969; Schein, 1968). Peer group interaction is also associated with reduced turnover (Evan, 1963).

The peer group is often the employee's main emotional link to the organization; often he comes to value the organization only because of his regard for his peers. For example, much of the zeal and bravery of Marine troops is based on their devotion to their buddies rather than a general commitment to Marine Corps values. Therefore, an organization would do well to examine the nature of work group interaction patterns, norms, and values.

If these norms and values run counter to the organization's goals, a serious problem may exist, and an organizational diagnosis might be conducted to determine the probable reasons. If the work group culture is supportive (or perhaps neutral) vis-a-vis organizational goals, it would be useful to create structures which would encourage work-related peer interaction—such as weekly problem-solving sessions, an informal morning coffee break, team projects, or older "coaches" assigned to new men.

The important point here is that because the peer group is a potent force, there is a certain amount of risk attached to utilizing it. A group of employees can very accurately diagnose a "poor" organizational climate and can effectively transmit this awareness and quota-restricting pressures to new members. Thus, the peer group can be either strongly functional or strongly dysfunctional for organizational identification.

CONCLUSION

Perhaps one common element among most of these lever points for facilitating careers is that they have high potential value in either causing or curing problems. There is much in the way of energy and resources in both the new recruit and the organization he enters. In nature, when two systems in different states interact—as in a value gap or an electrical voltage differential—potential energy is available. By applying what we know about organizations and careers to the so-called generation gap, we may develop its potential rather than short circuit it.

REFERENCES

Argyris, C. *Integrating the individual and the organization*. New York: Wiley, 1964.

Becker, H., Geer, B., Hughes, E., & Strauss, A. *Boys in white*. Chicago: University of Chicago Press, 1961.

Becker, H., Geer, B., & Strauss, A. *Making the grade*. Chicago: University of Chicago Press, 1969.

Behavioral Research Service. *A comparison of a work planning program with the annual performance appraisal interview approach*. Crotonville, N.Y.: General Electric Company, undated.

Berlew, D., & Hall, D. T. The socialization of managers: Effects of expectations on performance. *Administrative Science Quarterly*, 1966, 11, 207-223.

Bowlby, J. *Maternal care and mental health*. Geneva: World Health Organization, 1951.

Campbell, R. Career development: The young business manager. In J. R. Hackman (Chm.), Longitudinal approaches to career development. Symposium presented at the American Psychological Association, San Francisco, August 1968.

Cox, R. D. *Youth into maturity*. New York: Materials for Mental Health Center, 1970.

Evan, W. M. Peer-group interaction and organizational socialization. *American Sociological Review*, 1963, 28, 436-440.

Hall, D. T., The impact of peer interaction during an academic role transition. *Sociology of Education*, Spring 1969, 42, 118-140.

Hall, D. T. A theoretical model of career sub-identity development in organizational settings. *Organizational Behavior and Human Performance*, 1970, in press.

Hall, D. T., & Lawler, E. E. III. Unused potential in research and development organizations. *Research Management,* 1969, 12, 339-354.

Hall, D. T., & Nougaim, K. An examination of Maslow's need hierarchy in an organizational setting. *Organizational Behavior and Human Performance,* 1968, 3, 12-35.

Hall, D. T., & Schneider, B. Work assignment characteristics and career development in the priesthood. In L. W. Porter (Chm.), Traditional bureaucratic organizations in a changing society. Symposium presented at the American Psychological Association, Washington, D.C., August 1969.

Levinson, D. J. A psychological study of the male mid-life decade. Unpublished research proposal, Department of Psychiatry, Yale University, 1968.

Lewin, K. The psychology of success and failure. *Occupations,* 1936, 14, 926-930.

L.I.A.M.A. *Recruitment, selection, training, and supervision in life insurance.* Hartford: Life Insurance Agency Management Association, 1966.

Maslow, A. *Motivation and personality.* New York: Harper, 1954.

McGregor, D. *The human side of enterprise.* New York: McGraw-Hill, 1960.

Ondrack, D. A. An examination of the generation gap: Attitudes toward authority. *Personnel Administration,* May-June 1971, vol. 34, pp. 8-17.

Pelz, D. C., & Andrews, F. M. *Scientists in organizations.* New York: Wiley, 1966.

Roe, A., & Baruch, R. Occupational changes in the adult years. *Personnel Administration,* July-August 1967, 30, 26-32.

Schein, E. H. Attitude change during management education: A study of organizational influences on student attitudes. *Administrative Science Quarterly,* 1967, 11, 601-628.

Schein, E. H. The first job dilemma. *Psychology Today,* March 1968, 1, 27-37.

Schein, E. H. Personal change through interpersonal relationships. In W. Bennis, E. Schein, F. Steele, & D. Berlew (Eds.), *International dynamics.* (Rev. ed.) Homewood, Ill.: Dorsey, 1968, 333-369.

Schein, E. H. How graduates scare bosses. *Careers Today,* charter issue, 1968, 89-96.

Schein, E. H. The generation gap: Implications for education and management. Working paper #326-68. Massachusetts Institute of Technology, 1969.

Slater, P. *The pursuit of loneliness: American culture at the breaking point.* Boston: Beacon, 1970.

White, R. W. *Lives in progress.* New York: Holt, Rinehart, and Winston, 1952.

White, R. W. Motivation reconsidered: The concept of competence. *Psychological Review,* 1959, 66, 297-323.

part TWO
Classical School of
Management

The classical school refers to the literature which began to emerge in the late 1800s and which reported the first efforts to study systematically the process of management. The men who first studied and wrote about management are the pioneers of the field. They are, in this sense of the term, classicists. We refer to F. W. Taylor, Henry Gantt, Frank and Lillian Gilbreth, Harrington Emerson, Morris Cooke, Mary Parker Follett, James Mooney, Henri Fayol, Lyndall Urwick, and many others as major contributors to the classical school of management. They defined the field and its problems and they paved the way for subsequent analyses and research. But, in another sense of the word, the classical school includes contemporary writers.

The term classical can also be used to refer to the recurring and fundamental issues of a field of study; the term can refer to efforts to discover underlying principles and processes. Thus, much contemporary literature which seeks understanding of work and the work environment and which analyzes the underlying nature of coordination through planning, organizing, and controlling can be included in the classical school. The literature which we have included in this section illustrates this contemporary expression of the classical school. It is our contention that the classical school is not a historical artifact which can be used as a foil by critics who fail to understand it; rather, it is the core of contemporary management literature.

Lyndall Urwick, the author of "Are the Classics Really Out of Date?" pens a sharp indictment of those who degrade the work of the classicists. The basis of his position is that contemporary management scholars tend to criticize classical management literature from a position of ignorance: Urwick believes that many critics of the classical school have simply not read the classical literature. At the same time he criticizes some current writings and writers for having dodged the basic problem of field definition—What is management? To what ends should knowledge about management be pursued? We previously observed these questions being raised by Professor Koontz. Whether Mr. Urwick's criticism of the critics of the classical theories is accurate can be measured by subsequent dialogue and debate; his comments should not go unheeded.

The second article in this section, "The Relationship Between Scientific Management and Personnel Policy in North American Administrative Systems" by V. Seymour Wilson, provides a brief overview of the historical context of scientific management. He also demonstrates the impact of this part of the Classical Management School on the very practical problems of position classification in business and government personnel management practice. Wilson concludes that much of the philosophy and many of the methods of scientific management are permanently imbedded in the work environments of North America.

An important contribution of the classical school is the identification of planning as a fundamental managerial function. Taylor and other early writers differentiated between planning and executing. More recent writers have directed our attention to the broad purposes of planning.

"Shaping the Master Strategy of Your Firm" expresses Professor William H. Newman's ideas about the necessity for managers to develop a master plan, or master strategy, which deals with the firm's mission. As Newman observes, every firm must express its central purpose in terms of services, resources, cooperation and competition, change, growth and adaptation. Through the use of a number of examples he demonstrates how actual firms have succeeded or failed because of the success or failure of managers to develop and re-develop master strategy.

The article by Stewart Thompson presents his analysis of staff planning departments in organizations. In "What Planning Involves," he begins by specifying and discussing three kinds of business planning—plans for current business, plans for continuing in business, and plans for business development and growth. Based upon interviews conducted in various firms, Thompson outlines a framework of business planning utilized by business decision makers. He then presents an actual business experience which points out the changes in the firm's manner of doing business and how plans had to be developed to cope with the changes. In the final section of the article Thompson deals with planning for the future.

An important tool in classical organization theory is the organization chart. Harold Stieglitz examines in "What's Not on the Organization Chart," the current use of such charts and concludes that their advantages outweigh their disadvantages when used correctly. Indeed, the principal criticism is in terms of what it does not show rather than in what it shows. The chart shows the division of work and superior-subordinate relationships, but it does not show degrees of responsibility and authority, distinction between line and staff, relative status, communication channels, and the informal organization. But despite these inadequacies the organization chart is better than currently available substitutes.

The final article reports Allan T. Demaree's analysis of "The Age of Anxiety at A.T. & T." This is a case study of a large complex organization which is beset by numerous problems. Although the causes of many of its difficulties were beyond the influence of AT&T's management, the cause of some can no doubt be traced to the company's overemphasis on centralized authority. Demaree describes the control procedures which corporate management exercises over line (operating) management. These procedures prevent the company from responding to changes. It is a lucid illustration of the overuse of control at the expense of creativity.

5

Are the Classics Really Out of Date?*

LYNDALL F. URWICK

In 1910 Louis D. Brandeis was briefed by the shippers on the Eastern seaboard of the United States to appear before the Interstate Commerce Commission to oppose an application by the railway corporations to raise rates. He determined to base part of his "case" on the contention that if the railway corporations would listen to the new ideas about managing which had been discussed at various meetings of the American Society of Mechanical Engineers over the previous 25 years, they could save so much money there would be no need for them to raise rates.

He wanted a slogan, a catchy phrase to express these new ideas as a whole. At a meeting at Henry Laurence Gantt's apartment in New York in the Autumn of 1910, it was decided to adopt the title "Scientific Management." Frederick Winslow Taylor was not present at this meeting. He did not give evidence in "the Eastern Rates Case," as it came to be called.

But, Brandeis' tactics were brilliantly successful. Almost overnight, the press of the United States was full of articles about the new ideas. And, since Taylor was popularly, and rightly, regarded as the leading mind among the group which had fostered these ideas, he found himself famous as their author. He called his second paper on the subject, published in 1911, "The Principles of Scientific Management." When he died, a few years later, early in 1915, his admirers engraved on his tomb "The Father of Scientific Management."

The phrase "Scientific Management" is, however, highly ambivalent. It can mean two very different things. It can be interpreted as a claim that managing is or can be an exact science. Or it can imply that managing is a task which can be studied in the scientific temper and spirit. There is no question that Taylor used the phrase in the second meaning. He knew, none better, that in his day knowledge about dealing with people was not an exact science.

Since, however, his ideas excited a great deal of opposition, especially in some academic and trade union circles, it was convenient for a great many people to misrepresent him, to claim that his words meant a great deal more—or a great deal less—than he had ever contemplated.

*Source: Reprinted by permission from *S.A.M. Advanced Management Journal* (July 1969), pp. 4-12.

TAYLOR'S ATTITUDE

Thus, we find Taylor himself protesting, as early as 1912, that the adjective "scientific" did not apply to the *whole process* of managing. It applied solely to the method of analyzing and measuring individual tasks which he had introduced:

> A very serious objection has been made to the use of the word "science" in this connection. I am much amused to find that this objection comes chiefly from the professors of this country. They resent the use of the word science for anything quite so trivial as the ordinary every-day affairs of life. I think the proper answer to this criticism is to quote the definition given by a professor who is, perhaps, as generally recognized as a thorough scientist as any man in this country—Professor McLaurin, of the Institute of Technology, of Boston. He recently defined the word science as "classified or organized knowledge of any kind." And surely the gathering in of knowledge, which, as previously stated, has existed, but which was in an unclassified condition in the minds of workmen, and then the reducing of this knowledge to laws and rules and formulae, certainly represents the organization and classification of knowledge, even though it may not meet with the approval of some people to have it called science.[1]

On the other hand he was modest in avoiding personal claims. To the question "You do not claim a monopoly on scientific management?" he replied, "I should say not. . . . I do not believe there is any man connected with scientific management who has the slightest pride of authorship in connection with it. Every one of us realizes that this has been the work of a hundred men or more, and that the work which any one of us may have done is but a small fraction of the whole. This is a movement of large proportions and no one man counts for much of anything in it. It is a matter of evolution, of many men, each doing his proper share in the development, and I think any man would be disgusted to have it said that he had invented scientific management, or that he was very much of a factor in scientific management. Such a statement would be an insult to the whole movement. It is not an affair of one man or of ten or twenty men."[2]

Such was the attitude of Taylor—a man, who, whether one agrees with his views or not, was, by all the evidence, a big man, both intellectually and ethically. Yet the abuse of him and his ideas still continues. It seems to have become almost traditional in much academic writing in the United States.

1/"Testimony," pp. 41, 42. Originally published 1912. Reprinted as Pt. ii. of *Scientific Management* (New York: Harper & Bros., 1947). This volume contains Taylor's three main contributions to management thought, "Shop Management" 1903, "The Principles of Scientific Management" 1911, and his "Testimony" before the Committee of Investigation appointed by the House of Representatives 1912. The three parts are paged separately.

2/Ibid., "Testimony," p. 282.

Only the other day the author came across a passage which cited as evidence that Taylor was hostile to the trade unions in that he objected to "herding men into gangs." Historically speaking, this is nonsense. Taylor never used this phrase with reference to the trade unions. He used it of the yard labor at Bethlehem Steel, where, previously, men had been employed in gangs. He was writing in favor of the task idea, giving each individual a specified task to perform and rewarding him highly if he achieved standard. He was not referring to trade unions at all.[3]

"Now He Belongs to the Ages"

As Professor Peter Drucker observed, when he was presented with the Society for Advancement of Management's Taylor Key in 1967,

> The popular game of belittling Taylor makes not much more sense than a belittling of Newton because all he did was to create the science of physics without, 300 years ago, being able to anticipate quantum mechanics. Indeed, just as we can only have quantum mechanics because a Newton gave us classical physics, we can only have today all the new, shiny tools and concepts of modern management theory because a Taylor founded the study of work and the study of organization 75 years ago.[4]

Perhaps some of the Professors who delight in belittling Taylor might reflect occasionally that, but for Taylor, there would be no "Chairs" for them to occupy.

"So Wise We Grow"

But it is not only Taylor who is subjected to this kind of attack. Almost all the earlier writers on management have come under fire as dogmatic, inaccurate or unscientific. Their work is described as "classical," "traditional," and so on. In the fast-moving climate of American academic opinion these epithets are, of course, pejorative. They imply "fuddy-duddy, out-of-date." They are, in short, an endorsement of the most crashing denial of intellectual values ever uttered publicly—the late Henry Ford's "History is Bunk."[5] They are examples of the conceit neatly summarized in Alexander Pope's couplet:

> We think our fathers fools, so wise we grow;
> Our wiser sons, no doubt, will think us so.[6]

3/Ibid., "Principles," pp. 68, 69, 70, 72.
4/Peter F. Drucker, "Frederick Winslow Taylor—The Professional Management Pioneer," *Advanced Management Journal,* vol. 32, no. 4, Oct. 1967, p. 8.
5/Henry Ford. In the witness box during his libel suit v. The Chicago Tribune, July 1919.
6/Alexander Pope, *Essay on Criticism,* Pt. ii, L. 237.

"Space Programs" and Semantic Rocketry

Most of this unfriendly comment comes from two sources:—

(1) The work on operational research which made an impact in the Second World War and has abrogated to itself the title Management Science. It has led some people to think that any human problem can be reduced to a mathematical "model." This, combined with the development of the computer, has issued in an outbreak of utopianism among some academic minds in the United States. Intellectually, as well as astronautically, a number of people are dreaming of "space programs." The very slow speed at which exact knowledge develops which is applicable practically to the art of living seems, to such thinkers, intolerable. They are under compulsion to search for short cuts.

(2) The invasion of the field of management in the last thirty years by a whole galaxy of so-called "behavioral sciences." Many of these bodies of knowledge are, scientifically speaking, in their infancy. So they cry out loud a great deal. More important, their own terminology has not yet settled down. As an unkind reviewer noted in *The Wall Street Journal* a few years ago, "Sociology is the use of a jargon invented for that purpose."[7] They have infected the study of management with their own semantic immaturity.

JUNGLE WARFARE

The consequence has been that the teaching of management has been frustrated and complicated by warring theories to a degree which reduces men who are trying genuinely to equip the next generation for their tasks, almost to despair.[8] In particular, the terminology of the subject is in acute confusion.

So bad had the situation become that in 1962, Professor Harold Koontz, speaking officially as President of the American Academy of Management, felt compelled to say:

What is upsetting to practicing managers, and, in fact, to all who see great social good emanating from improved management, is that the varied approaches to management theory have led to a kind of confused and destructive jungle warfare. Particularly in academic writings the primary interests of many would-be cult leaders seem to be to carve out a distinct (and hence original) approach to management. To defend this originality and hence to gain a place in posterity (or at least to gain a publication which will justify academic status or promotion), these writers seem to

---

7/"The Job and Jargon of Sociology," *Wall Street Journal,* May 14, 1959.

8/Cf. John M. Pfiffner & Frank C. Sherwood, *Administrative Organization* (Englewood Cliffs, New Jersey: Prentice-Hall, Inc., 1960, 5th printing 1964), pp. 462, 463. "The Bridge Between Practice and Research . . . every researcher and theorist has his own set of categories."

have become overly concerned with downrating, and sometimes misrepresenting what anyone else has said or thought or done.[9]

Following on Koontz' comment, a symposium of distinguished teachers and practitioners of management was invited to the University of California, Los Angeles Campus, in 1962 to discuss the subject. The proceedings were published in 1964. "Throughout the discussions," as Professor Koontz commented in summing up, "semantic confusion was evident."[10]

LACK OF DEFINITION

One comment came from the only Englishman present, Wilfred Brown. Brown is not uninstructed in sociology. In collaboration with Dr. (now Professor) Elliott Jaques, he had tried consistently over a period of years to apply modern sociological ideas to the organization of the Glacier Metal Co. Ltd. Between them they have written quite a series of well-known books on the subject.[11]

Brown said: "Frankly, I have not been able to follow much of what's been said in the discussion."[12] And, "You can't start up here without the definitions that initiate the process. The British Institute of Management, the American Management Association, and the Business Schools of America haven't any definitions. How can you instruct a theory about management when you haven't got a definition of the word—of the role of the manager?"[13]

A DEFENSE OF JARGON

The only dissenting voice came from Professor Herbert Simon of the Carnegie Institute of Technology. He defended elaborate jargon under two heads:

(1) That some of the older professions such as medicine and the law have jargon. "They do this in part to impress us. I don't think perhaps we ought to be too sensitive about doing a little bit on our own part to impress others."[14]

9/Harold Koontz, "Making Sense of Management Theory," *Harvard Business Review*, vol. 40, no. 4, July-August 1962.

10/*Toward Unified Theory of Management,* ed. Harold Koontz (New York: McGraw-Hill, 1964), p. 238.

11/E. G. Wilfred Brown, (a) *Exploration in Management,* 1960, (b) *Piece Work Abandoned,* 1962 (both London: Heinemann Educational Books, and New York: John Wiley); Elliott Jaques, (c) *The Changing Culture of a Factory,* 1951 (London: Tavistock Publications, New York: Dryden Press), (d) *Measurement of Responsibility,* 1956 (Tavistock Publications, London and Harvard University Press), (e) Brown and Jaques, *Product Analysis Pricing,* 1964 (London: Heinemann Educational Books Ltd.), and *Glacier Project Papers,* 1965 (London: Heinemann Books Ltd.).

12/Op. cit., N(13), p. 231.

13/Ibid., p. 105.

14/Ibid., p. 104.

(2) New knowledge "develops a new vocabulary to describe the new distinctions it is making."

The trouble with which Professor Simon did *not* deal is that it is impossible for the layman to know with which of these two alternatives he is dealing. Is jargon being used to express new truths or merely, by impressing the public, to conceal the fact that a writer has no new truths to express? Giving quite ordinary jobs longer titles in order to make them sound more important is an old trick. The rat-catcher becomes a "rodent officer"; the lift boy blossoms into an "elevator-attendant." Even quite small children play the game of having "a secret language." Its point is that no one who is not an initiate can understand what the little rascals are talking about. They can then make derisory comments about their elders while escaping the normal penalties for impertinence.

SEMANTIC SEDUCTION

Professor Simon himself has mounted a couple of scathing attacks upon his predecessors:

(a) In the second chapter of his *Administrative Behavior* first published in 1945, entitled "Some Problems of Administrative Theory."[15]
(b) In the first two chapters of the later book *Organizations*, which he wrote in conjunction with Professor James G. March, in 1958. These are entitled "Organizational Behavior" and "Classical Organization Theory."[16]

Both are examples of what can only be described as semantic seduction.

What Are "Principles"?

In the first example the whole sense of the chapter turns on the meaning assigned to the word *principle*. Now, admittedly, in the early days of scientific management there was a good deal of confusion as between laws, principles and methods. The author called attention to this point in 1928, seventeen years before Professor Simon's chapter appeared.

Following the famous Cambridge economist, Alfred Marshal, it was stated that "A law is a relationship between cause and effect which, so far as the total of existing experience goes, has been proved to be valid in all cases. It is specific. A principle, on the other hand, does not involve any relationship. It is a general proposition sufficiently applicable to the series of phenomena under consideration to provide a guide to action. A law is a statement of fact. A principle is a

15/Herbert Simon, *Administrative Behavior* (New York: The Macmillan Co., 1947), pp. 20-44.
16/James G. March and Herbert A. Simon, *Organizations* (New York: John Wiley & Sons, 1958).

mechanism of thought." In other words "a principle is a law in its sophomore year."[17]

Indeed, Professor Simon himself has no objection to the word "principle." In the second edition of his book, and referring to his experience with the Economic Cooperation Administration, he writes, "In the course of the first few weeks of E.C.A.'s existence its top administrators were able to develop a set of guiding *principles* that provided some of the key decision premises on which its activity rested."[18]

So it is only other people's "principles" to which Professor Simon objects. But he does not quote those "other people." He merely restates their "principles" in his own words and, by prefacing each of them with the phrase "administrative efficiency is increased by," turns them into laws. In at least one of his statements—"Proponents of a restricted span of control . . . have nowhere explained the reasoning which led them to the particular number they selected"[19]—he is manifestly inaccurate. Graicunas had stated "reasons" eight years before Professor Simon's chapter was published.[20]

Indeed, Professor Simon himself seems to have realized that, in this chapter, he had exceeded the bounds of legitimate criticism. For, having devoted some fifteen pages to pulling his predecessors to pieces, he asks "Can anything be salvaged?" And he replies to his own question:

> As a matter of fact almost everything can be salvaged. The difficulty has arisen from treating as principles of administration what are really only criteria for describing and analyzing administrative situations.[21]

The 1967 edition of the unabridged *Random House Dictionary of the English Language* defines the word CRITERION as "a standard of judgment or criticism; an established rule or *principle* for testing anything."[22]

Thus, on his own showing, Professor ˋSimon's scathing attack on his predecessors turns on the difference in meaning between two words which the most up-to-date dictionary likely to be found in most American homes defines as synonymous.

A CHANGE OF DIRECTION

It is not surprising that in his second book, Professor Simon has somewhat shifted his direction of attack. It is not possible in a brief article to enumerate all

17/L. Urwick, "The Principles of Direction and Control" in *Pitman's Dictionary of Industrial Administration* (London: Pitman, 1928).

18/Op. cit., N(18), 2d ed. 1957, p. xxi.

19/Op. cit., N(18), 1st ed. p. 28, 2d ed. p. 28.

20/A. V. Graicunas, "Relationship in Organization" in *Papers on the Science of Administration,* ed. Luther Gulick and L. Urwick (New York: Columbia University Press, 1937), pp. 183-87.

21/Op. cit., N(18), pp. 35, 36 1st ed. and 'do' 2d ed.

22/*The Random House Dictionary of the English Language,* "The Unabridged Edition" (New York: Random House, Inc., 1967), p. 344.

the dubious statements about other people's work which litter the first two chapters of *Organizations*. By the time it was published, the invasion of management by the so-called "behavioral sciences," already noted, was in full swing.

Three points are interesting:

(1) *The Organization of "Organizations."* The title of the book is "Organizations," *not* Organization. It opens with a paragraph in which the authors refuse to define the meaning in which they are using that term—"the world has an uncomfortable way of not permitting itself to be fitted into clean classification."[23] Almost all their predecessors did make an attempt at some classification of the processes of management, however inadequate. And they used the term *organization* as *one* of those processes, the process concerned with dividing up all the activities necessary to any common purpose into positions or posts and relating those posts to each other.

In the American vernacular the word *organization,* preceded by the article—"the or an organization"—is often used of an institution *as a whole.* But this is the vernacular, not science. In the vernacular, a child is sometimes spoken of as "a little anatomy." But this does not lead students of other disciplines to criticize anatomists because they have not dealt with, say, the biochemistry of the child's nervous system. They appreciate that anatomy and biochemistry are separate subjects.

Indeed, even in the vernacular, it is appreciated that the term organization has two meanings. If A. speaks of the General Motors Corporation as "an organization" or "the organization," everyone understands that A. is using the term *organization* in a meaning different to that implied in the phrase "the organization of the General Motors Corporation." Yet, in this book the authors play Box and Cox between these two meanings of the word. For instance:

> Statements about organizations are statements about human behavior, and imbedded in every such proposition, explicitly or implicitly, is a set of assumptions as to what properties of human beings have to be taken into account to explain their behavior in organizations.[24]

Statements about organization made by their predecessors were *not* generalizations about human behavior. They made one assumption about human behavior and one only, namely that human beings can only cooperate effectively if they can communicate accurately. That is what *organization,* as used by previous students of management, is about. An "organization chart" is a wiring diagram: it is *not* a complete description of how an institution works.

(2) *Ignoring Chester Barnard.* Professor Simon is a great admirer of the late Chester Barnard. He invited him to write an introduction to his first book and, in this one, speaks of "the Barnard-Simon theory of organizational equilibrium."[25] Barnard, in his *The Functions of the Executive,* makes the point

23/Op. cit., N(19), p. 1.
24/Ibid., p. 6.
25/Ibid., p. 84.

half-a-dozen times or more that *the* reason for formal organization is the need for exact communication.[26] Incidentally, there is also a passage in Barnard's book, which endorses the principle of the span of control, though not under that title.[27]

(3) *The Sorcery of "Scientific Method."* The wand of "scientific method" is waved to throw doubt upon earlier work. For instance, "much of what we know or believe about organization is distilled from common sense and from the practical experience of executives. The great bulk of this wisdom and lore has never been subjected to the rigorous scrutiny of scientific method. The literature contains many assertions but little evidence to determine—by the usual scientific standards of public testability and reproducibility—whether these assertions really hold up in the world of fact."[28]

If reproducibility and public testability are the only tests of scientific method then we are a long way from a scientific knowledge of the government of human groups, if we are ever likely to get there with our present techniques. You cannot reproduce an experiment on a group of human beings. A group of the same individuals is a different group on Tuesday to what it was on Monday: the individuals composing it will have changed. As for public testability, the individual is entitled to some privacy. And it is right for the individual and for society that he should have it. I cannot imagine Professor Simon asking each member of a test group on Tuesday, publicly, mark you!, "Who were you with last night?" Yet such factors unquestionably influence individuals and thus their group-behavior.

As he himself has said elsewhere, "It hardly seems necessary to add that the sum total of knowledge we have accumulated about human behavior in organizations is still a pail of water in an ocean of ignorance."[29] But we are adrift on that ocean and we can either sink or do our best to swim.

In the meanwhile those who have made some attempt to swim, are discouraged by the perpetual chorus from academic halls that they should change their style, a chorus moreover in which there is little harmony.

Nor are Professor Simon's tests of "public testability" and "reproducibility" the only criteria of scientific method. Many years ago Henri le Chatelier, the French physicist who introduced the ideas of Frederick Winslow Taylor to France and Europe, observed that scientific method involves six steps—definition, analysis, measurement, hypothesis, experiment, proof—*in that order.*

Professors March and Simon in their *Organizations* have deliberately discarded the first of those steps. In doing so they have cut across the efforts of their predecessors to make some headway with the second. Without them the remaining steps are useless and, indeed, often misleading. In doing this they

---

26/Chester I. Barnard, *The Functions of the Executive* (Cambridge, Mass.: Harvard University Press, 1938), pp. 82, 89, 91, 94/5, 106, 113, 175, 217.
27/Ibid., p. 289 and footnote.
28/Op. cit., N(19), p. 5.
29/Op. cit., N(13), p. 80.

have added to the confusion in which the terminology of management currently labors.

THE YOGIS AND THE COMMISSARS

Forty years ago, the late J. B. S. Haldane, the biochemist, remarked that "mechanics became a science when physicists said what they meant by such words as weight, velocity and force, *but not till then.*"[30] It is a remark which those who seek to contribute to our knowledge of management might take to heart.

The simple fact is that managing is, as is medicine, a practical art. Like medicine it depends on a wide range of underlying sciences from anatomy to zoology. Again like medicine, no laboratory experiments or theoretical formulations are of use to practitioners till they have been tried in the fire of "clinical experience."

In medicine this necessary unity of theory and practice is achieved largely through the teaching hospitals. Some embryonic equivalents are beginning to develop in the management field. But on the whole, theorists and practitioners live in different worlds. It is ridiculous that a man should be able to write "Ph.D., M.B.A., B.Sc.," all in management subjects, after his name, when anyone acquainted with him is well aware that his temperament renders him incapable of managing a school picnic without muddling up the buns and the tennis balls.

This essential unity of theory and practice is made more difficult each time a theorist, a yogi, for whatever reasons, starts to wrap up his knowledge in an esoteric jargon. It may gain him prestige among his fellow yogis. But only at the price of reducing the practical people, the commissars, to fury, contempt and despair.

Management is not yet sufficiently established as an academic subject to be able to afford these "frills." Its semantics are a mess. Every sincere teacher of the subject should regard it as one of his primary responsibilities to assist in cleaning up that mess.

30/J. B. S. Haldane, "Science and Politics" in *Possible Worlds* (London: Chatts & Windus, 1928), p. 186. Italics added.

6

The Relationship between Scientific Management and Personnel Policy in North American Administrative Systems*

V. SEYMOUR WILSON

Some time ago in an article in *[Public Administration]* Dr. V. Subramaniam made reference to the impact of scientific management on the attitudes to administration found in the United States and Canada.[1] The philosophy had a significant influence on the environment of North American industry and government and, as Subramaniam has argued, it stressed the preeminence of practical specialists' skills over those of the generalists.

The full historical sequence leading to the introduction of many aspects of scientific management in the United States of America has been comprehensively treated elsewhere, and a recent volume on the Canadian federal bureaucracy deals, in part, with the events surrounding the introduction of the philosophy in the Canadian environment.[2] This paper is restricted to first analysing those aspects of the philosophy dealing with human resources within organizations, and second to making the connection between the philosophy and the system of personnel administration introduced into both the Canadian and American bureaucratic environment during the reform era of the early part of this century.

*Source: Reprinted by permission from *Public Administration* (Summer 1973), 193-205.

1/V. Subramaniam, 'The Relative Status of Specialists and Generalists: An Attempt at a Comparative Historical Explanation', *Public Administration* (London), Autumn 1968, pp. 336-7.

2/See J. E. Hodgetts, W. McCloskey, R. Whitaker and V. Seymour Wilson, *The Biography of an Institution: The Civil Service Commission of Canada* 1908-1967, Montreal: McGill-Queen's Press, 1972. Two historical analyses exploring the impact of scientific management on the American environment are Samuel Haber, *Efficiency and Uplift: Scientific Management in the Progressive Era* (Chicago: University of Chicago Press, 1964), and Hugh G. J. Aitken, *Taylorism at Watertown Arsenal: Scientific Management in Action*, 1908-1915 (Cambridge, Mass.: Harvard University Press, 1960). For the application of scientific management to the European environment see Charles S. Maier, 'Between Taylorism and Technology: European Ideologies and the Vision of Industrial Productivity in the 1920's', *Journal of Contemporary History*, vol. 5, no. 2, 1970, pp. 27-61; Hyacinth Dubreuil, *Des Robots? Ou des Hommes?: l'oeuvre et l'influence de l'ingénieur Taylor* (Paris: Bernard Grasset, 1956).

A Brief Analysis of the Philosophy

The genesis of scientific management and the reasons for its widespread popularity have been the subject matter of many books on managerial ideology.[3] During the latter part of the nineteenth century the great expansion of industrial enterprise brought economic prosperity to the capitalist entrepreneur but misery to the underprivileged, and intense organizational conflict between management and the unions.[4] With this growing problem of chaos and disorganization, it soon became readily apparent to many observers that much of the misery and suffering was due to an unplanned economic and organizational expansion, the effects of which could be mitigated by some form of bureaucratic rationalization.[5] It is hardly surprising then, as Mouzelis has indicated, that 'with mechanization of production, the mechanical engineers came to acquire a strategic position in the social structure of enterprise'.[6] But, as Subramaniam has noted, their role was, from the beginning, one of a limited instrumental character, subject to direction by, and subservience to the self-made industrial tycoon:

> The entrepreneur knew what he wanted, and what he did not want in the early stage of an industry was advice from others as to what he should want. Combining in himself the functions of the owner, as well as manager, he was, however, prepared to take advice, from the engineer about *how* to do things and pay him well for doing them.[7]

Thus the staff role in organization was created: to answer the 'how' meant that the engineer had to be released from the routine aspects of organization work and given ample time for creative thinking. This structural change in the organizational environment soon produced the desired results: it was a paper read to the American Society of Mechanical Engineers in 1886 entitled 'The Engineer as Economist' which first started Frederick Taylor, himself an engineer, thinking about management as a scientific phenomenon, leading to the formation of the 'classical school' or 'scientific management school' of organizational theory.[8] It should be stressed, however, that Taylor's contribution to

3/The literature on scientific management is fairly extensive. Apart from Frederick W. Taylor's own writings on the subject, two studies are worth specific mention: Nicos Mouzelis, *Organization and Bureaucracy: An Analysis of Modern Theories,* London: Routledge & Kegan Paul, 1964, and Reinhard Bendix, *Work and Authority in Industry: Ideologies of Management in the Course of Industrialization,* 2d ed., New York: Harper & Row, 1963.

4/For a comprehensive treatment of this theme, particularly in the English environment, see R. Bendix, Ibid., pp. 34-116.

5/N. P. Mouzelis, op. cit., pp. 79-81.

6/Ibid., p. 80, Professor Subramaniam also concurs: 'It was thus characteristic of America that the first great writer on Scientific Management was Taylor, a former engineer. It was characteristic, too, of America that for quite some time the Scientific Management movement was in the hands of engineers'. V. Subramaniam, op. cit., p. 336.

7/Ibid., p. 336.

8/C. S. George, *The History of Management Thought,* Englewood Cliffs, N.J.: Prentice-Hall, 1968.

this school of thought, though significant, was by no means exclusive: Taylor was one student among many who adopted and amplified the classical approach. Nevertheless, it is tacitly agreed by admirers and critics alike, that a focus on Taylor's contributions would generally provide a comprehensive conception of this school of management thought.[9]

The manipulative mind, utilizing the assumptions of mechanics, was strikingly evident in this school of thought, for the concept of systems as applied to machinery was adopted for the study of man within organizations.[10] The need for rationalization in organizations meant that the entire factory structure was to be visualized as a complex productive mechanism with the various parts harmonizing to create a distinct, precision-working harmonious whole, creating an output in the most expeditious and cheapest manner known possible. Furthermore the worker within the organization was considered as a machine, whose part in the conversion process could be quantitatively measured and rated, and whose overall efficiency could be improved through simple mechanical adjustments such as reducing the number of superfluous motions involved in any given action.[11] These analogies can be made much more evident in an examination of Taylor's 'workshop management' practices. Taylor first applied his concepts to the loading of ingots of pig iron for shipment by rail. Under the old conditions, he noted that the handling of ingots yielded an average daily work load of less than thirteen tons per man. Taylor then concluded that a first-class workman should be able to handle forty-seven tons per day, by instituting the following changes:

(1) that only able-bodied men be selected for this type of work;
(2) that premium rates be paid to these men;
(3) that the work pattern must be planned and prescribed in detail;
(4) that rest periods be instituted so as to permit the more efficient distribution to the men's expendable energies.[12]

This form of rationalization paid rich dividends: line production was increased threefold, and the unit cost of handling the pig iron was substantially reduced. This initial success led to an albeit slow but steady increase in enthusiasm for Taylor's overall philosophy and the dividends accruing from it. Taylor adopted the approach that his work could be the catalyst for the needed revolution in the study and practice of administrative efficiency. Philosophy and practice were to be meshed in his three main levels of concern:[13] (1) 'mechanisms' or 'techniques'; (2) 'underlying principles'; and (3) 'fundamental philosophy'.

9/See R. T. Golembiewski, *Behaviour and Organization: O and M and the Small Group*, Chicago: Rand McNally & Co., 1962.

10/James G. March and Herbert A. Simon, *Organizations*, New York: Wiley, 1958, pp. 12-22.

11/Ibid.

12/Frederick W. Taylor, *The Principles of Scientific Management*, New York: Harper, 1911, pp. 126-130.

13/Dwight Waldo, *The Administrative State*, New York: Roland, 1948, pp. 48-51.

The 'mechanisms' or 'techniques' of Taylor's work have borne the brunt of much criticism for what they imply about man in the working environment. Taylor emphasized the mechanical aspects of work, referring to the organizational milieu as 'a complex and delicate machine', the social experience of the worker requiring an overall control when he is in this environment. Consistent with this emphasis on mechanics, Taylor concentrated on the physiological characteristics of the worker rather than his whole being which he brings to the daily work environment.[14] In effect, Taylor was interested in 'abstract functions' which he organized in the 'one best way' of handling the job: the worker was of interest only insofar as he performed such functions. This fact is illustrated by Taylor's oft-repeated dictum that: 'In the past man has been first; in the future the system must be first'.[15]

Another related factor was the tacit assumption that all work must be segmentalized into minute specializations. This 'rationalization process' of the work environment assumed that a surgeon's activities were as easily dissectible as those of a stenographer or a messenger.[16] As one commentator puts it: 'The aim, then was to break jobs into component specialties, to integrate these specialties as the wheels and levers of a watch, and to control men in the consistent performance of their simple function'.[17] Herein lies the practical implications of much of Taylor's work, for this aim has led to the detailed conceptions of job analysis and classification, to which we will return later in this paper.

Scientific management, however, went far beyond the obvious, a sophistication which most writers fail to accord to Taylor and his disciples. Taylor realized that techniques, in themselves, provided no direction for 'workshop management', for in essence they were neutral tools. He therefore buttressed his practical concerns with the 'underlying principles of management', namely, a norma-

14/A. Etzioni, *Modern Organizations,* New Jersey: Prentice-Hall, 1964, pp. 21-22.

15/F. W. Taylor, op. cit., p. 7. This dictum dovetailed rather neatly with the concerns of American management for workers in industry to be content with their allocated positions in the work environment. Sociologist Bendix argues that: 'Scientific management was both a cause and a consequence of a changing image of the ideal industrial worker, and by the 1920's this was beginning to tell in the growing emphasis of representative statements upon the virtues of work and compliance rather than of initiative and competitive drive.' Bendix, op. cit., p. 285.

16/This assumption of 'New Taylorism' profoundly affects North American managerial philosophy and practice up to the present day. It is clearly evident, for example, in the rationalization process associated with the current fad of Programme Planning and Budgeting in North America, and the employment of industrial psychologists by both big industry and government to extract the 'essence' of managerial functions by closely studying every minute of the senior executive's time as he performs his daily duties. The recent attempt by the Nixon Administration to stop-watch the working time of lawyers at the Justice Department in Washington is illustrative of this orientation. To fully describe the movement whereby scientific management became the ready bedfellow of this rationalization sought by industry and government would require an art beyond this writer—that of comedy. For a perceptive study of the 'New Taylorism' see Victor A. Thompson, *Bureaucracy and Innovation,* Alabama: University of Alabama Press, 1969.

17/R. T. Golembiewski, *Behaviour and Organization: O and M and the Small Group,* Chicago: Rand McNally, 1962, p. 14.

tive consideration for the purposes to which the techniques of scientific management were to be applied. As Mouzelis has emphasized, Taylor conceptualized at least four great underlying principles in his philosophy:

(1) Replacing rule of thumb methods with scientific determination of each element of a man's work.
(2) The scientific training and selection of workmen.
(3) Co-operation of management and labour to ensure the accomplishment of work in accordance with the scientific method.
(4) A more equal division of responsibility between management and workers, with management taking responsibility for planning and organizing of work.

It must however be conceded that this philosophy remained vague in Taylor's writings. Because of the organizational chaos into which Taylorism was born, perhaps these principles were meant to be proscribed limits on the techniques of the new 'science'. For example, 'co-operation of management and labour' could be interpreted as a limit on the inclination of management to coerce labour into higher production simply by the use of the manipulative techniques of the new 'science'.

The classical approach, as Amitai Etzioni has indicated, contained both a theory of organization and a theory of motivation. The latter was a natural concomitant to the general mechanistic analogy in Taylor's work: man was conceived as a Hobbesian automaton, his whole being motivated by a fear of deprivation and an unsatiable appetite for the things of Mammon. This logic, argues Etzioni, compelled Taylor 'to view human and machine resources not so much as mutually adaptable, but rather man functioning as an appendage to the industrial machine'.[18] Perhaps this judgement of Taylor's work is too harsh in its assessment. A careful reading of Taylor indicates that he envisaged scientific management as a compendium of two general classes of factors, normative and empirical. The arguments above about philosophy and practice are indicative of this: the empirical factors were more concerned with the objectivity of the work situation, while the normative factors attempted to prescribe certain limits for the development of models of efficient and economical systems. Taylor repeatedly emphasized that his followers were not at liberty to develop a system of forced manipulation of labour, no matter what its efficiencies of cost, for such a system was precluded by the normative factors mentioned above. Thus his 'underlying principles' and 'mechanisms' or 'techniques' were compatible with each other: both carried a decided commitment to transcend conflicts of interest. As Charles S. Maier so succinctly puts it 'Taylorism promised an escape from zero-sum conflict, in which the gain of one party could be extracted only from the equal sacrifice of the other'.[19]

On the one hand Taylor's fundamental philosophy suggested a system of

18/A. Etzioni, op. cit., p. 21.
19/Charles S. Maier, op. cit., p. 31.

authority highly appealing to American entrepreneurs at the turn of the cen-
turn, and positing a smoothly functioning universe, mechanistic in its conception, and Newtonian in its regularity and predictability. It was, as March and
Simon stated:

> . . . a set of operating procedures that could be employed in each concrete
> situation to discover the methods that would be efficient in that situation
> and to secure their application. Taylor's invention of time study is more
> accurately compared to the invention of the microscope than, say, to the
> cell hypothesis'.[20]

Less obvious, on the other hand, was the suggestion that by applying its
normative considerations, and by removing the evaluation of the worker's performance from its mundane day to day environment, and applying motion study
in isolation, an analytical separation was made between *techniques* and *the
persons* who possessed the techniques. Michael Oakeshott best described these
two inseparable but analytically distinct types of knowledge combined in all
human activity: technique meaning all forms of knowledge which can be
separated from the person and formulated into abstract rules; and practical
knowledge which exists 'only in use, is not reflective and (unlike technique)
cannot be formulated into rules'.[21]

The implications of this distinction, however, were much more subtle for
nineteenth century capitalism. The Horatio Alger concept of 'from office boy
to President' or 'from log cabin to the White House' implied outstanding personal qualities which could be attributed to the great entrepreneurial wizards
of the day—the Vanderbilts, Carnegies and Rockefellers to name among the
most prominent. Scientific management, by separating techniques from persons,
implicitly demystified this cult of success. Methodology, its advocates exclaimed,
and not charisma, would supply the answers so badly required for the rationalization of industrial enterprises. It was perhaps this subconscious threat to their
personal authority which caused much of the hostility American entrepreneurs
initially displayed towards scientific management.

This hostility soon disappeared when the potentialities of scientific management became increasingly evident. 'Institutionalization of charisma' had some
far-reaching implications for the routinization of organizational procedures and
practices.[22] While demystifying the cult of success, it reinforced the notion that
the organization is a great hierarchy of superior-subordinate relations in which
the person at the top issues the general order that initiates all activity. All

20/J. March and H. Simon, op. cit., p. 20.
21/Michael Oakeshott, *Rationalism in Politics, and Other Essays,* London: Methuen,
1962, p. 8. Michael Polanyi has also made this important distinction in his discussion of
tacit knowledge. For a comprehensive treatment of this theme see Michael Polanyi, *The
Tacit Dimension.* New York: Doubleday & Co., 1966.
22/Reinhard Bendix significantly identifies bureaucratization as routinization. See
Bendix, op. cit., pp. 198-253.

authority and initiation are cascaded down by successive delegations.[23] This emphasis on merit, routinization of organizational activity, and a formalistic impersonality, gave new insights to the social engineers regarding ways whereby the energies of human beings could best be made malleable for the purposes of organizational activity. As March and Simon put it: 'First, in general there is a tendency to view the employee as an inert instrument performing the task assigned to him. Second, there is a tendency to view personnel as a given rather than as a variable in the system'.[24]

This organizational framework fitted remarkably well to the prior assumptions which production-oriented management had of human nature. What Charles Lindblom has called 'synoptic rationality'[25]—complete coordination of all activities, no overlapping and duplication, and the eradication of variances due to human defections by mechanizing or programming all activities—increasingly became part and parcel of the intellectual apparatus of American capitalism. Its influence remains with us up to the present day.

The Taylorites, despite their later protestation to the contrary, unwittingly gave respectability to these inviolate credos of the entrepreneurs. Indeed, Taylor in one of his most memorable passages argued that personnel within the organization must 'do what they are told promptly and without asking questions or making suggestions . . . It is absolutely necessary for every man in an organization to become one of a train of gear wheels'.[26] For industry the great American tycoon Henry Ford corroborated this sentiment: 'All that we ask of the men is that they do the work which is set before them'.[27] A philosophy which was once viewed as antithetical to management's interest increasingly obtained popular support in business circles.

This orientation encouraged American management to view the job not as a means for individual advancement and fulfilment, but rather as an end in itself with specific skills attached to it. In effect, personnel was taken as a given rather than as a variable in the scientific management system. 'The worker', comments Samuel Haber, 'was no longer thought to be an individualist. He was most comfortable and could be dealt with most productively, in a group. He usually had little desire to rise or to increase his income by very much. What he did want was security and enough pay to satisfy his comparatively limited wants'.[28] 'The booming profession of personnel management' was, in part, given the task to oversee these wants.

23/Victor Thompson, op. cit., pp. 15-16.

24/J. March and H. Simon, op. cit., p. 29.

25/David Braybrooke and Charles E. Lindblom, *A Strategy of Decision*, New York: The Macmillan Company, 1963, pp. 37-57.

26/Samuel Haber, op. cit., p. 24.

27/Quoted by Rensis Likert, 'Motivation and Increased Productivity', *Management Record*, vol. 18, no. 4, April, 1956, p. 128.

28/H. Haber, op. cit., p. 165.

Position Classification as an Aspect of Scientific Management

The shadow of Taylorism on the practices of the new profession of personnel advisers to management became much more pronounced as North America moved into the second decade of the twentieth century. Indeed 'shadow' is, as R. T. Golembiewski has expressed it, 'from one point of view, a rather deficient figure of speech to apply to the philosophy of Taylorism; it is as substantial as the proverbial broad side of a barn'.[29] The links between scientific management and the classification of positions within organizations are substantial.[30] It is to a brief exploration of classification that we now turn.

Because of its preoccupation with the 'one best way' concept of doing a task, and 'equal pay for equal work', scientific management was inevitably to centre some thought on job analysis and evaluation. According to C. W. Lytle, the original reason for job analysis was to study 'definite jobs to ascertain what kind and what degree of man-qualities are necessary to make man-job units operate satisfactorily'.[31] Interest in job analysis became of central focus to the organizational analysts as a direct result of the 1910 publication of Taylor's *Shop Management* in book form. It was one of Taylor's major recommendations that a 'centralized' employment department be created in each organization, enabling the accurate collection of job statistics to guide management in the hiring activity. Thus, 'the planning department', as Taylor then called personnel activity, was brought into being:

> No doubt inspiration ... came from Taylor's practices: his further specialization of jobs, his 'science of work' studies, his more careful selection and placement of operatives, and his examples of increasing unit labour cost to reduce unit total cost. Apparently Taylor and other engineers were too busy with the improvement of methods to go far into this (job analysis), the last step of job study. In fact, the pioneers in developing better shop management were putting most jobs on incentive payment and were content to work backwards from total earnings to derive basic rates'.[32]

But underlying this analysis there was a much more profound reason for its necessity than the sheer advocacy of a 'planning department'. Mouzelis suggests that Taylorism, when utilized to create formal theories of administration, makes 'the basic assumption that in spite of the great variety of goals and environments

29/R. T. Golembiewski, op. cit., p. 11.
30/Thomas W. Wood, 'The Contributions of F. W. Taylor to Scientific Personnel Management' (unpublished Ph.D. dissertation, University of North Carolina, 1941); Cyril C. Ling, *The Management of Personnel Relations: History and Origins,* Illinois: Irwin Col., 1965, pp. 285-6; Charles W. Lytle, *Job Evaluation Methods,* New York: Roland Press, 1946, pp. 102-103.
31/C. W. Lytle, Ibid., p. 11.
32/Ibid., p. 11.

in which organizations operate, it is possible to identify basic similarities in *structure* and *process* which can be conceptually analysed and made explicit'.[33] In the consideration of structure the formal theories make 'a clear distinction between the position (the office) and the person who occupies it. The responsibilities of different positions and the relations among them can be defined and delineated independently from the persons who will assume them'.[34] This separation between the office and its incumbent, together with the search for universal generalizations about organizations, made it possible for the construction of a rational-efficient framework for management. But to discover these generalizations or 'principles', a basic precondition must be a clear understanding of the structural features common to *all* existing organizations. This, Mouzelis concludes, makes it imperative that the formation of principles be 'preceded by a descriptive and conceptual analysis of how an organization is structured'.[35]

> [For such an analysis, we are told:] . . . the main concepts generally used
> are those of authority and position. Vertically, the organization structure
> is conceived as a hierarchy which is created by the delegation of authority
> and responsibility from the top to the bottom of the organization. Hori-
> zontally, the differentiation is analysed in terms of functions'.[36]

Process, on the other hand, is related to 'getting things done by people who operate in organized groups'[37]—in effect, the development of managerial skills on the job. Classification analysis was, therefore, much more concerned with structure than with process.

Unanimous acknowledgement has been accorded to E. O. Griffenhagen of Chicago for having grasped this distinction between structure and process and applying his energies towards an understanding of structure.[38] Primarily due to his foresight and energy Griffenhagen soon became the leading American expert on job analysis. Beginning with his initial work for the Commonwealth Edison Company in Chicago between 1909 and 1912, Griffenhagen's fame was to spread quickly throughout North America. By 1914, banks, insurance companies and other industrial enterprises were requesting the classification of the clerical positions in their establishments.[39] By the 1920's Griffenhagen's initial pioneering work had spearheaded similar exploits in the states of Illinois, Ohio, New Jersey, Nebraska, Massachusetts, the cities of Oakland, Pittsburgh, St. Paul, Milwaukee, New York, Cleveland, St. Louis, Dayton, Baltimore and Detroit, the counties of Milwaukee and Los Angeles, and the federal civil service in Ottawa, Canada.[40]

33/Mouzelis, op. cit., p. 88. Italics for emphasis.
34/Ibid., pp. 88-89.
35/Mouzelis, op. cit., p. 89.
36/Ibid., p. 89.
37/Ibid., p. 90.
38/W. E. Mosher and J. D. Kingsley, *Public Personnel Administration,* New York: Harper & Bros., 1936, pp. 356-7.
39/Lytle, op. cit., p. 102.
40/Mosher and Kingsley, op. cit., pp. 356-7.

The concept of job analysis was seen as one aspect of the classification 'movement'.[41] Essentially, classification consisted of two processes: job analysis and job specification. E. O. Griffenhagen explains:

Where it is difficult to describe the common characteristics of a group of positions that are to be allocated to the same class in the process of classification, it is often possible to adopt the expedient of explaining the kind of ability, kind of experience, kind of skills, etc., that a person qualified to handle the work must possess. The first step in the process of classification is, therefore, to learn all that is practical to learn regarding the duties of each position in the service. The term job analysis, if it is to persist, ought to be restricted to this process'.[42]

The result of this process was called job specification, that is, the utilization of the conglomerate data obtained in job analysis by first dividing up the job positions within an organization into a preliminary series of broad general divisions, and then smaller groups, until the smallest working unit is derived. This small unit was called 'the class'. Essentially it was:

a group of positions that are sufficiently alike to justify common treatment from the standpoints both of selection and of compensation. By this it is meant that persons chosen as qualified to enter upon the duties of one position in a class are necessarily qualified to enter upon the duties of any other position in the same class, and also that a scale of pay fairly applicable to any position in the class will be equally applicable to any other position in the class'.[43]

The classification process was, therefore, the practical fulfilment of the analytical distinction of structure made by Mouzelis and described previously: first a difference was conceived between the position (the office) and the person who occupies it. Job analysis then proceeded by identifying the basic functions necessary for the realization of the purposes for which the position was created. Specification then entailed the further subdivision of this material into specific subcategories, arriving at individual tasks or classes which were then finally grouped together to achieve maximum productivity and efficiency with the minimum of cost.[44]

Within a period of two decades the classification movement was transformed, in management eyes, from the ugly duckling of 'theory' into the beautiful Cinderella of practicality, advantageous to American capitalism. Just as scien-

41/Ibid., p. 355.
42/E. O. Griffenhagen, 'Job Analysis for Position Classification', American Management Association, 1931, in *Handbook of Business Administration,* New York: Kraus Publishing Co., 1931, p. 1139.
43/E. O. Griffenhagen, 'The Principles and Technique of Preparing an Occupational Classification of Positions in the Public Service', *Public Personnel Studies,* vol. II, no. 8, November 1924, Baltimore: Johns Hopkins Press, p. 241.
44/E. Brech, *Organization: The Framework of Management,* London: Longmans, Green Co., 1957, pp. 27-29.

tific management purported to 'bring about the Christian philosophy of love and welfare among all nations',[45] so too did the proponents of classification develop an evangelical fervour for their cause.[46] This significant growth in popularity of a managerial ideology has been attributed to many factors, chief among them being the war psychosis of the Western world in the second decade of the twentieth century. Cyril Ling has argued that since America was engaged in a total war effort such as she had never experienced before, the massive mobilization of economic resources required an expanded bureaucracy, both public and private. More particularly, the armed services were faced with tremendous personnel problems which had to be solved if success in the war effort was to be ensured. Consequently, it became mandatory to pay particular regard to personnel, hence the new standardized personnel specifications and interest in the need for specialization.[47]

Others indicate that the 'hot gospellers' of the Progressive Movement adopted and popularized both scientific management and its practical implications, for both were attuned to the concerns of the Progressives. Scientific management, it was claimed, implicitly called for the eradication of patronage by its orderly classification of duties, and its emphasis on the need for competent trained personnel to fill these classified positions. Moreover, both scientific management exponents and the Progressives saw the hope that 'science', as a method, would be the panacea for societal ills.[48] And no doubt, this was a contributory element to the growth of the movement, for, as Professor Leonard D. White implies, it was one of the central objectives of the scientific movement to 'lay the foundation for equitable treatment for public employees by the accurate definition, orderly arrangement, and fair examination of positions in the public service'.[49]

In any event the classification movement grew steadily in importance, first being popularized in private industry and then in government. The reason for this growth was explained by the leading expert in the field to Canadian federal civil servants, as he completed the task of classifying the Canadian federal bureaucracy:

> The tendency of recent years in the realm of political science towards an expansion and extension of the functions and activities of the government, as interested in the greatest good of the greatest number in the community, has caused a corresponding enlargement of the organization of governmental bodies and has introduced numerous problems of the exact kinds that privately-controlled businesses have had to cope with and have in many respects solved. It has been a natural development that those engaged in the field of industrial engineering should be called in from time to time to assist public officials in the application of those principles and

45/Quoted in Mouzelis, op. cit., p. 84.
46/Mosher and Kingsley, op. cit., p. 355.
47/Ling, op. cit., pp. 322-37.
48/Samuel Haber, op. cit., pp. 99-134.
49/Leonard White, *Introduction to the Study of Public Administration,* New York: Macmillan Co., 1952, p. 279.

methods that have been developed in the field of industry under the pressure and stress of competition'.[50]

The foregoing analysis attempts to indicate how the philosophy of scientific management has become closely associated with some of the most powerful conceptions existing in North American society. In the work environment the philosophy emphasized specialism: specific qualifications were required of candidates for each position to be filled, and only those persons who would successfully meet these requirements by virtue of certain educational achievements, training and experience were chosen for positions in industry or government. Since the selection standards were primarily based on the candidate's achievements, productivity, special abilities and skills in relation to the immediate demands of the specific position in question, the long-range potential of the employee tended to receive relatively less emphasis in the overall selection process. However, the latter criterion was never considered crucial at the time scientific management was adopted. To the moral reformers position classification was indeed a blessing, for it served as a means to eradicate the 'venal practices' of patronage, substituting in its stead the rational criteria of utilitarianism, achievement and performance.

Second, there are assumptions about the individual within the organization flowing from the demand for obedience and deference to authority. The organizational milieu is supposed to foster personnel who conceive their role as merely that of implementing whichever policies are defined by policy makers. The occupational code of the personnel recruited by 'scientific methods' constrains him to accept a dependent role *vis-à-vis* his policy-making betters in the political executive: the political bosses supply the goals whereas the administrative personnel, on the basis of expert knowledge, indicate alternative means for reaching these ends. So controlling and pervasive is this occupational code built into the writings on scientific management that for many years it has led civil service personnel and academics alike, to abide by this sharp distinction between ends and means.

The hey-day of scientific management is certainly over: indeed much of its success lies in the fact that quite a number of its philosophical tenets are today assumed as a matter of course in the North American work environment. This does not mean that all aspects of the philosophy have been unquestionably accepted: what Victor Thompson calls the 'New Taylorism' is still subject to much criticism in the North American literature on bureaucracy.[51] However the practical implications of many of these tenets have been so deeply ingrained in North American society that it is difficult to envisage any substantial changes in these tenets taking place. The North American commitment to specialism in the work environment is certainly one of these.

50/Griffenhagen and Associates, 'A Farewell Contribution from Griffenhagen and Associates Ltd.', *The Civilian*, February, 1921, p. 69.
51/See Victor A. Thompson, op. cit., pp. 54-60.

7

Shaping the Master Strategy
of Your Firm*

WILLIAM H. NEWMAN

Every enterprise needs a central purpose expressed in terms of the services it will render to society. And it needs a basic concept of how it will create these services. Since it will be competing with other enterprises for resources, it must have some distinctive advantages—in its services or in its methods of creating them. Moreover, since it will inevitably cooperate with other firms, it must have the means for maintaining viable coalitions with them. In addition, there are the elements of change, growth, and adaptation. Master strategy is a company's basic plan for dealing with these factors.

One familiar way of delving into company strategy is to ask, "What business are we in or do we want to be in? Why should society tolerate our existence?" Answers are often difficult. A company producing only grass seed had very modest growth until it shifted its focus to "lawn care" and provided the suburban homeowner with a full line of fertilizers, pesticides, and related products. Less fortunate was a cooperage firm that defined its business in terms of wooden boxes and barrels and went bankrupt when paperboard containers took over the field.

Product line is only part of the picture, however. An ability to supply services economically is also crucial. For example, most local bakeries have shut down, not for lack of demand for bread, but because they became technologically inefficient. Many a paper mill has exhausted its sources of pulpwood. The independent motel operator is having difficulty meeting competition from franchised chains. Yet in all these industries some firms have prospered—the ones that have had the foresight and adaptability (and probably some luck, too) to take advantage of their changing environment. These firms pursued a master strategy which enabled them to increase the services rendered and attract greater resources.

Most central managers recognize that master strategy is of cardinal importance. But they are less certain about how to formulate a strategy for their particular firm. This article seeks to help in the shaping of master strategies. It outlines key elements and an approach to defining these. Most of our illustra-

*Source: Copyright 1967 by the Regents of the University of California. Reprinted from *California Management Review*, vol. 9, no. 3, 77-88, by permission of The Regents.

tions will be business enterprises; nevertheless, the central concept is just as crucial for hospitals, universities, and other nonprofit ventures.

A practical way to develop a master strategy is to:

Pick particular roles or niches that are appropriate in view of competition and the company's resources.

Combine various facets of the company's efforts to obtain synergistic effects.

Set up sequences and timing of changes that reflect company capabilities and external conditions.

Provide for frequent reappraisal and adaptation to evolving opportunities.

New Markets or Services

Picking Propitious Niches. Most companies fill more than one niche. Often they sell several lines of products; even when a single line is produced an enterprise may sell it to several distinct types of customers. Especially as a firm grows, it seeks expansion by tapping new markets or selling different services to its existing customers. In designing a company strategy we can avoid pitfalls by first examining each of these markets separately.

Basically, we are searching for customer needs—preferably growing ones—where adroit use of our unique resources will make our services distinctive and in that sense give us a competitive advantage. In these particular spots, we hope to give the customer an irresistible value and to do so at relatively low expense. A bank, for example, may devise a way of financing the purchase of an automobile that is particularly well-suited to farmers; it must then consider whether it is in a good position to serve such a market.

Identifying such propitious niches is not easy. Here is one approach that works well in various situations: Focus first on the industry—growth prospects, competition, key factors required for success—then on the strengths and weaknesses of the specific company as matched against these key success factors. As we describe this approach more fully, keep in mind that we are interested in segments of markets as well as entire markets.

The sales volume and profits of an industry or one of its segments depend on the demand for its services, the supply of these services, and the competitive conditions. (We use "service" here to include both physical products and intangible values provided by an enterprise.) Predicting future demand, supply, and competition is an exciting endeavor. In the following paragraphs, we suggest a few of the important considerations that may vitally affect the strategy of a company.

Elements of Demand

Demand for Industry Services. The strength of the *desire* for a service affects its demand. For instance, we keenly want a small amount of salt, but care little for additional quantities. Our desire for more and better automobiles does not have this same sort of cut-off level, and our desires for pay-television (no commercials, select programs) or supersonic air travel are highly uncertain, falling in quite a different category from that of salt.

Possible *substitutes* to satisfy a given desire must be weighed—beef for lamb, motorboats for baseball, gas for coal, aureomycin for sulfa, weldments for castings, and so forth. The frequency of such substitution is affected, of course, by the relative prices.

Desire has to be backed up by *ability to pay,* and here business cycles enter in. Also, in some industries large amounts of capital are necessarily tied up in equipment. The relative efficiency, quality of work, and nature of machinery already in place influence the money that will be available for new equipment. Another consideration: If we hope to sell in foreign markets, foreign-exchange issues arise.

The *structure of markets* also requires analysis. Where, on what terms, and in response to what appeals do people buy jet planes, sulphuric acid, or dental floss? Does a manufacturer deal directly with consumers or are intermediaries such as retailers or brokers a more effective means of distribution?

Although an entire industry is often affected by such factors—desire, substitutes, ability to pay, structure of markets—a local variation in demand sometimes provides a unique opportunity for a particular firm. Thus, most drugstores carry cosmetics, candy, and a wide variety of items besides drugs, but a store located in a medical center might develop a highly profitable business by dealing exclusively with prescriptions and other medical supplies.

All these elements of demand are subject to change—some quite rapidly. Since the kind of strategic plans we are considering here usually extends over several years, we need both an identification of the key factors that will affect industry demand and an estimate of how they will change over a span of time.

Supply Situation

Supply Related to Demand. The attractiveness of any industry depends on more than potential growth arising from strong demand. In designing a company strategy we also must consider the probable supply of services and the conditions under which they will be offered.

The *capacity* of an industry to fill demand for its services clearly affects profit margins. The importance of over- or undercapacity, however, depends on the ease of entry and withdrawal from the industry. When capital costs are high, as in the hotel or cement business, adjustments to demand tend to lag. Thus, overcapacity may depress profits for a long period; even bankruptcies do not remove the capacity if plants are bought up—at bargain prices—and operated by new owners. On the other hand, low capital requirements—as in electronic assembly work—permit new firms to enter quickly, and shortages of supply tend to be short-lived. Of course, more than the physical plant is involved; an effective organization of competent people is also necessary. Here again, the case of expansion or contraction should be appraised.

Costs also need to be predicted—labor costs, material costs, and for some industries, transportation costs or excise taxes. If increases in operating costs affect all members of an industry alike and can be passed on to the consumer in the form of higher prices, this factor becomes less significant in company strategy. However, rarely do both conditions prevail. Sharp rises in labor costs in Hawaii, for example, place its sugar industry at a disadvantage on the world market.

A highly dynamic aspect of supply is *technology*. New methods for producing established products—for example, basic oxygen conversion of steel displacing open-hearth furnaces and mechanical cotton pickers displacing century-old hand-picking techniques—are part of the picture. Technology may change the availability and price of raw materials; witness the growth of synthetic rubber and industrial diamonds. Similarly, air cargo planes and other new forms of transportation are expanding the sources of supply that may serve a given market.

For an individual producer, anticipating these shifts in the industry supply situation may be a matter of prosperity or death.

Climate of Industry

Competitive Conditions in the Industry. The way the interplay between demand and supply works out depends partly on the nature of competition in the industry. *Size, strength, and attitude of companies* in one industry—the dress industry where entrance is easy and style is critical—may lead to very sharp competition. On the other hand, oligopolistic competition among the giants of the aluminum industry produces a more stable situation, at least in the short run. The resources and managerial talent needed to enter one industry differ greatly from what it takes to get ahead in the other.

A strong *trade association* often helps to create a favorable climate in its industry. The Independent Oil Producers' Association, to cite one case, has been unusually effective in restricting imports of crude oil into the United States. Other associations compile valuable industry statistics, help reduce unnecessary variations in size of products, run training conferences, hold trade shows, and aid members in a variety of other ways.

Government regulation also modifies competition. A few industries like banking and insurance are supervised by national or state bodies that place limits on prices, sales promotion, and the variety of services rendered. Airlines are both regulated as a utility and subsidized as an infant industry. Farm subsidies affect large segments of agriculture, and tariffs have long protected selected manufacturers. Our patent laws also bear directly on the nature of competition, as is evident in the heated discussion of how pharmaceutical patents may be used. Clearly, future government action is a significant factor in the outlook of many industries.

Crucial Factors

Key Factors for Success in the Industry. This brief review suggests the dynamic nature of business and uncertainties in the outlook for virtually all industries. A crucial task of every top management is to assess the forces at play in its industry and to identify those factors that will be crucial for future success. These we call "key success factors." Leadership in research and development may be very important in one industry, low costs in another, and adaptability to local need in a third; large financial resources may be a *sine qua non* for mining whereas creative imagination is the touchstone in advertising.

We stressed earlier the desirability of making such analyses for narrow segments as well as broad industry categories. The success factors for each segment are likely to differ in at least one or two respects from those for other segments. For example, General Foods Corporation discovered to its sorrow that the key success factors in gourmet foods differ significantly from those for coffee and Jello.

Moreover, the analysis of industry outlook should provide a forecast of the *growth potentials* and the profit prospects for the various industry segments. These conclusions, along with key success factors, are vital guideposts in setting up a company's master strategy.

The range of opportunities for distinctive service is wide. Naturally, in picking its particular niche out of this array a company favors those opportunities which will utilize its strength and bypass its limitations. This calls for a candid appraisal of the company itself.

Position in Market

Market Strengths of Company. A direct measure of *market position* is the percentage that company sales are of industry sales and of major competitors' sales. Such figures quickly indicate whether our company is so big that its activities are likely to bring prompt responses from other leading companies. Or our company may be small enough to enjoy independent maneuverability. Of course, to be most meaningful, these percentages should be computed separately for geographical areas, product lines, and types of customer—if suitable industry data are available.

More intangible but no less significant are the relative standing of *company products* and their *reputation* in major markets. Kodak products, for instance, are widely and favorably known; they enjoy a reputation for both high quality and dependability. Clearly, this reputation will be a factor in Eastman Kodak Company strategy. And any new, unknown firm must overcome this prestige if it seeks even a small share in one segment of the film market. Market reputation is tenacious. Especially when we try to "trade up," our previous low quality, service, and sharp dealing will be an obstacle. Any strategy we adopt must have enough persistence and consistency so that our firm is assigned a "role" in the minds of the customers we wish to reach.

The relationship between a company and the *distribution system* is another vital aspect of market position. The big United States automobile companies, for example, are strong partly because each has a set of dealers throughout the country. In contrast, foreign car manufacturers have difficulty selling here until they can arrange with dealers to provide dependable service. A similar problem confronted Whirlpool Corporation when it wanted to sell its trademarked appliances publicly. (For years its only customer had been Sears, Roebuck and Company.) Whirlpool made an unusual arrangement with Radio Corporation of America which led to the establishment of RCA-Whirlpool distributors and dealers. Considering the strong competition, Whirlpool could not have entered this new market without using marketing channels such as RCA's.

All these aspects of market position—a relative share of the market, comparative quality of product, reputation with consumers, and ties with a distributive system—help define the strengths and limitations of a company.

Service Abilities

Supply Strengths of a Company. To pick propitious niches we also should appraise our company's relative strength in creating goods and services. Such ability to supply services fitted to consumer needs will be built largely on the firm's resources of labor and material, effective productive facilities, and perhaps pioneering research and development.

Labor in the United States is fairly mobile. Men tend to gravitate to good jobs. But the process takes time—a southern shoe plant needed ten years to build up an adequate number of skilled workers—and it may be expensive. Consequently, immediate availability of competent men at normal industry wages is a source of strength. In addition, the relationships between the company and its work force are important. All too often both custom and formal agreements freeze inefficient practices. The classic example is New England textiles; here, union-supported work habits give even mills high labor costs. Only recently have a few companies been able to match their more flourishing competitors in the South.

Access to *low-cost materials* is often a significant factor in a company's supply position. The development of the southern paper industry, for example, is keyed to the use of fast-growing forests which can be cut on a rotational basis to provide a continuing supply of pulpwood. Of course, if raw materials can be easily transported, such as iron ore and crude oil by enormous ships, plants need not be located at the original source.

Availability of materials involves more than physical handling. Ownership, or long-term contracts with those who do own, may assure a continuing source at low cost. Much of the strategy of companies producing basic metals—iron, copper, aluminum, or nickel—includes huge investments in ore properties. But all sorts of companies are concerned with the availability of materials. So whenever supplies are scarce a potential opportunity exists. Even in retailing, Sears, Roebuck and Company discovered in its Latin American expansion that a continuing flow of merchandise of standard quality was difficult to assure, but once established, such sources became a great advantage.

Physical facilities—office buildings, plants, mines—often tie up a large portion of a company's assets. In the short run, at least, these facilities may be an advantage or a disadvantage. The character of many colleges, for instance, has been shaped by their location, whether in a plush suburb or in a degenerating urban area, and the cost of moving facilities is so great that adaptation to the existing neighborhood becomes necessary. A steel company, to cite another case, delayed modernizing its plant so long that it had to abandon its share of the basic steel market and seek volume in specialty products.

Established organizations of highly talented people to perform particular tasks also give a company a distinctive capability. Thus, a good research and development department may enable a company to expand in pharmaceuticals, whereas a processing firm without such a technical staff is barred from this profitable field.

Perhaps the company we are analyzing will enjoy other distinctive abilities to produce services. Our central concern at this point is to identify strengths and see how these compare with strengths of other firms.

Finances and Management

Other Company Resources. The propitious niche for a company also depends on its financial strength and the character of its management.

Some strategies will require large quantities of capital. Any oil company that seeks foreign sources of crude oil, for instance, must be prepared to invest millions of dollars. Five firms maintain cash reserves of this size, so *financial capacity* to enter this kind of business depends on: an ability to attract new capital—through borrowing or sale of stock—or a flow of profits (and depreciation allowances) from existing operations that can be allocated to the new venture. On the other hand, perhaps a strategy can be devised that calls for relatively small cash advances, and in these fields a company that has low financial strength will still be able to compete with the affluent firms.

A more subtle factor in company capacity is its *management.* The age and vitality of key executives, their willingness to risk profit and capital, their urge to gain personal prestige through company growth, their desire to insure stable employment for present workers—all affect the suitability of any proposed strategy. For example, the expansion of Hilton Hotels Corporation into a worldwide chain certainly reflects the personality of Conrad Hilton; with a different management at the helm, a modification in strategy is most appropriate because

Conrad Hilton's successors do not have his particular set of drives and values.

Related to the capabilities of key executives is the organization structure of the company. A decentralized structure, for instance, facilitates movement into new fields of business, whereas a functional structure with fine specialization is better suited to expansion in closely related lines.

Picking a Niche

Matching Company Strengths with Key Success Factors. Armed with a careful analysis of the strengths and limitations of our company, we are prepared to pick desirable niches for company concentration. Naturally, we will look for fields where company strengths correspond with the key factors for success that have been developed in our industry analyses described in the preceding section. And in the process we will set aside possibilities in which company limitations create serious handicaps.

Potential growth and profits in each niche must, of course, be added to the synthesis. Clearly, a low potential will make a niche unattractive even though the company strengths and success factors fit neatly. And we may become keenly interested in a niche where the fit is only fair if the potential is great.

Typically, several intriguing possibilities emerge. These are all the niches—in terms of market lines, market segments, or combinations of production functions—that the company might pursue. Also typically, a series of positive actions is necessary in order for the company to move into each area. So we need to list not only each niche and its potential, but the limitations that will have to be overcome and other steps necessary for the company to succeed in each area. These are our propitious niches—nestled in anticipated business conditions and tailored to the strengths and limitations of our particular company.

An enterprise always pursues a variety of efforts to serve even a single niche, and, typically, it tries to fill several related niches. Considerable choice is possible, at least in the degree to which these many efforts are pushed. In other words, management decides how many markets to cover, to what degree to automate production, what stress to place on consumer engineering, and a host of other actions. One vital aspect of master strategy is fitting these numerous efforts together. In fact, our choice of niches will depend in part, on how well we can combine the total effort they require.

Synergy is a powerful ally for this purpose. Basically, synergy means that the combined effect of two or more cooperative acts is greater than the sum which would result if the actions were taken independently. A simple example in marketing is that widespread dealer stocks *combined with* advertising will produce much greater sales volume than widespread dealer stocks in, say, Virginia and advertising in Minnesota. Often the possibility of obtaining synergistic effects will shape the master strategy of the company—as the following examples will suggest.

Combination of Services

Total Service to Customer. A customer rarely buys merely a physical product. Other attributes of the transaction often include delivery, credit terms, return privileges, repair service, operating instructions, conspicuous consumption, psychological experience of purchasing, and the like. Many services involve no physical product at all. The crucial question is what combination of attributes will have high synergistic value for the customers we serve.

International Business Machines, for instance, has found a winning combination. Its products are well designed and of high quality. But so are the products of several of its competitors. In addition, IBM provides salesmen who understand the customer's problems and how IBM equipment can help solve them, and fast, dependable repair service. The synergistic effect of these three services is of high value to many customers.

Each niche calls for its own combination of services. For example, Chock Full o' Nuts expanded its restaurant chain on the basis of three attributes: good quality food, cleanliness, and fast service. This combination appealed to a particular group of customers. A very limited selection, crowded space, and lack of frills did not matter. However, if any one of the three characteristics slips at an outlet, the synergistic effect is lost.

Adding to Capabilities

Fuller Use of Existing Resources. Synergistic effects are possible in any phase of company operations. One possibility is that present activities include a "capability" that can be applied to additional uses. Thus, American watch companies have undertaken the manufacture of tiny gyroscopes and electronic components for spacecraft because they already possessed technical skill in the production of miniature precision products. They adopted this strategy on the premise that they could make both watches and components for spacecraft with less effort than could separate firms devoted to only one line of products.

The original concept of General Foods Corporation sought a similar synergistic effect in marketing. Here, the basic capability was marketing prepared foods. By having the same sales organization handle several product lines, a larger and more effective sales effort could be provided and/or the selling cost per product line could be reduced. Clearly, the combined sales activity was more powerful than separate sales efforts for each product line would have been.

Vertical Integration

Expansion to Obtain a Resource. Vertical integration may have synergistic effects. This occurred when the Apollo Printing Machine Company bought a foundry. Apollo was unsatisfied with the quality and tardy delivery of its castings and was looking for a new supplier. In its search, it learned that a nearby foundry could be purchased. The foundry was just breaking even, primarily because the volume of its work fluctuated widely. Following the purchase, Apollo gave the foundry a more steady backlog of work, and through close technical cooperation the quality of castings received by them was improved. The consolidated set-up was better for both enterprises than the previous independent operations.

The results of vertical integration are not always so good, however; problems of balance, flexibility, and managerial capacity must be carefully weighed. Nevertheless, control of a critical resource is often a significant part of company strategy.

Unique Services

Expansion to Enhance Market Position. Efforts to improve market position provide many examples of "the whole being better than the sum of its parts." The leading can companies, for example, moved from exclusive concentration on metal containers into glass, plastic, and paper containers. They expected their new divisions to be profitable by themselves, but an additional reason for the expansion lay in anticipated synergistic effects of being able to supply a customer's total container requirements. With the entire packaging field changing so rapidly, a company that can quickly shift from one type of container to another offers a distinctive service to its customers.

International Harvester, to cite another case, added a very large tractor to its line a few years ago. The prospects for profit on this line alone were far from certain. However, the new tractor was important to give dealers "a full line"; its availability removed the temptation for dealers to carry some products of competing manufacturers. So, when viewed in combination with other International Harvester products, the new tractor looked much more significant than it did as an isolated project.

Negative Synergy

Compatibility of Efforts. In considering additional niches for a company, we may be confronted with negative synergy—that is, the combined effort is worse than the sum of independent efforts. This occurred when a producer of high quality television and hi-fi sets introduced a small color television receiver. When first offered, the small unit was as good as most competing sets and probably had an attractive potential market. However, it was definitely inferior in performance to other products of the company and, consequently, undermined public confidence in the quality of the entire line. Moreover, customers had high expectations for the small set because of the general reputation of the company, and they became very critical when the new product did not live up to their expectations. Both the former products and the new product suffered.

Compatibility of operations within the company should also be considered.

A large department store, for instance, ran into serious trouble when it tried to add a high-quality dress shop to its mass merchandising activities. The ordering and physical handling of merchandise, the approach to sales promotion, the sales compensation plan, and many other procedures which worked well for the established type of business were unsuited to the new shop. And friction arose each time the shop received special treatment. Clearly, the new shop created an excessive number of problems because it was incompatible with existing customs and attitudes.

Broad Company Goals

Summarizing briefly: We have seen that some combinations of efforts are strongly reinforcing. The combination accelerates the total effect or reduces the cost for the same effect or solidifies our supply or market position. On the other hand, we must watch for incompatible efforts which may have a disruptive effect in the same cumulative manner. So, when we select niches—as a part of our master strategy—one vital aspect is the possibility of such synergistic effects.

Master strategy sets broad company goals. One firm may decide to seek pre-eminence in a narrow specialty while another undertakes to be a leader in several niches or perhaps in all phases of its industry. We have recommended that this definition of "scope" be clear in terms of:

Services offered to customers.

Operations performed by the company.

Relationships with suppliers of necessary resources.

The desirability of defining this mission so as to obtain synergistic effects.

But master strategy involves more than defining our desired role in society. Many activities will be necessary to achieve this desired spot, and senior executives must decide what to do first, how many activities can be done concurrently, how fast to move, what risks to run, and what to postpone. These questions of sequence and timing must be resolved to make the strategy operational.

Strategy of Sequence

Choice of Sequence. Especially in technical areas, sequence of actions may be dictated by technology. Thus, process research must precede equipment designs, product specifications must precede cost estimation, and so forth. Other actions, such as the steps necessary to form a new corporation, likewise give management little choice in sequence. When this occurs, normal programming or possibly PERT analysis may be employed. Little room—or need—exists for strategy.

Preordained sequences, however, are exceptional in the master strategy area. A perennial issue when entering a new niche, for instance, is whether to develop markets before working on production economies, or vice versa. The production executive will probably say, "Let's be sure we can produce the product at a low cost before committing ourselves to customers," whereas the typical marketing man will advise, "Better be sure it will sell before tooling up for a big output."

A striking example of strategy involving sequence confronted the Boeing company when it first conceived of a large four-engine jet plane suitable for handling cargo or large passenger loads. Hindsight makes the issue appear simple, but at the time, Air Force officers saw little need for such a plane. The belief was that propeller-driven planes provided the most desirable means for carrying cargo. In other words, the company got no support for its prediction of future market requirements. Most companies would have stopped at this point. However, Boeing executives decided to invest several million dollars to develop the new plane. A significant portion of the company's liquid assets went into the project. Over two years later, Boeing was able to present evidence that caused the Air Force officials to change their minds—and the KC 135 was born. Only Boeing was prepared to produce the new type of craft which proved to be both faster and more economical than propeller-driven planes. Moreover, the company was able to convert the design into the Boeing 707 passenger plane which, within a few years, dominated the airline passenger business. Competing firms were left far behind, and Convair almost went bankrupt in its attempt to catch up. In this instance, a decision to let engineering and production run far ahead of marketing paid off handsomely.

No simple guide exists for selecting a strategic sequence. Nevertheless, the following comments do sharpen the issue:

Resist the temptation to do first what is easiest simply because it requires the least initiative. Each of us typically has a bias for what he does well. A good sequence of activities, however, is more likely to emerge from an objective analysis.

If a head start is especially valuable on one front, start early there. Sometimes, being the first in the market is particularly desirable (there may be room for only one company). In other cases, the strategic place to begin is the acquiring of key resources; at a later date limited raw materials may already be bought up or the best sites occupied by competitors. The importance of a head start is usually hard to estimate, but probably more money is lost in trying to be first than in catching up with someone else.

Move into uncertain areas promptly, preferably before making any major commitments. For instance, companies have been so entranced with a desired expansion that they committed substantial funds to new plants before uncertainties regarding the production processes were removed.

If a particular uncertainty can be investigated quickly and inexpensively, get it out of the way promptly.

Start early with processes involving long lead-times. For example, if a new synthetic food product must have government approval, the tedious process of testing and reviewing evidence may take a year or two longer than preparation for manufacturing and marketing.

Delay revealing plans publicly if other companies can easily copy a novel idea. If substantial social readjustment is necessary, however, an early public announcement is often helpful.

In a particular case, these guides may actually conflict with each other, or other considerations may be dominant. And, as the Boeing 707 example suggests, the possible gains may be large enough to justify following a very risky sequence. Probably the greatest value of the above list is to stimulate careful thought about the sequence that is incorporated into a company's master strategy.

Resource Limitations

Straining Scarce Resources. A hard-driving executive does not like to admit that an objective cannot be achieved. He prefers to believe, "Where there's a will there's a way." Yet, an essential aspect of master strategy is deciding what can be done and how fast.

Every enterprise has limits—perhaps severe limits—on its resources. The amount of capital, the number and quality of key personnel, the physical production capacity, or the adaptability of its social structure—none of these is boundless. The tricky issue is how to use these limited resources to the best advantage. We must devise a strategy which is feasible within the inherent restraints.

A household-appliance manufacturer went bankrupt because he failed to adapt his rate of growth to his financial resources. This man had a first-rate product and a wise plan for moving with an "economy model" into an expanding market (following rural electrification). But, to achieve low production costs, he built an oversized plant and launched sales efforts in ten states. His contention was that the kind of company he conceived could not start out on a small scale. Possibly all of these judgments were correct, but they resulted in cash requirements that drained all of his resources before any momentum was achieved. Cost of the partially used plant and of widely scattered sales efforts was so high that no one was willing to bail out the financially strapped venture. His master strategy simply did not fit his resources.

The scarce resource affecting master strategy may be managerial personnel. A management consulting firm, for instance, reluctantly postponed entry into the international arena because only two of its partners had the combination of interest, capacity, and vitality to spend a large amount of time abroad, and these men were also needed to assure continuity of the United States practice. The firm felt that a later start would be better than weak action immediately—even though this probably meant the loss of several desirable clients.

The weight we should attach to scarce resources in the timing of master strategy often requires delicate judgment. Some strain may be endured. But, how much, how long? For example, in its switch from purchased to company-produced tires, a European rubber company fell behind on deliveries for six months, but, through heroic efforts and pleading with customers, the company weathered the squeeze. Now, company executives believe the timing was wise! If the delay had lasted a full year—and this was a real possibility—the consequence would have approached a catastrophe.

Forming Coalitions. A cooperative agreement with firms in related fields occasionally provides a way to overcome scarce resources. We have already referred to the RCA-Whirlpool arrangement for distributing Whirlpool products. Clearly, in this instance, the timing of Whirlpool's entrance into the market with its own brand depended on forming a coalition with RCA.

Examples of Coalitions

The early development of frozen foods provides us with two other examples of fruitful coalitions. A key element in Birdseye master strategy was to obtain the help of cold-storage warehouses; grocery wholesalers were not equipped to handle frozen foods, and before the demand was clearly established they were slow to move into the new activity. And the Birdseye division of General Foods lacked both managerial and financial resources to venture into national wholesaling.

Similarly, Birdseye had to get freezer cabinets into retail stores, but it lacked the capability to produce them. So, it entered into a coalition with a refrigerator manufacturer to make and sell (or lease) the cabinets to retail stores. This mutual agreement enabled Birdseye to move ahead with its marketing program much faster. With the tremendous growth of frozen foods, neither the cold storage warehouse nor the cabinet manufacturer continued to be necessary, but without them in the early days widespread use of frozen foods would have been delayed three to five years.

Coalitions may be formed for reasons other than "buying time." Nevertheless, when we are trying to round out a workable master strategy, coalitions—or even mergers—may provide the quickest way to overcome a serious deficiency in vital resources.

The Right Time to Act

Receptive Environment. Conditions in a firm's environment affect the "right time" to make a change. Mr. Ralph Cordiner, for example, testifies that he launched his basic reorganization of General Electric Company only when he felt confident of three years of high business activity because, in his opinion, the company could not have absorbed all the internal readjustments during a period of declining volume and profits.

Judging the right time to act is difficult. Thus, one of the contributing factors to the multimillion-dollar Edsel car fiasco was poor timing. The same automobile launched a year or two earlier might have been favorably received. But buyer tastes changed between the time elaborate market research studies were made and the time when the new car finally appeared in dealer showrooms. By then, preference was swinging away from a big car that "had everything" toward compacts. This mistake in timing and associated errors in strategy cost the Ford Motor Company over a hundred million dollars.

A major move can be too early, as well as too late. We know, for instance, that a forerunner of the modern, self-service supermarket—the Piggly Wiggly—was born too soon. In its day, only a few housewives drove automobiles to shopping centers; and those that could afford cars usually shunned the do-it-yourself mode so prevalent today. In other words, the environment at that time simply was not receptive to what now performs so effectively. Other "pioneers" have also received cool receptions—prefabricated housing and local medical clinics are two.

No Simple Rules

The preceding discussions of sequence and timing provide no simple rules for these critical aspects of basic strategy. The factors we have mentioned for deciding which front(s) to push first (where is a head start valuable, early attention to major uncertainties, lead-times, significance of secrecy) and for deciding how fast to move (strain on scarce resources, possible coalition to provide resources, and receptivity of the environment) bear directly on many strategy decisions. They also highlight the fundamental nature of sequence and timing in the master strategy for a firm.

Master strategy involves deliberately relating a company's efforts to its particular future environment. We recognize, of course, that both the company's capabilities and its environment continually evolve; consequently, strategy should always be based, not on existing conditions, but on forecasts. Such forecasts, however, are never 100 per cent correct; instead, strategy often seeks to take advantage of uncertainty about future conditions.

This dynamic aspect of strategy should be underscored. The industry outlook will shift for any of numerous reasons. These forces may accelerate growth in some sectors and spell decline in others, may squeeze material supply, may make old sources obsolete, may open new possibilities and snuff out others. Meanwhile, the company itself is also changing—due to the success or failure of its own efforts and to actions of competitors and cooperating firms. And with all of these internal and external changes the combination of thrusts that will provide optimum synergistic effects undoubtedly will be altered. Timing of actions is the most volatile element of all. It should be adjusted to both the new external situation and the degrees of internal progress on various fronts.

Consequently, frequent reappraisal of master strategy is essential. We must build into the planning mechanisms sources of fresh data that will tell us how well we are doing and what new opportunities and obstacles are appearing on the horizon. The feedback features of control will provide some of these data. In addition, senior managers and others who have contact with various parts of the environment must be ever-sensitive to new developments that established screening devices might not detect.

Hopefully, such reappraisal will not call for sharp reversals in strategy. Typically, a master strategy requires several years to execute and some features may endure much longer. The kind of plan I am discussing here sets the direction for a whole host of company actions, and external reputations and relations often persist for many years. Quick reversals break momentum, require repeated relearning, and dissipate favorable cumulative effects. To be sure, occasionally a sharp break may be necessary. But, if my forecasts are reasonably sound, the adaptations to new opportunities will be more evolution than revolution. Once embarked on a course, we make our reappraisal from our new position—and this introduces an advantage in continuing in at least the same general direction. So, normally, the adaptation is more an unfolding than a completely new start.

Even though drastic modification of our master strategy may be unnecessary, frequent incremental changes will certainly be required to keep abreast of the times. Especially desirable are shifts that anticipate change before the pressures build up. And such farsighted adjustments are possible only if we periodically reappraise and adapt present strategy to new opportunities.

Master strategy is the pivotal planning instrument for large and small enterprises alike. The giant corporations provide us with examples on a grand scale, but the same kind of thinking is just as vital for small firms.

An Example

A terse sketch of the central strategy of one small firm will illustrate this point. The partners of an accounting firm in a city with a quarter-million population predicted faster growth in data processing than in their normal auditing and tax work, yet they knew that most of their clients were too small to use an electronic computer individually. So they foresaw the need for a single, cooperative computer center serving several companies. And they believed that their intimate knowledge of the procedures and the needs of several of these companies, plus the specialized ability of one partner in data processing, put them in a unique position to operate such a center. Competition was anticipated from two directions: New models of computers much smaller in size would eventually come on the market—but even if the clients could rent such equipment they would still need programmers and other specialized skills. Also, telephonic hook-ups with International Business Machines service centers appeared likely— but the accounting firm felt its local and more intimate knowledge of each company would give it an advantage over such competition. So, the cooperative computer center looked like a propitious niche.

The chief obstacle was developing a relatively stable volume of work that would carry the monthly rental on the proposed computer. A local insurance company was by far the best prospect for this purpose; it might use half the computer capacity, and then the work for other, smaller companies could be fitted into the remaining time. Consequently, the first major move was to make a deal—a coalition—with the insurance company. One partner was to devote almost his entire time working on details for such an arrangement; meanwhile, the other two partners supported him through their established accounting practice.

We see in this brief example:

The picking of a propitious niche for expansion.

The anticipated synergistic effect of combining auditing services with computing service.

The sequence and timing of efforts to overcome the major limiting factor.

The project had not advanced far enough for much reappraisal, but the fact that two partners were supporting the third provided a built-in check on the question of "how are we doing."

REFERENCE

This article is adapted from a new chapter in *The Process of Management,* second edition, Prentice-Hall, Inc., 1967. Executives who wish to explore the meaning and method of shaping master strategies still further can consult the following materials: E. W. Reilley, "Planning the Strategy of the Business," *Advanced Management,* 20 (Dec. 1955), 8-12; T. Levitt, "Marketing Myopia," *Harvard Business Review,* 38:4 (July-August 1960), 45-66; F. F. Gilmore and R. G. Brandenburg, "Anatomy of Corporate Planning," *Harvard Business Review,* 41:6 (November-December 1962), 61-69; and H. W. Newman and T. L. Berg, "Managing External Relations," *California Management Review,* 5:3 (Spring 1963), 81-86.

8
What Planning Involves*

STEWART THOMPSON

The contribution of the business planner is this: despite the impossibility of accurately forecasting the future, he identifies a range of possibilities and prepares for them. Once this is understood, the difference between planning and forecasting becomes clearer. "Forecasting" is the attempt to find the most probable course of events or a range of probabilities. "Planning" is deciding what one will do about them.

Specialists in market research and economic forecasting can be useful in gathering information on which plans for the business can be based. But decisions on what is to be achieved, and why, are business decisions, to be made by top management. This view was generally supported by the managers who participated in this research project. Most of those interviewed in firms which have staff planning departments emphasized that the work of these departments is not that of making business decisions. Instead, they declared, these departments help top management by gathering information, by identifying problems, by recommending procedures to be followed in formulating and reviewing plans. It is top management that decides the kinds of work to be performed, the kinds of material to be used, and the needs of specific customers to be satisfied. Top management decides the risks the company is willing to take and states whether the future of the firm is to be staked on one or more products, on one or more markets. Top management decides what things the company will do as a side line and what things it will do as a life-or-death commitment.

Characteristics of a Business Plan

Even though the future is largely unknown, work in the present takes on added significance when it is performed in contemplation of future results. A business plan states what results are to be achieved and states things that people actually can and should do to achieve them. It also provides for the evaluation and measurement of results.

Underlying the use of planning in business is the insight that management is not only "feel" or experience, but also choice of a rational course of action. The

*Source: Reprinted by permission of the publisher from AMA Research Study no. 54, *How Companies Plan,* copyright 1962 by the American Management Association, Inc.

decisions and actions of business men are based on certain ideas regarding the kind of business they manage, the market and economy in which they operate, the resources at their disposal, and the effect of their actions upon the business and upon persons outside the business.

Objectives, assumptions, and risks are always present in the thoughts, decisions, and acts of a manager. Even though these elements may not be always clear to him, he must act on the basis of some ideas about the character of his business: its environment, its resources, its potential. No matter how important intuition and experience may be, business decisions and actions can be rational. A major purpose and contribution of a business plan is to bring out and sharpen this rationality.

A business plan is a preparation for action. It involves making decisions and scheduling results.

Scheduling takes into account the magnitude of the problems in bringing about a result. Scheduling tests the feasibility of a plan. For example, it may show that results needed "immediately" would, in fact, require three years of preparation. Thoughtful scheduling extends the possibility of making business decisions effective. Without schedules, business plans may be only unrealistic dreams. Scheduling has to do with such questions as these: "What must I have completed on what date?" "What stages can be accelerated?" "What stages can be got under way concurrently with other stages?" Scheduling starts with the knowledge of what is desired and works backward.

By tying business decisions to specific times and results, a plan for management can be formulated which, when used imaginatively, can aid in maintaining and augmenting the value of a business to the society of which it is a part.

Three Kinds of Business Planning

In different ways, the experience of managers reported here shows three kinds of business plans: (1) plans for doing current business, (2) plans for continuing in business, and (3) plans for business development and growth. The major emphasis of this study is on business plans of the kinds listed as (2) and (3).

Plans for doing current business are related to creating today's business and to scheduling today's work in accordance with time and quality standards. These are the operating plans of the manager and the supervisor and the worker, piece by piece, order by order. Since they concern customer service and operating efficiency in an immediate way, effective planning and scheduling of today's business are essential to future survival and growth. The importance of this point has been emphasized by David Packard, President of Hewlett-Packard Company, in these words:

The keystone of our entire program at Hewlett-Packard Company can be summarized in the statement that we believe tomorrow's success is based on today's performance. In our opinion, this is so obvious a statement as hardly to require repetition, but we often see other firms which are so busy worrying about tomorrow that they never quite seem to do otherwise, and the first order of business is almost always to make sure that current operations are on a sound and profitable basis. It is true that this approach is fairly conservative and that our rate of progress has probably been somewhat limited by our desire to avoid overcommitments to the future, but on the other hand we find that, when we have our current situation under firm control, all our key people seem to have a little more time to look constructively toward the future.[1]

Plans for continuing in business are those that deal with the changing character of the customer's business, with the changing habits and expectations of workers and society at large. These plans do not deal specifically with only one order or one customer. Rather, they are plans reasoned from the manager's assumptions on long-term trends and the changes in those trends. These are plans to build the changing values of the customer into the products and services of the business.

In addition to—or instead of—plans made to perpetuate a business in the markets it already serves, the chief executive may see opportunities his business could logically exploit in other areas. Plans made by the top management of Harris-Intertype Corporation to move into electronics are of this kind, in part at least. Plans for business development and growth sometimes involve preparation to open markets different from those traditionally served by the business, with products different from those the business itself makes. Or, the plans may be to serve essentially the same customers with different or more expanded products and services.

For many companies, business planning is the act of making decisions in one or more of these areas. By thinking of plans to meet needs in each of these three areas, a manager can identify the areas in his own company in which planning ought to be accelerated.

Planning as Practiced by Most Companies

An analysis of the remarks of the business men who participated in this study shows that their business planning usually involves the following steps:

a. Gathering information on both the external environment and the company internally, in order to see the major problems facing the business.

b. Identifying and studying the factors which may limit the company's efficiency and growth in the future.

c. Formulating basic assumptions (such as, for example, "No major war within the next five years," or "A continuation of the present economic trends for

---

1/David Packard, "Assuring the Company's Future," American Management Association, General Management Series, no. 175, New York, 1955, p. 27.

the planning period"). It may also involve determination of several plans for the future, based on a set of markedly different assumptions.

d. Laying down the objectives or the goals of the business, based on information gathered, assumptions, predictions, and a study of major problems.

e. Determining the actions which must be taken to achieve the objectives.

f. Setting up a timetable for these actions. . . .

THE CONCEPT OF THE BUSINESS BOUNDARY

Through planning, a manager creates a strategy for the survival and growth of his business. What must he do to assure the health of his firm as a growing enterprise? His answer commits money, knowledge, and skills to specific tasks in order to accomplish specific results. These results change the circumstances of the business, change its problems and its opportunities, and may create the need for changes in its character and its plans for the future.

The manager plans his business by defining a particular relationship of work-product-customer to highlight those factors that are of greatest importance to his business. In effect, the manager defines boundaries within which his business will operate. The effectiveness of a business plan depends largely upon the ability of the manager to select appropriate boundaries. A clear statement of business boundaries has the value of concentrating thought on the problems that are vital to the business.

Mason Smith, Vice President and Treasurer of Whirlpool Corporation, emphasized this point when he spoke of the manager's need for a frame of reference for his business:

A frame of reference is essential for long-range planning—and by "frame of reference" I mean, specifically, the definition and statement of the company's broad objectives and policies in such a way that they are understood clearly by all personnel. I am convinced that any attempt to initiate and maintain a long-range planning program without some general, company-wide understanding of the kind of business that the management is attempting to build will yield very few tangible benefits. In addition to a cold, clear acknowledgment of the company's financial limitations, these objectives and policies should provide some indication of whether the company will intensify within one industry or diversify; whether or not it will integrate; whether it will attempt only to maintain the Number One position in its industry or try to balance size with other considerations; whether it will assume a posture of statesmanship in its industry or operate under short-run principles. Decisions regarding such matters are, of course, subject to review and revision by the board and by management at any time. When they are revised, however, management should be sure that the long-range planning program is following whatever new statement of policy is laid down.[2]

In solving operating problems, the manager reasons from agreed-on boundaries to implications for the particular problem. If seemingly promising lines of action conflict with accepted boundaries, there are two solutions: change the boundaries or drop the action. So it may be said that business planning covers (1) exploration and improvement within boundaries that have been laid down, and (2) the questioning, evaluation, and restructuring of the boundaries themselves.

This testing and correcting of the boundaries is a vital part of business planning. "Who are our customers?" "Why?" "Under what circumstances does a customer become a non-customer?" "To our customers Jackson, Jones, and Johnson, what is the function and value of our product?" "What consulting services does our special competence enable us to provide that our competitors cannot provide?" "Is our main strength in making the product, or in our methods of selling it, or in our company image, or in our knowledge supplied to the customer on how to use, store, and maintain the product?" These are some of the questions that the participants in this study have answered or tried to answer.

The Need for Boundaries

According to a statement by one of its executives, the top management of one company which took part in this research had no clear idea of the boundaries of the business. Eventually, a situation arose that sharply pointed up the need for well-defined boundaries. Although some aspects of the situation have been altered in the telling, in order to comply with this firm's desire for anonymity, the problem was essentially as reported here.

A researcher came up with a device to aid surgeons by measuring the oxygen content of blood continuously while surgery was in progress. When a vice president discovered that almost $100,000 had been spent on the instrument he ordered the work to be discontinued. Recalled an official of the firm:

> We stopped work on that project, but we did not know why. Nobody, not even the president or the officer who issued the order, seemed to know why. I raised the question: "O.K.," I said, "let's stop work on the project, but let's be sure we know why. Do we not want to do medical research? Do we not have the money to finish the project? Do we want to make only radio and TV sets?" Nobody was prepared to get down to some careful thinking on the issue. We just stopped. The researcher left us,

2/Mason Smith, "How to Initiate Effective Long-Range Planning," *The Dynamics of Management,* American Management Association, Management Report, no. 14, New York, 1958, p. 70.

taking his ideas with him. In time, the failure to examine the possibilities the researcher was opening up for us may prove to be one of the greatest fumbles we ever made. As I see it, the fumble was not so much the decision to stop the project, unfortunate as that may have been, but the larger issue of failing to thoroughly consider the areas in which the competence of those in the firm can best be applied. We still lack a central concept about our business. It is badly needed here.

The System Boundary

There are two concepts of business boundaries. The one just discussed involves the choice of objectives and behavior for the firm. In this case the boundary marks off the area of business purpose and conduct selected by the top management for present or future operations of the company.

The other concept relates to changes in the dynamic structure or climate within which the managerial decisions and plans must be made. This dynamic structure, or "system," consists of the variables affecting and affected by the business. The system includes the interaction of individuals within the firm, the interaction of the firm with its customers and with other businesses, and influences within the society of which the firm is a part. In this context the boundary—more specifically, the system boundary—is the moment of significant change in the variables of the system.

Let us assume that at some point in the operation of a particular business one of its essential variables (for example, its most important customer) does not continue as before. This discontinuity can be described as a system boundary. The business might have to dissolve, or at least its managers would be faced with a grave problem. The business could perhaps establish a new relationship with another type of customer in order to survive. If this were done, a new climate or business system would operate and new variables would govern the company. There would be new factors (or a re-weighting of old factors) to be considered in the new business plan. Business planning seeks to identify such points of major change and to enable the manager to make preparations in case of need. In some cases, proper response may require very significant changes in company concepts, with such results as adding new products, hiring a new president, or selling a division of the company.

A Company Experience

The following case illustrates an evolution of a business and a change in the boundaries within which it operated. This firm's experience points out that changes in the way the firm did business created a new business system. These changes were subtle, not easy to recognize, not easy to define precisely. The president did not call them "boundaries," but he did recognize that at different points in time an isolated change created new stages in his firm's growth and gave rise to new kinds of opportunities and problems and a need for new plans. The firm made storage racks, hand trucks, and other equipment used in handling and storing materials.

The owners of the firm hired a new president to help achieve higher profits. As the president examined sales records and visited customers, he found that his competitors gained considerable business from the use of attractively prepared and well-illustrated catalogues. It seemed to him highly desirable to have such catalogues, but he felt that his company could not afford them.

The president proceeded to expand his product line to some extent and redesigned much of it to approximate closely the products of one of his principal competitors, a much larger company. In the course of soliciting business, particularly from those firms he knew well, he used his competitor's catalogue, sometimes offering lower prices and usually providing earlier delivery. In addition, he studied the utilization of his equipment in the customer's plants. As his profits increased, he later brought out his own descriptive catalogue, added some especially designed devices, and concentrated on the technical training of his firm's salesmen. His sales proceeded to match and then outstrip the business of even his largest competitors. Salesmen of the competitor sold from the catalogue in a routine way ("Order by number, please"), but this president had his salesmen bring special problem-solving skills to his customers' operations. Incidentally, for many of his salesmen this change in the character of their work launched them on a new career in the firm.

Recognizing an opportunity to depart still further from the traditional marketing methods of "the industry" and to publicize the unique character of his company, the president offered his own help and that of his salesmen to aid customers to solve problems of layout and utilization in their plants. Some of the customers began to request his aid in training members of their own staffs in his techniques of analysis. These requests came with such frequency that for a time he seriously considered setting up another business to deal with the consultations. However, he decided against this idea.

Hearing of his success in his own line, manufacturers of other related products sought to have his firm distribute all or some of their lines. The directors of the firm, well pleased with operations under their president, recommended diversification into other businesses.

A major problem became that of planning and controlling the growth of the business in order to utilize effectively the evolving skills and growing reputation of the firm while avoiding, as far as possible, an uncontrolled dissipation of energy.

Company Character

Business decisions that clarify the boundaries within which the business will operate, and a timetable of results, imply as well as a plan a particular conception of "management." The way in which this conception is defined by the individual manager gives "planned character" to his firm. The president's concept of the firm he is managing, for example, largely defines the kind of planning he will do.

There is a difference between financial manipulation and business management. There is a difference between a corporation and its individual components. Sometimes confusion exists as to what kind of planning the managers should do, because the kind of business the chief executive is managing or creating is not clear.

Some managers believe their company operates as a federalized enterprise with a central office and various decentralized divisions, when in actual fact the characteristics of the company are more those of a financial trust. As a financial trust, the primary concern of the central management is the investment of shareholders' capital in various businesses. These investments may be, for the most part, in minority interests. Buying and selling of interests in various firms is done for appreciation of capital rather than for building an enterprise with a logic of its own. Planning in a financial trust type of operation requires different knowledge and skills and addresses itself to kinds of problems which are different from those in a decentralized company.

A "federalized company," as the term is used here, is a firm which has a headquarters office for two or more enterprises, each of which has its unique products, processes, and markets and complements the others. In an enterprise of this type, planning within the divisions applies to the exploration of markets and improved efficiency, within the boundaries laid down. Plans would also include means for clarifying the boundaries of the divisions and of the total enterprise in the light of new problems and opportunities. Problems relating to new product ideas and new markets that do not fall clearly within the scope of one or more of the divisions would have to be resolved. Headquarters as well as divisional management may have parts to play in planning for action to be taken by two or more divisions that may form together a single unit in order to achieve a specific purpose. Business planning at headquarters may involve the raising of capital and the strengthening of management competence in the subsidiary and affiliated businesses, as well as provision for assuring that continuous development of managerial competence is energized within the divisions by themselves. The orientation of management at headquarters may aim to do less and less in the way of managing the divisions, so that top management can concentrate on identifying and planning for those events that most affect the whole firm.

Another form of business that has special planning needs of its own is the holding company. Such firms own either a substantial minority interest or a controlling interest in various enterprises, no single one of which may relate to the markets, products, or processes of the others. The central concern of management of a holding company often is to acquire capital at the most favorable terms. The capital is utilized by the subsidiary enterprises for their growth and expansion and may represent funds which the subsidiaries could not have acquired had they not had affiliation with the holding company. Planning at headquarters may emphasize the appropriation of acquired capital (and regular profits) among the affiliated businesses. Very often, management at headquarters is skilled in dealing with the financial problems of the business but incompetent to deal with the more specialized plans of individual affiliated businesses. To distinguish the areas of competence of headquarters management and to define the kinds of contributions headquarters can make to the profit-producing end of the enterprise (the divisions) is a matter for careful planning and of large consequence.

In addition to the federalized corporation and the holding company, there is the business that does not have a relationship to a central headquarters. This is the one-plant, one-management business. It may or may not be owned by its managers. It may or may not be a large corporation. With regard to planning for this kind of business—as for the others—difference in size is not in itself so major a consideration as is the difference in the kind of problems with which top management must deal. Even a small company, like its larger counterparts, may have many circles of affiliation with other businesses, and these should be recognized in the business plan. There are many forms of affiliation that are becoming increasingly common.[3]

It is most unlikely that any enterprise will fit neatly into such arbitrary classifications as those given here. Nonetheless, managers of individual companies must continually think of their businesses according to some structure of ideas in order to know what they are really doing and whether they are doing the essential things. A manager—of whatever business—cannot do everything. He needs some rational framework for determining which kinds of decisions he will leave for others and which ones he is to decide for himself. In clarifying the definition of this framework, top managers must carefully examine the nature of their relationship to the operating executives. The classification just listed, while oversimplified, may enable managers to question their assumptions regarding the main issues they habitually retain—perhaps without conscious examination—for their own attention.

Inadequacies of Planning

The objective of this report is to describe the kinds of business planning done, and the methods followed, in a selected group of companies. This implies

3/In this regard the following articles are worthy of note: Robert Hershey, "No Job Is Too Big . . . The Multiple Organization: Management's Answer to Complexity," *The Management Review*, February, 1959, p. 9; John J. Corson, "Government and Business: Partners in the Space Age," *The Management Review*, September, 1959, p. 9; and Robert G. Sproul, Jr., "Developing Profitable Partnerships in Overseas Operations," *The Management Review*, October, 1960, p. 4.

differences in personal preference, from one company to another (or even within the same company), on how planning ought to be done. It implies as well that examples of both good and not-so-good planning are to be found in this report.

Some companies, for example, are currently enamored of change, accelerating change, and innovations and new developments. The intoxicating enthusiasm for change and "new frontiers" sometimes leads to neglect of the stable elements which do not change. Anticipation of and planning for change is fruitless unless it is coupled with anticipation of and planning for factors which will be stable. It is probably a matter of individual emphasis, but the examples in this study weigh heavily on the side of managements' concern for change. They do not express equal awareness of the stable elements of the businesses.

Along the same line is the emphasis on new developments and acquisitions, as contrasted with improved efficiency within existing markets. Commented an official of one firm, "Farming the same farm more efficiently usually has a better chance, I'll wager, than new products or other expansion." He was right in going on to suggest that many companies do not seem to study the possibility of becoming more efficient within the current boundaries of the business with the same thoroughness that characterizes plans for diversification into other fields—which often prove later to be beyond their competence.

Clarifying boundaries and areas of competence is a pressing need in many companies, including some of those represented in this study. . . . [One company's] "Ten-Year Forward-planning Program" . . . does not meet the definition of a plan as proposed in the text. It is a rather vague declaration of intention. A plan stipulates courses of action to produce measurable results. This document does not. A plan must be operational in the sense that it describes actions in terms of things people actually can do. This document does not. The document does speak of improved results. But it will be a plan only when the desired improvement is stated as a recognized standard. A plan states that certain results must be obtained (for example, reduced costs) and states specifically what those results are and what will be done to achieve them.

This is not to say that a document of intention is of no value; such a document may be the precursor of specific and realistic plans. It is sometimes essential to think through, in broad terms, what one intends to do. Good intentions can lead to sound and effective action. (In fact, all action ought to be based on "good intentions.") Still, the manager ought to distinguish a business plan from a statement limited to the expression of good intentions.

In other situations, top management participation in business planning is entirely lacking. Plans are called for from various division and department heads and "coordinated" (a word which is often used but seldom defines clearly the work performed) at the top. A clear view of what the division and department heads must contribute is often lacking. Asking department heads or even senior officers in a firm what it is they would like to do in the coming year or in ten years may be one way to attempt to capture their interest. But it is not business planning. To limit the formulation of a business plan to this kind of procedure is to do little more than make an opportunity for people to do what they want to do, undisciplined by clear purposes and concrete objectives vital to the whole. In such a case, planning is in the nature of recreation or play, where people plan to do the things they enjoy. It is the task of top management to provide the purpose and to set the boundaries, using as directly as possible the best brains in the business (and outside it, too) to do so. But it is correct to view the interests and skills of its people as the company's special strengths. A business plan should include thinking on the numbers and levels of skills required and how they can best be related to each other in order to get the vital work of the business done. Presidents and managers interviewed spoke also of a number of other problems and inadequacies associated with making plans for a business—for example, the following:

a. The manager may confine his thinking to largely obsolete or contemporary ideas.
b. The manager may be unwilling or unable to see that this plan was either ill-conceived or well-conceived but, in any case, not feasible. He won't believe he is headed for failure until his business is liquidated.
c. There is danger of "throwing good money after bad." One may be inclined to invest another $100,000 to try to save a $50,000 investment that is not producing. More thought might bring to mind a more profitable avenue in which to direct the $100,000.
d. It is often difficult to stop work on a planned project, even when instructions to do so have been given. In one company a project had been officially stopped because the results planned were not being realized. But it took an additional (and unplanned) $250,000 to bring the works finally to a halt.
e. To plan to make something out of a company, if it cannot possibly be made, can be extremely costly if the plan is followed.
f. A business plan in itself is no guarantee that desired results will be realized. While deliberate planning is one aspect of good management, it is not a substitute for it.

How Far into the Future?

Certain characteristics of every business must be identified in order to determine what needs to be planned and for what period of time. The reader will find that many companies that participated in this research study state they plan five years into the future and make annual or half-yearly reviews of accomplishments, with an eye to altering the plan if necessary. Thus each year (or each six months) an entirely new five-year plan may be devised. Other firms establish a five-year plan but make no changes in it except as changes of great magnitude may require, such as unforeseen opportunities and drastic changes in the nation's economy.

A public utility which plans as far as 25 years in advance in order to provide future sites for its system may be exercising no more foresight than another firm, manufacturing consumer products, which plans six months in advance. Both companies have needs to be met in the future which must be prepared for in the present. The wisdom of a lumber business in providing now for wood to be available 100 years hence does not mean that its managers are gifted with some special talent; the fact that they embark on a reforestation program to assure (insofar as possible) that there will be trees does not prove that they are clairvoyant. To be sure, in such cases, the managers would be exercising good judgment. At the same time, it would not be good judgment to lay elaborate plans for an advertising or sales-training program 100 years in advance.

A few managers in this study mention plans for the next ten years. A number of firms have very long-range plans in addition to their basic five- or ten-year plans, but these are more often in the nature of statements of ultimate objectives than of detailed plans.

Insofar as a norm could be discerned among all the company statements, five years seems to be the planning period for many of the participating firms. This does not mean that plans for all aspects of the business are made for a five-year period. Rather, it means that when certain managers spoke of their "long-range plan" they had in mind marketing and product plans (sometimes, other kinds of plans as well) that looked to certain results in five years or intermediate periods. This does not indicate that every business should have a five-year plan. Two of the reasons why some managers think of planning in terms of five years may be that (1) this period is as far in the future as they can or need to anticipate; and (2) constant repetition of the phrase "five-year plan" by commentators speaking and writing about the U.S.S.R. and certain other countries may have had its influence.

Deciding on a range of time for planning is associated with the problems of evaluating the success of a manager. If one evaluates a man's work today, the result may be different than the result of an evaluation in five, ten, or 25 years. In formulating objectives, the manager must visualize the results as he expects them to be in the future. The range of time to be considered is a decision of large consequence in formulating a plan. Planning has to do with identifying what Peter Drucker calls "the futurity of today's decisions." There are some guides to be followed in deciding the "length of futurity" appropriate for the plans of a particular business or special unit within a business.

There are certain characteristics of the operations of each firm that lead to the selection of a particular span of time for planning. Long-range planning for a manufacturer of women's wear may be practically yesterday for the capital goods producer or the large public utility. Factors which lead to a selection of the proper planning time span are the following:

1. Lead time. This is the length of time it takes from the realization that major new products are needed to the completion of their design, production, and

distribution, plus a major period of utilization before the product is obsoleted.

2. The length of time required to recover the capital funds invested in plant and equipment and in training skilled personnel. A plan should provide for recovery of the capital funds invested in the actual physical construction of the plant and equipment and in hiring and training managers and skilled personnel. For example, a firm with a heavy investment in manufacturing and other facilities would have to base some of its plans on a period of time during which the machines would remain useful. Often this time span would be well in excess of the time required to manufacture one line of products.

3. The expected future availability of customers. For manufacturers of machinery and equipment used by other manufacturers, this is the time period up to the expected obsolescence of the customers' products.

4. The expected future availability of raw materials and components. If it takes 99 years to grow a forest to replace the trees the company uses in its manufacture of wood products, someone has to think about planting seedlings now. In this area, the planning span would be 99 years. Research may possibly shorten such long planning spans by providing entirely new raw materials.

As previously stated, one useful concept in determining the planning span is lead time. If one is driving a car, for example, and decides to turn a corner, there is either enough time to do it or there is not. If a firm is supplying a foreign market by sea, the manager must make the decision to ship the goods well before the material is at dockside and ready to be loaded.

Lead time should be defined in relation to the kind of action one is willing to take. In situations where the process of production or transportation is familiar, lead time is readily determined. If a ship takes five days to cross the Atlantic and five days are needed to load and unload, the lead time is ten days. This can be shortened, if necessary, by using air express. As another example, a driver can stop an automobile by exerting ordinary pressure on the brakes, or he can come to an emergency stop. Normally, when driving one does not want to make a series of emergency stops; he allows for routine stops. "Lead time," therefore, may be best defined as the period between decision and arrival at the final results. If routine methods are used, the period or range of time would be considered normal lead time.

With respect to planning, the appropriate ranges of time may also be described in terms of lead time. If, for instance, the building of facilities is being considered, one could thus express the relevant lead time required to decide what to build and where to build, plus the time needed to complete the construction.

In planning within the basic direction and limits of company growth, however, a lead time of even 20 to 30 years for facilities construction is not long enough. There is the additional time which represents the useful life of the building or facility. A firm does not normally plan to put up a building and scrap it shortly thereafter. The planning span might well be the total time the facilities are expected to be of use to the firm.

In some cases the time span of the business plan may end with the discontinuation of the business as it is presently conceived. A plan should provide for discontinuing work and jobs that do not need to be done, just as it should provide for discontinuing products and divisions that fail to advance the firm toward its goals. A business plan may have to include an estimate of the date on which the design of products, method of production, and kind of customer to be served will be altered to such a degree that the manager will need to reconceive his aims in terms of being in a new business.

It is evident, then, that the study of lead-time requirements can help in determining the planning span. But a carefully laid plan with a lengthy lead time may become a short-term expedient—if not altogether useless—if the actions of competitors (or of customers or others) create new situations not provided for in the plan. One manufacturer of tacks and nails suddenly found large segments of his market vanishing because of new kinds of adhesives being produced by firms he had never before thought of as competitors. An economic recession may cause the managers of a business to restudy their business plan and the span of time it covers. Vital decisions need to be made: Should the managers cut back on growth plans, thereby keeping outgo commensurate with income? Should they go ahead, with faith in the company, pursuing long-range goals established at a time of abundance? These are questions to be answered by business men who have large areas of responsibility for shaping the future of their businesses and of society as a whole.

9

What's Not on the Organization Chart*

HAROLD STIEGLITZ

Organization charts come in various sizes, colors and even textures. Most are black and white and printed on paper. Some are affixed to office walls—and made of materials that are easily changed. Some charts are highly detailed; some are very sketchy. Some are stamped *confidential* and secreted in the desks of a chosen few; others are broadly distributed and easily available. Despite these and other variations that might be noted, all organization charts have at least one thing in common: they don't show how the organization works. Or, as some people say, they don't show the *real* organization.

Such a statement, which usually emerges as a criticism of organization charts, goes beyond the fact that the organization chart, like milk, may be dated but not fresh. For it is increasingly understood that no organization chart is 100% current. Rather, the criticism is that even the most current chart is utterly inadequate as a diagram of the organization.

Few organization planners, even those whose major preoccupation is drawing charts, argue too vehemently against this criticism. They just go on drawing their charts. Most often, the charts they draw are of the conventional type made up of boxes and lines. These usually end up in a pyramidal shape with a box (generally larger) at the top to represent the chief executive.

However, behind the preparation and issuance of the chart, there is, presumably, this basic understanding: An organization chart is not an organization. And there is far more to an organization—even in the limited sense of an organization structure—than can ever be put on a chart.

But while the chartist himself may be aware of it, this knowledge is seldom pervasive. Some companies recognize this and attempt to underscore the fact that a chart is just a two-dimensional representation by placing the following caution at the bottom of the chart:

Level of boxes shows reporting relationships and has no significance with regard to importance of position or status.

*Source: Reprinted by permission from *The Conference Board Record* (November 1964), 7-10.

Such a caution or demurrer is seldom sufficient to quiet the critics or unruffle ruffled feathers, and is quite often taken with a large grain of salt—sometimes because the chart does show some of the very things that the demurrer may say it doesn't. If nothing else, for example, the head of a unit that doesn't appear on an organization chart can be reasonably sure that his unit is not rated important enough to merit inclusion.

Actually, the conventional organization chart (see Figure 1) shows very little. It implies a little more than it shows. But the inferences that are drawn from it are limited only by the experience, imagination and biases of the beholder—in or outside of the company. In other words, one of the troubles with charts seems to be the people who read them.

FIGURE 1
A Conventional Organization Chart

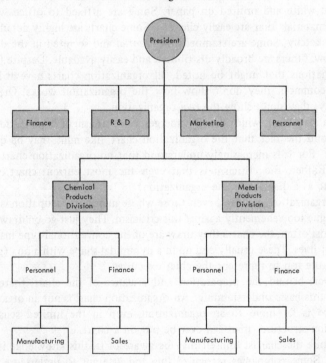

WHAT IT SHOWS

The organization chart of most companies shows—indeed is designed to show—just two things:

1. Division of work into components. These components may be divisions or departments or they may be individuals. Boxes on the conventional chart represent these units of work.

departments or they may be individuals. Boxes on the conventional chart represent these units of work.
2. Who is (supposed to be) whose boss—the solid lines on the chart show this superior-subordinate relationship with its implied flow of delegated responsibility, authority and attendant accountability.

Implicit in these two are several other things that the chart is designed to show:

3. Nature of the work performed by the component. Depending upon the descriptive title placed in the box, what this shows may be specific (Facilities Engineering), speculative (Planning) or spurious (Special Projects).
4. Grouping of components on a functional, regional or product basis. This is also conveyed to some extent by the labels in the boxes.
5. Levels of management in terms of successive layers of superiors and subordinates. All persons or units that report to the same person are on the one level. The fact that they may be charted on different horizontal planes does not, of course, change the level.

It is rather difficult to pinpoint anything else about a structure that is actually shown on an organization chart. Some may argue whether, in fact, even the few items above can be read directly from any or some charts.

WHAT THE CHART DOESN'T SHOW

What an organization chart doesn't show is often the most interesting part of the chart—at least to the internal personnel. And it is the inferences that arise from what's missing which companies attempt to deal with in their demurrers or cautions. The demurrers, as already suggested, don't always scotch the inferences. In many cases, the warnings may be erroneous or incomplete.

Degree of Responsibility and Authority

Take, for example, this caution: "Size and position of boxes do not indicate degree of responsibility or authority." Well, it is quite possible that they do. Indeed in the mere process of showing superior-subordinate relationships, the chart does clearly imply varying degrees of responsibility and authority. This is implicit in the process of delegation.

A possibly more accurate demurrer might be "any relationship between size and position of boxes and degree of responsibility and authority may be coincidental, accidental or just plain odd." For what the chart clearly does not show is the degree of responsibility and authority exercised by positions on the same management level. Two persons on the same management level may have vastly different degrees of authority. A man on the third level may have more or less authority than a second-level manager in a different chain of delegation.

Of course, because the chart cannot adequately begin to depict varying degrees of authority, it cannot show the degree of decentralization. Decentralization, organizationally speaking, has relevance only in terms of delegation of decision-making authority. Almost by definition, it refers to the level at which decisions are made.

Inferences about decentralization are often drawn from charts; the company chart that shows activities grouped into product divisions or regional divisions as opposed to a purely functional grouping is often referred to as decentralized. That may or may not be the case. The view from the top may be of a highly decentralized company; the view from the bottom or intermediate layers may be quite the opposite. And a functionally organized company can be as highly decentralized as a divisionally organized company. It all depends on the level at which decisions are being made. The chart cannot depict that, nor can it depict the extent of the restrictions—in the form of policies, budgets, procedures, reports, audits—that make for more or less decentralization.

Staff and Line

Distinguishing between staff and line is an arduous, hazardous, and so far as some organization planners are concerned, an academic chore. Attempting to determine line and staff from an organization chart presents similar hazards. Titles or functional labels alone won't do it. What one company considers line may be staff to another. Again, it depends on the responsibility and authority delegated to the units.

Of course, the nature of the company's business may give clues to what is staff or line. In a manufacturing company, for example, certain functions are traditionally viewed as staff: personnel administration, public relations, legal and secretarial, and finance are examples. In a services company the arrangement may be quite different. But reliance on the nature of the business can be misleading. In manufacturing, for example, divisionalization has brought into being staff units with labels such as manufacturing and marketing—labels that typically would belong to line components in a functionally organized firm.

In some companies, charting methods are used to attempt to distinguish what these firms consider to be line and staff (or service and operating) units. Sometimes the so-called staff units are charted on one horizontal plane, line on another. Other companies use skinny little lines to connect staff, healthier looking lines to connect line or operating units. Still others add labels to underscore this visual aid.

With all these visual distinctions, a chart reader might readily infer what is obviously being implied: there is a difference between the two types of units. To try to interpret these differences in terms of line-staff responsibilities, authorities, and relationships presents the same difficulties as reading the degree of decentralization from the chart.

Status or Importance

To some people, inclusion on the organization chart is, in itself, a status symbol. The physical location on the chart—the linear distance from the chief executive—is viewed as a measure of importance. And there's the rub. Given the limitations of a piece of paper, not everyone can be charted equidistant from the chief executive. Reassurances like "size and position of boxes do not reflect importance or status" are seldom reassuring enough. The incumbent charted in a particular spot may realize the truth of this statement; but he may fear that the "other fellows may not," or vice versa.

There is little question but that position on an organization chart, in some companies, does imply relative importance and status. But it has the same limitations in implying (or covering up lack of) importance as do size of office, titles, parking lot space, etc. Most people still rely on the pay envelope as a more accurate reflection of relative importance. And the organization chart just isn't designed to reflect the pay structure of the company.

In short, the organization chart may imply relative importance or status, but, to rephrase a caution that might appear on a chart, "Any inferences drawn from this chart regarding relative importance or status may or may not be correct."

Lines of Communication

Another caution that shows up is: "This chart does not indicate channels of contact." Actually it does. What it doesn't show is *all* the channels of contact or communication. Possibly a more appropriate warning might be: "This chart indicates a few of the major channels of contact—but if the organization sticks to only these, nothing will get done." For it is a truism of organization that no one unit or individual operates in isolation from all the others. All are linked by an intricate network of communication. (Maze may be a more apt term than network.) Proper organization performance relies on this network and on each unit and individual becoming party to it. To chart the total network is practically impossible. To attempt to chart it—and thus introduce certain rigidities into it—might easily frustrate its workings.

Relationships

In a real sense, lines of communication are really relationships. "You can't have one without the other"—and the picture of either that shows up on the chart is that of only a few key links in the total network.

Any organization is a hotbed of relationships. Not all of them, of course, necessarily grow out of the nature of the work of the company. Even those that do, however, do not show up on the conventional or even unconventional organization chart.

On occasion a company has noted: "This chart shows relationships only and does not represent levels of management." The caution may have been on the wrong chart, for on the chart in question the opposite seemed true.

More frequently the company notes: "This chart shows reporting relationships only. . . ." Even this seems questionable—it is accurate only if the phrase reporting relationships is understood to mean superior-subordinate reporting relationships.

Organizational relationships—as opposed to social, etc. relationships within a company—grow out of the division of work and delegation of responsibility and authority. A number of functional relationships, authority relationships, staff-line relationships, and just plain work relationships may come into play in reaching any decision or in completing any given piece of work. Most companies long ago gave up any attempt to even begin to show all of these relationships on a chart.

The "Informal" Organization

To some people, that mystical entity known as the "informal" organization is the *real* organization. *It* is how things really get done.

The *it* referred to, however, may be any number of things, depending upon the point of view. To narrow it to just two types—there is the "informal" organization and the *informal* organization.

The "informal" organization, in this makeshift dichotomy, encompasses all relationships and channels of communication that mature, reasonable people are expected to develop and use in order to meet organizational objectives. As mature, reasonable people, they are expected, of course, to also respect their superior's need to be kept informed of matters affecting his area of accountability. This "informal" organization is viewed as a logical and necessary extension of the formal organization. It is informal only in the sense that nobody has found it necessary to inundate the organization with memorabilia that fully spell out its workings.

The *informal* organization, on the other hand, encompasses all the relationships, communication channels, and influences or power centers that mature, reasonable people develop because a lot of other people in the organization are not mature and reasonable—"especially the bosses who needn't be informed because they'll only say 'no.' " Rather than being a logical extension of the formal organization, it comes into being because the formal organization is viewed as being illogical or inflexible or inefficient or just plain inconsistent with the personal and possibly organizational objectives being worked toward. This *informal* organization, according to "informal" organization specialists, gets work done in spite of the formal organization.

Neither shows up on the organization chart: the "informal" because it's too complex to be reduced to a two-dimensional chart; the *informal* because that would make it formal—a heresy that would immediately give rise to another *informal* organization.

For those not fully satisfied with this dichotomy, there may be a third type—the INFORMAL organization. It includes parts of the "informal" and *informal*. By definition, it covers everything not shown on the organization chart; by definition, it can't be charted.

THE INADEQUATE CHART

Attempts to revamp the conventional organization chart in order to overcome these and other limitations have produced many examples of modern, non-objective art (Alexander Calder's mobiles have been mistaken for organization charts). There is the circular chart (and its variants) designed to better convey internal relationships and to better camouflage "status." There is the chart with the vertical lines between boxes stretched to reflect similar levels of responsibility or similar levels of pay (scrapped after first attempt—required too long a sheet of paper). There is the chart with the pyramid up-ended to reflect the true flow of authority—from subordinates to superiors (scrapped after first attempt—"That's rubbing it in").

Despite all its limitations, the conventional chart is increasingly used to depict the skeletal structure of the organization. For more complete documentation of what this chart means, companies rely on position guides, linear responsibility charts, statements of general responsibilities and relationships—indeed, the whole organizational manual.

The essential value of the chart seems to lie in the fact that it does strip the organization to the skeletal framework. In so doing, it serves a useful purpose both as a tool of organizational analysis and a means of communication.[1] As a complete picture of the organization, it is recognized as being completely inadequate. But it evidently is less inadequate than most substitutes.

1/See "Charting the Company Organization Structure," *Studies in Personnel Policy,* no. 168, for detailed description of charts and their uses.

10

The Age of Anxiety at AT&T*

ALLAN T. DEMAREE

On the brink of the Seventies, as trouble convulsed the once well-ordered world of Haakon Ingolf Romnes, the tall, angular engineer who heads American Telephone & Telegraph composed a letter to his managers. He urged them to have confidence in the face of an uncertain future: "confidence in ourselves—in each other—confidence in our ability to do the kind of intelligent, realistic, and sensitive management job the times demand." That uncharacteristic exhortation is light-years from the mood of AT&T a decade ago, when the formidable communications giant seemed so impeccably managed and impervious to criticism that it did not permit itself even the briefest moment of self-doubt. "It would be naive," wrote Romnes, "to assert that the unclouded optimism with which we confronted the Sixties would serve us well today."

So fundamental a change at AT&T is epochal. For AT&T is more than the biggest monopoly in the U.S., a corporation controlling greater wealth than any other in the world ($47 billion in assets at the end of 1969). It is also a kind of subculture all its own, encompassing nearly one million employees and filled with its own myths and mores, prides and prejudices, that only momentous events can call into question.

Myriad events combined to confront AT&T with crisis. An unprecedented decline in the quality of telephone service subjected the company to widespread criticism unparalleled in its history. Service in New York City is abominable, with lesser degrees of degradation in Boston, Miami, Detroit, Washington, and Pittsburgh. The reason for the service troubles was management's failure to anticipate demand, but the root cause of that failure stemmed from the interplay of many more subtle forces, both financial and psychological. The fortunes of the telephone business swing on management's ability to strike a precarious balance between profit and service, stockholder and customer, the efficient use of capital plant and the maintenance of enough spare capacity to meet unforeseen demands. And in the mid-Sixties, events conspired to knock that balance out of kilter.

As inflation drove up costs, profits came under pressure, and earnings on total capital declined steadily. Strangely enough, the operating companies were

*Source: Reprinted by permission from *Fortune* (May 1970), 156-59, 261, 264, 266, 269, 272.

reluctant to seek rate increases, and in order to keep profits up telephone-company presidents felt increasing pressures to cut costs. These pressures were especially intense in companies like New York Telephone that had a low rate of return to begin with and, consciously or unconsciously, they began narrowing the margins of spare capacity and taking risks with the quality of service they provided.

Not even Bell's awesome technology could free telephone-company managers from their pains. Bell reaped the major gains of automation by 1963 in local service, the biggest chunk of the business, and it is back coping with people problems; its work force is increasing rapidly, reaching 956,000 at the end of 1969. The quality of that enormous force has declined dramatically as Bell has had to hire and train uneducated and undisciplined workers, causing efficiency to plunge and turnover to climb. At the same time, policy changes at the Federal Communications Commission opened the way for eager competitors, armed with technology that Bell itself had pioneered, to chisel away at multibillion-dollar hunks of the telephone empire.

The cumulative effect of these troubles has been to plunge AT&T's proud executives deep into introspection. Historically, the communications giant merrily expanded its monopoly, fending off would-be competitors with restrictive tariffs, refusals to interconnect, and selective rate cuts, which it could subsidize from its monopoly markets. Now groups of Bell officials gather in conference behind the classical granite façade of 195 Broadway, the corporate headquarters in lower Manhattan, to brood over the fundamental question: "What is our business?"

The answer is by no means clear; they are torn between pushing ahead and pulling back. The tug of war is waged not so much between individuals as within them. On the one hand, old-line telephone men reject, as if by reflex, the notion that they should cut back to their monopoly telephone business, leaving the rest of communications to others. "If we do, we'll make the same mistake the railroads did," says Vice Chairman John deButts, evoking an analogy to the railroad that is heard repeatedly in the Bell System. "Ours is a communications business, not just a telephone business."

On the other hand, the shock of severe criticism has increasingly brought telephone people to the realization that even Bell's vast reserves of capital, manpower, and management acumen are limited, and that the areas they serve on the periphery of their monopoly business must be judiciously chosen. "We can't be all things to all people," they tell one another, speaking softly lest the admission be heard outside. Thus, Bell is now wavering between its railroad syndrome and a new-found humility. If its actions are occasionally out of step with its words, or its words out of step with each other, the explanation is likely to be found in a kind of corporate schizophrenia.

Bell now faces many challenges, any one of which would sorely tax the resources of a lesser corporation. It must restore telephone service to the high standards its customers once expected. It must decide what markets it should serve beyond its basic telephone monopoly and cope with the competition there. And in an age of labor scarcity, it must hire, train, motivate, and keep more skilled men and women than ever before. How well it meets these challenges will depend largely on the unique culture of the corporation itself, a culture that contains great strengths and serious shortcomings.

The corporate empire of AT&T comprises twenty-four operating companies, most of them big enough to rank on *Fortune's* list of the fifty largest utilities; Western Electric, AT&T's manufacturing arm, ranked eleventh among the 500 largest manufacturers; and Bell Telephone Laboratories, the biggest corporate research organization in the world. All these companies are majority-owned by AT&T with three exceptions, Bell of Canada (2 percent owned), Southern New England Telephone (18 percent), and Cincinnati Bell (27 percent).

It would be natural to conclude that such concentration of ownership would yield concentration of control—that AT&T is one great monolith, and that all the crucial decisions are made at the pinnacle of power. The truth is more complicated. Bell is a strange, perhaps unique, blend of independence and conformity. In mood and atmosphere, a great gulf separates the operating companies from corporate headquarters. Operating executives have the zest of men doing things—laying cables, installing phones, "operating in real time," as one of them puts it. AT&T's huge superstaff, entangled in task forces and committees galore, is far more contemplative, soul-searching, and all too frequently ponderous, deliberate, and painfully slow.

The conformity that pervades the Bell System has its dangers. Practices, habits, traditions, ways of thinking, inarticulate assumptions have overgrown the entire company and they are glacially slow to change. Not all, by any means, are bad. Older employees, especially, have an uncommon loyalty to the company and an unabashed pride in its traditional excellence of service to the public. But there is also the feeling, undisturbed for years, that the way Bell has always done things must necessarily be the best way. Someone once likened the Bell System to a great dragon: you could chop off its tail and it would take five years to feel it in the head.

This comfortable feeling of security and permanence has been reinforced by decades of inbreeding that virtually excludes all influence from outside the telephone business itself. Bell managers generally rotate through various companies and diverse jobs in the system, but few of those who reach the top have had much work experience elsewhere. They never seem to get fired, rarely are they demoted, and a shake-up is virtually beyond imagination. AT&T's twenty-one top officers average thirty-three years with the company. Of 148 top officers at Western Electric in 1968, all but one started their careers in the Bell System. "You're all right when you get hired," says a man who quit Southern Bell, "but as the years go by your head becomes more and more Bell-shaped."

Many dispassionate outsiders think it's high time for a breath of fresh air. "If I had a chance to make just one recommendation to Romnes," says Professor Richard Vancil, an expert in long-range planning at Harvard Business School, "it would be that he take a vice president from Xerox, IBM, even U.S. Steel, and make him president of an operating company. It would shake the industry to its boots." AT&T has itself felt the need of outside advice. Upon occasion, operating companies have hired management consultants like McKinsey & Co., and AT&T has its own board of independent economic advisers.

But "Hi" Romnes is not of a mind to make sweeping changes. His role, as he sees it, is largely advisory. He does not try to second-guess the top officers of the operating companies—indeed, he may not even talk to a company president for months at a time. "They don't have to check their decisions," he says. "Performance is what counts."

Bell measures the performance of each company and each area within each company by dozens of technical indexes that are compiled in green, orange, white, gray, and brown books, published monthly, quarterly, and annually, and distributed variously throughout the system. From headquarters pours volume upon volume of "Bell System Practices," or B.S.P.s as they are called, prescribing everything from authorized methods for splicing cable to sales pitches for marketing switchboards. Conformity is not all bad. Because of standard procedures, emergency crews were easily borrowed from other Bell companies to repair the damage caused by Hurricane Camille. But many employees claim standardization is carried to the point of stultification. Operators are taught to get into their chairs on the left and out on the right, whether they work in New York or San Francisco. "If you figure out a better way of doing something," says an engineer from New York Tel, "forget it—they'd have to change all the manuals."

A Gadfly Measures by the Cent

For all this uniformity, the presidents of the operating companies still have broad discretion to make critical decisions affecting their business. The single most important decision they make is how much to invest in new capital equipment—the trunks that carry telephone calls, the central offices that switch them, and so forth. The capital budget, at least $6.5 billion this year for the whole Bell System, or 8 percent of all corporate capital expenditures in the U.S., determines the ability of each operating company to provide acceptable service. Solely responsible for their own forecasts of demand and investment projections, the operating companies submit these three times yearly to AT&T, beginning about two years before the equipment is slated for installation.

Albert M. Froggatt, sixty-three, a genial, English-born engineer in charge of AT&T's department of engineering economics, helps oversee the capital budgets. Froggatt checks the companies' plans against past performance by a variety of indicators and jaunts around the country acting as the corporate gadfly, asking questions, offering suggestions. He knows it takes $1 of investment in telephone plant to earn 33 cents in annual revenue. So if a company forecasts 25 cents of new revenue for each dollar invested, Froggatt says: "I would yowl and look into it and see if I can find out what is wrong. . . . Very frequently the companies are willing to make a further review of their program and modify it as they think it should be modified. But it is their ultimate responsibility.

When it comes to raising money for their investment programs, the operating companies must work closely with AT&T. They generate a little more than half their funds from depreciation and retained earnings. The rest comes from two sources—about one-third from issuing bonds and two-thirds from selling stock to AT&T. Since one Bell company or another is in the bond market every three weeks, the offerings have to be timed by John J. Scanlon, AT&T's treasurer. Scanlon, in turn, goes to the capital market on AT&T's behalf to help raise money to buy the operating companies' stock and to finance Western Electric, the Long Lines division, and Bell Labs.

What is truly surprising is that AT&T has never directed its operating companies to cut back on capital expenditures. To keep from doing so, Scanlon has performed remarkable feats. A usually reserved fellow whose face seems cast in a perpetual smile, Scanlon glows with puckish delight when he talks high-flying finance. The nearly $1.6-billion package of bonds he put on the market last month is the biggest corporate debt financing in history, and the Bell System is expected to issue nearly one-fifth of the total long-term corporate debt this year. Since AT&T's investment plans will require $35 billion or more in new capital over the next five years, Scanlon will probably fashion another gigantic package of debt or equity next year. After that, Scanlon thinks, AT&T's use of accelerated depreciation, which it adopted for tax purposes this year, will begin generating enough cash flow to diminish its reliance on outside financing.

As Solid as a Post in Concrete

It might seem that any manager fortunate enough to enjoy an almost unlimited supply of capital is sitting in the catbird seat. But it doesn't work quite that way in the Bell family. If an operating-company president builds more plant than is needed to meet demand, service may be superb but excess capacity will devour his profits. If he builds too little, profits may be high but service will suffer the multitude of ills caused by overloads on the lines and switching centers. The act of balancing service against profit is never easy, and when costs rise, putting pressure on profits, it takes uncommon dexterity. Romnes himself concedes under questioning: "We talk and talk about service at every meeting we have, but I have to say there have been times when, in the minds of some, the investors were given greater consideration."

The official view at AT&T is that poor service resulted from strikes, difficulties in hiring skilled workers in a tight labor market, and unanticipated growth in demand (e.g., some welfare clients received allowances for telephones, and brokerage calls increased as trading boomed on the New York Stock Exchange). All these had an important bearing, but they are only part of the story. The crunch was severe because the growth in demand came at a time when some operating companies were under intense pressure to cut costs and failed to invest enough money in new plant and equipment and in the people to maintain it. AT&T's reluctance to admit the extent to which cost cutting figured in its service problems is an understandable part of Bell System mores. "Service comes first," Bell people say again and again, and they honestly believe it. The thought is imbedded in their consciousness like a post in concrete, for providing good service is the *sine qua non* of Bell's legitimacy, the company's pledge of performance in return for the privilege of monopoly.

Saddled with fixed rates in a time of galloping inflation, the operating companies could, of course, have applied for increases. But telephone men have built up a psychological reluctance to go running to the regulators; they hate to admit that they can't keep ahead of costs. In startling contrast to electric utilities, the Bell companies averaged eleven years without rate increases before they started knocking on commission doors, late in 1968.

Forecasting and the Shell Game

As the screws began to tighten, operating companies took risks with service in various ways. Some began adding equipment to meet only short-term growth. This saves money in the short run but ultimately increases costs and shaves the margin of spare capacity dangerously thin. Company presidents also cut back forecasts of future demand that were sent up to them from the field, thereby reducing the amount planned for investment. Since men in the field generally played safe by padding their forecasts, it was common practice for top executives to cut them; but when profit pressures mounted, managers tended to cut closer to the bone. In this world of imprecision, the risks executives took were frequently uncertain—hidden like the pea in a shell game.

"You start taking risks that you won't get greater growth than you think you are likely to get," says Alfred W. Van Sinderen, president of Southern New England Telephone. "We took some calculated risks in the latter part of the Sixties. Some paid off, some didn't. We knew we were doing it, but felt we had to." The results, while at first imperceptible to the public, could be statistically measured at some companies as early as 1966, when dial tones slowed and installation backlogs lengthened.

New York Tel appears to have been an extreme case of overzealous cost cutting, yet officials there seemed blissfully unaware of the risks they were taking. To start with, officials had an unclear idea of what their margins were because they kept only loose track of calling rates, which increased and cut into spare capacity more than they realized. Then they tightened maintenance budgets and cut back capital expenditures two years running, 1966 and 1967, even though their own forecasts predicted ever increasing demand. Thus the company's spare capacity had been chopped to the peril point when, late in 1968, it was hit with an unexpected surge of demand that overloaded nearly half its central offices in downstate New York.

William G. Sharwell, New York Tel's operating vice president, who was moved into that key post at the height of the crisis, now concedes, in hindsight, that the company put too much emphasis on earnings at the expense of service. "But at the time I didn't think they were doing wrong," says Sharwell. "I'm sure there was no sense of the enormity of risk involved—we were not playing it fast and loose—no one was conscious of taking any risk of particular consequence."

Pessimists see the mistake as fatal. "I don't think they're ever going to recover from it," says one of the most highly respected men at the FCC. A perceptive executive with another communications carrier foresees this scenario for AT&T: increasing costs leading to a decline in service, declining service resulting in the loss of public sympathy, public criticism culminating in reluctance by the states to allow a fair profit—on and on in an ever descending spiral.

That dreadful specter is visible to Romnes, too, and he is pressing hard to avoid it: "I think we should put all our emphasis on the service side," he says. His view is widespread among telephone-company managers, many of whom are tasting severe public criticism for the first time and feel hurt, shaken, and challenged. Still, the tremendous increase in capital spending itself brings untoward side effects on service. The rapid buildup has siphoned some of the best skilled craftsmen into construction work and away from vital jobs in maintenance and repair. Many new workers have been hired quickly and efficiency has dropped. Productivity for the whole Bell System—measured in the number of employees per 10,000 telephones—declined last year for the first time since 1946. Unfortunately, both stockholders and customers will end up paying for Bell's error in judgment, and even if service is restored as predicted, Bell's vaunted reputation may be permanently marred.

Stealing Mother Bell's Cream

Just at the time when Bell was grappling with its internal problems, its monopoly position was challenged. In 1968 the FCC ruled that Bell must for the first time allow phones, switchboards, data sets, and other terminal equipment produced by outside manufacturers to be connected to its network. Then the FCC permitted new competition to enter the common-carrier market, supplying point-to-point microwave radio transmission, like the private lines Bell rents to companies, at cheaper rates. And currently the FCC has pending an application from a subsidiary of University Computing Co. to build a switched network to carry data transmission.

These markets are big and growing fast. The market is estimated at more than $1 billion a year for switchboards and accessory equipment. Bell's private-line business is about $500 million a year and growing at 10 percent annually. Data traffic over the switched network is estimated by Bell to be only about 1 percent of all traffic today, but its rate of growth is phenomenal. Just as important as gross revenues, the new competition for the first time provides communications buyers with a yardstick to measure Bell's performance.

Bell's pricing policies invite competition. Bell widely practices what it calls rate averaging, which it does in two ways. It lumps together the low costs of modern microwave with the high costs of old wire and cable, so that its charges for service bear no necessary relationship to the cost of providing service solely with the latest technology. Second, within any regulatory jurisdiction, Bell charges uniform rates for all calls of equivalent distance, even though the actual costs of transmission can vary by as much as a factor of ten. Rate averaging has been encouraged by state and federal regulators because it makes for easy-to-understand tariffs, minimizes squabbling over which customers are favored by using low-cost equipment, and provides equal charges to city and country dwellers despite differences in costs. Once competition enters the picture, however, Bell is subjected to what it calls "cream-skimming." Rivals can steal customers on Bell's most profitable routes.

Romnes makes it clear that he is willing to break the old pattern of rate averaging and cut rates to compete if necessary. As long as the competition comes in interstate long-distance transmission, AT&T may have a decisive advantage. The costs of long-distance transmission are still declining, and Bell has earned more than the authorized rate of return on long-distance service, prompting the FCC to demand rate cuts. So AT&T has plenty of leeway to cut rates without hurting profits. But the FCC will be watching carefully to see that Bell doesn't subsidize competitive price cuts with profits earned in its monopoly markets—a tactic AT&T has been accused of in the past.

Bell also faces strong competition in highly profitable optional-equipment markets like the PBX boards for businesses and the phones connected to them. One Bell company has computed that it earns 3 to 4 percent on standard residential service and 13 to 15 percent on optional equipment, which means profits on optionals subsidize residential service to some extent. Major rival suppliers of optional equipment include ITT, Philips' Norelco, RCA, and several Japanese companies. When they install PBXs and other equipment for businesses, Bell's is summarily ripped out by the roots. As competition intensifies, operating companies will be forced to lower their prices, and state regulators will be faced with the question of whether residential customers should continue to be subsidized.

To protect their markets, some operating companies are beginning to react like seasoned competitors. New Jersey Bell requires its customer representatives to file a report to headquarters whenever a customer considers buying a competitor's equipment. "Now they are sharpening up their sales force instead of just taking orders," says an official of Norelco. Southern New England Tel is eager to supply customers with new types of equipment that Western Electric hasn't offered, and it will install more than 100 Nippon Electric PBXs in the next few months. "They're more versatile than anything Western makes and the price is right," says O. Haydn Owens, general marketing manager. "We think it will keep us competitive." Other Bell companies are beginning to shop outside, too.

An ironic twist is that Bell, which opposed competition fiercely, will reap some of its benefits. Western has been hard-pressed to keep up with the demands of data processors for a varied supply of data sets. If Western did not produce a particular data set, Bell's refusal to permit outside equipment on its lines became a barrier to the increased use of the telephone network. Now Romnes and others at the top finally realize that Bell can get greater network usage if smaller manufacturers supply some of these specialized devices. But Bell's change in its position has come as a cultural shock to telephone people who have been steeped in the idea that devices supplied by outsiders, or "foreign attachments" as Bell dubs them, are as desirable as Indonesian parasites.

Case of the Creeping Girdle

As it struggled to meet new competition, Bell was beset by personnel problems. One of the largest employers of minorities, Bell hired black and Spanish-speaking workers whom its standards would have barred a few years ago. Many fledgling operators have never made a long-distance call before and some need speech therapy. Independent-minded young people with lots of job options are quickly dissatisfied with boring tasks and reject Bell's traditional regimentation. "If a girl's girdle is creeping up," says a union man describing the new attitude, "she's going to stand up and pull it down without asking the chief operator."

Turnover has shot up and is costing Bell dearly. Bell had to interview a million women last year, hired 125,000, and ended up with a net gain of 15,000. Operators are quitting at twice the rate they did in the early Sixties; switchmen, frame men, and other key craftsmen are quitting four times as fast. The money Bell has invested in training these workers is lost forever when they leave, and training costs are rising as equipment becomes more complex.

Efficiency has plunged as inexperienced and ill-qualified workers take the place of old-timers. More than a quarter of the craftsmen have less than two years' experience, up from 7 percent ten years ago. The drop in quality feeds back on morale. "The company puts more pressure on the supervisors for efficiency," says a former Ohio Bell manager, "but the supervisors have less dedicated people, so they get disgruntled."

Another cause of morale problems is Bell's most controversial management tool, the dozens of indexes it uses to measure performance. Observers tap the lines long enough to grade operators (Is she polite? Does she give correct information?), and electronic devices gather other data, such as dial-tone speed, that are used in the index ratings. Employees distrust the indexes and consider them dehumanizing. Supervisors complain that indexes are used too rigidly in judging their chances for promotion. Some managers won't take the risk of innovating lest it hurt their rating, and others over-react, such as the tense young supervisor who, upon seeing his service index drop, asked his workers to take a pledge to give good service or quit. The indexes' accuracy and effect on productivity are open to question because employees have found scores of ways to "game" them and cheat the system.

AT&T is moving to combat its personnel problems. It has supplemented the indexes with new methods of measuring service quality, such as customer surveys, and officials report they use index ratings in determining promotions less than they did, say, five years ago. AT&T has set up a manpower laboratory to learn how to cope with the changed attitudes of new employees. And Robert N. Ford, a personnel director who once likened Bell's problem of keeping people in dull jobs to "that faced by a general who commands mercenary troops," has run a number of trials to make jobs more interesting, abandoning pat routines and letting workers make better use of their native abilities.

The dimensions of AT&T's personnel problems are growing, however, as laborsaving automation, which cut the number of operators needed in the late Fifties and early Sixties, is now proving less potent. AT&T's projections show that by 1980 it must *increase* its complement of operators by 130,000, more than RCA's entire work force.

Adapting the Corporate Culture

Beset by troubles at every turn, AT&T is entering an age of anxiety. In the years ahead, its leaders will have to strike the tenuous balance between service and profits in an atmosphere of rising costs and intense public concern with the quality of the System's performance. They must cope with competition they never faced before and train new workers they wouldn't have hired a few years ago. The future of the Bell System hangs on its leaders' ability to adapt AT&T's great corporate culture to its emphatically new environment. Among the assets AT&T brings to the task are the dedication of its management and the challenge its executives feel in the face of criticism. Change will come hard, however, because the company is slowed by great size, bound by tradition, encumbered by years of inbreeding. Overcoming these internal liabilities is the biggest struggle AT&T executives face.

part THREE

Behavioral School
of Management

The classical approach is depicted by behavioralists as being narrow, noncontemporary, and incomplete because of its lack of analysis of the human element in work organizations. Whether this view is accurate is not really an important issue. Instead it clearly points out that there are other approaches than the classical that are considered viable for studying management.

The Behavioral School of Management has become the antithesis to the Classical School of Management. There are certainly some overlapping issues and interpretations but basically they are different. The behavioral approach has two major time reference points that are important. First, there is the "human relations" theme which became popular in the 1940s and 1950s. Second, there is the "behavioral science" theme, which came into popular use in the early 1950s and today is the most publicized in the literature.

Human Relations Theory

Human relations theory brought to the attention of management the important role that individuals play in determining the success or failure of an organization. The human relations approach took the basic premises of the classical school as givens, and tried to show how these premises should be modified because of individual behavior differences and the influence of work groups upon the individual, and vice versa. Human relations theory concentrated on the social environment surrounding the job whereas the major emphasis of classical writers was on the physical environment.

The human relations movement began as a result of the famous Hawthorne Studies conducted at the Chicago Hawthorne Plant of Western Electric.[1] The researchers originally set out to study the relationship between productivity and physical working conditions. Instead they found that the human element in the

1/For a complete account of these studies, see Fritz J. Roethlisberger and W. J. Dickson, *Management and the Worker* (Boston: Harvard University Press, 1939).

work environment apparently had a significantly greater impact on the rate of productivity than the technical and physical aspects of the job.

Probably the major contribution of the Hawthorne studies is that they generated a great deal of interest in human problems of the workplace and were the catalyst for a number of future studies of human behavior in organizational settings. Although the assumptions and methods of human relations and behavioral science are not the same, it was the human relations movement that provided the impetus for the present day behavioral science emphasis in management theory.

The Behavioral Science Approach

The behavioral science approach to the study of management can be defined as the study of human attitudes and behavior in laboratories or actual organizational settings using scientific procedures. It focuses on people as individuals, in groups, and in the total organizational system. It is also interdisciplinary in that it borrows heavily from three disciplines, psychology, sociology, and anthropology.

Many advocates of the behavioral science approach claim that both practicing managers and scholars have blindly accepted without scientific validation many of the management theories and prescriptions that preceded them. They emphasize that scientific procedures should be used to test and validate these theories and prescriptions. Because of the work and philosophy espoused by behavioralists some of the theories and prescriptions have been modified or discounted, while in other cases they have met the test of scientific validation.

The articles in this section of the book are designed to present a panoramic view of the Behavioral School of Management as well as examine in detail key concepts such as participative management, management by objectives, motivation, leadership, and organizational development. The presentation of a complete viewpoint of the behavioral science school is beyond the scope and space limitations of this book.

Most organizations have numerous goals, and the relative importance of each of these goals changes over time. In fact, problems may arise because some of the goals may be competing or incompatible. In the opening article in this part, "Criteria of Organizational Effectiveness," Stanley E. Seashore notes that a strategy of optimal realization of goals cannot be determined unless there exists some conception of the dimensions of performance, their relative importance, and their relationships with one another. He proposes a framework for conceptualizing organizational performance, with distinctions among several different classes of performance dimensions and with consideration for several types of relationships among them.

The second article is "Participative Management: Time for a Second Look" by Robert C. Albrook. He examines the concept and ideas associated with a popular behaviorally-oriented approach called participative management. He examines a number of issues dealing with management style and custom designing the style to fit the company or industry. Included in the article is a diagnostic exercise which can be used to assess the style of management being used in a particular company.

Henry Tosi and Steve Carroll in "Management by Objectives" discuss what is currently one of the most discussed and most scientifically studied approaches found in the literature—MBO. The authors clearly caution the reader not to consider management by objectives an easy-to-apply approach. They emphasize some of the difficulties of implementing MBO and the need to link it to other organizational programs such as wage and salary systems.

Robert N. Ford in "Motivation Through the Work Itself" emphasizes new ideas in job design that American Telephone and Telegraph Company has implemented. He employs the "Herzbergian" concept of job enrichment to improve the morale of and the performance of employees. Ford generally believes that through job enrichment the worker can reduce many negative features of work such as lack of challenge and boredom.

One area in which the Behavioral School of Management has made significant contributions is in the study of work groups. The fifth article in this section, "Peer Leadership Within Work Groups," is concerned with this area. In it, the authors, David G. Bowers and Stanley E. Seashore, attempt to answer two questions: (1) What are the dimensions of leadership within a work group? and (2) What are the critical issues in leadership research? In order to answer these questions the authors report the results of a study which they conducted.

An article by Wendell French, "Organization Development Objectives, Assumptions, and Strategies" discusses organization development which to some people is in a "state of confusion" and to other people is a revolutionary concept that can result in improved attitudes, behavior, and effectiveness. French provides a systematic action research model of organization development (OD).

Two case studies illustrate behavioral concepts being applied in actual organizational settings. "Armstrong Cork Company" is a case study that describes a seminar in human behavior that is used to develop managers in the company. It illustrates some of the positive features of the program.

The second case is "Hotel Corporation of America." A reorganization of the company has fostered a need for integration which is being attempted through the use of what is called "organic OD." This case stresses such concepts as involving subordinates, dissent, and reevaluation of early OD practices.

11

Criteria of Organizational Effectiveness*

STANLEY E. SEASHORE

Multiple, Conflicting Goals

The aim of the following discussion is to outline a way of viewing the relationships among the numerous criteria that might be considered in the evaluation of the performance of an organization. To understand such relationships we shall need to make some distinctions between different kinds of criterion measures. We shall need to create some encompassing conceptions that serve to aid the evaluation of performance when some desired measures are not available, or when the number of measures is inconveniently large.

The issues taken up here arise because most organizations have multiple goals rather than a single goal, and goal achievement may not be directly measurable. The formal objectives of the organizations may themselves be multiple and, in any case, there are multiple short-run goals and subgoals that need to be examined. The matter would be simple if the various goals were all of similar priority and combinable in some simple additive way; but this is not the situation. The manager making decisions that rest upon multivariate assessments of the performance of his organization has to calculate the weights and the correlation values that he will apply when estimating the net outcome of a course of action.

A typical example would be the case of a manager who wishes his firm to obtain a substantial profit, and at the same time to grow in size, to insure future profit by product improvements, to avoid financial risk, to pay a substantial annual dividend to his investors, to have satisfied employees, and to have his firm respected in the community. He cannot maximize all of these simultaneously, as increasing one (e.g., dividends or risk avoidance) may imply reduced achievement on another (e.g., growth, product research). He must consider their "trade-off" value, their contingencies, and the presence of negative correlations among them. To estimate an optimum course of action he has to evaluate the dependability and relevance of the various measures and then estimate the way

*Reprinted by permission from the July, 1965, issue of the *Michigan Business Review*, published by the Graduate School of Business Administration, The University of Michigan.

in which they combine to provide an overall evaluation of performance or a prediction of future change in performance. This task will be easier when we have for his use a theory to describe the performance of organizations. The following suggestions are a step in that direction.

CRITERIA AND THEIR USES

To begin with we need to make some distinctions among different kinds of criteria and their uses.

1. *Ends vs. Means.* Some criteria are close to the formal objectives of the organization in the sense that they represent ends or goals that are valued in themselves; others have value mainly or only because they are thought to be necessary means or conditions for achieving the main goals of the organization. Substantial profit, for example, may be a goal sought by a business organization, while employee satisfaction may be valued because it is thought to be an aid in reaching the goal of substantial profit.

2. *Time Reference.* Some criterion measures refer to a past time period (profit for the past year), others to current states (net worth), and still others to anticipated future periods (projected growth). Whatever their time reference, all may be used for drawing inferences about past or future conditions or changes.[1]

3. *Long vs. Short Run.* Some criterion measures refer to a relatively short period of time, others to a longer period; they may refer to performances that are relatively stable (do not change much in the short run) or relatively unstable (erratic or highly variable in the short run). The usefulness of a criterion measure is limited if the period covered is not appropriate to the usual or potential rate of change in the variable.

4. *"Hard" vs. "Soft."* Some criteria are measured by the characteristics of, or number or frequency of, physical objects and events, while others are measured by qualitative observation of behavior or by evaluative questions put to people. Dollar measures, for example, or tons of scrap, or number of grievances, are "hard" measures; while employee satisfaction, motivation to work, and cooperation, product quality, customer loyalty, and many others are usually "soft." *The distinction is useful, but it contains a trap,* for we commonly think of the hard variables as being in some way inherently more valid, more reliable, and more relevant to the performance evaluation problem, when this is not necessarily true. Profit rate, for example—a popular hard variable—is a rather vague concept to begin with (accountants dispute about definition and about conventions for measurement) and it is often in the short run unreliable as a

1/Many firms' current operating and financial statistics, although appropriate for control and accounting purposes, prove to be of little value for performance evaluation for the reason that they are short-period measures of unstable performances. Monthly plant maintenance costs, for example, may be extremely variable (perhaps seasonal) and may be useful as a performance criterion measure only when applied to longer periods of time. In the short run, apart from other considerations, low maintenance costs may or may not be a favorable indicator.

performance indicator and thus quite irrelevant to the evaluation problem, even for an organization whose long-run goals include making a profit. Similarly, a soft variable, such as one representing the intentions of key executives to stay with the organization, may be measured with high reliability in some circumstances and may be vital in the assessment of the organization's performance.

5. *Values.* Some variables appear to have a linear value scale (more is always better than less), while others have a curvilinear scale (some optimum is desired; more and less are both to be avoided). The shape of the curves determines in part the trade-off relationships among assessment variables under conditions where simultaneous optimization is not possible. Examples: profit rate is usually linear in value in the sense that more is better than less; maintenance costs, by contrast, are usually curvilinear in value in the sense that either excessively high or low costs may be judged to diminish overall firm performance.

THE HIERARCHY OF CRITERIA

A full accounting for the performance of an organization requires consideration for (1) achievement of the organization's main goals over a long span of time, (2) performance over shorter periods on each of those criteria that represent ends valued in themselves, and which, jointly, as a set, determine the net ultimate performance, and (3) performance on each of a number of subsidiary criteria that provide an immediate or current indication of the progress toward, or probability of achieving, success on end-result variables. The network of criteria of performance can be viewed as a pyramid-shaped hierarchy:

1. *At the top* is the "ultimate criterion"—some conception of the net performance of the organization over a long span of time in achieving its formal objectives, whatever they may be, with optimum use of the organization's environmental resources and opportunities. The ultimate criterion is never measured (except possibly by historians); yet some concept of this kind is the basis for evaluation of lesser criteria of performance.

2. *In the middle* are the penultimate criteria. These are shorter run performance factors or dimensions comprised by the ultimate criterion. They are "output" or "results" criteria: things sought for their own value and having trade-off value[2] in relation to each other. Their sum, in some weighted mixture, determines the ultimate criterion. Typical variables of this class for business organizations are: sales volume, productive efficiency, growth rate, profit rate, and the like. There may be included some "soft" (usually behavioral) variables such as employee satisfaction or customer satisfaction. In the case of some non-business organizations these penultimate criteria might be predominantly of the behavioral kind, as in the case of a school whose output is judged in terms of

2/By trade-off value we mean only that an amount of one kind of performance may be substituted for an amount of another; for example, an increase in sales volume may be judged to offset a decline in profit rate per sales unit.

learning rates, proportion of students reaching some standard of personal growth or development, etc.[3]

3. *At the bottom* of the hierarchy of assessment criteria are measures of the current organizational functioning according to some theory or some empirical system concerning the conditions associated with high achievement on each of the penultimate criteria. These variables include those descriptive of the organization as a system and also those representing subgoals or means associated with penultimate criteria. The number of criteria in this class is very large (over 200 have been used in some studies without sensing that the limits were being approached), and they are interrelated in a complex network that includes causal, interactional, and modifier types of relationships. Included are some criteria that are not valued at all except for their power to reduce the amount of uncontrolled variance in the network. Among the "hard" criteria at this level, for a business organization, might be such as: scrappage, short-run profit, productivity against standards, meeting of production schedules, machine downtime, ratio of overtime to regular time, product return rate, rate of technological innovation, and the like. Among the "soft" criteria at this level may be such as these: employee morale, credit rating, communication effectiveness, absenteeism, turnover, group cohesiveness, customer loyalty, pride in firm, level of performance motivation, and others.

CHARACTERISTICS OF BEHAVIORAL CRITERIA

Such a model locates the behavioral criteria—those descriptive of the members (in this context, customers and clients are also "members") of the organization and of their values, attitudes, relationships, and activities—mainly in the lower regions of the network of assessment criteria, distant and perhaps only indirectly related to the ultimate goals by which the organization is eventually judged.

If behavioral criteria appear near the top of the network, it is because they are valued in themselves and have trade-off value in relation to other priority goals of the organization. In general, however, the hard—non-behavioral—criteria are the preferred ones for most business organizations for the good reason that they are more relevant to the formal objectives of the organization.

The behavioral measures are presumed to have some stable relationships to the various non-behavioral measures; these relationships may be causal, interactional, or merely one of co-variance. It is further presumed that the criteria and their relationships are not entirely unique to each organization, nor transient, but are to some degree stable and to some extent common to all or many

---

3/One large U.S. firm has published what appears to be a carefully considered formulation of its own roster of assessment criteria at this penultimate level. It includes one behavioral category, "employee attitudes," which is further defined in operational terms in a manner compatible with the system outlined here.

organizations. These presumptions appear to have some partial confirmation from analyses performed so far.[4]

We now come to the question of the role of behavioral criteria in the light of this broader conception of the evaluation of organizational performance. It appears that behavioral criteria are not likely, for most business organizations, to have a prominent place in the roster of penultimate criteria although they may and do appear there. Their chief role will arise from their power to improve the prediction of future changes in the preferred "hard" criteria, i.e., their power to give advance signals of impending problems or opportunities.

A second use they may commonly have is to complement the available hard criteria in such a way as to give the manager a more balanced and more inclusive informational basis for his decisions in the case where the hard variable measures are incomplete or not reliable for short-run evaluation.[5]

In some rare instances, the behavioral criteria have to be used exclusively instead of the preferred hard criteria of organizational performance for the reason that measurements of hard criteria are not available at all or not at reasonable cost.

There are three basic strategies that may be applied in formulating a unique version of this general scheme that may be appropriate for a particular organization.

1. There exist several partially-developed general theories concerning the survival requirements of organizations. These assumed requirements may be defined in performance terms and posited as the roster of penultimate criteria or organizational goals. From this starting point, a set of subsidiary goals and performance criteria may be constructed on empirical grounds, on theoretical grounds, or on some combination of the two.

2. The existing personal values of the owners of a firm, or of the managers as representatives, may be pooled to form an agreed-upon roster of penultimate criteria together with their corresponding performance indicators, and from this starting point the set of subsidiary goals and performance criteria can be constructed.

3. Comparative empirical study can be made of the performance characteristics of a set of organizations assumed to share the same ultimate criterion but clearly differing in their overall success as judged by competent observers (for

4/See "Applying Modern Management Principles to Sales Organizations," Foundation for Research on Human Behavior seminar report, 1963, for an illustration of the similarity across three sales organizations in the relevance of behavioral measures to hard penultimate criteria of organizational performance. Also, "Models of Organization Performance," an unpublished MS by Basil Georgopoulos, Stanley Seashore, and Bernard Indik; and "Relationships Among Criteria of Job Performance," by Stanley Seashore, Bernard Indik, and Basil Georgopoulos, *Journal of Applied Psychology, 44,* 1960, 195-202.

5/An example, a decision to raise prices is likely to rest not only upon estimates of hard performances, past and future, but also upon estimates of political and economic climate, of customer loyalty, of the feasibility of alternatives such as employee collaboration in cost reduction, etc.

example, such a study might be made of a set of insurance sales agencies, some clearly prospering and others clearly headed for business failure). Using factorial analysis methods and actual performance data to identify the sets of lower-order performance criteria, and using trend and correlational analyses to detect the relationships among these sets of criteria over time, one can, in principle, draw conclusions about the penultimate components of performance that bear upon organizational survival or failure in that particular line of business.

ALTERNATIVE THEORETICAL APPROACHES

These three approaches can and do produce strikingly different systems for describing the network of criteria to be used in evaluating organizational performance. One of the general theories, for example, proposes that there are nine basic requirements to be met, or problems to be continuously solved, for an organization to achieve its long run goals; these include such requirements as adequate input of resources, adequate normative integration, adequate means of moderation of organizational strain, adequate coordination among parts of the organization, etc. Theories of this kind are produced mainly by general organizational sociologists and stem from the view that an organization is a living system with intrinsic goals and requirements that may be unlike those of individual members. By contrast, the second mentioned approach stems from the personal values of managers. The resulting networks of criteria are different.[6]

A start has been made at the Institute for Social Research in exploring such alternative strategies. With respect to the first approach, two theoretical models have been tested against empirical data from a set of organizations in a service industry, using executive judgments of unit overall effectiveness as the ultimate criterion. Both models proved to be about equally valid, but of limited utility in explaining variance on the ultimate criterion; each "accounted for" about half of the ultimate criterion variance, with the unexplained portion arising from measurement errors and/or faulty theory. An attempt to apply the wholly-empirical approach to the same set of data proved to be a failure in the sense that it was not more powerful in explaining variance on the ultimate criterion than were the simpler, theory-based models, and furthermore the resulting roster of performance dimensions was not very satisfactory in common-sense terms.

A third effort is now in progress, using objective data about the performance of a set of insurance sales agencies over a span of twelve years; the early results look very promising on first examination. It appears that there will be identified a roster of about ten penultimate criteria of agency performance, each inde-

---

6/To illustrate, take the criterion of profit: in one case, profit is likely to be treated as one of a few penultimate criteria (ends valued in their own right), while in the other case profit is relegated to a subsidiary role as one of several alternative means for insuring adequate input of resources. If this seems implausible, note that some organizations—government, educational, and religious organizations, for example—have survived and prospered without profit from their own activities.

pendent of the others and of varying weight in relation to ultimate performance, and each associated with a roster of subsidiary criteria of kinds that lend themselves to ready measurement and statistical combination. It remains to be seen whether these criteria are unique to this particular line of business, or have some applicability to other kinds of organizations.

12

Participative Management: Time for a Second Look*

ROBERT C. ALBROOK

The management of change has become a central preoccupation of U.S. business. When the directors have approved the record capital budget and congratulated themselves on "progress," when the banquet speaker has used his last superlative to describe the "world of tomorrow," the talk turns, inevitably, to the question: "Who will make it all work?" Some people resist change. Some hold the keys to it. Some admit the need for new ways but don't know how to begin. The question becomes what kind of management can ease the inevitable pains, unlock the talent, energy, and knowledge where they're needed, help valuable men to contribute to and shape change rather than be flattened by it.

The recipe is elusive, and increasingly business has turned to the academic world for help, particularly to the behavioral scientists—the psychologists, sociologists, and anthropologists whose studies have now become the showpieces of the better business schools. A number of major corporations, such as General Electric, Texas Instruments, and Standard Oil (N.J.), have brought social scientists onto their staffs. Some companies collaborate closely with university-based scholars and are contributing importantly to advanced theoretical work, just as industry's physicists, chemists, and engineers have become significant contributors of new knowledge in their respective realms. Hundreds of companies, large and small, have tried one or another formulation of basic behavioral theory, such as the many schemes for sharing cost savings with employees and actively soliciting their ideas for improved efficiency.

For forty years the quantity and quality of academic expertise in this field have been steadily improving, and there has lately been a new burst of ideas which suggest that the researchers in the business schools and other centers of learning are really getting down to cases. The newest concepts already represent a considerable spin-off from the appealingly simple notions on which the behavioral pioneers first concentrated. The essential message these outriders had for business was this: recognize the social needs of employees in their work, as well as their need for money; they will respond with a deeper commitment and

*Source: Reprinted by permission from *Fortune* (May 1967), 166-70, 197-200; Copyright 1967, Time, Inc.

better performance, help to shape the organization's changing goals and make them their own. For blue-collar workers this meant such steps as organizing work around tasks large enough to have meaning and inviting workers' ideas; for middle and upper management it meant more participation in decision making, wider sharing of authority and responsibility, more open and more candid communication, up, down, and sideways.

The new work suggests that neither the basic philosophy nor all of the early prescriptions of this management style were scientifically sound or universally workable. The word from the behavioral scientists is becoming more specific and "scientific," less simple and moralistic. At Harvard, M.I.T., the University of Michigan, Chicago, U.C.L.A., Stanford, and elsewhere, they are mounting bigger, longer, and more rigorous studies of the human factors in management than ever before undertaken.

One conclusion is that the "participative" or "group" approach doesn't seem to work with all people and in all situations. Research has shown that satisfied, happy workers are sometimes more productive—and sometimes merely happy. Some managers and workers are able to take only limited responsibility, however much the company tries to give them. Some people will recognize the need to delegate but "can't let go." In a profit squeeze the only way to get costs under control fast enough often seems to be with centralized, "get tough" management.

Few, if any, behaviorists espouse a general return to authoritarian management. Instead, they are seeking a more thorough, systematic way to apply participative principles on a sustained schedule that will give the theory a better chance to work. Others are insisting that management must be tailor-made, suited to the work or the people, rather than packaged in a standard mixture. Some people aren't and never will be suited for "democracy" on the job, according to one viewpoint, while others insist that new kinds of psychological training can fit most executives for the rugged give-and-take of successful group management.

As more variables are brought into their concepts, and as they look increasingly at the specifics of a management situation, the behaviorists are also being drawn toward collaboration with the systems designers and the theorists of data processing. Born in reaction to the cold scientism of the earlier "scientific management" experts with their stopwatches and measuring tapes, the "human relations" or behavioral school of today may be getting ready at last to bury that hatchet in a joint search for a broadly useful "general theory" of management.

Why Executives Don't Practice What They Preach

Before any general theory can be evolved, a great deal more has to be known about the difficulty of putting theory into practice—i.e., of transforming a simple managerial attitude into an effective managerial style. "There are plenty of executives," observes Stanley Seashore, a social psychologist at the University of Michigan's Institute for Social Research, "who'll decide one morning they're going to be more participative and by the afternoon have concluded it doesn't work."

What's often lacking is an understanding of how deeply and specifically management style affects corporate operations. The executive who seeks a more effective approach needs a map of the whole terrain of management activity. Rensis Likert, director of the Michigan institute, has developed a chart to assist managers in gaining a deeper understanding of the way they operate. A simplified version is presented in Figure 1.[1] By answering the questions in the left-hand column of the chart (e.g., "Are subordinates' ideas sought and used?"), an executive sketches a profile of the way his company is run and whether it leans to the "authoritative" or the "participative." Hundreds of businessmen have used the chart, under Likert's direction, and many have discovered a good deal they didn't realize about the way they were handling people.

Likert leads his subjects in deliberate steps to a conclusion that most of them do not practice what they say they believe. First, the executive is asked to think of the most successful company (or division of a company) he knows intimately. He then checks off on the chart his answers as they apply to that company. When the executive has finished this exercise, he has nearly always traced the profile of a strongly "participative" management system, well to the right on Likert's chart. He is next asked to repeat the procedure for the least successful company (or division) he knows well. Again, the profiles are nearly always the same, but this time they portray a strongly "authoritative" system, far to the left on the chart.

Then comes the point of the exercise. The executive is asked to describe his own company or division. Almost always, the resulting profile is that of a company somewhere in the middle, a blend of the "benevolent authoritative" and the "consultative"—well to the left of what the executive had previously identified as the most successful style. To check out the reliability of this self-analysis, Likert sometimes asks employees in the same company or division

1/This figure is adapted from a technique developed by Rensis Likert, director of the Institute for Social Research at the University of Michigan, to help businessmen analyze their companies' management style. Anyone—executive or employee—can use it to diagnose his own company or division. Check the appropriate answers, using guide marks to shade your emphasis. After the first question, for example, if your answer is "almost none," put the check in the first or second notch of the "none" box. Regard each answer as a sort of rating on a continuous scale from the left to the right of the chart. When you have answered each question, draw a line from the top to the bottom of the chart through the check marks. The result will be a profile of your management. To determine which way management style has been shifting, repeat the process for the situation as it was three, five, or ten years ago. Finally, sketch the profile you think would help your company or division to improve its performance. Likert has tried the chart on a number of business executives. Most of them rated their own companies about in the middle—embracing features of Systems 2 and 3. But nearly all of them also believe that companies do best when they have profiles well to the right of the chart, and worst with profiles well to the left. (Adapted, with permission, from *The Human Organization: Its Management and Value*, by Rensis Likert, published in April, 1967, by McGraw-Hill.)

FIGURE 1
Diagnose Your Management

	SYSTEM 1 Exploitive authoritative	SYSTEM 2 Benevolent authoritative	SYSTEM 3 Consultative	SYSTEM 4 Participative group
LEADERSHIP				
How much confidence is shown in subordinates?	None	Condescending	Substantial	Complete
How free do they feel to talk to superiors about job?	Not at all	Not very	Rather free	Fully free
Are subordinates' ideas sought and used, if worthy?	Seldom	Sometimes	Usually	Always
MOTIVATION				
Is predominant use made of 1 fear, 2 threats, 3 punishment, 4 rewards, 5 involvement?	1,2,3, occasionally 4	4, some 3	4, some 3 and 5	5,4, based on group set goals
Where is responsibility felt for achieving organization's goals?	Mostly at top	Top and middle	Fairly general	At all levels
COMMUNICATION				
How much communication is aimed at achieving organization's objectives?	Very little	Little	Quite a bit	A great deal
What is the direction of information flow?	Downward	Mostly downward	Down and up	Down, up, and sideways
How is downward communication accepted?	With suspicion	Possibly with suspicion	With caution	With an open mind
How accurate is upward communication?	Often wrong	Censored for the boss	Limited accuracy	Accurate
How well do superiors know problems faced by subordinates?	Know little	Some knowledge	Quite well	Very well
DECISIONS				
At what level are decisions formally made?	Mostly at top	Policy at top, some delegation	Broad policy at top, more delegation	Throughout but well integrated
What is the origin of technical and professional knowledge used in decision making?	Top management	Upper and middle	To a certain extent, throughout	To a great extent, throughout
Are subordinates involved in decisions related to their work?	Not at all	Occasionally consulted	Generally consulted	Fully involved
What does decision-making process contribute to motivation?	Nothing, often weakens it	Relatively little	Some contribution	Substantial contribution
GOALS				
How are organizational goals established?	Orders issued	Orders, some comment invited	After discussion, by orders	By group action (except in crisis)
How much covert resistance to goals is present?	Strong resistance	Moderate resistance	Some resistance at times	Little or none
CONTROL				
How concentrated are review and control functions?	Highly at top	Relatively highly at top	Moderate delegation to lower levels	Quite widely shared
Is there an informal organization resisting the formal one?	Yes	Usually	Sometimes	No--same goals as formal
What are cost, productivity, and other control data used for?	Policing, punishment	Reward and punishment	Reward, some self-guidance	Self-guidance, problem solving

to draw its profile, too. They tend to rate it as slightly more "authoritative" than the boss does.

Likert believes that the predominant management style in U.S. industry today falls about in the middle of his chart, even though most managers seem to know from personal observation of other organizations that a more participative approach works better. What accounts for their consistent failure to emulate what they consider successful? Reaching for a general explanation, Likert asks his subjects one final question: "In your experience, what happens when the senior officer becomes concerned about earnings and takes steps to cut costs, increase productivity, and improve profits?" Most reply that the company's management profile shifts left, toward the authoritarian style. General orders to economize—and promptly—often result in quick, across-the-board budget cuts. Some programs with high potential are sacrificed along with obvious losers. Carefully laid, logical plans go down the drain. Some people are laid off—usually the least essential ones. But the best people in the organization sooner or later rebel at arbitrary decisions, and many of them leave.

At the outset, the arbitrary cost cutting produces a fairly prompt improvement in earnings, of course. But there is an unrecognized trade-off in the subsequent loss of human capital, which shows up still later in loss of business. In due course, management has to "swing right" again, rebuilding its human assets at great expense in order to restore good performance. Yet the manager who puts his firm through this dreary cycle, Likert observes, is often rewarded with a bonus at the outset, when things still look good. Indeed, he may be sent off to work his magic in another division!

Likert acknowledges that there are emergencies when sharp and sudden belt-tightening is inescapable. The trouble, he says, is that it is frequently at the expense of human assets and relationships that have taken years to build. Often it would make more sense to sell off inventory or dispose of a plant. But such possibilities are overlooked because human assets do not show up in the traditional balance sheet the way physical assets do. A company can, of course, lose $100,000 worth of talent and look better on its statement than if it sells off $10,000 worth of inventory at half price.

A dollars-and-cents way of listing the value of a good engineering staff, an experienced shop crew, or an executive group with effective, established working relations might indeed steady the hand of a hard-pressed president whose banker is on the phone. Likert believes he is now on the trail of a way to assign such values—values that should be at least as realistic as the often arbitrary and outdated figures given for real estate and plant. It will take some doing to get the notion accepted by bankers and accountants, however sophisticated his method turns out to be. But today's executives are hardly unaware that their long payrolls of expensive scientific and managerial talent represent an asset as well as an expense. Indeed, it is an asset that is often bankable. A merely more regular, explicit recognition of human assets in cost-cutting decisions would help to ensure that human assets get at least an even break with plant and inventory in time of trouble.

Likert and his institute colleagues are negotiating with several corporations to enlist them in a systematic five-year study, in effect a controlled experiment, that should put a firmer footing under tentative conclusions and hypotheses. This study will test Likert's belief that across-the-board participative management, carefully developed, sustained through thick and thin, and supported by a balance sheet that somehow reckons the human factor, will show better long-run results than the cyclical swing between authoritarian and participative styles reflected in the typical middle-ground profile on his chart.

Conversion in a Pajama Factory

Already there's enough evidence in industry experience to suggest that participative management gets in trouble when it is adopted too fast. In some cases, an authoritarian management has abruptly ordered junior executives or employees to start taking on more responsibility, not recognizing that the directive itself reasserted the fact of continuing centralized control. Sometimes, of course, a hard shove may be necessary, as in the recent experience of Harwood Manufacturing Corp. of Marion, Virginia, which has employed participative practices widely for many years. When it acquired a rival pajama maker, Weldon Manufacturing Co., the latter's long-held authoritarian traditions were hard to crack. With patient but firm prodding by outside consultants, who acknowledge an initial element of "coercion," the switch in style was finally accomplished.

Ideally, in the view of Likert and others, a move of this kind should begin with the patient education of top executives, followed by the development of the needed skills in internal communication, group leadership, and the other requisites of the new system. Given time, this will produce better employee attitudes and begin to harness personal motivation to corporate goals. Still later, there will be improved productivity, less waste, lower turnover and absence rates, fewer grievances and slowdowns, improved product quality, and, finally, better customer relations.

The transformation may take several years. A checkup too early in the game might prove that participative management, even when thoroughly understood and embraced at the top, doesn't produce better results. By the same token, a management that is retreating from the new style in a typical cost squeeze may still be nominally participative, yet may already have thrown away the fruits of the system. Some research findings do indicate that participation isn't producing the hoped-for results. In Likert's view, these were spot checks, made without regard to which way the company was tending and where it was in the cycle of change.

A growing number of behaviorists, however, have begun to question whether the participative style is an ideal toward which all management should strive. If they once believed it was, more as a matter of faith in their long struggle against the "scientific" manager's machine-like view of man than as a finding from any new science of their own, they now are ready to take a second look at the proposition.

It seems plain enough that a research scientist generally benefits from a good deal of freedom and autonomy, and that top executives, confronted every day by new problems that no routine can anticipate, operate better with maximum consultation and uninhibited contributions from every member of the team. If the vice president for finance can't talk candidly with the vice president for production about financing the new plant, a lot of time can be wasted. In sales, group effort—instead of the usual competition—can be highly productive. But in the accounting department, things must go by the book. "Creative accounting" sounds more like a formula for jail than for the old behaviorists' dream of personal self-fulfillment on the job. And so with quality control in the chemical plant. An inspired adjustment here and there isn't welcome, thank you; just follow the specifications.

In the production department, automation has washed out a lot of the old problem of man as a prisoner of the assembly line, the kind of problem that first brought the "human relations" experts into the factories in the 1920's and 1930's. If a shop is full of computer-controlled machine tools busily reproducing themselves, the boy with the broom who sweeps away the shavings may be the only one who can put a personal flourish into his work. The creativity is all upstairs in the engineering and programing departments. But then, so are most of the people.

"Look what's happened in the last twenty years," says Harold J. Leavitt, a social psychologist who recently moved to Stanford after some years at Carnegie Tech. "Originally the concern of the human-relations people was with the blue-collar worker. Then the focus began to shift to foremen and to middle management. Now it's concentrated in special areas like research and development and in top management. Why? Because the 'group' style works best where nobody knows exactly and all the time what they're supposed to be doing, where there's a continuous need to change and adapt."

Democracy Works Better in Plastics

One conclusion that has been drawn from this is that management style has to be custom-designed to fit the particular characteristics of each industry. The participative approach will work best in those industries that are in the vanguard of change. A Harvard Business School study has compared high-performance companies in three related, but subtly different, fields: plastics, packaged food, and standard containers. The plastics company faced the greatest uncertainties and change in research, new products, and market developments. The food company's business was somewhat more stable, while the container company encountered little or no requirement for innovation. The three achieved good results using markedly different management styles. The plastics firm provided for wide dispersal of responsibility for major decisions, the food company for moderate decentralization of authority, and the container company operated with fairly centralized control.

Less successful enterprises in each of the three industries were also examined, and their managements were compared with those of the high-performance companies. From this part of the study, Harvard researchers Paul Lawrence and Jay Lorsch drew another conclusion: not only may each industry have its own appropriate management style, but so may the individual operations within the same company. The companies that do best are those which allow for variations among their departments and know how to take these variations into account in coordinating the whole corporate effort.

Both the sales and the research departments in a fast-moving plastics company, for example, may adopt a style that encourages employees to participate actively in departmental decision making. But in special ways the two operations still need to differ. The research worker, for example, thinks in long-range terms, focusing on results expected in two or three years. The sales executive has his sights set on results next week or next month. This different sense of time may make it hard for the two departments to understand each other. But if top management recognizes the reasons and the need for such differences, each department will do its own job better, and they can be better coordinated. On the other hand, if top management ignores the differences and insists, for example, on rigidly uniform budgeting and planning timetables, there will be a loss of effectiveness.

It seems an obvious point that sales must be allowed to operate like sales, accounting like accounting, and production like production. But as Lawrence comments, "The mark of a good idea in this field is that as soon as it is articulated, it does seem obvious. People forget that, five minutes before, it wasn't. One curse of the behavioral scientist is that anything he comes up with is going to seem that way, because anything that's good *is* obvious."

People, Too, Have Their Styles

Other behavioral scientists take the view that management style should be determined not so much by the nature of the particular business operation involved, but by the personality traits of the people themselves. There may be some tendency for certain kinds of jobs to attract certain kinds of people. But in nearly any shop or office a wide range of personality types may be observed. There is, for example, the outgoing, socially oriented scientist as well as the supposedly more typical introverted recluse. There are mature, confident managers, and there are those who somehow fill the job despite nagging self-doubt and a consuming need for reassurance.

For a long time, personality tests seemed to offer a way to steer people into the psychologically right kind of work. Whether such testing for placement is worthwhile is now a matter of some dispute. In any case, the whole question of individual differences is often reduced to little more than an office guessing game. Will Sue cooperate with Jane? Can Dorothy stand working for Jim? Will Harry take suggestions?

The participative approach to management may be based upon a greatly oversimplified notion about people, in the view of psychologist Clare Graves of Union College in Schenectady, New York. On the basis of limited samplings, he tentatively concludes that as many as half the people in the northeastern U.S., and a larger proportion nationwide, are not and many never will be the eager-beaver workers on whom the late Douglas McGregor of M.I.T. based his "Theory Y." Only some variation of old-style authoritarian management will meet their psychological needs, Graves contends.

Graves believes he has identified seven fairly distinct personality types, although he acknowledges that many people are not "purebreds" who would fit his abstractions perfectly and that new and higher personality forms may still be evolving. At the bottom of his well-ordered hierarchy he places the childlike "autistic" personality, which requires "close care and nurturing." Next up the scale are the "animistic" type, which must be dealt with by sheer force of enticement; the "ordered" personality that responds best to a moralistic management; and the "materialistic" individual who calls for pragmatic, hard bargaining. None of these are suited for the participative kind of management.

At the top of Graves's personality ladder are the "sociocentric," the "cognitive," and the "apprehending" types of people. They are motivated, respectively, by a need for "belonging," for "information," and for an "understanding" of the total situation in which they are involved. For each of these levels some form of participative management will work. However, those at the very top, the unemotional "apprehending" individuals, must be allowed pretty much to set their own terms for work. Management can trust such people to contribute usefully only according to their own cool perception of what is needed. They will seldom take the trouble to fight authority when they disagree with it, but merely withdraw, do a passable but not excellent job, and wait for management to see things their way. In that sense, these highest-level people are probably not ideal participators.

Graves believes most adults are stuck at one level throughout their lifetimes or move up a single notch, at best. He finds, incidentally, that there can be bright or dull, mature or immature behavior at nearly all levels. The stages simply represent psychological growth toward a larger and larger awareness of the individual's relationship to society.

If a company has a mixture of personality types, as most do, it must somehow sort them out. One way would be to place participative-type managers in charge of some groups, and authoritarian managers in charge of others. Employees would then be encouraged to transfer into sections where the management style best suits them. This would hardly simplify corporate life. But companies pushing the group approach might at least avoid substituting harmful new rigidities—"participate, or else!"—for the old ones.

The Anthropological View

Behaviorists who have been studying management problems from an anthropological viewpoint naturally stress cultural rather than individual differences. Manning Nash, of the University of Chicago's business school, for example, observes that the American emphasis on egalitarianism and perform- ance has always tempered management style in the U.S. "No matter what your role is, if you don't perform, no one in this country will defer to you," he says. "Americans won't act unless they respect you. You couldn't have an American Charge of the Light Brigade." But try to export that attitude to a country with a more autocratic social tradition, and, in the words of Stanley Davis of Harvard, "it won't be bought and may not be workable."

Within the U.S. there are many cultural differences that might provide guides to managerial style if they could be successfully analyzed. Recent research by Lawrence and Arthur N. Turner at the Harvard Business School hints at important differences between blue-collar workers in cities and those in smaller towns, although religious and other factors fog the results. Town workers seem to seek "a relatively large amount of variety, autonomy, interaction, skill and responsibility" in their work, whereas city workers "find more simple tasks less stress-producing and more satisfying."

In managerial areas where democratic techniques *are* likely to work, the problem is how to give managers skill and practice in participation. The National Education Association's National Training Laboratories twenty years ago pioneered a way of doing this called "sensitivity training" (see "Two Weeks in a T-Group," *Fortune,* August, 1961). Small groups of men, commonly drawn from the executive ranks, sit down with a professional trainer but without agenda or rule book and "see what happens." The "vacuum" draws out first one and then another participant, in a way that tends to expose in fairly short order how he comes across to others.

The technique has had many critics, few more vocal than William Gomberg of the University of Pennsylvania's Wharton School. Renewing his assault recently, he called the "training" groups "titillating therapy, management development's most fashionable fad." When people from the same company are in the group, he argues, the whole exercise is an invasion of privacy, an abuse of the thera- peutic technique to help the company, not the individual. For top executives in such groups, Gomberg and others contend, the technique offers mainly a catharsis for their loneliness or insecurity.

"Psyching Out the Boss"

Undoubtedly the T-group can be abused, intentionally or otherwise. But today's sensitivity trainers are trying to make sure the experience leads to useful results for both the individual and his firm. They realize that early groups, made up of total strangers gathered at some remote "cultural island," often gave the executive little notion of how to apply his new knowledge back on the job. To bring more realism to the exercise, the National Training Laboratories began ten years ago to make up groups of executives and managers from the same company, but not men who had working relationships with one another. These "cousin labs" have led, in turn, to some training of actual management "families," a boss and his subordinates. At the West Coast headquarters of the T-group movement, the business school at U.C.L.A., some now call such training "task-group therapy."

Many businessmen insist T-groups have helped them. Forty-three presidents and chairmen and hundreds of lesser executives are National Training Laboratories alumni. U.C.L.A. is besieged by applicants, and many are turned away.

Sensitivity training is supposed to help most in business situations where there is a great deal of uncertainty, as there is in the training sessions themselves. In such situations in the corporate setting there is sometimes a tendency for executives to withdraw, to defer action, to play a kind of game with other people in the organization to see who will climb out on a limb first. A chief ploy is "psyching out the boss," which means trying to anticipate the way the winds of ultimate decision will blow and to set course accordingly.

The aim of sensitivity training is to stop all this, to get the executive's nerve up so that he faces facts, or, in the words of U.C.L.A.'s James V. Clark, to "lay bare the stress and strain faster and get a resolution of the problem." In that limited sense, such therapy could well serve any style of management. In Clark's view, this kind of training, early in the game, might save many a company a costly detour on the road to company-wide "democracy." He cites the experience of Non-Linear Systems, Inc., of Del Mar, California, a manufacturer of such electronic gear as digital voltmeters and data-logging equipment and an important supplier to aerospace contractors. The company is headed by Andrew Kay, a leading champion of the participative style. At the lower levels, Kay's application of participative concepts worked well. He gave workers responsibility for "the whole black box," instead of for pieces of his complex finished products. Because it was still a box, with some definite boundaries, the workers seized the new opportunity without fear or hesitation. The psychological magic of meaningful work, as opposed to the hopelessly specialized chore, took hold. Productivity rose.

Vice Presidents in Midair

But at the executive level, Kay moved too quickly, failing to prepare his executives for broad and undefined responsibilities—or failing to choose men better suited for the challenge. One vice president was put in charge of "innovation." Suspended in midair, without the support of departments or functional groups and lacking even so much as a job description, most of the V.P.s became passive and incapable of making decisions. "They lost touch with reality—including the reality of the market," recalls Clark. When the industry suffered a general slump and new competition entered the field, Non-Linear wasn't ready. Sales dropped 16 percent, according to Kay. In time he realized he was surrounded with dependent men, untrained to participate in the fashion he had peremptorily commanded. He trimmed his executive group and expects to set a new sales record this year.

Sheldon Davis of TRW Systems in Redondo Beach, California, blames the behavioral scientists themselves for breakdowns like Non-Linear's. Too often, he argues, "their messages come out sounding soft and easy, as if what we are trying to do is build happy teams of employees who feel 'good' about things, rather than saying we're trying to build effective organizations with groups that function well and that can zero in quickly on their problems and deal with them rationally."

To Davis, participation should mean "tough, open exchange," focused on the problem, not the organizational chart. Old-style managers who simply dictate a solution are wrong, he argues, and so are those new-style managers who think the idea is simply to go along with a subordinate's proposals if they're earnestly offered. Neither approach taps the full potential of the executive group. When problems are faced squarely, Davis believes, the boss—who should remain boss—gets the best solution because all relevant factors are thoroughly considered. And because everyone has contributed to the solution and feels responsible for it, it is also the solution most likely to be carried out.

One of the most useful new developments in the behavioral study of management is a fresh emphasis on collaboration with technology. In the early days of the human-relations movement in industry, technology was often regarded as "the enemy," the source of the personal and social problems that the psychologists were trying to treat. But from the beginning, some social scientists wanted to move right in and help fashion machines and industrial processes so as to reduce or eliminate their supposedly antihuman effects. Today this concept is more than mere talk. The idea is to develop so-called "socio-technical" systems that permit man and technology *together* to produce the best performance.

Some early experimentation in the British coal mines, by London's Tavistock Institute, as well as scattered work in this country and in Scandinavia, have already demonstrated practical results from such a collaboration. Tavistock found that an attempt to apply specialized factory-style technology to coal mining had isolated the miners from one another. They missed the sense of group support and self-direction that had helped them cope with uncertainty and danger deep in the coal faces. Productivity suffered. In this case, Tavistock's solution was to redesign the new system so that men could still work in groups.

In the U.S. a manufacturer of small household appliances installed some highly sophisticated new technical processes that put the company well in the front of its field. But the engineers had broken down the jobs to such an extent that workers were getting no satisfaction out of their performance and productivity declined. Costs went up and, in the end, some of the new machinery had to be scrapped.

Some technologists seem more than ready to welcome a partnership with the human-relations expert. Louis Davis, a professor of engineering, has joined the U.C.L.A. business-school faculty to lead a six-man socio-technical research group that includes several behaviorists. Among them is Eric Trist, a highly respected psychologist from the Tavistock Institute. Davis hopes today's collaboration will lead in time to a new breed of experts knowledgeable in both the engineering and the social disciplines.

"It's Time We Stopped Building Rival Dictionaries"

The importance of time, the nature of the task, the differences within a large organization, the nature of the people, the cultural setting, the psychological preparation of management, the relationship to technology—all these and other variables are making the search for effective managerial style more and more complex. But the growing recognition of these complexities has drained the human-relations movement of much of its antagonism toward the "super-rationalism" of management science. Humanists must be more systematic and rational if they are to make some useful sense of the scattered and half-tested concepts they have thus far developed, and put their new theories to a real test.

A number of behaviorists believe it is well past time to bury the hatchet and collaborate in earnest with the mathematicians and economists. Some business schools and commercial consulting groups are already realigning their staffs to encourage such work. It won't be easy. Most "systems" thinkers are preoccupied with bringing all the relevant knowledge to bear on a management problem in a systematic way, seeking the theoretically "best" solution. Most behaviorists have tended to assume that the solution which is *most likely to be carried out* is the best one, hence their focus on involving lots of people in the decision making so that they will follow through. Where the "experts" who shape decisions are also in charge of getting the job done, the two approaches sometimes blend, in practice. But in many organizations, it is a long, long road from a creative and imaginative decision to actual performance. A general theory of management must show how to build systematic expertise into a style that is also well suited to people.

The rapprochement among management theorists has a distinguished herald, Fritz J. Roethlisberger of Harvard Business School, one of the human-relations pioneers who first disclosed the potential of the "small group" in industrial experiments forty years ago. He laughs quickly at any suggestion that a unified approach will come easily. "But after all, we are all looking at the same thing," he says. "It's time we stopped building rival dictionaries and learned to make some sentences that really say something."

13

Management by Objectives*

HENRY L. TOSI
and
STEPHEN CARROLL

Management by objectives has been described as a general process in which ". . . The superior and the subordinate manager of an organization jointly define its common goals, define each individual's major areas of responsibility in terms of the results expected of him and use these measures as guides for operating the unit and assessing the contribution of each of its members." (Odiorne, 1965).

The logic of MBO is, indeed, attractive. There is an intrinsic desirability to a method which motivates performance and enhances measurement while at the same time increases the participation and involvement of subordinates.

The Elements of MBO

There are three basic aspects of MBO which will affect its success: goals and goal setting; participation and involvement of subordinates; and, feedback and performance evaluation.

Goals and Goal Setting. A number of studies[1] have clearly demonstrated that when an individual or group has a specific goal, there is higher performance than when the goals are general, or have not been set. Generally, high performance can be associated with higher individual or group goals. A number of studies[2] also suggest that performance improvement occurs when an individual is successful in achieving past goals. When there is previous goal success, the individual is more likely to set higher goals in future periods, and he is more likely to attain them.

*Source: Reprinted from *Personnel Administration* (July-August 1970), 44-8, by permission of the International Personnel Management Association.

1/See for instance Bryan, J. F. and Locke, E. A., "Goal Setting as a Means of Increasing Motivation," *Journal of Applied Psychology,* 1967, vol. 51, pp. 274-277; Locke, E. A., "Motivational Effects of Knowledge of Results: Knowledge or Goal Setting?" *Journal of Applied Psychology,* 1967, vol. 51, pp. 324-329.

2/See Lockette, R. R., *The Effect of Level of Aspiration upon the Learning of Skills.* Unpublished doctoral dissertation, University of Illinois, 1956; Yacorzynski, G. K., "Degree of Effort III. Relationship to the Level of Aspiration," *Journal of Experimental Psychology,* 1941, 30 pp. 407-413; Horowitz, M., et al., *Motivational Effects of Alternative Decision Making Processes in Groups.* Bureau of Educational Research, University of Illinois, 1953.

Participation. There have been a number of diverse findings about the relationship of participation in decision-making and productivity. These apparently contradictory findings have been resolved by concluding that if the subordinate perceives the participation to be legitimate, it will have positive effects on productivity. In addition, participation does seem to have an effect on the degree of acceptance of decisions reached mutually. There is also evidence[3] that involvement and participation are positively correlated with the level of job satisfaction.

Feedback. Both laboratory and field research have demonstrated that relatively clear, unambiguous feedback increases problem solving capacities of groups and improves the performance of individuals.[4] Positive attitudes, increased confidence in decisions, and greater certainties of superior's expectations were found to be related to communications which clarified roles and role expectancies with more and better information.

Feedback, in the form of formal appraisal in a work setting, when based on relatively objective performance standards, tends to be related to a more positive orientation by subordinates of the amount of supervision their boss exercises. Positive actions are more likely to be taken by subordinates when feedback is viewed as supportive and is objectively based.

MBO and Employee Motivation

Studies of the MBO process in organizations strongly suggest that changes in performance and attitude, which seem positive and desirable, appear to be associated with how it is formally implemented. The implementation of MBO alters the expectations of organization members about performance appraisal and evaluation. These expectations, if not met, may affect the degree of acceptance of the MBO approach. (See Raia, 1965; and Tosi and Carroll, 1968).

This problem may be resolved, to some degree, through proper setting of objectives and use of the MBO process. We believe certain minimal conditions must prevail if MBO is to have its motivational effect:

Goal Clarity and Relevance. Few managers would quarrel with the notion that organizational goals should be made known to the members. Individual perceptions of the goal are important here. Tosi and Carroll (1968) have suggested some dimensions of goals which need to be communicated to members. First, goals should represent the unit's needs. The members must be aware of the

---

3/Vroom, Victor, *Some Personality Determinants of the Effects of Participation*, Englewood Cliffs: Prentice-Hall; Tosi, Henry, "A Reexamination of Some Personality Determinants of the Effects of Participation," *Personnel Psychology* (forthcoming).

4/See Wertz, J. A., Antoinetti, and Wallace, S. R., "The Effect of Home Office Contact on Sales Performance," *Personnel Psychology,* 1954, vol. 7, pp. 381-384; Smith, E. E., "The Effects of Clear and Unclear Role Expectations on Group Productivity and Effectiveness," *Journal of Abnormal and Social Psychology,* 1957, vol. 55, pp. 213-217; and, Hand Mueller, A., "Some Effects of Feedback on Communication," *Human Relations,* 1951, vol. 4, pp. 401-410.

importance of the goals. The development of relatively objective criteria increases the perception of goal clarity. If goals have these properties, they are more likely to have effects upon the individual working towards them.

Managerial Use and Support. "Top management support" is important for the success of any program. The best evidence of support is the use of the technique by the manager himself. Formulating goals, discussing them with subordinates, and providing feedback based on these goals will have substantially greater effect on a subordinate than simply saying "this has the support of top management." Many managers mistakenly feel the verbalization of support for a policy is adequate enough. They send a memo to subordinates stating that top management wishes a program to be implemented. This, obviously, does not insure compliance. "Do as I say, not as I do" will not work. Verbalized policy support must be reinforced by the individual's perception of the superior's action and behavior in using an objective approach. It is of little or no use to support MBO philosophy orally and not use it!

The Need for Feedback. While a number of studies have concluded that goals have a greater impact on performance than just feedback alone we do not believe it to be an either/or situation. Feedback about well-developed goals seems a fundamental requirement for behavior change. It may be that the subordinate's perception of the specificity, objectivity and frequency of feedback is interpreted as a measure of the superior's support of an objectives approach.

Some Other Cautions. There are other significant points that cut across those made above: there are personal as well as organization constraints which must be taken into consideration in the development of goals. The organizational unit and the organization level affect the nature of the goals which can, and will, be set. Goals at lower levels may be more precise and probably more objectively measured. The goals of one functional area, engineering for instance, may be much more general than those of another, say the marketing department.

MBO and the Compensation Process

If, as McClelland (1961) suggests, individuals high in need achievement will expend more effort in reaching challenging goals irrespective of external rewards associated with goal accomplishment, MBO may supplement or complement standard compensations procedures. Tying MBO into the financial reward system could have a handsome pay-off. It is for this reason that we suggest how information obtained from MBO can be used in making improved compensation decisions.

Internal Wage Administration. MBO can be of assistance in developing salary differentials within a particular job class. By assessing the level of difficulty and contribution of the goals for a particular job and comparing them with similar jobs, better determination of the appropriateness of basic compensation differentials may be made.

MBO may be useful in providing information about changes in job requirements which may necessitate re-evaluation and adjustment of compensation levels for different positions. By observing changes in objectives over time, changes in job requirements may be detected which could lead to revisions in compensation schedules.

The objectives approach can aid in determining supplementary compensation levels such as stock options, bonus plans, and administration of profit sharing plans. This type of compensation is usually given when performance exceeds the normal position requirements. A properly developed objectives approach will take into account both normal job duties as well as goals and activities which extend beyond them. The extent to which an incumbent is able to achieve these non-routine objectives should be one, but perhaps not the only, factor in ranking unit members in order of their additional contribution to group effectiveness. It will provide a sound basis for determining what the level of supplemental compensation should be. Needless to say, goals which extend beyond normal job requirements should contribute importantly to organizational success.

A possible problem needs to be noted here. When goals go substantially beyond the current job requirements it may be due to the individual's initiative and aggressiveness. If this happens, it may be more appropriate strategy to change the position of the individual, not to redefine his job and change his compensation levels. A method must be developed which takes this possibility into consideration, as well as the fact that different managers will have different goals. This does not seem to be the appropriate place to detail such a device. A weighing approach which considers the capability of the manager, the difficulty of the goal, and its importance to the unit might resolve this problem.

Performance-Linked Rewards. If goals are developed properly, their achievement may be more readily associated with an individual so that appropriate individual rewards may be given. The *goal statement* is the heart of the "objectives approach." It is a description of the boss's expectancies which will be used in the feedback and evaluation process. It is a communicative artifact which spells out, for both the boss and the subordinate, the objectives *and* the manner in which they will be obtained. It should *contain two elements,* the *desired goal level* and the *activities* required to achieve that level of performance. This permits not only a comparison of performance against some criterion, but also allows determination of whether or not events, which are presumed to lead to goal achievement, have taken place if appropriate criteria are not available.

This has important implications for the problems of assessment, evaluation, and compensation. Some goals may be neither measurable nor adequately verifiable. Yet, intuitively we know what must be done to achieve them. If this is the case, and we have distinguished between goals and activities, we can at least determine whether activities which are presumed to lead to desired ends have taken place.

It is important to recognize the distinction between measuring the achievement of a goal level and determining whether or not an event presumed to lead to goal achievement has taken place. If we are unable to quantify or specify a goal level in a meaningful way, then we must simply assume that the desired level will be achieved if a particular event, or set of activities, has taken place. For example, it is very difficult to find measurable criteria to assess a manager's capability in developing subordinates, yet we can determine if he has provided them with development opportunities. If they have participated in seminars, attended meetings or gone to school it may be *assumed* that the development activities are properly conducted.

Promises and Problems

By its very nature, MBO seems to be a promising vehicle for linking performance to the evaluation process and the reward system in order to encourage both job satisfaction and productivity. It appears that higher performance and motivation is most likely when there is a link between performance and the reward systems. (Tosi and Carroll, 1968; Porter and Lawler, 1968). It may be that this link can be achieved through the process of feedback regarding goal achievement and the association of rewards and sanctions to achievement. Goal attainment should be organizationally reinforced, and the reinforcement should be different for individuals, as a function of their own attainment. The use of an "objectives" approach in conjunction with a compensation program may also result in less dissatisfaction with the allocation of compensation increases made. Certainly there is virtually universal agreement among managers that rewards should go for actual accomplishments rather than for irrelevant personal characteristics and political or social standing.

There may be problems arising from the use of MBO and its emphasis on goals and goal achievement. Many organizations have adopted the objectives approach because it seems to be a better appraisal device, and they have used it primarily in this manner. But, an appraisal system should furnish information needed to make other personnel decisions, such as promotion and transfer. Information furnished by the objectives approach may not be adequate for these purposes. Accomplishment of goals at a lower level job may be a good indicator of capability in the current job and/or level of motivation, but not of the individual's abilities to perform at higher levels of responsibility, especially if the requirements on the higher level job are much different from the current position.

Conversely, goals accomplished at a lower level may be indicative of promotability to a particular high level job if there is high goal congruence between the two positions. At any rate, there is certainly no reason to rely strictly upon the objectives approach for these decisions. It can be used along with other criteria, such as assessment of traits, when this is deemed an important dimension by the decision makers. Another potential difficulty should be pointed out. If the objectives approach becomes the basic vehicle for the determination of compensation increases, then managers may quickly learn to "beat the system."

Unless higher level managers are skilled in the use of MBO, subordinates may set objectives which have high probabilities of achievement, refraining from setting high risk goals. When any system becomes too formalized, managers learn how to beat it, and those using it become more concerned with simply meeting the formal benefits for both the individual and the organization are probably no different from earlier more traditional methods of appraisal.

The "objectives approach" seems to be a practical way of motivating organization members, but it is not an easy path to follow. It requires a considerable amount of time and energy of *all managers,* in addition to extensive organization support to make it work. MBO may lose some of its mystique, value, importance, and significance when it must be translated into a formal policy requirement. It is too easy to consider a formal MBO program as merely another thorn in the manager's side, with no positive gains for implementing it. To succeed, an MBO program must be relevant, applicable, helpful, and receive organization support and reinforcement. One way in which this can be done is to link it to other elements of the structural system which reinforce behavior, such as compensation and reward programs.

REFERENCES

Drucker, Peter. *The Practice of Management.* New York: Harper and Brothers, 1954.

McClelland, D. C. *The Achieving Society.* Princeton: Van Nostrand, 1961.

McGregor, Douglas. *The Human Side of Enterprise.* New York: McGraw-Hill, 1960.

Odiorne, George. *Management by Objectives.* New York: Pitman, 1965.

Porter, Lyman and Lawler, Edward. *Managerial Attitudes and Performance.* Homewood, Illinois: Richard D. Irwin, 1968.

Raia, Anthony. "Goal Setting and Self Control," *Journal of Management Studies,* II-1, February 1965, pp. 34-35.

Tosi, H. and Carroll, S. "Managerial Reactions to Management by Objectives," *Academy of Management Journal.* December 1968, pp. 415-426.

14

Motivation through the Work Itself*

ROBERT N. FORD

This closing chapter consists solely of the author's ideas and opinions, not those of the Bell System, although the corporation does not necessarily disagree with the basic position set forth here. The statement of the problem, the strategy employed to meet it, and the results are scarcely open to question. But the final sections of the chapter are interpretations of data and one man's point of view about the nature of work.

THE PROBLEM OF JOBS

The problem that precipitated these studies is employee dissatisfaction with work, which is evidenced in steadily mounting turnover rates. That this problem is widespread was shown by the many inquiries about these studies from other businesses.

Careful exit interviewing brought out the usual wide range of reasons for quitting—inadequate pay, undesirable hours, bad transportation, home problems, poor supervision, and undesirable work. The Bell System has worked reasonably hard to correct these problems or, when they cannot be corrected, to alleviate them. Take night work, for example. Night tours of duty for some employees are facts we have to live with in any business that operates around the clock every day, without time off even for Christmas. This is a limiting factor in any effort to decrease dissatisfaction. Does this limiting condition apply to the *jobs* we do, also? Must they, like the tours of duty, be what they are? Are they causing trouble unnecessarily?

Strategy for Improving Jobs

The work of Professor Herzberg and others suggested strongly that the work itself was a powerful motivator of employees under certain conditions. The Herzberg survey study of 200 management men probed the causes of job satisfaction and dissatisfaction. AT&T's experimental studies started where the

*Source: Reprinted by permission of the publisher from *Motivation Through the Work Itself,* by Robert N. Ford. Copyright 1969 by the American Management Association, Inc.

Herzberg study left off; they involved several thousand employees in achieving groups spread across nine different nonsupervisory jobs in ten associated companies of the Bell System.

In all cases the work itself—the task—was the variable in the experimental groups and was held as constant as possible in the control groups. In both experimental and control groups the factors that surround the work itself—variously labeled maintenance or hygiene items—were also held constant.

In each of the experimental trials, a family of immediate supervisors tried to solve this problem: How can we shape a particular job so that the job incumbent has, not more work, but more responsibility for the work? How can we make him feel that a part of the business is his alone, that he can make decisions regarding it and personally identify with it? If we can do this, the employee will have a heightened chance for individual achievement and for recognition of his achievement. In addition, he will have a chance to learn and to grow on his job, perhaps to be promoted. Furthermore, if we can do this, we can make the employee's working life a more meaningful human experience. If we succeed, he will not feel impelled to look elsewhere for good work or to become so unproductive as to be useless to the company.

Here are two illustrations of how employees are given *more* responsibility. In the first, a service representative usually decided when a customer's service should be cut off for failure to pay a bill. She reported her decision to her supervisor, who checked the facts and the reasoning and usually obtained the signature of someone still higher in management. Then service was discontinued until the customer paid his bill. In the work-itself program, after the representative has repeatedly demonstrated her good judgment, she orders the cutoff directly. If the customer pays the overdue bill, the representative involved can really feel that *she* was successful. And if she has made an error in judgment, it is her error, not the supervisor's. Thus responsibility, a major motivator, is increased for the employee.

The second illustration comes from a large foreign chemical company where six studies similar to those reported in this book are in progress. Although the sales volume in dollars is high for a certain line of chemicals, the profit margin is dropping. The salesmen have been doing an excellent job of selling chemicals that have low margins and competitively favorable prices but they have not done well at selling lines with better profit margins. However, the salesmen were not aware of this.

In this project, the experimental group was given pricing information, including the lower and upper bounds that have to be observed in setting the price of any chemical. Next, they were acquainted with the profitability problem and were asked, in effect, to "act for the company. Set the price at the level that you think will result in a sale and help to overcome the profitability slide." After six months of applying this technique the experimental group is reported to be running almost three-quarters of a million dollars ahead of the control group in profitability of sales. The control group, in contrast, is still merely following the book in setting prices. In the service representative illustration and in this one, the challenge is to find ways, big or little, whereby an employee can earn the right to act for the company.

As these sessions with families of supervisors proceeded (never cross-sectional or interdepartmental groups), the technique of greenlighting was developed whereby highly specific items or ideas were produced to make a job more meaningful and more interesting. For competent people with demonstrated ability, jobs can be improved by steps such as these:

1. Give the employee a good module of work.

   Pull responsibilities back down to this job level if they have been assigned higher up only for safety's sake.

   Gather together the responsibilities that are now handled by people whose work precedes or follows, including verifying and checking.

   Push certain routine matters down to lower-rated jobs.

   Automate the routine matter completely if possible.

   Rearrange the parts and divide the total volume of work, so that an employee has a feeling of "my customers," "my responsibility."
2. Once an employee has earned the right, let him really run his job.
3. Develop ways for giving employees *direct* individual feedback on their own performance (not group indexes).
4. Invent ways of letting the job expand so that an employee can grow psychologically. ("There's always something new coming up on this job!")

Such steps as these four principles of job improvement should result in better jobs for employees. Since employees want meaningful work, they should like the improved job better, and turnover should drop in locations where it once was high. In other jobs that are handled by older people who don't quit but who do give other evidences of job dissatisfaction (low productivity, grievances, and so on) improvement should be attainable simply by concentrating on the question: How can we made this as good a task or assignment as possible and practical?

Some Surprisingly Good Results

Of the nineteen studies nine were rated "outstandingly successful," one was a complete "flop," and the remaining nine were "moderately successful." The most striking single piece of evidence was a 13 percent drop in the turnover rate among a large sample of service representatives at a time when the control group rate increased by 9 percent. Other technical results (productivity, quality of performance, customer reaction, and so on) either improved slightly or at least held their own. If the turnover rate across the Bell System could be dropped by only 10 percentage points (to use a conservative figure) the savings in training costs on this one job alone would be in millions of dollars.

The biggest error one could make in interpreting the data would be to contend that these good results came from increased skill at "keeping people busy." In the first place, a typical service representative is never "unbusy." She is always very busy indeed. But supervisors in the test locations found ways of letting trained service representatives be *more* responsible for their customers in a meaningful way than they had ever been before. As a result, the desire to quit apparently dropped and other indicators improved slowly.

While permanence of the gains is still to be established for 18 of the 19 studies, the original Treasury Department results show *excellent* long-range promise. After three years, the Treasury correspondents' service index for all units (achieving and control alike) is now in the upper 90's.

No claim is made that these 19 trials cover a representative sample of jobs and people within the Bell System. For example, there were no trials among the manufacturing or laboratory employees, nor were all operating companies involved. There are more than a thousand different jobs in the Bell System, not just the nine in these studies. What to make of the results, then?

Even this limited sample of the universe of jobs shows that significant changes can be made in some jobs and that striking improvements will result. In other cases, not much will happen, although no losses will occur in the effort to improve jobs. These are the most likely probabilities if we take more samples of the same jobs, but there is no way of predicting whether good results will occur with a new job.

The Future of the Effort

What will be done with the findings in the companies that conducted the studies? The reaction throughout the Bell System has generally been, "We don't see how we can afford not to go ahead." There is to be no crash program; we made it clear that these results usually required eight months to a year of patient, persistent work. In general, any department in any location, systemwide, may go ahead *with the active support and concurrence of headquarters*. Men in all departments at headquarters have been made available to help start either projects or programs in the field.

For the most part, however, the project stage is past. Most departments, both at headquarters and in the field, now ask to start *programs*. This implies that no data will be collected from a control group; that is, no group will be asked to "hold still" for a year. Therefore, evaluation will generally be in terms of a group's own past performance.

A small manpower utilization group with these explicit responsibilities has been set up at AT&T headquarters.

1. Spread current knowledge and techniques.
2. Act as consultants on current job structures.
3. Continue to probe for new understanding of the reasons jobs go wrong; get the principles refined.
4. Serve as consultants to field people who are setting up new jobs, a never-ending process in such an expanding industry as communications.

Quite clearly AT&T is settling down for the long haul. Seventy-seven new programs have been started. No one expects all jobs to be equally improvable, nor is every job in need of assistance. And, since there are so many requests, the accepted view is, "Don't push any manager who is uncertain or lukewarm in his interest. Reach him later."

At this writing, more than 50 companies outside the Bell System have requested further information about the studies. Some were already conducting their own studies; others have now started here in the United States and abroad. A reasonably safe prediction is that much more information will be available within the next ten years as to how one bridges the gap from theory to fact. Experimental studies, not surveys, will probably make the difference as knowledge in this field accumulates.

SOME TRUTHS ABOUT WORK

One reason not all managers rush into this program is that it means extensive change and not trivial change at that. Placing his photograph above each employee's work position won't suffice, but it is a project that could be set up in one "crash" week. Making basic changes in a well-established job is hard work, mentally and emotionally. After working on improving the jobs of the people they supervise, managers have often been heard to say, "What am I doing to my own job!"

Many a supervisor rose to his present job by performing well on each job in turn on the way up. To have kept these jobs rather than to have become a turnover statistic himself might be viewed as a reflection on his own ability. But, in spite of the likelihood of emotional involvement when changing a familiar job, personal feelings do not get in the way very frequently either in workshop sessions or among the highly placed managers when proposals for change are brought to them. Even the man who may be responsible for the fix a job is in is usually glad to find a solution. Occasionally, a particular executive has struggled too hard to save an old job rather than accept the changes proposed by lower-level supervisors in the greenlight sessions, but this is the exception.

There are no villains, no evil people who deliberately deprive employees of job satisfaction. When past steps have resulted in inadvertent job denuding, these steps were usually taken to achieve other desirable ends.

Still another basic truth is uncovered when we ask, "Why have these projects gone well?" We let it be known that six new projects were needed in order to check out the original Treasury study. We got three times that number in a matter of weeks, even though the executive level had only the results of one study to judge by. And, since the new programs are doing very well indeed, many other managers want to start.

The basic truth here is that managers *want* employees to do well and to have good jobs. "After all," one said, "I work here too." John W. Gardner suggests that *there can be no institutional change without aspiration*.[1] The fact that managers reach toward the work-itself goal indicates that they do aspire to present their employees with rich job opportunities.

The aspiration of good jobs for all employees is matched by similar aspirations for the other two legs of the corporate stool. There is no doubt at all that a sensible corporation aspires to give better service to *customers* also. More than 15,000 employees in the Bell Telephone Laboratories, for example, are working essentially toward new and better services. And on the *shareholder's* side, in an era when his equity can erode because of rapid inflation, the corporation has given repeated evidence that it aspires to keep its shareholder financially above the tide of inflation.

There is a direct connection between job improvement projects and one of Gardner's statements:

> The release of human potential, the enhancement of individual dignity, the liberation of the human spirit—those are the deepest and truest goals to be conceived by the hearts and minds of the American people. And those are ideas that sustain and strengthen a great civilization—if we believe in them, if we are honest about them, if we have the courage and the stamina to live for them.[2]

What is the connection? The studies were founded on the premise that jobs could be improved—and then set out to do it by releasing human potential more completely. In Gardner's words:

> Of all the ways in which society serves the individual, few are more meaningful than to provide him with a decent job. . . . It isn't going to be a decent society for any of us until it is for all of us. If our sense of responsibility fails us, our sheer self-interest should come to the rescue.[3]

Some people may assume that Gardner was talking about the hard-core unemployed. Actually, he was talking about a just society for all; but in any case his words amply support the aphorism, "A difference which makes no difference is not different."

A statement of deep truth that appeared at the time of these studies was made by the Negro psychologist Kenneth B. Clark, who said:

> The roots of the multiple pathology in the dark ghetto are not easy to isolate. They do not lie primarily in unemployment. In fact, if all of its residents were employed it would not materially alter the pathology of the community. More relevant is the status of the jobs held . . . more important than merely having a job, is the kind of job it is.[4]

1/John W. Gardner, *No Easy Victories,* Harper & Row, New York, p. 44.
2/Ibid., p. 16.
3/Ibid., p. 25.
4/Kenneth B. Clark, "Explosion in the Ghetto," *Psychology Today,* September 1967.

Ultimately there is no truth for the black employee that is not equally a truth for the white. To help a hard-core person get started management may want to take a job apart for a while. It may at first give him not the whole module or task—the installation and repair of telephones, for example—but the recovery of telephone handsets that were left in apartments, homes, or offices when tenants moved. Then he can learn how to install a telephone and eventually perform the more difficult task of figuring out why an instrument refuses to work.

Nothing more will be said here about minority problems, differences between male and female employees, or college graduates versus high school or grade school graduates simply because we have not found *(in these studies)* that the differences make a difference. Even the question of how to improve jobs for older employees as distinct from younger ones has not proved to be a critically important problem. *The major problem* is how to improve the job for any human being. That's why work itself, not the manipulation of people, has been repeatedly presented as the crucial variable.

And Gardner is quite right when he says, "our sheer self-interest should come to the rescue." This is one employee program that can be cost-free in as little as one year. In contrast, most employee programs end up as added costs of doing business.

There are still some people who would debate these issues. One spokesman explicitly said that these work-itself studies are misdirected. In his opinion, what employees need is "more close-order drill, more discipline." He said that the lack of discipline in American industry today is causing excessive turnover, grievances, and strikes. Although he made no suggestion as to how to achieve this discipline, one might observe that all it takes is military conscription (a kind of compulsory employment office), prisons for poor performers and objectors to the proposed employment, and, in some countries, a wall against which to stage executions.

Still another view of work that needs to be dealt with holds that the "work ethic" or "Protestant ethic" idea is outdated. By 1985, Americans will be able to live at the level of their present standard of living by working only six months a year. Or, alternatively, if a man chooses to work year-round, he will be able to retire from work at age 38.[5] Enough rise in the gross national product is expected to make this feasible. People must get ready for handling leisure, and the unmistakable implication of the report is that the work ethic has prepared us poorly for such a life.

And so it has. The disputable point is not the accuracy of the prediction; it is the implication that work is not or cannot be as enjoyable as is a hobby or a sport such as golf or fishing. Gardner states the case for the potential satisfactions of work:

What could be more satisfying than to be engaged in work in which

5/*The New York Times,* April 7, 1968, report of a new study conducted by Southern California Research Council.

every capacity or talent one may have is needed, every lesson one may have learned is used, every value one cares about is furthered?

No wonder men and women who find themselves in that situation commonly overwork, pass up vacations, and neglect the less exciting games such as golf.

It is one of the amusing errors of human judgment that the world habitually feels sorry for overworked men and women—and doesn't feel a bit sorry for the men and women who live moving from one pleasure resort to the next. As a result, the hard workers get not only all the real fun but all the sympathy too, while the resort habitués scratch the dry soil of calculated diversion and get roundly criticized for it. It isn't fair.[6]

What seems likely is that people of the future will learn to struggle against jobs that are unnecessarily bad. The willingness of management in many companies to improve the work itself should give courage to those who believe men should not write off the work portion of their lives while getting ready for the new leisure. Obviously one portion yields money, the other does not. But the point is this: Both the work *and* the leisure portions should be and can be challenging and interesting. The right mix will vary from person to person.

How Long Will It Last?

The concept of work just outlined grew out of the studies, as have the views as to how long a person will find his job improved, a question that arises repeatedly. In the first place, not all jobs have equal potential for yielding satisfaction. Some will be fairly routine even when we have reshaped them as best we can. In this case, the goal is still to give the employee all the responsibility possible in running the job.

A woman in one of our studies volunteered to take on a routine clerical assignment that recurred four times a year, a job that involved replacing lost, mislaid, or mutilated checks—the sort of job that automation can never eliminate. When asked why she volunteered for a second time to perform this "dum-dum" job, she replied, "Well, it may be a dum-dum job, but at least it's *my* dum-dum job the way we now run it." An important implication of these studies is that routine work, especially if everyone recognizes that it must be done, can be made more acceptable if we maximize the personal responsibility component. Although this may not be the world's greatest job, employees will find it worthwhile if they are allowed to run it in a self-responsible way.

The substantial reduction in turnover indicates that we can slow down the onset of dissatisfaction. Part of the long-range job of a supervisory family is to plan a *series* of steps so that an employee can feel he is still learning, still growing. He should be able to advance within his current job, as well as upward to the next job level. Unless a job has very elastic boundaries and psychological

6/Gardner, op. cit., p. 32.

growth and learning can occur, it will eventually bore its incumbents. People, like plants, may need to be repotted occasionally, at least until the pot is big enough for the specimen to grow without stunting. Once we have done our best to make a good and challenging job, the onset of boredom will vary with the ability of the incumbents. For some, the job may be good for a lifetime; for others, only a few years. If we have been reasonably good at selection, placement, and training, as well as job shaping, no one will be bored in only a few weeks or months.

The whimsical "Peter Principle" holds that men rise in a business hierarchy until they reach their own level of incompetence. There they stay, since they are incompetent to go ahead. If a battle of principles were to break out, we would present in opposition the Ford Principle, which is that "a man tends to repot himself until he finds a pot that is big enough." Not all people succeed in finding such a pot, of course. This puts men (or employees) into three classes.

> Class 1—Men in pots that are too big for them (as suggested by the Peter Principle).
> Class 2—Men in pots that are just right.
> Class 3—Men in pots too small for them.

Class 1 is no cause for worry; surely not too many men are in it. Those men in Class 2 are to be envied. It's Class 3 that is bothersome.

Applying the Ford Principle, we should not cut men down to fit the pots we need to fill; we should instead get bigger pots—enlarge the jobs—and let our men grow to fill them. To put it another way, if our round pegs (people) do not fit our square holes (jobs) ream the holes to the pegs; don't ram the pegs into the holes any which way or cut them down to fit. In other words, change the shape of the jobs and you improve the level of employee satisfaction; cut the employees down to fit the job and you perpetuate existing troubles and perhaps breed new ones.

WILL FUTURE STUDIES TURN OUT AS WELL?

Progress over the past two or three years has led us to conclude that the measured results, are an understatement of what can be achieved eventually. Some handicaps were built into the study designs for scientific reasons, such as the need to minimize the Hawthorne effect. Experience shows that if employees know that they are part of a special study or campaign, results drop off again when the campaign is over. Therefore, we never told the employees that studies were under way or that we were going to try to improve their jobs. We simply did it, at first not very expertly. In 16 of the 19 studies, we did not tell even the first-level supervisors that systematic approach to job improvement was under way simply to block their being either for or against the idea of improving motivation through the work itself.

In the future, either projects or programs *should* provide richer yields for these reasons:

1. First-level supervisors can be informed, along with upper levels. The complete family will have better greenlight ideas than the smaller supervisory family we used (second, third, and fourth levels). Acts inconsistent with the principles will occur less frequently once the immediate supervisor is both informed and included.
2. The topmost levels should be informed also so that inconsistent ideas, orders, and plans do not come down from above.
3. Sometimes good ideas for improving one job are blocked unless other jobs, even other departments, are involved. In the project stage, we had to forgo involving other jobs and departments; but they should be involved in future programs.
4. When supervisory people in *many* locations are working simultaneously to reshape a given job, cross-fertilization of ideas actually occurs. In only one study were we able to take advantage of this.
5. The training workshops have improved because of the early trials.
6. Only after the studies were well along did we discover the crucial importance of devising feedback schemes for individual employees (as opposed to group indexes).

Considering all these factors, future efforts should be more productive than the original trials, especially if they are programs available to any supervisory family, rather than limited to a trial or project group. This does not imply that a program will be *any easier* than the trials; good greenlight items will always be hard to come by. But results should be at least as striking, if not more so.

THE PRINCIPLES OF JOB ENRICHMENT

At the start of this series of studies, many tape recordings were made wherein employees talked about their jobs, especially upon quitting. Many remarks were heard repeatedly: "I'm tired of being treated like a child." "I didn't think this would be like school, but it is." "I don't want to be simply a 'hey-boy' for someone else." There is no indication that times will change, that people will once again come to employment offices begging for work, or that they will stay when they don't want to, as they have at times in the past. The roots of the disenchantment must be dealt with. Much of the disenchantment can be traced to the early 1900's, when industry went through a period of job engineering and stopwatch analyses of work flow. Then job designs, job specifications, job rules, job regulations, and highly detailed work practices were developed. In many interviews, employees specifically complain about being caged in by these rules.

In such a work situation, the supervisor's job may seem to be that of keeper of the caged-in people. And his major motivational task might be viewed as that of rattling the cages so that the drowsy animals "look alive." In this analogy motivation is from *outside:* the keeper does it. Many managers now believe that this approach to work motivation has had its day.

How to go forward, then? How to view employees? The data from these studies show that it is possible to get an order-of-magnitude change, not just a small increment. Modern employees are bright, healthy, well fed, and well educated compared to those in the time-and-motion study days. They will not accept dull jobs unless the jobs are their very own. We must set the conditions of work so as to gradually maximize the responsibility thrust upon the worker. To do this we must ask ourselves these questions:

What do I do for him that he could now do for himself?

What thinking can he now do for himself?

What goals could we now set *jointly*?

What advanced training or skill could he now have?

What job could he work toward now? How could I help him?

Is there a way of combining this job with another one that he would like? Is the module right?

Is there anything he does that could be given to a lower-rated job?

Can anything be automated out of the job?

The trouble, then, with a straight engineering approach to work flow, job layout, and job specifications is that employees won't stay on these jobs—as evidenced by turnover rates for highly rationalized, tightly structured jobs. We must learn to trade off engineering economies for human values and not to assume that this will be costly. Actually, every day beyond the old median length of tenure that a service representative, for example, stays on a newly reshaped job is of cash value to the business. We are quite sure that she *will* stay if she can get more satisfaction from her work.

Job satisfaction is hard to describe, hard to visualize. It will not make an employee go around with a big, happy grin on his face. More typical of his expression would be that of the golfer, the athlete, the chess player, trying to make a good shot or to perform well. The face and attitude of any well-motivated worker confronted by a difficult, challenging situation are more like those of the athlete than those of the relaxed watchers in the stands.

Job satisfaction may or may not be tied to happiness. But we will know that we are doing something right if we can change the conditions of the job so that employees will stay on and work productively. For the older workers, the test will be whether they are with us in spirit as well as in body. The way to achieve this end, for new or old employees, is not to confront them with demands, but to confront them with demanding, meaningful work. And the employee will always have the last word as to whether the work is meaningful.

15

Peer Leadership within Work Groups*

DAVID G. BOWERS
and
STANLEY E. SEASHORE

One of the current tasks in industrial psychology is to relate concepts of group process and leadership to the performance of work groups. This paper emphasizes several issues that are of critical importance for the interpretation of research results in this area and for the guidance of future research. The comments are based on the research program of the Institute for Social Research. The Institute for several years has had an active program of theory development and field observation focused upon factors, such as leadership and group activity, that bear upon the effectiveness and survival of work groups and their organizations. In addition to mentioning five central issues, the article will refer briefly to the results obtained in one recent field study.

Conceptions of Leadership

The conception of "leadership" in this discussion rests on social-psychology (rather than sociology or individual psychology). That is, it is concerned with the behavior of persons insofar as it influences the behavior of others in ways such that the occurrence of "leadership" may be inferred. An act of leadership is any behavior of one person within the context of organizational life that influences the behavior of others with reference to achievement of organization goals. This is a familiar conception, so there is no need to discuss it further except to note that under this definition (1) leadership may be exercised by any person within an organization or work group, whether or not he is in a position of formal authority, and (2) leadership acts may be of many kinds.

Much of our work has been concerned with the creation and use of a system of variables or characteristics that will allow the description of the amount and kind of leadership that occurs within a work group, and the comparison of work

*Source: Reprinted from *Personnel Administration* (September-October 1967), 45-50, by permission of the International Personnel Management Association.

groups in these respects. The variables currently in use are four in number. These have been identified through factor analysis methods coupled with correlational analyses to confirm the meaning and predictive power of the resulting conceptual dimensions of leadership. An appended table shows that the four proposed dimensions of leadership are compatible with those proposed independently by others working on related issues. The four leadership dimensions are thought to comprise the basic conceptual structure of the phenomenon called "leadership." Additional and subsidiary dimensions will be found necessary for the description in detail of the leadership found in any particular work group. The proposed dimensions are:

1. *Support:* behavior which serves the function of increasing or maintaining the individual member's sense of personal worth and importance in the context of group activity;
2. *Interaction facilitation:* behavior which serves the function of creating or maintaining a network of interpersonal relationships among members of the group;
3. *Goal emphasis:* behavior which serves the function of creating, changing, clarifying, or gaining member acceptance of group goals;
4. *Work facilitation:* behavior which serves to provide effective work methods, facilities, and technology for the accomplishment of group goals.

It should be noted that these dimensions of leadership correspond to some extent to the dimensions of individual motivation proposed by several recent writers (Angyal, Bronfenbrenner, Nuttin). "Support" and "interaction facilitation" appear to be related to the need to be an accepted part of a group of beings like oneself (broadly, a need for affiliation). "Goal emphasis" and "work facilitation" appear related to the need to master one's environment or control one's fate (broadly, a need for achievement).

Crude but useful scales for measurement of these dimensions of leadership have been developed based upon interview and questionnaire data obtained from members of many groups and organizations. Each member is asked to report his perceptions as to whether (or how frequently) certain specific acts occur, these specific acts being chosen to represent each of the four dimensions of leadership.

It should be noted that while the four dimensions of leadership are conceptually independent, they rarely occur as factors in pure form. A single act may carry implications for two or more of the leadership dimensions. For example, a discussion between supervisor and subordinate about production may serve simultaneously to provide support for the employee, to reinforce group goals, to facilitate work and to reinforce the interaction network. The problem of measurement of the four dimensions accordingly rests upon the choice of acts which represent, in relatively pure form, only one of the dimensions. This is sometimes made difficult by the fact that the leadership qualities of an act are inherent in the group member's perceptions of it rather than in the act itself, and the same act may occasionally be differently perceived.

Comparison of Leadership Concepts of Different Investigators

	Hemphill & Coons[a]	Halpin & Winer[b]	Kahn[c]	Cartwright & Zander[d]	Likert[e]
Support	Maintenance of membership character	Consideration	Employee orientation		Principle of supportive relationships
Interaction facilitation	Group interaction facilitation	Sensitivity	----	Group maintenance functions	Group methods of supervision
Goal emphasis	Objective attainment behavior	Production emphasis	Production orientation	Goal achievement functions	High performance goals
Work facilitation		Initiation of structure			Technical knowledge planning scheduling coordinating

[a] Hemphill, J. K. & Coons, A. E. Development of the leader behavior description questionnaire. In R. M. Stogdill & A. E. Coons (Eds.), Leader behavior: Its description and measurement. Res. Monog. No. 88. Columbus, Ohio: Bureau of Business Research, the Ohio State University, 1957, 6-38.

[b] Halpin, A. W. & Winer, J. A factorial study of the leader behavior descriptions. In R. M. Stogdill & A. E. Coons (Eds.), Leader behavior: Its description and measurement. Res. Monog. No. 88. Columbus, Ohio: Bureau of Business Research, the Ohio State University, 1957, 39-51.

[c] Kahn, R. L. The prediction of productivity. J. Soc. Issues, 1956, 12, 41-49.
Kahn, R. L., Human relations on the shop floor. In E. M. Hugh-Jones (Ed.), Human relations and modern management. Amsterdam, Holland: North-Holland Publishing Co., 1958, 43-74.

[d] Cartwright, D. & Zander, A. Group dynamics research and theory. Evanston, Ill.: Row, Peterson & Co., 1960.

[e] Likert, R. New patterns of management. New York: McGraw-Hill Book Co., 1961.

Some Issues

Given this conception of the dimensions of leadership, and means for measuring them, it becomes possible to approach systematically and quantitatively some issues that until recently were approached only on a speculative basis. Five such issues or questions are mentioned here in the context of work group performance.

1. *The Issue of Concentration or Dispersion of Leadership.* Classical theories of leadership hold that leadership is and should be exercised mainly by persons in positions of formal authority and responsibility—by the supervisor in the case of a work group. Contrary views are expressed in the notions concerning the phenomenon of dual leadership (for group maintenance functions and for group task functions, respectively), and in notions concerning informal leadership or peer leadership. Despite all of the speculation on this issue, coupled with some ingenious research, we still do not have dependable information about the dispersion of leadership acts among members of work groups or about the conditions that lead to various degrees of dispersion.

2. *The Issue of Generality of Leadership Dimensions.* If we assume for the moment that leadership acts are performed by persons other than the formally designated leaders, then several questions arise. Are the conceptual dimensions developed for describing formal leadership equally applicable to informal leadership? Do informal leaders within a group carry out some kinds of leadership functions but not others? Do informal leaders engage in categories of leadership behavior that are not relevant for describing the behavior of the formal leaders? Our own tentative belief on these questions is that the leadership behavior of supervisors and of group members is indistinguishable except with respect to pattern of emphasis.

3. *The Issue of Relationships between Supervisory Leadership and Peer Leadership.* On this issue, there exist several competing views and little factual information. Does the supervisor's pattern of leadership get *replicated* in the leadership behavior of subordinates (that is, do subordinates tend to provide leadership in much the same way as does the formal leader), or is there instead a *compensatory* process such that peer leadership adapts to offset any deficiencies arising from the behavior of the supervisor? In instances in which both supervisor and subordinates engage in the same class of leadership behavior, are the effects additive, multiplicative or substitutive? Are the relationships circular, or causal in one direction?

4. *The Issue of Relative Potency of Supervisory and Peer Leadership with Respect to Group and Organizational Criteria.* Is group performance more influenced by supervisory leadership or by peer leadership? Is the relative potency different for different dimensions of group performance or uniform for all?

5. *The Issue of Selective Impact on Performance.* If one assumes that group performance is itself a complex of several dimensions or categories of performance, then the question arises whether a specified leadership act contributes

to a specific performance criterion, whether performed by the supervisor or by a group member. It is possible that certain criteria of performance are determined by supervisory leadership alone, others by member leadership alone, or by some combination of the two.

Results from a Recent Study

We wish now to refer briefly to the results from a recent field study in which data relevant to these issues were obtained. Our purposes are (1) to illustrate a method for the resolution of these issues and (2) to advance some tentative conclusions.[1]

The study was carried out in an insurance sales organization system comprising 78 sales groups. Each of the groups studied is composed of an owner-manager together with his salesmen, numbering from 10 to 50 men. Each group is located in a different city. All sell the same kinds of insurance under the same general business policies and with approximately equal opportunities for business success. These groups were selected for study because they provide an unusual set of conditions: a large population of autonomous groups that are nearly identical in their formal structure and purpose but highly variable in their performance, thus allowing the effective comparative study of group leadership phenomena in relation to performance.

Data were obtained through interviews and questionnaires from over 2,000 salesmen and their supervisors, including measures of our four dimensions of leadership behavior as they are perceived to occur in the case of the owner-manager and in the case of group members. A number of measures were obtained to represent the performance of the sales groups. These include five measures representing dimensions of group member satisfaction; three representing objective business achievement, such as volume of sales, cost of sales, growth in business volume; two variables describing the local group's choice of business style or strategy; and one describing group membership stability.

The following comments indicate our interpretation of the data with reference to each of the issues previously mentioned.

1. Our data sustain the idea that group members do engage in behavior which can be described as leadership, and that in these groups, it appears likely that the total quantity of peer leadership is at least as great as the total quantity of supervisory leadership. The groups varied greatly from one another with respect to the degree and the pattern of emphasis in peer leadership behavior.

2. The four dimensions of leadership developed initially for the description of formal leaders appear to be equally applicable to the description of leadership by group members.

3. The supervisor's pattern of leadership (i.e., relative degree of emphasis on

---

1/For a complete description of this study, see "Use of a Four-Factor Theory of Leadership To Predict Organizational Effectiveness," by D. Bowers and S. Seashore, *Administrative Science Quarterly*, September 1966, *11*, 2, pages 238-63.

each of the four dimensions) tends to be replicated in the leadership behavior of his subordinates; that is, the subordinates tend to provide leadership in much the same way as does the formal leader. This correspondence of pattern, however, is not so great as to preclude the possibility that some compensatory member leadership is occurring. Proof is lacking on this point. The joint effects of peer and supervisory leadership are mixed, with some instances of an additive relationship, some of substitution. None of the tested cases appears to involve a multiplicative relationship.

4. With respect to the issue of relative potency, the peer leadership variables are at least as potent as supervisory leadership variables, and possibly more so, in predicting group achievement of goals.

5. Selective impact on performance clearly occurs. Each of the peer leadership variables and each of the supervisory leadership variables appear to be selective in its impact. For example, the variable "peer goal emphasis" relates significantly to group cost performance, to the group's style of business (larger policies, sold to more affluent clients, etc.) and to member satisfaction with fellow agents, but it does not relate significantly to such performance variables as volume of business, business growth rate, satisfaction with job. Peer goal emphasis appears in the case of these groups to play a central role, as it is either the best single predictor or a significant additive predictor in relation to a majority of our criteria of group performance.

CONCLUSION

The results briefly reported here must be taken as suggestive, as they come from an organization that is not typical. Nevertheless, the study provides confirmation for certain ideas that are of importance in understanding the role of the small group or work team in business and industry.

One of the functions of the group is to provide leadership to its own members and to supplement the leadership provided by the formal hierarchy of the organization. This factor aids in the explanation of the common research finding that the effectiveness of large organizations often depends closely upon the character and functioning of the work groups of which they are composed.

16

Organization Development Objectives, Assumptions, and Strategies*

WENDELL FRENCH

Organization development refers to a long-range effort to improve an organization's problem solving capabilities and its ability to cope with changes in its external environment with the help of external or internal behavioral-scientist consultants, or change agents, as they are sometimes called. Such efforts are relatively new but are becoming increasingly visible within the United States, England, Japan, Holland, Norway, Sweden, and perhaps in other countries. A few of the growing number of organizations which have embarked on organization development (OD) efforts to some degree are Union Carbide, Esso, TRW Systems, Humble Oil, Weyerhaeuser, and Imperial Chemical Industries Limited. Other kinds of institutions, including public school systems, churches, and hospitals, have also become involved.

Organization development activities appear to have originated about 1957 as an attempt to apply some of the values and insights of laboratory training to total organizations. The late Douglas McGregor, working with Union Carbide, is considered to have been one of the first behavioral scientists to talk systematically about and to implement an organization development program.[1] Other names associated with such early efforts are Herbert Shepard and Robert Blake who, in collaboration with the Employee Relations Department of the Esso Company, launched a program of laboratory training (sensitivity training) in the

---

*Source: Copyright 1969 by the Regents of the University of California. Reprinted from *California Management Review*, vol. 12, no. 2, 23-34, by permission of The Regents.

1/Richard Beckhard, W. Warner Burke, and Fred I. Steele, "The Program for Specialists in Organization Training and Development," mimeographed, NTL Institute for Applied Behavioral Science, December 1967, p. ii; and John Paul Jones, "What's Wrong with Work?" in *What's Wrong with Work?* (New York: National Association of Manufacturers, 1967), p. 8. For a history of NTL Institute for Applied Behavioral Science, with which Douglas McGregor was long associated in addition to his professorial appointment at M.I.T. and which has been a major factor in the history of organization development, see Leland P. Bradford, "Biography of an Institution," *Journal of Applied Behavioral Science*, 3:2 (1967), 127-143. While we will use the word "program" from time to time, ideally organization development is a "process," not just another new program of temporary quality.

company's various refineries. This program emerged in 1957 after a head-quarters human relations research division began to view itself as an internal consulting group offering services to field managers rather than as a research group developing reports for top management.[2]

Objectives of Typical OD Programs. Although the specific interpersonal and task objectives of organization development programs will vary according to each diagnosis of organizational problems, a number of objectives typically emerge. These objectives reflect problems which are very common in organizations:

1. To increase the level of trust and support among organizational members.
2. To increase the incidence of confrontation of organizational problems, both within groups and among groups, in contrast to "sweeping problems under the rug."
3. To create an environment in which authority of assigned role is augmented by authority based on knowledge and skill.
4. To increase the openness of communications laterally, vertically, and diagonally.
5. To increase the level of personal enthusiasm and satisfaction in the organization.
6. To find synergistic solutions[3] to problems with greater frequency. (Synergistic solutions are creative solutions in which 2 + 2 equals more than 4, and through which all parties gain more through cooperation than through conflict.)
7. To increase the level of self and group responsibility in planning and implementation.[4]

Difficulties in Categorizing. Before describing some of the basic assumptions and strategies of organization development, it would be well to point out that one of the difficulties in writing about such a "movement" is that a wide variety of activities can be and are subsumed under this label. These activities have varied all the way from inappropriate application of some "canned" management development program to highly responsive and skillful joint efforts between behavioral scientists and client systems.

Thus, while labels are useful, they may gloss over a wide range of phenomena. The "human relations movement," for example, has been widely written about as though it were all bad or all good. To illustrate, some of the critics of the

2/Harry D. Kolb, Introduction to *An Action Research Program for Organization Improvement* (Ann Arbor: Foundation for Research in Human Behavior, 1960), p. i.

3/Cattell defines synergy as "the sum total of the energy which a group can command." Daniel Katz and Robert L. Kahn, *The Social Psychology of Organizations* (New York: John Wiley and Sons, 1966), p. 33.

4/For a similar statement of objectives, see "What is OD?" *NTL Institute: News and Reports from NTL Institute for Applied Behavioral Science,* 22 (June 1968), 1-2. Whether OD programs increase the overall level of authority in contrast to redistributing authority is a debatable point. My hypothesis is that both a redistribution and an overall increase occur.

movement have accused it of being "soft" and a "hand-maiden of the Establishment," of ignoring the technical and power systems of organizations, and of being too naively participative. Such criticisms were no doubt warranted in some circumstances, but in other situations may not have been at all appropriate. Paradoxically, some of the major insights of the human relations movement, e.g., that the organization can be viewed as a social system and that subordinates have substantial control over productivity have been assimilated by its critics.

In short, the problem is to distinguish between appropriate and inappropriate programs, between effectiveness and ineffectiveness, and between relevancy and irrelevancy. The discussion which follows will attempt to describe the "ideal" circumstances for organization development programs, as well as to point out some pitfalls and common mistakes in organization change efforts.

Relevancy to Different Technologies and Organization Subunits. Research by Joan Woodward[5] suggests that organization development efforts *might be more relevant to certain kinds of technologies and organizational levels, and perhaps to certain workforce characteristics, than to others.* For example, OD efforts may be more appropriate for an organization devoted to prototype manufacturing than for an automobile assembly plant. However, experiments in an organization like Texas Instruments suggest that some manufacturing efforts which appear to be inherently mechanistic may lend themselves to a more participative, open management style than is often assumed possible.[6]

However, assuming the constraints of a fairly narrow job structure at the rank-and-file level, organization development efforts may inherently be more productive and relevant at the managerial levels of the organization. Certainly OD efforts are most effective when they start at the top. Research and development units—particularly those involving a high degree of interdependency and joint creativity among group members—also appear to be appropriate for organization development activities, if group members are currently experiencing problems in communicating or interpersonal relationships.

Basic Assumptions. Some of the basic assumptions about people which underlie organization development programs are similar to "Theory Y" assumptions[7] and will be repeated only briefly here. However, some of the assumptions about groups and total systems will be treated more extensively. The following assumptions appear to underlie organization development efforts.[8]

5/Joan Woodward, *Industrial Organization: Theory and Practice* (London: Oxford University Press, 1965).

6/See M. Scott Myers, "Every Employee a Manager," *California Management Review*, 10 (Spring 1968), pp. 9-20.

7/See Douglas McGregor, *The Human Side of Enterprise* (New York: McGraw-Hill Book Company, 1960), pp. 47-48.

8/In addition to influence from the writings of McGregor, Likert, Argyris, and others, this discussion has been influenced by "Some Assumptions About Change in Organizations," in notebook "Program for Specialists in Organization Training and Development," NTL Institute for Applied Behavioral Science, 1967; and by staff members who participated in that program.

About People

Most individuals have drives toward personal growth and development, and these are most likely to be actualized in an environment which is both supportive and challenging.

Most people desire to make, and are capable of making, a much higher level of contribution to the attainment of organization goals than most organizational environments will permit.

About People in Groups

Most people wish to be accepted and to interact cooperatively with at least one small reference group, and usually with more than one group, e.g., the work group, the family group.

One of the most psychologically relevant reference groups for most people is the work group, including peers and the superior.

Most people are capable of greatly increasing their effectiveness in helping their reference groups solve problems and in working effectively together.

For a group to optimize its effectiveness, the formal leader cannot perform all of the leadership functions in all circumstances at all times, and all group members must assist each other with effective leadership and member behavior.

About People in Organizational Systems

Organizations tend to be characterized by overlapping, interdependent work groups, and the "linking pin" function of supervisors and others needs to be understood and facilitated.[9]

What happens in the broader organization affects the small work group and vice versa.

What happens to one subsystem (social, technological, or administrative) will affect and be influenced by other parts of the system.

The culture in most organizations tends to suppress the expression of feelings which people have about each other and about where they and their organizations are heading.

Suppressed feelings adversely affect problem solving, personal growth, and job satisfaction.

The level of interpersonal trust, support, and cooperation is much lower in most organizations than is either necessary or desirable.

"Win-lose" strategies between people and groups, while realistic and appropriate in some situations, are not optimal in the long run to the solution of most organizational problems.

9/For a discussion of the "linking pin" concept, see Rensis Likert, *New Patterns of Management* (New York: McGraw-Hill Book Company, 1961).

Synergistic solutions can be achieved with a much higher frequency than is actually the case in most organizations.

Viewing feelings as data important to the organization tends to open up many avenues for improved goal setting, leadership, communications, problem solving, intergroup collaboration, and morale.

Improved performance stemming from organization development efforts needs to be sustained by appropriate changes in the appraisal, compensation, training, staffing, and task-specialization subsystem—in short, in the total personnel system.

Value and Belief Systems of Behavioral Scientist-Change Agents. While scientific inquiry, ideally, is value-free, the applications of science are not value-free. Applied behavioral scientist-organization development consultants tend to subscribe to a comparable set of values, although we should avoid the trap of assuming that they constitute a completely homogeneous group. They do not.

One value, to which many behavioral scientist-change agents tend to give high priority, is that the needs and aspirations of human beings are the reasons for organized effort in society. They tend, therefore, to be developmental in their outlook and concerned with the long-range opportunities for the personal growth of people in organizations.

A second value is that work and life can become richer and more meaningful, and organized effort more effective and enjoyable, if feelings and sentiments are permitted to be a more legitimate part of the culture. A third value is a commitment to an action role, along with a commitment to research, in an effort to improve the effectiveness of organizations.[10] A fourth value—or perhaps a belief—is that improved competency in interpersonal and intergroup relationship will result in more effective organizations.[11] A fifth value is that behavioral science research and an examination of behavioral science assumptions and values are relevant and important in considering organizational effectiveness. While many change agents are perhaps overly action-oriented in terms of the utilization of their time, nevertheless, as a group they are paying more and more attention to research and to the examination of ideas.[12]

The value placed on research and inquiry raises the question as to whether the assumptions stated earlier are values, theory, or "facts." In my judgment, a

10/Warren G. Bennis sees three major approaches to planned organizational change, with the behavioral scientists associated with each all having "a deep concern with applying social science knowledge to create more viable social systems; a commitment to action, as well as to research . . . and a belief that improved interpersonal and group relationships will ultimately lead to better organizational performance." Bennis, "A New Role for the Behavioral Sciences: Effecting Organizational Change," *Administrative Science Quarterly*, 8 (September 1963), 157-158; and Herbert A. Shepard, "An Action Research Model," in *An Action Research Program for Organization Improvement*, pp. 31-35.

11/Bennis, "A New Role for the Behavioral Sciences," 158.

12/For a discussion of some of the problems and dilemmas in behavioral science research, see Chris Argyris, "Creating Effective Relationships in Organizations," in Richard

182 FUNDAMENTALS OF MANAGEMENT: SELECTED READINGS

substantial body of knowledge, including research on leadership, suggests that there is considerable evidence for these assumptions. However, to conclude that these assumptions are facts, laws, or principles would be to contradict the value placed by behavioral scientists on continuous research and inquiry. Thus, I feel that they should be considered theoretical statements which are based on provisional data.

This also raises the paradox that the belief that people are important tends to result in their being important. The belief that people can grow and develop in terms of personal and organizational competency tends to produce this result. Thus, values and beliefs tend to be self-fulfilling, and the question becomes "What do you choose to want to believe?" While this position can become Pollyanna-ish in the sense of not seeing the real world, nevertheless, behavioral scientist-change agents, at least this one, tend to place a value on optimism. It is a kind of optimism that says people can do a better job of goal setting and facing up to and solving problems, not an optimism that says the number of problems is diminishing.

It should be added that it is important that the values and beliefs of each behavioral science-change agent be made visible both to himself and to the client. In the first place, neither can learn to adequately trust the other without such exposure—a hidden agenda handicaps both trust building and mutual learning. Second, and perhaps more pragmatically, organizational change efforts tend to fail if a prescription is applied unilaterally and without proper diagnosis.

Strategy in Organization Development: An Action Research Model. A frequent strategy in organization development programs is based on what behavioral scientists refer to as an "action research model." This model involves extensive collaboration between the consultant (whether an external or an internal change agent) and the client group, data gathering, data discussion, and planning. While descriptions of this model vary in detail and terminology from author to author, the dynamics are essentially the same.[13]

Figure 1 summarizes some of the essential phases of the action research model, using an emerging organization development program as an example. The key aspects of the model are *diagnosis, data gathering, feedback to the client group, data discussion and work by the client group, action planning, and action.* The sequence tends to be cyclical, with the focus on new or advanced problems as the client group learns to work more effectively together. Action research should also be considered a process, since, as William Foote Whyte says, it involves ". . . a continuous gathering and analysis of human relations research

N. Adams and Jack J. Preiss, eds., *Human Organization Research* (Homewood, Ill.: The Dorsey Press, 1960), pp. 109-123; and Barbara A. Benedict, et al., "The Clinical Experimental Approach to Assessing Organizational Change Efforts," *Journal of Applied Behavioral Science* (November 1967), 347-380.

13/For further discussion of action research, see Edgar H. Schein and Warren G. Bennis, *Personal and Organizational Change Through Group Methods* (New York: John Wiley and Sons, 1966), pp. 272-274.

FIGURE 1
An Action Research Model for Organization Development

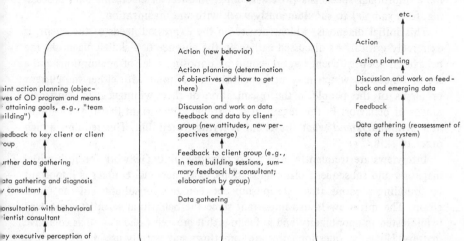

data and the feeding of the findings into the organization in such a manner as to change behavior."[14] (Feedback we will define as nonjudgmental observations of behavior.)

Ideally, initial objectives and strategies of organization development efforts stem from a careful *diagnosis* of such matters as interpersonal and intergroup problems, decision-making processes, and communication flow which are currently being experienced by the client organization. As a preliminary step, the behavioral scientist and the key client (the president of a company, the vice president in charge of a division, the works manager or superintendent of a plant, a superintendent of schools, etc.), will make a joint initial assessment of the critical problems which need working on. Subordinates may also be interviewed in order to provide supplemental data. The diagnosis may very well indicate that the central problem is technological or that the key client is not at all willing or ready to examine the organization's problem-solving ability or his own managerial behavior.[15] Either could be a reason for postponing or moving slowly in the direction of organization development activities, although the technological problem may easily be related to deficiencies in interpersonal relationships or

14/William Foote Whyte and Edith Lentz Hamilton, *Action Research for Management* (Homewood, Ill.: Richard D. Irwin, 1964), p. 2.
15/Jeremiah J. O'Connell appropriately challenges the notion that there is "one best way" of organizational change and stresses that the consultant should choose his role and intervention strategies on the basis of "the conditions existing when he enters the client system" (*Managing Organizational Innovation* [Homewood, Ill.: Richard D. Irwin, 1968], pp. 10-11).

decision making. The diagnosis might also indicate the desirability of one or more additional specialists (in engineering, finance, or electronic data processing, for example) to simultaneously work with the organization.

This initial diagnosis, which focuses on the expressed needs of the client, is extremely critical. As discussed earlier, in the absence of a skilled diagnosis, the behavioral scientist-change agent would be imposing a set of assumptions and a set of objectives which may be hopelessly out of joint with either the current problems of the people in the organization or their willingness to learn new modes of behavior. In this regard, it is extremely important that the consultant *hear and understand* what the client is trying to tell him. This requires a high order of skill.[16]

Interviews are frequently used for *data gathering* in OD work for both initial diagnosis and subsequent planning sessions, since personal contact is important for building a cooperative relationship between the consultant and the client group. The interview is also important since the behavioral scientist-consultant is interested in spontaneity and in feelings that are expressed as well as cognitive matters. However, questionnaires are sometimes successfully used in the context of what is sometimes referred to as survey feedback, to supplement interview data.[17]

Data gathering typically goes through several phases. The first phase is related to diagnosing the state of the system and to making plans for organizational change. This phase may utilize a series of interviews between the consultant and the key client, or between a few key executives and the consultant. Subsequent phases focus on problems specific to the top executive team and to subordinate teams. (See Figure 2.)

Typical questions in data gathering or "problem sensing" would include: What problems do you see in your group, including problems between people, that are interfering with getting the job done the way you would like to see it done?; and what problems do you see in the broader organization? Such openended questions provide wide latitude on the part of the respondents and encourage a reporting of problems as *the individual sees them.* Such interviewing is usually conducted privately, with a commitment on the part of the consultant that the information will be used in such a way as to avoid unduly embarrassing anyone. The intent is to find out what common problems or

16/For further discussion of organization diagnosis, see Richard Beckhard, "An Organization Improvement Program in a Decentralised Organization," *Journal of Applied Behavioral Science,* 2 (January-March 1966), 3-4, "OD as a Process," in *What's Wrong with Work?,* pp. 12-13.

17/For example, see Floyd C. Mann, "Studying and Creating Change," in Timothy W. Costello and Sheldon S. Zalkind, eds., *Psychology in Administration—A Research Orientation* (Englewood Cliffs: Prentice-Hall, 1963), pp. 321-324. See also Delbert C. Miller, "Using Behavioral Science to Solve Organization Problems," *Personnel Administration,* 31 (January-February 1968), 21-29.

FIGURE 2
Organization Development Phases in a Hypothetical Organization

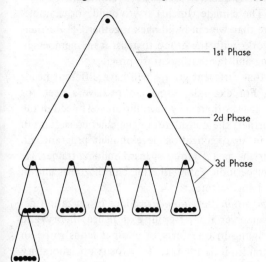

1st Phase

2d Phase

3d Phase

1st phase. Data gathering, feedback and diagnosis—consultant and top executive only.

2nd phase. Data gathering, feedback, and revised diagnosis—consultant and two or more key staff or line people.

3rd phase. Data gathering and feedback to total top executive team in "team-building" laboratory, with or without key subordinates from level below.

4th and additional phases. Data gathering and team-building sessions with 2nd or 3rd level teams.

Subsequent phases. Data gathering, feedback, and interface problem-solving sessions across groups.

Simultaneous phases. Several managers may attend "stranger" T-Groups; courses in the management development program may supplement this learning.

themes emerge, with the data to be used constructively for both diagnostic and feedback purposes.

Two- or three-day offsite *team-building or group problem-solving sessions* typically become a major focal point in organization development programs. During these meetings the behavioral scientist frequently provides feedback to the group in terms of the themes which emerged in the problem-sensing interviews.[18] He may also encourage the group to determine which items or themes should have priority in terms of maximum utilization of time. These themes usually provide substantial and meaningful data for the group to begin work on. One-to-one interpersonal matters, both positive and negative, tend to emerge spontaneously as the participants gain confidence from the level of support sensed in the group.

Different consultants will vary in their mode of behavior in such sessions, but will typically serve as *"process" observers and as interpreters of the dynamics of the group interaction* to the degree that the group expresses a readiness for such intervention. They also typically encourage people to take risks, a step at a

18/For a description of feedback procedures used by the Survey Research Center, Univ. of Michigan, see Mann and Likert, "The Need for Research on the Communication of Research Results," in *Human Organization Research,* pp. 57-66.

time, and to experiment with new behavior in the context of the level of support in the group. Thus, the trainer-consultant(s) serves as a stimulant to new behavior but also as a protector. The climate which I try to build, for example, is: "Let's not tear down any more than we can build back together."[19] Further, the trainer-consultant typically works with the group to assist team members in improving their skills in diagnosing and facilitating group progress.[20]

It should be noted, however, that different groups will have different needs along a task-process continuum. For example, some groups have a need for intensive work on clarifying objectives; others may have the greatest need in the area of personal relationships. Further, the consultant or the chief consultant in a team of consultants involved in an organization development program will play a much broader role than serving as a T-group or team-building trainer. He will also play an important role in periodic data gathering and diagnosis and in joint long-range planning of the change efforts.[21]

Laboratory Training and Organization Development. Since organization development programs have largely emerged from T-group experience, theory, and research, and since laboratory training in one form or another tends to be an integral part of most such programs, it is important to focus on laboratory training per se. As stated earlier, OD programs grew out of a perceived need to relate laboratory training to the problems of ongoing organizations and a recognition that optimum results could only occur if major parts of the total social system of an organization were involved.

Laboratory training essentially emerged around 1946, largely through a growing recognition by Leland Bradford, Ronald Lippitt, Kenneth Benne, and others, that human relations training which focused on the feelings and concerns of the participants was frequently a much more powerful and viable form of education than the lecture method. Some of the theoretical constructs and

19/This phrase probably came from a management workshop sponsored by NTL Institute for Applied Behavioral Science.

20/For a description of what goes on in team-building sessions, see Beckhard, "An Organizational Improvement Program," 9-13; and Newton Margulies and Anthony P. Raia, "People in Organizations—A Case for Team Training," *Training and Development Journal*, 22 (August 1968), 2-11. For a description of problem-solving sessions involving the total management group (about 70) of a company, see Beckhard, "The Confrontation Meeting," *Harvard Business Review*, 45 (March-April 1967), 149-155.

21/For a description of actual organization development programs, see Paul C. Buchanan, "Innovative Organizations—A Study in Organization Development," in *Applying Behavioral Science Research in Industry* (New York: Industrial Relations Counselors, 1964), pp. 87-107; Sheldon A. Davis, "An Organic Problem-Solving Method of Organizational Change," *Journal of Applied Behavioral Science*, 3:1 (1967), 3-21; Cyril Sofer, *The Organization from Within* (Chicago: Quadrangle Books, 1961); Alfred J. Marrow, David G. Bowers, and Stanley E. Seashore, *Management by Participation* (New York: Harper and Row, 1967); Robert R. Blake, Jane S. Mouton, Louis B. Barnes, and Larry E. Greiner, "Breakthrough in Organization Development," *Harvard Business Review*, 42 (November-December 1964), 133-155; Alton C. Bartlett, "Changing Behavior as a Means to Increased Efficiency," *Journal of Applied Behavioral Science*, 3:3 (1967), 381-403; Larry E. Greiner, "Antecedents of Planned Organization Change," ibid., 3:1 (1967), 51-85; and Robert R. Blake and Jane Mouton, *Corporate Excellence Through Grid Organization Development* (Houston, Texas: Gulf Publishing Company, 1968).

insights from which these laboratory training pioneers drew stemmed from earlier research by Lippitt, Kurt Lewin, and Ralph White. The term "T-Group" emerged by 1949 as a shortened label for "Basic Skill Training Group"; these terms were used to identify the programs which began to emerge in the newly formed National Training Laboratory in Group Development (now NTL Institute for Applied Behavioral Science).[22] "Sensitivity Training" is also a term frequently applied to such training.

Ordinarily, laboratory training sessions have certain objectives in common. The following list, by two internationally known behavioral scientists,[23] is probably highly consistent with the objectives of most programs:

Self Objectives

Increased *awareness* of own feelings and reactions, and own impact on others.

Increased *awareness* of feelings and reactions of others, and their impact on self.

Increased *awareness* of dynamics of group action.

Changed *attitudes* toward self, others, and groups, i.e., more respect for, tolerance for, and faith in self, others, and groups.

Increased *interpersonal competence,* i.e., skill in handling interpersonal and group relationships toward more productive and satisfying relationships.

Role Objectives

Increased *awareness* of own organizational role, organizational dynamics, dynamics of larger social systems, and dynamics of the change process in self, small groups, and organizations.

Changed *attitudes* toward own role, role of others, and organizational relationships, i.e., more respect for and willingness to deal with others with whom one is interdependent, greater willingness to achieve collaborative relationships with others based on mutual trust.

Increased *interpersonal competence* in handling organizational role relationships with superiors, peers, and subordinates.

Organizational Objectives

Increased *awareness* of, *changed attitudes* toward, and increased *interpersonal competence* about specific organizational problems existing in groups or units which are interdependent.

Organizational improvement through the training of relationships or groups rather than isolated individuals.

22/From Bradford, "Biography of an Institution." See also Kenneth D. Benne, "History of the T Group in the Laboratory Setting," in Bradford, Jack R. Gibb, and Benne, eds., *T/Group Theory and Laboratory Method* (New York: John Wiley and Sons, 1964), pp. 80-135.

23/Schein and Bennis, p. 37.

Over the years, experimentation with different laboratory designs has led to diverse criteria for the selection of laboratory participants. Probably a majority of NTL-IABS human relations laboratories are "stranger groups," i.e., involving participants who come from different organizations and who are not likely to have met earlier. However, as indicated by the organizational objectives above, the incidence of special labs designed to increase the effectiveness of persons already working together appears to be growing. Thus terms like "cousin labs," i.e., labs involving people from the same organization but not the same subunit, and "family labs" or "team-building" sessions, i.e., involving a manager and all of his subordinates, are becoming familiar. Participants in labs designed for organizational members not of the same unit may be selected from the same rank level ("horizontal slice") or selected so as to constitute a heterogeneous grouping by rank ("diagonal slice"). Further, NTL-IABS is now encouraging at least two members from the same organization to attend NTL Management Work Conferences and Key Executive Conferences in order to maximize the impact of the learning in the back-home situation.[24]

In general, experienced trainers recommend that persons with severe emotional illness should not participate in laboratory training, with the exception of programs designed specifically for group therapy. Designers of programs make the assumptions, as Argyris states them,[25] that T-Group participants should have:

1. A relatively strong ego that is not overwhelmed by internal conflicts.
2. Defenses which are sufficiently low to allow the individual to hear what others say to him.
3. The ability to communicate thought and feelings with minimal distortion.

As a result of such screening, the incidence of breakdown during laboratory training is substantially less than that reported for organizations in general.[26] However, since the borderline between "normalcy" and illness is very indistinct, most professionally trained staff members are equipped to diagnose severe problems and to make referrals to psychiatrists and clinical psychologists when appropriate. Further, most are equipped to give adequate support and protection to participants whose ability to assimilate and learn from feedback is low. In addition, group members in T-Group situations tend to be sensitive to the emotional needs of the members and to be supportive when they sense a person

24/For further discussion of group composition in laboratory training, see Schein and Bennis, pp. 63-69. NTL-LABS now include the Center for Organization Studies, the Center for the Development of Educational Leadership, the Center for Community Affairs, and the Center for International Training to serve a wide range of client populations and groups.

25/Chris Argyris, "T-Groups for Organizational Effectiveness," *Harvard Business Review*, 42 (March-April 1964), 60-74.

26/Based on discussions with NTL staff members. One estimate is that the incidence of "serious stress and mental disturbance" during laboratory training is less than one percent of participants and in almost all cases occurs in persons with a history of prior disturbance (Charles Seashore, "What Is Sensitivity Training," *NTL Institute News and Reports*, 2 [April 1968], 2).

experiencing pain. Such support is explicitly fostered in laboratory training.

The duration of laboratory training programs varies widely. "Micro-Labs," designed to give people a brief experience with sensitivity training, may last only one hour. Some labs are designed for a long weekend. Typically, however, basic human relations labs are of two weeks duration, with participants expected to meet mornings, afternoons, and evenings, with some time off for recreation. While NTL Management Work Conferences for middle managers and Key Executive Conferences run for one week, team-building labs, from my experience, typically are about three days in length. However, the latter are usually only a part of a broader organization development program involving problem sensing and diagnosis, and the planning of action steps and subsequent sessions. In addition, attendance at stranger labs for key managers is frequently a part of the total organization development effort.

Sensitivity training sessions typically start with the trainer making a few comments about his role—that he is there to be of help, that the group will have control of the agenda, that he will deliberately avoid a leadership role, but that he might become involved as both a leader and a member from time to time, etc. The following is an example of what the trainer might say:

> This group will meet for many hours and will serve as a kind of laboratory where each individual can increase his understanding of the forces which influence individual behavior and the performance of groups and organizations. The data for learning will be our own behavior, feelings, and reactions. We begin with no definite structure or organization, no agreed-upon procedures, and no specific agenda. It will be up to us to fill the vacuum created by the lack of these familiar elements and to study our group as we evolve. My role will be to help the group to learn from its own experience, but not to act as a traditional chairman nor to suggest how we should organize, what our procedure should be, or exactly what our agenda will include. With these few comments, I think we are ready to begin in whatever way you feel will be most helpful.[27]

The trainer then lapses into silence. Group discomfort then precipitates a dialogue which, with skilled trainer assistance, is typically an intense but generally highly rewarding experience for group members. What goes on in the group becomes the data for the learning experience.

Interventions by the trainer will vary greatly depending upon the purpose of the lab and the state of learning on the part of the participants. A common intervention, however, is to encourage people to focus on and own up to their own feelings about what is going on in the group, rather than to make judgments about others. In this way, the participants begin to have more insight into their own feelings and to understand how their behavior affects the feelings of others.

While T-Group work tends to be the focal point in human relations labora-

27/Ibid., 1.

tories, laboratory training typically includes theory sessions and frequently includes exercises such as role playing or management games.[28] Further, family labs of subunits of organizations will ordinarily devote more time to planning action steps for back on the job than will stranger labs.

Robert J. House has carefully reviewed the research literature on the impact of T-Group training and has concluded that the research shows mixed results. In particular, research on changes as reflected in personality inventories is seen as inconclusive. However, studies which examine the behavior of participants upon returning to the job are generally more positive.[29] House cites six studies, all of which utilized control groups, and concludes: *All six studies revealed what appear to be important positive effects of T-Group training. Two of the studies report negative effects as well . . . all of the evidence is based on observations of the behavior of the participants in the actual job situations. No reliance is placed on participant response; rather, evidence is collected from those having frequent contact with the participant in his normal work activities.*[30]

John P. Campbell and Marvin D. Dunnette,[31] on the other hand, while conceding that the research shows that T-Group training produces *changes in behavior,* point out that the usefulness of such training in terms of *job performance* has yet to be demonstrated. They urge research toward "forging the link between training-induced behavior changes and changes in job-performance effectiveness."[32] As a summary comment, they state: *. . . the assumption that T-Group training has positive utility for organizations must necessarily rest on shaky ground. It has been neither confirmed nor disconfirmed. The authors wish to emphasize . . . that utility for the organization is not necessarily the same as utility for the individual.*[33]

At least two major reasons may account for the inconclusiveness of research

28/For a description of what goes on in T-groups, see Schein and Bennis, pp. 10-27; Bradford, Gibb, and Benne, pp. 55-67; Dorothy S. Whitaker, "A Case Study of a T-Group," in Galvin Whitaker, ed., *T-Group Training: Group Dynamics in Management Education,* A.T.M. Occasional Papers (Oxford: Basil Blackwell, 1965), pp. 14-22; Irving R. Weschler and Jerome Reisel, *Inside a Sensitivity Training Group* (Berkeley: University of California, Institute of Industrial Relations, 1959); and William F. Glueck, "Reflections on a T-Group Experience," *Personnel Journal,* 47 (July 1968), 501-504. For use of cases or exercises based on research results ("instrumented training") see Robert R. Blake and Jane S. Mouton, "The Instrumented Training Laboratory," in Irving R. Weschler and Edgar H. Schein, eds., *Five Issues in Training* (Washington: National Training Laboratories, 1962), pp. 61-76; and W. Warner Burke and Harvey A. Hornstein, "Conceptual vs. Experimental Management Training," *Training and Development Journal,* 21 (December 1967), 12-17.

29/Robert J. House, "T-Group Education and Leadership Effectiveness: A Review of the Empiric Literature and a Critical Evaluation," *Personnel Psychology,* 20 (Spring 1967), 1-32. See also Dorothy Stock, "A Survey of Research on T-Groups," in Bradford, Gibb, and Benne, pp. 395-441.

30/House, ibid., pp. 18-19.

31/John P. Campbell and Marvin D. Dunnette, "Effectiveness of T-Group Experiences in Managerial Training and Development," *Psychological Bulletin,* 70 (August 1968), 73-104.

32/Ibid., 100.

33/Ibid., 101. See also the essays by Dunnette and Campbell and Chris Argyris in *Industrial Relations,* 8 (October 1968), 1-45.

on the impact of T-Group training on job performance. One reason is simply that little research has been done. The other reason may center around a factor of cultural isolation. To oversimplify, a major part of what one learns in laboratory training, in my opinion, is how to work more effectively with others in group situations, *particularly with others who have developed comparable skills.* Unfortunately, most participants return from T-Group experiences to environments including colleagues and superiors who have not had the same affective (emotional, feeling) experiences, who are not familiar with the terminology and underlying theory, and who may have anxieties (usually unwarranted) about what might happen to them in a T-Group situation.

This cultural distance which laboratory training can produce is one of the reasons why many behavioral scientists are currently encouraging more than one person from the same organization to undergo T-Group training and, ideally, *all* of the members of a team and their superior to participate in some kind of laboratory training together. The latter assumes that a diagnosis of the organization indicates that the group is ready for such training and assumes such training is reasonably compatible with the broader culture of the total system.

Conditions and Techniques for Successful Organization Development Programs. Theory, research, and experience to date suggest to me that *successful* OD programs tend to evolve in the following way and that they have some of these characteristics (these statements should be considered highly tentative, however):

There is strong pressure for improvement from both outside the organization and from within.[34]

An outside behavioral scientist-consultant is brought in for consultation with the top executives and to diagnose organizational problems.

A preliminary diagnosis suggests that organization development efforts, designed in response to the expressed needs of the key executives, are warranted.

A collaborative decision is made between the key client group and the consultant to try to change the culture of the organization, at least at the top initially. The specific goals may be to improve communications, to secure more effective participation from subordinates in problem solving, and to move in the direction of more openness, more feedback, and more support. In short, a decision is made to change the culture to help the company meet its organizational goals and to provide better avenues for initiative, creativity, and self-actualization on the part of organization members.

Two or more top executives, including the chief executive, go to laboratory training sessions. (Frequently, attendance at labs is one of the facts which precipitates interest in bringing in the outside consultant.)

34/On this point, see Larry E. Greiner, "Patterns of Organization Change," *Harvard Business Review,* 45 (May-June 1967), 119-130.

Attendance in T-Group program is voluntary. While it is difficult to draw a line between persuasion and coercion, OD consultants and top management should be aware of the dysfunctional consequences of coercion (see the comments on authentic behavior below). While a major emphasis is on team-building laboratories, stranger labs are utilized both to supplement the training going on in the organization and to train managers new to the organization or those who are newly promoted.

Team-building sessions are held with the top executive group (or at the highest point where the program is started). Ideally, the program is started at the top of the organization, but it can start at levels below the president as long as there is significant support from the chief executive, and preferably from other members of the top power structure as well.

In a firm large enough to have a personnel executive, the personnel-industrial relations vice president becomes heavily involved at the outset.

One of two organizational forms emerges to coordinate organization development efforts, either (a) a coordinator reporting to the personnel executive (the personnel executive himself may fill this role), or (b) a coordinator reporting to the chief executive. The management development director is frequently in an ideal position to coordinate OD activities with other management development activities.

Ultimately, it is essential that the personnel-industrial relations group, including people in salary administration, be an integral part of the organization development program. Since OD groups have such potential for acting as catalysts in rapid organizational change, the temptation is great to see themselves as "good guys" and the other personnel people as "bad guys" or simply ineffective. Any conflicts between a separate organization development group and the personnel and industrial relations groups should be faced and resolved. Such tensions can be the "Achilles heel" for either program. In particular, however, the change agents in the organization development program need the support of the other people who are heavily involved in human resources administration and vice versa; what is done in the OD program needs to be compatible with what is done in selection, promotion, salary administration, appraisal, and vice versa. In terms of systems theory, it would seem imperative that one aspect of the human resources function such as any organization development program must be highly interdependent with the other human resources activities including selection, salary administration, etc. (TRW Systems is an example of an organization which involves top executives plus making the total personnel and industrial relations group an integral part of the OD program.[35])

35/See Sheldon A. Davis, "An Organic Problem-Solving Method."

Team-building labs, at the request of the various respective executives, with laboratory designs based on careful data gathering and problem diagnosis, are conducted at successively lower levels of the organization with the help of outside consultants, plus the help of internal consultants whose expertise is gradually developed.

Ideally, as the program matures, both members of the personnel staff and a few line executives are trained to do some organization development work in conjunction with the external and internal professionally trained behavioral scientists. In a sense, then, the external change agent tries to work himself out of a job by developing internal resources.

The outside consultant(s) and the internal coordinator work very carefully together and periodically check on fears, threats, and anxieties which may be developing as the effort progresses. Issues need to be confronted as they emerge. Not only is the outside change agent needed for his skills, but the organization will need someone to act as a "governor"—to keep the program focused on real problems and to urge authenticity in contrast to gamesmanship. The danger always exists that the organization will begin to punish or reward involvement in T-Group kinds of activities per se, rather than focus on performance.

The OD consultants constantly work on their own effectiveness in interpersonal relationships and their diagnostic skills so they are not in a position of "do as I say, but not as I do." Further, both consultant and client work together to optimize the consultant's knowledge of the organization's unique and evolving culture structure, and web of interpersonal relationships.

There needs to be continuous audit of the results, both in terms of checking on the evolution of attitudes about what is going on and in terms of the extent to which problems which were identified at the outset by the key clients are being solved through the program.

As implied above, the reward system and other personnel systems need to be readjusted to accommodate emerging changes in performance in the organization. Substantially improved performance on the part of individuals and groups is not likely to be sustained if financial and promotional rewards are not forthcoming. In short, management needs to have a "systems" point of view and to think through the interrelationships of the OD effort with the reward and staffing systems and the other aspects of the total human resources subsystem.

In the last analysis, the president and the "line" executives of the organization will evaluate the success of the OD effort in terms of the extent to which it assists the organization in meeting its human and economic objectives. For example, marked improvements on various indices from one plant, one division, one department, etc., will be important indicators of program success. While human resources administration indices are not yet perfected, some of the measuring devices being developed by Likert, Mann, and others show some promise.[36]

Summary Comments

Organization development efforts have emerged through attempts to apply laboratory training values and assumptions to total systems. Such efforts are organic in the sense that they emerge from and are guided by the problems being experienced by the people in the organization. The key to their viability (in contrast to becoming a passing fad) lies in an authentic focus on problems and concerns of the members of the organization and in their confrontation of issues and problems.

Organization development is based on assumptions and values similar to "Theory Y" assumptions and values but includes additional assumptions about total systems and the nature of the client-consultant relationship. Intervention strategies of the behavioral scientist-change agent tend to be based on an action-research model and tend to be focused more on helping the people in an organization learn to solve problems rather than on prescriptions of how things should be done differently.

Laboratory training (or "sensitivity training") or modifications of T-group seminars typically are a part of the organizational change efforts, but the extent and format of such training will depend upon the evolving needs of the organization. Team-building seminars involving a superior and subordinates are being utilized more and more as a way of changing social systems rapidly and avoiding the cultural-distance problems which frequently emerge when individuals return from stranger labs. However, stranger labs can play a key role in change efforts when they are used as part of a broader organization development effort.

Research has indicated that sensitivity training generally produces positive results in terms of changed behavior on the job, but has not demonstrated the link between behavior changes and improved performance. Maximum benefits are probably derived from laboratory training when the organizational culture supports and reinforces the use of new skills in ongoing team situations.

Successful organization development efforts require skillful behavioral scientist interventions, a systems view, and top management support and involvement. In addition, changes stemming from organization development must be linked to changes in the total personnel subsystem. The viability of organization development efforts lies in the degree to which they accurately reflect the aspirations and concerns of the participating members.

In conclusion, *successful organization development tends to be a total system effort; a process of planned change—not a program with a temporary quality; and aimed at developing the organization's internal resources for effective change in the future.*

36/See Rensis Likert, *The Human Organization: Its Management and Value* (New York: McGraw-Hill Book Company, 1967).

17

Armstrong Cork Company*

Armstrong Cork Company has a long history of industrial training and management development. Because the company has sought to take the best of the various training aids and technologies for its multifaceted training courses, its approach has been characterized as eclectic. So has its approach to the use of behavioral science concepts.

Armstrong sent a training executive to one of the earliest sensitivity training laboratories for industry. Today it employs sensitivity training mainly to strengthen the corporate management-development staff's skills in interpersonal relations, including group-discussion leading.

To cite another example of the eclectic nature of its involvement, the company has used some form of psychological tests for about twenty years and has recently been updating the validity studies on the test batteries at several plants; but at no time has the use of psychological tests been to the point of "total saturation." Generally speaking, Armstrong has tried to adapt programs and techniques from a wide variety of sources to its needs at any given time, and there has been a continual updating of the many general and specialized courses offered throughout the company, e.g., the incorporation of "in-basket" exercises in some recent management development seminars.

As stated by the general manager of management development and plant personnel services: "We have tried to keep abreast of continuing developments of all sorts in the field of training and education. Certainly the behavioral sciences are making an important contribution now—possibly the most important contribution of all—and we sought some way to give our managers knowledge of these newer contributions in order to help the organization become more effective."

SEMINAR IN HUMAN BEHAVIOR

In taking the eclectic approach to behavioral science, almost all training programs at Armstrong have some inputs from behavioral research even though only one program is actually labeled "behavioral science": an in-house developed and conducted program called "Seminar in Human Behavior."

The impetus for this special course in human behavior actually came from the

*Source: Reprinted by permission from *Behavioral Science: Concepts and Management Application* (New York: The Conference Board, Inc., 1969), 87-92.

higher-level managers themselves as a result of a company-wide survey of managers on their future training needs in their respective organizations. Armstrong felt that a wealth of behavioral research has a direct bearing on the manager's job, but that most of the research findings suffered from an important weakness: jargon and overtechnical reporting. As stated by one Armstrong manager: "There's nothing mysterious about behavioral research, but so much of it is couched in a self-perpetuating jargon that frightens most managers. But it can be understood if translated properly—not only understood but directly applied to their jobs."

So the general manager of management development and plant personnel services set out to find someone who could "examine and evaluate existing research, analyze and sift the data, and translate it into the language of business." He found and hired a psychologist for the job in 1965.

Cull and Translate

Once he joined the staff, the psychologist, in collaboration with the employee relations research department, began reviewing research reports ranging from the Hawthorne studies to recent research in job satisfaction and job enrichment. His first task was to cull from the complete research writings the essentials of the problem in each study, describe the method of research, and condense the research findings into a summary of the most pertinent details. He then set about translating or transliterating each study into understandable business terminology.

The studies he selected covered a wide range of management concerns and several facets of individual and group behavior. Initially, seven pieces of research were selected to form the nucleus for a seminar based on behavioral research, and the data to be presented were placed on transparencies for slide projection, along with a recorded narrative.

Classic Studies

The seven studies include, for example, Frederick Herzberg's 1957 research on identifying factors in the work situation that lead to employee satisfaction or dissatisfaction. This research found that factors that produce job satisfaction tend to be separate and distinct from the factors that produce job dissatisfaction. That is, satisfying factors in the job are not the polar opposites of dissatisfying factors, but are discrete entities. It was out of these studies that Herzberg developed his now famous Motivation-Hygiene Theory.

Another in the series is a condensation and adaptation of the study by the University of Michigan's Institute for Social Research of the effect of leadership (and leadership style) on productivity, which was performed on first-line supervisors on the Chesapeake and Ohio Railroad in 1947. Basically the study found that high-producing foremen tended to regard the attainment of productivity as a problem of human motivation, and, therefore, conceived themselves primarily as motivators; these high producers also spent most of their time and energy in actual supervision. The low-producing foremen tended to do little supervision—in the sense of managing—but worked along with the men, doing the same tasks, and spending relatively little time in work planning or managing.

From the original conception of the format through the graphics and production work, all of the materials were prepared in-house. The central management development staff also prepared a leader's guide and a workbook for each of the participants. The workbooks contain, in addition to summaries of the materials covered in the slides, general readings from some of the better known behavioral science literature, such as Douglas McGregor's *The Human Side of Enterprise* and Rensis Likert's *New Patterns of Management* as well as background readings related to the specific pieces of research, and a series of questions about managing human resources.

Each of the studies is prefaced with an overview and summary of the research report. Exhibit 1, for example, is based on specifics and details of the problem,

EXHIBIT 1
ARMSTRONG CORK COMPANY
Summary of "Overcoming Resistance to Change"

Problem

One of the most serious production problems faced by a clothing manufacturing company was the resistance of its production workers to necessary changes in methods and jobs. This resistance expressed itself in several ways, such as:

1. Grievances about piece rates that went with new methods
2. High turnover
3. Low efficiency
4. Restriction of output
5. Strong hostility toward management

Study

Because of these problems, management decided to conduct a research study to find out what could be done to overcome this resistance. This study included the use of two procedures in handling work groups to be transferred to new jobs:

I. The first procedure involved *participation through group representatives* of the employees in designing the changes to be made in the jobs.
II. The second procedure consisted of *total participation by all the employees* in the group in designing the changes to be made in the jobs.
III. The production records of these two groups were later compared with the record of a third group that had been transferred in the usual way: this group had not participated either totally or through representatives in designing the changes in the job to which they were transferred.

Results

The most important finding of this comparison was that the employees who had *all participated* in designing the job to which they were transferred *learned the new job faster, had fewer grievances, less turnover, and higher efficiency* than was the case among the employees who were handled through either the use of group representatives or through the usual method.

*Based on a study by Lester Coch and J. R. P. French: "Overcoming Resistance to Change."

and research methods. The principal results are then presented on slides (see Exhibit 2). Next questions about the implications of the research results and their relevance to the day-by-day managing at Armstrong are projected (see Exhibit 3). These questions serve as a kick off for general discussion.

Although the specific research studies form the central part of the seminars, Armstrong's management development staff felt that other materials on human behavior would add to the effectiveness of the seminar by giving the participants a broader view of the field and its contribution to the world of work. In addition to the excerpts from popular books and essays, films were added to the program. These include "The Eye of the Beholder,"[1] which is designed to encourage participants to examine how they arrive at judgments about other people; two films from the "Dynamics of Leadership" series,[2] which encourage analysis of the structure and behavior of groups; and "Something to Work For,"[3] which is geared to trigger introspection and self-evaluation of the individual's leadership style.

With the first seminars packaged, the management development staff was ready to begin giving the Seminar in Human Behavior in late 1966. It was

EXHIBIT 2
ARMSTRONG CORK COMPANY
Typical Sample of Sequence of Slides–"Overcoming Resistance to Change"

Slide 18

In summary, resistance to change among the employees was interpreted to be the result of a combination of individual reactions to frustration and strong forces of group loyalty. On the basis of this interpretation, management felt that the best methods for overcoming resistance to change would be group methods. These involved three procedures for handling work groups to be transferred to new jobs. Here is what was done:

Slide 19

Group One was transferred in the way that had usually been used before . . .

Slide 20

Group Two underwent a procedure that involved the use of group representatives in planning the changes to be made in the jobs to which they were to be transferred.

Slide 21

In Group Three, *all* of the members of the group participated in designing these changes. Let's see how these procedures worked, starting with the group that was transferred in the usual way.

Slide 22

As usual, the job was modified by the production department, and a new piece rate was set. Then a meeting was held in which the group was told that the change was necessary because of competitive conditions. These explanations were made by the time study man . . . questions were answered . . . and the meeting dismissed.

1/Stuart Reynolds Films.
2/Produced for National Educational Television by Malcolm Knowles.
3/Roundtable Films.

EXHIBIT 3
Sample Questions Posed to Begin Discussion—"Overcoming Resistance to Change"

Discussion Questions

1. What are some of the characteristics of industry that make changes in products and methods of doing things necessary?
2. What are some of the reasons why people resist changes in their jobs?
3. Why do you think the total participation approach resulted in higher production than did participation by representatives?
4. Are there work situations in which participation might not be the best way of planning job changes?
5. Are there any other ways that the pajama plant problem might have been solved?

decided that the seminars would require a full three days. Some have been conducted at the general office for employees there and for sales personnel who travel to Lancaster. Others have been conducted throughout the country at various plant locations. A training specialist from headquarters usually conducts the seminar; he is often assisted by the training and development analyst who developed the program.

Before participants arrive for the seminar they have received the workbook containing background materials, summaries of the pieces of behavioral research, and case problems. When the seminar convenes the leader explains the nature of the program, its purpose, and its goals. He then begins by presenting the films and slides, preparatory to group discussion.

Discussion, as a rule, is intended to center initially around the questions at the end of the slide series, but it may be open-end, and the company trainers take a nondirective stance in their discussion-leader roles because they hope also to develop free and easy communication within the group. The psychologist who authored the series says, "We want to make people think about the dynamics of personality and motivation, so they will manage their people with documented knowledge about how people behave, instead of on the basis of 'old wives tales.' But, at least as important as giving them this information, is the need for them to conceptualize their jobs by gaining insight into themselves and how their behavior affects others. It is only by accomplishing the latter that managers actually become more effective, for information at the intellectual level is not the same as an understanding of themselves and a sensitivity to other people."

From Classroom to Job

At least one built-in feature of the seminar, "team projects," is geared to help participants to observe the group behavior and the interaction of the individuals who constitute the group, and, at the same time, to come to grips with "people problems" as they might exist back on the job. As part of preseminar preparation, each participant outlines an on-the-job problem involving relationships among people and brings the problem with him to the course. Early in the program, participants are divided into small groups of five or six persons. Their assignment requires them to function as a task force—one hour each of the three days—while they do the following:

(1) Choose one of the five or six problems represented in the group
(2) Analyze the interpersonal and organizational aspects of the problem
(3) Develop the ramifications of each solution presented—the pros and cons, the relative values, and the concomitant problems that might develop should any of the solutions be adopted—and give this estimation of how the organization involved would receive each solution.

Solutions developed represent group consensus before they are presented at a plenary session at the end of the seminar. The jobs of the task forces, coupled with the "Dynamics of Leadership" films and other parts of the seminar, are oriented toward observation of behavioral interaction as a group works toward problem identification and solution. This orientation is demonstrated as each group presents and defends its solutions at the final session.

Mixed Groups

Armstrong's plant and office managers select participants for the Seminar in Human Behavior, and whether or not a particular unit will make use of the seminar for its management personnel is left up to the local manager. Thus, the corporate "teaching" staff works "on call" like consultants. The composition of the attendees at any given seminar is heterogeneous: more than one plant has been represented, and usually there are many levels of management in each seminar. (A seminar group may be composed of a plant manager, office staff, line foremen, and a staff department head.) According to one training executive, this seminar is the first company training course in some twenty years made up of truly vertical organizational groups.

Since the inception of the Seminar in Human Behavior in late 1966, Armstrong has conducted 36 sessions. There have been about 720 graduates. Five of the six plants participating so far have been "completely exposed," which means that every manager at these plants has attended a Seminar in Human Behavior.

Program Expansion

Armstrong views the Seminar in Human Behavior, not so much as a *fait accompli* or a one-shot training effort, as the beginning of a continuing program of company applications of behavioral concepts. So far, Armstrong reports, the seminars have met with tremendous success and managers are asking for more assistance from the corporate staff in digging deeper into the field of behavioral research as it relates to the management function.

The corporate development staff is responding by expanding its coverage of the company through the seminars.

In the meantime, plans are under way to develop a more advanced course for managers who are graduates of the original seminar. For example, Armstrong recently acquired from the Bureau of National Affairs its Saul Gellerman film series to serve as the core of the follow-up course. The course will deal with more specific motivational and communication problems; and it is expected that a modified sensitivity training method will characterize future seminars. And, finally, the central development group plans to do in-house research on subsequent seminar groups on the relationship between human behavior training and subsequent job satisfaction, productivity, and managerial effectiveness.

18

Hotel Corporation of America*

The Hotel Corporation of America is a relatively young company, both from the standpoint of the organization's history and from the standpoint of the average age of its managers. Formed in 1956, HCA has gone through a period of acquiring independently owned hotels, divesting itself of other hotels, building new hotels and motor hotels both in the United States and overseas, and enlarging its consumer food activities.

The collection of operations that eventually coalesced into what is now Hotel Corporation of America represents a wide range of management styles and a variety of operating approaches. There was, among these components little sense of belonging to a larger organization. Part of this situation is attributable to the history of the firm, which was a loose collection of separate operations in the past. Part of it was also a built-in problem in this kind of business—or what one vice president later termed the "hotel management syndrome," which to him connotes management of an autocratic nature, among other things. The situation that HCA found itself in could be called a natural outgrowth of the essentially entrepreneurial atmosphere that has traditionally characterized the business.

With the formation of the HCA organization, it was decided that the company would be decentralized, but it was also felt that each separate component and the total organization could derive benefits from an integrated strategy for managing, as well as from combining efforts in such specific areas as purchasing, marketing, finance, and management development. The real problem was how to do it—how to impress on the organization's managers that they were, indeed, now part of an organization with common purposes; moreover, as members of this organization they had to learn to work together for their common good.

Need for Integration

Preliminary concern over the organization's future influenced top management to begin studying the underlying problems that exist when a loosely structured collection of separate operations becomes a corporate entity, along with those problems that may either result from the amalgamation or be aggravated by it. The company's approach to its own "organizational diagnosis," as well as its subsequent organizational improvement efforts, was initiated and

*Source: Reprinted by permission from *Behavioral Science: Concepts and Management Application* (New York: The Conference Board, Inc., 1969), 106-12.

influenced by contemporary behavioral research–haltingly at first but increasingly as the activity progressed.

The initial spark of interest in the behavioral sciences was generated when HCA's president attended a two-day seminar that the late Douglas McGregor held in 1955 for a small group within the Young Presidents' Organization. Here McGregor explored with the young presidents his "Theory Y" concept and its implications. HCA's president recalled, "I guess I realized then that Theory Y represented more than a series of programs or gimmicks, and that it had to be a way of life." He remembers that he felt he would like the new HCA to be a Theory Y company, but he added, "I really didn't know what to do with Theory Y."

The president's impression of the newly formed company was that of an organization with the traditional values of "Theory X," and, moreover, with more than the usual amount of "win-lose" attitudes. (One vice president agreed with his evaluation and ascribed the existing situation to "the in-keeper mentality.")

After exposure to McGregor's Theory Y, the president tried to put into practice one of the theory's principles, namely open communication within the system to gain commitment and involvement. As the president perceived the situation in HCA, many of the firm's problems were related to the lack of communication among its managers. The most glaring lack of communication appeared to be between the central office staff and the operating executives at the various hotels.

Meetings Not Enough

The president had been holding quarterly management meetings that brought together both corporate staff and operations executives. These meetings were designed to give top management an opportunity to report on the current state of affairs and to give both management segments–line and staff–an opportunity to participate in planning and decision making. Although these managers met together regularly, it was apparent to the president that the meetings were not accomplishing their purpose. In fact, the president reports, they often increased the competition and antagonism that already existed between these two groups of managers. At the very least, the meetings had not helped the managers to open up and communicate with each other. Listening with the "third ear" the president heard the corporate staff complaining that line managers, instead of finding ways to put into effect new ideas or improvements, purposely found reasons against them. Furthermore, corporate staff members complained that, in some hotels, they were not able to deal with their counterparts at all, since the general managers of these hotels required that corporate staff communicate and deal with the operations personnel *only* through the general manager.

On the other hand, the general managers complained that the corporate men only created "confusion." They called it "interference in local matters on the part of people who do not know our particular problems." In everyday practice, some general managers had gone so far as to bar central staff from their hotels unless the general manager himself specifically requested their assistance.

Although these feelings of mutual resentment came through at the quarterly management meetings, they were usually expressed in the form of defensiveness and complaining. There was no evidence that the managers could, or would, deal openly and objectively with the underlying problems and their causes.

Entrepreneur versus Organization Man

This stand-off at the top between the essentially entrepreneurial general managers and the essentially organization-minded men from the corporate staff filtered downward in the firm, according to the president. As a result, a second major area of communication difficulties was identified by the president: relationships involving the hotel general managers and the next level of supervision. The president stated that based on his observations of the hotels in operation, there was a tendency among the general managers to keep information "close to the chest," sometimes even when that information was vital to the hotel's operation. The social distance between general managers and second-level managers was reinforced in a number of other ways. One of the most illustrative was the matter of compensation. For example, general managers' salaries were about 100 percent more than the salaries of the next level of managers.

These problems within HCA, along with related ones, seemed insurmountable to the young president, since they appeared to be a part of the basic fabric of the organization. Still trying to put his understanding of Theory Y into practice, he persisted in holding management meetings—despite the fact that he realized he was having little success in developing a team concept among the managers.

In the third year of his presidency, something happened to shed some new light on the situation. He attended a "laboratory" workshop (a form of sensitivity training) in the spring of 1958. He relates, "It was an emotionally jarring experience for me. . . . Among many things, I learned a lot about myself and about the ways groups work. In trying to relate the experience to the organization I headed, I realized that I had been trying to work with our managers as a group, when a group didn't exist." He continues, "I'd been trying to get them to communicate honestly and openly and objectively and that, in itself, was probably perceived as manipulative. What was missing was the essential ingredient of a true group: trust."

At the workshop, HCA's president discussed the company's difficulties, as he saw them, with a management consultant who was a trainer for the laboratory. Concurring with the manager's opinion that the company's problems were probably both organizational and interpersonal, the consultant agreed to enter the picture as a diagnostician working toward eventual organizational improvement.

Tackle Communication Problems First

The consultant and an associate began their work by holding extensive and intensive interviews throughout the organization and with varying management levels. Anonymity of the respondents was assured; furthermore, to ensure accuracy, the consultants fed back to each manager what he had reported. During the interviews, which were unstructured, managers were asked to talk about any problems that they saw within the corporation. As had been assumed, most of the problems boiled down to communication. The two consultants categorized these data into five problem areas:

(a) Communication between the president and subordinates
(b) Line/staff communications
(c) Location of decision making
(d) Official communication procedures
(e) Confusion over roles.

Armed with these data and analyses, the consultants met with the top management of HCA at an off-site three-day conference. Management was represented by the president, the central staff heads, and the general managers of the hotels. Initially the consultants systematically fed back the material they had obtained through their interviews, stressing the above-mentioned areas of concern as well as relevant individual comments about dissatisfaction with the organization. It took half a day merely to report their findings.

After receiving the consultants' report, the group set mutually agreeable priorities for dealing with the problems. They began to explore the possible causal factors in each of the problem areas, which included areas of conflict between individuals as well as general areas of conflict between the various segments of the corporation.

Throughout this meeting, the method of operation had been similar to that of a laboratory session. The members of the group were encouraged to deal openly with the information before them and to level with each other about their feelings. Furthermore, once they had presented their initial report, the consultants played an essentially nonparticipative role. However, in keeping with their posture of lab trainers, they reflected from time to time what was happening on the interpersonal level as it happened.

Reaction to Initial Session

Participants described this first meeting in such terms as "active," "volatile," and "tiring," but the consensus was that the time had been well spent, inasmuch as they had finally begun to get at the root causes of their organizational problems. Still they felt that this conference had been only a beginning and that some device was needed to carry them from this beginning into a long-range and continuing development program. Since it was also the consensus that, for the first time, they had begun to function as a working team, they decided to adopt the same general format at future sessions.

They had decided to develop themselves and their organization through a mechanism rooted in behavioral sciences.

This first meeting, for example, had been essentially a laboratory training session: the conference was held in a place away from work; it involved face-to-face confrontation on issues and feelings; the ground rules called for objectivity and leveling; the learning that took place was accomplished by the group itself, both in decision making and in interpersonal activities; the benefit that, the participants felt, was derived from the conference was believed to be the result of group interaction; and the sessions had made use of trainers as resource persons and analysts of what took place in the group process.

That first conference was not, however, a classic laboratory, since the group dealt with specific work-related problems and made some decisions about real-life situations within their own company. These activities were in addition to learning about themselves and how groups work, which is the primary, and sometimes exclusive, aim in a *pure* laboratory session.

"Organic" OD

The term for such organizational development effort is "organic," which usually implies a laboratory workshop composed exclusively of persons from the same organization (as opposed to a "stranger lab," which includes persons from various organizations). Also, in an organic lab the participants often deal with planning, decision making, and goal setting that relate directly to their jobs (as opposed to simulation exercises, which are designed to create a kind of *general* understanding about these components of the manager's jobs). HCA decided to make its continuing organizational development program an organic one, and one that would embrace not only the top-level managers, but second- and third- and fourth-level managers as well.

As one vice president put it, "I believe any kind of development, if it is to be effective, has to be geared to the organization it is supposed to serve. We in HCA weren't interested in another 'this year's training course.'"

Top management continued to meet on a regular basis under circumstances similar to their first off-site meeting. Since they had, in their analysis of their company problems, decided that both the lack of communication and the competitiveness that existed at the top were also prevalent at middle and lower levels of management, a similar series of laboratory-oriented workshops was set up for second-level managers from both the central office and from operating hotels.

Involving Subordinates

These second-echelon managers saw the company's problems as being basically the same as those isolated by their superiors. But they added two others that had special meaning to them as middle managers: (1) they felt that they had no idea of the corporation's future plans or what opportunities for advancement might exist for them personally, since "nobody at headquarters has given much thought to our career growth"; and (2) there was no corporate-wide communication among functional groups at the various isolated hotels, nor was there much communication between corporate staff and their counterparts at the operating level.

At the end of the second-level managers' first conference, the president met with them to hear their complaints and their suggestions for improvement, thus providing them with their first opportunity for direct upward feedback to the very top of the organization. The report was presented as a consensus of the group, without identification of any individuals who may have initiated any specific point. As the consultant-trainer confronted the president with each of the group's complaints, questions, requests, and recommendations, the president responded in terms of a decision for immediate action, assignment for further study, or referral to some other source where the action had to be taken (e.g., the general managers' meeting).

Like their superiors, the second-level managers unanimously agreed that they would like to continue these sessions. They, too, decided that subsequent sessions should also be group-process centered. They were encouraged by seeing top management begin to consider their needs and take some action on their recommendations; for example, there followed increased communication with them about the over-all plans of the firm and the establishment of a more extensive personal and career development program throughout the corporation. Also to meet their need for contact with their counterparts at the other hotels and at the central office, conferences were set up for managers within each of the major functional specialties within HCA, e.g., a series of meetings for food and beverage managers, another for room managers, another for sales managers.

Now convinced that the behavioral science route was beginning to build the organization into a more integrated firm with better communication, HCA followed up by holding additional laboratory-centered conferences for the top- and second-level managers, as well as for lower-level managers down to first-level supervisors. At first these conferences each involved managers from multiple locations, but eventually they took on a "family lab" nature by holding conferences comprised of whole departments that worked together on a daily basis in a given hotel.

Variations on a Theme

Substantively, these activities represent the origins and early progression of HCA's organizational development program. These group meetings still constitute a large part of the company's organizational development efforts; however, recent variations on the theme of open communication have been adapted to focus more accurately on the state of the organization as it has grown and as it has become more attuned to the behavioral science approach to managing.

Today the laboratory-oriented meetings may take the form of "D" development groups, or they may be called euphemistically "management seminars," but their basic form and content still could be categorized as a spin-off from sensitivity training. As the organization has changed (and HCA's top management attributes the change unequivocally to the use of behavioral science techniques), the company has also used other applications of behavioral sciences to supplement its basic, in-house, "D" groups. In several instances, management personnel have attended classic sensitivity-training laboratory sessions; and the company has also made use of the Managerial Grid. One of the most notable examples of the use of Grid training was in the Motor Hotel division, in which the management of a large motor hotel went through the basic Phase 1 laboratory and subsequent team-building sessions before they were assigned to work together in opening and running the new facility.

Selection a Part of OD

In addition to sensitivity training, Grid training, HCA's organic laboratories, and other modifications of the "group process" learning experiences, the company has continued to make use of a more widely recognized and accepted form of behavioral science technology, namely clinical psychology. HCA retains a national psychological consulting firm to interview and screen candidates for management positions. The screening interviews do not include the usual battery of psychological tests; instead, they are face-to-face interviews that cover general and specific areas of an applicant's interests and personality to ascertain whether he has the potential for working effectively within the atypical atmosphere of HCA. A vice president commented on the extensive use of the psychological consultants, "We aren't looking for people from the same mold, so that's not the purpose of having a professional psychologist do these interviews. We hope, rather, to learn if the potential employee has the flexibility to change and grow with the organization. In other words, we aren't sure everybody would be happy here, and we don't know if the existing organization could work with the average man who presents himself for employment." There is then, ostensibly, a tie-in with the screening interviews and the company's longer-range personal and organizational development objectives.

The psychological consulting firm, in addition to conducting employment interviews, works with HCA management by training its executives in assessment-interviewing techniques that include clues—that are not immediately and readily observable—to the personality make-up of individuals. The final decision on any job candidate is the responsibility of the manager who will supervise the employee, so HCA uses this extra training in the technique of interviewing as an adjunct to the manager's existing skill. This practice underscores the company's philosophy of decentralization and decision making at the point closest to the decision's impact. Since a manager decides initially who will work for him, HCA delegates to him the responsibility not only for selecting his employees but also for their personal and professional development. It is a widely accepted maxim that "development is a line function." The Hotel Corporation of America has tried to put that maxim into practice. Each manager decides, in consultation with the employee, who will receive what training, as is true in more traditional firms, but the managers themselves may be the persons who give the training. It is not uncommon, for example, to find line managers in HCA actually conducting D-groups or Grid seminars.

Since its organizational development program got under way in 1958, HCA has encouraged a deeper penetration of behavioral theory into its total management philosophy and practice. And there is a widespread feeling among HCA managers that the behavioral science route has been the most effective one for the organization, both from the standpoint of more effective communication and subsequent team action to reach corporate goals.

Metamorphosis Still in Process

But most executives at HCA would concede that the metamorphosis from a Theory X to a Theory Y company is far from complete. The going has been rough in many instances, and almost every one of the division heads can site a holdout or two in their respective segments of the firm—sometimes these holdouts are executives with considerable influence at the operating level. As one vice president explained, "We've been attempting to create a new way of doing almost everything related to managing, and it would be unrealistic to expect everybody to live with these changes and become committed overnight."

Dissent and Re-evaluation

While the change efforts at HCA have hardly been in effect only "overnight," there are some dissenters even among the managers whose primary job is to oversee the OD program. In fact, the turnover in vice presidents for human resources has been high enough to make even the most traditional management take notice. A vice president for human resources who left the company recently expressed a sense of frustration in his job, though he described himself as fully committed to the behavioral science value system. He summed up his impressions of HCA as follows: "Top management is committed to a meaningful business philosophy and is trying to live it; there is a deep belief that people are important; there is a genuine desire on most people's part to improve their performance; there is an extremely open and candid atmosphere at the top." He went on to say that while, in his opinion, the company has overcome some of its largest problems, notably lack of communication and competition among its managers, it has created some new problems or ignored other already existing ones. He feels that the company's strong insistence upon decentralization "has made control a dirty word," while central office "exerts more control than it admits," thereby blurring the whole concept of decentralization.

He pleads for more "nuts-and-bolts" personnel policies and practices to serve as a more solid foundation for the more sophisticated group-process activity that has, to date, been the sum and substance of HCA's human resources program. "We have gone at this whole OD effort backwards," he says. "We first need to attend to such things as long-range planning, manpower planning, and the establishment of some systematic means of ensuring information flow of all kinds. We also need to establish more consistent policies to take care of the mundane, but necessary, operation of personnel management.

Apparently, this former vice president is not alone in his thinking about the need for HCA to devote more effort and energy toward the traditional personnel concerns, for the company is currently reviewing its policy base and developing more written policies as a safeguard against sporadic administrative practices. The company is also beginning to concentrate more on the skills training aspects of employee and managerial development. Furthermore, HCA is paying more attention to manpower planning and career-development activities, as well as attempting to integrate the company's goal setting and long-range planning with its program of individual and organizational development.

In a total view of the developing and changing corporation, this recent emphasis on the "nuts-and-bolts" aspect of management and personnel admin-istration does not represent a backing away from its surge of behavioral-science activities. Indeed, HCA is beginning to view these two facets of management and organization development (traditional and behavioral) as both necessary and complementary. As the vice president of operations for the hotel division expressed it, "We are fortunate in being a young corporation because we don't have decades of encrusted thinking and outmoded practices to fight. Maybe we should have spent a little more time on the policy and control aspects of man-aging. But until you have an open, relating group of managers these older parts of the management system may only 'tie the hands' and restrict the imagination and innovativeness of a manager. Maybe now that we've begun to evolve into a Theory Y organization, we are in a better position to know where and why we need controls, because now we can be more objective and self-critical about our problems. Without objectivity and self criticism we cannot hope to develop further."

part FOUR
Management Science
School of Management

In the fourth part of the book the management science school will be the focal point. In the previous section we saw that a major goal of the behavioral science approach to management is that of applying scientific methodology to solving the *human problems* facing management. The major goal of the management science approach is to apply scientific methodology to solving *large-scale management problems.* This major school of management has formally existed for approximately the last 20 years although the idea of applying scientific methodology to large scale management problems is certainly much older. However, it was during this period that practitioners and scholars in this field began to have a noticeable impact on decision making in various types of organizations. Finally, it was also during this period that such professional societies as the Institute of Management Sciences, the Operations Research Society of America, and the American Institute for Decision Sciences were formed.

Boundaries of Management Science

While it is extremely difficult to place clear boundary lines around the management science school, it is possible to distinguish certain characteristics. It is generally agreed that a large number of management science applications possess the following characteristics:[1]

1. *A Primary Focus on Decision Making.* The principal end result of the analysis of a problem should have direct implications for managerial action. Hopefully, the analysis will enable the manager to plan, organize, and control more efficiently.

2. *An Appraisal Resting on Economic Effectiveness Criteria.* A comparison of the various feasible alternatives available to the manager should be based on

1/Harvey M. Wagner, *Principles of Management Science* (Englewood Cliffs, N.J.: Prentice-Hall, Inc., 1970), p. 5.

211

measurable values that reflect the future well-being of the firm. An example of a measurable value would be return on investment.

3. *Reliance on a Formal Mathematical Model.* The models used by management scientists are typically stated in mathematical form. The models utilize data and variables that are needed to aid in the decision making process.

4. *Dependence on an Electronic Computer.* This is a characteristic necessitated by either the complexity of the mathematical model, the volume of data to be manipulated, or the magnitude of computations needed to implement the model.

The essence of the four characteristics outlined is that the management scientist relies heavily upon (1) systematic analysis of problems and (2) the development and implementation of mathematical models or processes. The important point to recognize is that management science *is not* management. Systematic analysis and mathematical models are only useful insofar as they are an *aid* to the manager as he performs the functions of planning and controlling. The management science approach can aid the manager faced with making production, finance, marketing, personnel, and other similar decisions only if the manager understands the various models that exist in the management scientists' "tool bag."

The management science school is closely related to both the classical and behavioral schools. First, it can be considered as a basic extension of scientific management, the forerunner of the classical managerial philosophy. It is concerned with the effectiveness of the economic-technical system of the firm. Second, as more sophisticated mathematical models have been developed the management scientist has often had to communicate his recommendations to individuals that possess a weak mathematical background. Thus, in order to implement recommendations they have had to be concerned with such behaviorally oriented phenomena as communicating effectively, motivation, and group dynamics.

Six management science oriented articles have been selected to highlight the theme of the management science approach, and the interrelatedness of the management science approach to the classical and behavioral approaches. A brief summary of the main points discussed by the authors of the selected articles follows.

In the first article William J. Vatter assesses the extent and nature of the use of operations research techniques in American companies. The author surveyed a sample of the Financial Executives Institute. Replies were received from 360 respondents. The data received enabled Vatter to ascertain the following: (1) what firms use data processing and computer equipment; (2) when operations research was introduced as a major area of responsibility in the company; (3) which operations research models (linear programming, PERT, queueing) were being utilized; and (4) the reasons for not using operations research. This article indicated that there is a genuine and growing interest among executives in operations research.

The second article in this section "Quantitative Decision Making" by William A. Ruch summarizes very clearly what a supervisor should know about quantitative decision making. The author notes that its underlying rationale is to help replace the intuitive judgment in decisions with mathematical formulations in order to make sounder decisions. He stresses the importance of managers understanding some of the more basic mathematical concepts so they may make use of them as a tool and aid in decision making. The article concludes with a short case of how one supervisor used the sources of a mathematician to help him solve a management problem.

The third article by Donald G. Malcolm focuses upon the implementation of operations research recommendations. The author stresses the importance of properly implementing a problem solution. He emphasizes that the implementation phase consumes both time and money and is often completely neglected. Malcolm recommends that the implementation function should be the operations research and development function *(OR & D)*. The *OR & D* function would entail considering such factors as the criteria for evaluation and selection of operations research projects, developing a model to accomplish the project, establishing review period for project evaluation, and monitoring the implementation of the project.

The article by William F. Pounds entitled "The Process of Problem Finding" focuses upon the problem identification issue that often faces managers. Pounds emphasizes the point that research efforts over the past 20 years have resulted in the development of effective analytical techniques such as linear programming which deal with problem solving. He believes that problem solving methods have blurred the manager's vision concerning the identification of the problem. The author reports an empirical study of the process of managerial problem finding in a decentralized operating division of a large technically based corporation. The author's analysis of this study provides the reader with a relatively simple theoretical structure for problem finding.

An excellent article by Rex V. Brown entitled "Do Managers Find Decision Theory Useful?" presents a summary and discussion of a study which deals with hints and suggestions for future users of decision theory. The experiences of a number of companies that have found decision theory beneficial and others that have been disappointed with decision theory are discussed. Before discussing the company experiences Brown concisely reviews the elements of decision theory analysis. In his review the author explains how decision theory analysis works by using a "decision tree" example. The author also cites actual examples of companies currently using decision theory analysis for problem solving. Such company examples as General Electric, Ford, Du Pont, and Pillsbury are cited. Injected in these actual examples are Brown's and the company executives' analyses of both the positive and negative attributes of decision theory analysis.

The author ends the article by offering suggestions for implementing decision theory analysis into an organization.

The final article in this section "Technological Forecasting in the Decision Process" by Daniel D. Roman is concerned with a relatively new management concept known as technological forecasting. Basically, it represents an organized approach to selectively search for information. To date its greatest application and methodology development has been military oriented. Its proponents believe it can be extremely useful in deriving strategy to guide planning, programming, implementation, control and evaluation.

19

The Use of Operations Research in American Companies*

WILLIAM J. VATTER

In the last months of 1966, an attempt was made to learn something about the extent and nature of the use of operations research techniques in American companies. Inquiry forms were sent to the entire membership of the Financial Executives Institute, asking for information about OR activities within their companies. The choice of this broadside approach, as compared with a selected sample, was in part a matter of cost; but it was more intended to make it easy for any firm in the entire group of companies to contribute whatever information it could, under the protection of anonymity—for no attempt was made to identify respondents or companies.

There were some risks involved in this approach—for one thing, it is not unusual for a company to have more than one official who is a member of FEI, and it is therefore possible that more than one response could have been made for a given company. Comparison of the replies suggests that this is not the case, except that there may be certain autonomous divisions whose officers did reply separately. No one of the replies is in any sense a duplication of data shown on some other form; it seems fairly clear that the respondents took some steps to decide who should respond for the firm. Some of the replies were completed in part by a person other than the respondent—some associate or staff assistant who was more intimately concerned with OR methods and problems. But the forms were carefully filled in by people who knew and were interested in the issues; the way in which they rated their own results exhibited an objective and considered evaluation.

Other risks in such an approach were the obvious ones of getting a disproportionate number of replies from some one industry, geographic area, or an otherwise biased sample. It is possible that replies were made only by those companies sufficiently interested to contribute—because they had had such experience or encountered problems that could be dealt with by OR tools. It is also possible that other companies that had similar experience or interest did not reply because they preferred not to disclose what might easily be regarded as

*Source: Reprinted by permission from *The Accounting Review* (October, 1967), 721-30.

215

confidential information. But the approach used was intended to collect as much information as could be had by the most open and unrestricted means.

Replies were received from 360 respondents. This seems a very small number, when one considers that some 3,500 companies were represented in the original list. The size of the response makes it difficult to generalize from the reported information. Whether the failure to respond was because of reticence or preoccupation, or whether the non-responses merely indicate that those companies had no experience or interest in the subject, is impossible to establish. The attempt to preserve confidence by anonymity in the original approach made it difficult to engineer any kind of follow-up. However, the writer did make an attempt to re-check, by sending personal letters to that official deemed to be most concerned with such issues in each of 38 randomly selected companies. This letter indicated the concern of the writer about the limited reply, and asked as a special concession whether certain specified reasons had something to do with non-response, or whether the company had indeed replied to the inquiry. This correspondence revealed little to assist in the interpretation. Twenty-four of the thirty-eight letters evoked no response whatever. Of the fourteen who responded, four said they had not seen the inquiry form, six stated they made no use of OR techniques, three stated the form had been sent in, and one said that a reply had been intended, but was prevented by the pressure of other duties.

From this, one may gather some feeling that the ten percent response actually means that only a limited number of firms are using OR techniques or are interested in their use. For whatever reason, roughly only eleven percent of the thirty-eight addresses showed interest enough to get an inquiry form filled out, which is what was shown by the original approach. The agreement of the sample results with those of the overall survey suggests to the writer that any other approach would not have yielded much different results. This report therefore summarizes the 360 replies for what they are—the reports and comments of 360 people who were moved to contribute data. To those 360, the writer is indebted for whatever information may be contained in the results. To the others, he offers apologies for imposing on their time.

Company Classifications

The respondent group presents a fairly wide distribution by company size and industry affiliation. Using as the measure of size the gross revenues of the firm, Table 1 shows the make-up of the group. The class interval in this classification is admittedly a bit arbitrary, but it does spread the group over the range in a meaningful way.

Industry classifications are always difficult; in this day of diversification, acquisitions, and technological change, it is not easy to put a given company into the same group with very many others. But the descriptions by the respondents, and certain preconceptions of the writer, resulted in the tabulation in Table 2.

TABLE 1
Distribution of Respondents by Size
(gross revenue)

Amount of Annual Revenue	Number of Firms	%
Less than $1 million	13	4
$1–$24.9 million	64	18
$25–$49.9 million	49	14
$50–$99.9 million	45	12
$100–$499.9 million	122	34
$500–$999.9 million	37	10
Over 1 billion	30	8
Total	360	100%

The distinction between "heavy" and "light" manufacturing is not easy to draw, but steel, automobile, and machinery manufacturers are generally different from paper, plastics, wire products, and tires. An attempt to classify utilities was made difficult by combinations of service; transportation companies (airlines, railways, trucking) are included to make a group of regulated as opposed to unregulated business. Services include such things as printing, engineering, hotels, and hospitals. "Scientific" companies include chemicals, drugs, electronics, and aerospace, with petroleum thrown in because of its close affiliation with chemicals. "Consumer products" refers to the manufacturers of foods, houshold supplies, textiles, and clothing. Trading companies include wholesalers and retail chains (other than food producers), department-stores, and import-export firms. Financing companies include commercial and other banks, insurance, securities and investment firms.

TABLE 2
Distribution of Respondents by Industry Classification

	Number of Firms	%
Heavy manufacturing	56	15
Light manufacturing	38	11
Utilities, transportation	45	13
Services	30	8
"Scientific"	59	16
Consumer products	44	12
Financing	44	12
Wholesale, retail, trading	13	4
Construction and materials	27	7
Public authorities	2	1
Unidentified	2	1
Totals	360	100%

Data Processing Methods

A set of questions on the inquiry form elicited the data shown in Table 3. The respondents are generally heavy users of modern data-processing and computer equipment. Many firms use several kinds of equipment. Some lease the equipment, some own it, and many do both. 72% operate tape-driven computers, but 68% use electric accounting machines, and 57% use disc

TABLE 3
Data Processing Methods
(mentions)

Computers,	Tape	260	(Because of duplicate responses, these will add to more than 360.)
	Disc	202	
	Other . . .	62	
Punch cards	(EAM) . . .	243	(Only 24 firms do not use a computer.)
Other means		27	(Only 3 firms use neither punched cards nor computers.)

computers. Obviously, a considerable number (more than a third) use combinations of one kind or another. Only 24 firms (7%) do not use a computer (tape, disc, or card), and only 3 (less than 1%) use neither computers nor punched card systems. Many companies indicated that they were in the process of "modernizing" their data process system, to achieve better integration and more and prompter information. If equipment is a necessity for operations research, there is here no obvious impediment to OR work.

Formal OR Units in Organization

The inquiry form bore the question: "How long, if at all, has your company recognized operations research as a specific responsibility or function somewhere in the organization?" The answers appear in Table 4. It is of interest to note that the average use-period has been 3.6 years. This is especially striking, when it is noted that 36 companies have recognized operations research as a formal responsibility for 9 or more years. Table 3 suggests that there was an intensive start some years ago, a tapering off, and a subsequent growth period, which has been accentuated recently. The heavy upswing began apparently three or four years ago; but a quarter of the companies that now recognize operations research as an organizational responsibility have done so for *less* than one year. Table 4 also summarizes data about informal use and non-use of OR tools elicited from later questions in the inquiry form. As here tabulated, the figures for the group show 66% formal and 14% informal users of OR and 20% non-users. Table 5 shows the distribution of such companies (users and non-users) by size of firm.

TABLE 4
How Long, If at All, Has Your Company Recognized
Operations Research as a Specific Responsibility or
Function, Somewhere in the Organization?

Number of Years	Number of Firms
9 or more	36
8	8
7	5
6	11
5	25
4	14
3	23
2	32
1	24
Less than 1 year	59
Total formal users	237
Informal users	50
Non-users	73
Total	360

Weighted average period of use 3.6 years.

TABLE 5
Users and Non-Users by Size of Firm
(gross revenues)

Revenue Class	Users		Non-Users		Total	
	Number	%	Number	%	Number	%
Over 1 billion	30	100	—	—	30	100
$500–999.9 million	35	90	2	5	37	100
$100–499.9 million	111	91	11	9	122	100
$50–99.9 million	33	73	12	27	45	100
$25–49.9 million	36	73	13	27	49	100
$1–$24.9 million	33	52	31	48	64	100
Less than $1.0 million	9	69	4	31	13	100
Totals	287	80	73	20	360	100

Location of OR Responsibility

A question aimed at determining the location of formal OR activities educed
the results shown below. Accounting departments take a fair share of the overall
OR responsibility in 40% of the total 360 companies (62% of the users),
accounting departments are mentioned as having some part in the OR activities.

However, the responsibilities are spread fairly thin over the departmental operations. A centralized OR staff department (one that specializes in applying OR techniques) appears not to be a popular arrangement. Even if such titles as industrial engineering, information systems, and engineering (unqualified) are taken together, these represent only 41 firms, about 11% of the users.

TABLE 6
Where OR Work Is Done – Accounting, Production, Engineering, or Other Depts.
(formal recognition of OR functions)

Location or Combination	No. of Firms	% of Total	% of Users
Accounting (finance) only	48	13	20
Accounting, production, engineering	25	7	11
All departments	23	6	10
Data processing, information system	20	6	8
Accounting, engineering	19	5	8
Miscellaneous departments only	15	4	6
Accounting and production	13	4	5
Engineering only	11	3	5
Industrial engineering	10	3	4
Centralized OR department	9	3	4
Accounting and miscellaneous	9	3	4
Production and engineering	6	2	3
Engineering and miscellaneous	6	2	3
Production, engineering, and miscellaneous	6	2	3
Production department only	5	1	2
Accounting, production, and misc. depts.	5	1	2
Accounting, engineering, and misc. depts.	5	1	2
Production and miscellaneous depts.	2		
Total with formal departments	237	66%	100%
OR used informally	50	14%	
OR not used	73	20%	
TOTAL	360	100%	100%

Informal users show a similar concentration of activities, as shown in Table 7; but since some companies carry on both formal and informal activities in OR, the number of firms in Table 7 is 166; this includes 116 companies who have formally recognized departments to handle OR, as well as informal activities. Of these firms, 54% show accounting as involved with some OR activities. One rather striking bit of data is the apparent weakness of audit firm and consultant participation in OR. Only 8% of the companies (13 companies) mentioned the audit firm as a participant, while consultants (other than audit firm) were mentioned by 31% of the companies (50 out of 166). Of these, 22 associated accounting departments with the consultants.

TABLE 7
Patterns of Activity When Operations Research Is Used Informally

Combination		% of Firms
Accounting department alone	14%	
Accounting and some other department(s)	21	
One or more other departments (not accounting)	24	
Almost any or all departments (including accounting)	2	61%
Audit firm alone	3	
Audit firm and accounting department	3	
Audit firm and some non-accounting department(s)	1	
Audit firm, accounting, and some other department(s)	1	8%
Consultants alone	10	
Consultants and accounting department	6	
Consultants and some non-accounting department(s)	8	
Consultants, accounting, and some other department(s)	7	31%
Total (166 firms)		100%

Use of Specified OR Techniques

To get clear impressions of the degree to which OR tools were used by the companies, one must give some attention to the specific models or methods that are employed. These are obviously not "equivalent"; some tools require much more sophistication than others, and some are useful in only a few kinds of problems. On the other hand, the OR operator is one who uses whatever tools or models will fit his situation; what might be called an OR tool in one context is not so to be regarded in another. Nevertheless, it is possible to get a rough idea of the degree of use by counting the companies who use one, two, or more of these techniques. This tabulation appears in Tables 8 and 9.

TABLE 8
Extent of Use of Operations Research Techniques
(360 firms)

	Number	%
No use whatever	56	16
Use of one technique	37	10
Two	39	11
Three	49	14
Four	44	12
Five	34	9
Six	39	11
Seven	38	11
Eight	18	5
Nine or more	6	1
	360	100%

TABLE 9
Relative Use of Techniques, by Size of Firm
(revenues)

Revenue Class (millions)	No. of Firms	Percentage of Companies Using Indicated Number of OR Tools					
		Five or More	Four	Three	Two	One	None
$1,000	30	97	—	—	3	—	—
$500-999	37	65	14	11	5	5	—
$100-499	122	50	15	9	9	7	10
$50-99	45	13	11	30	13	11	22
$25-49	49	16	12	28	10	14	20
$1-24	64	6	13	9	19	20	33
$1 mil.	13	15	15	15	15	15	25
All	360	37	12	14	11	10	16

Respondents were asked to indicate which, if any, of the OR models or methods had been used by their company. The suggested list was:

1. Linear or other mathematical programming
2. Critical path scheduling (PERT)
3. Queueing (waiting line) models
4. Economic order size or other inventory models
5. Simulations
6. Factor analysis
7. Regression analysis
8. Statistical sampling
9. Other (specify)

This list is not a conclusive approach to decide whether or not a company is OR oriented. Economic order size models have been in use for many years; tools such as statistical sampling, factor analysis, and regression analysis could quite easily be used by firms who do not really subscribe to OR doctrines or methods generally. Critical path methods in the form of PERT are likely to be found widespread among government contractors. These tools exemplify, but do not define or establish the philosophy which is the essence of operations research.

Table 8 throws some light on the concepts of OR activity held by the respondents. Of them, 73 classified their firm as a non-user, yet some of them did actually use some of the tools—only 56 actually indicated complete non-use. But some firms classified as "users" indicated the use of only two or three techniques, some of which were of a fairly general nature. OR does not require a widespread use of many techniques; only six firms used more than eight, 24 more than seven, 62 more than six of these tools; half the companies (181) used only three or less. As might be expected, extensive use of OR techniques was more common in the larger companies. Table 9 shows the percentage of companies in each size group that make use—more or less— of the OR tools.

Extent of Use and Quality of Results

The inquiry form provided spaces to indicate whether each specific tool had been used only "sometimes" or "often"; it also provided for showing the relative success from using each tool. The replies are summarized in Table 10. The wide range of activity patterns among companies is evident, in that while 237 of the companies considered themselves "users" and 179 of them used four or more OR tools, the heaviest mention for any single tool was 226, for critical path scheduling. Relative rankings for individual tools used was not entirely unexpected. Factor analysis received the least mention; statistical sampling and inventory models received only slightly more emphasis than regression analysis and linear programming. Whatever may be one's expectations as to the use of individual tools, these figures reflect the companies' decisions as to which problems and tools were deemed most useful. The kinds of problems for which these tools were used covered a very wide range; an attempt to tabulate these by classifications would be impossible without more detailed information than could be provided in the form. One cannot look over the list of uses without recognizing the breadth and broad scope of problems dealt with.

In appraising the results of using OR tools, respondents were frank in their comments and apparently objective in their ratings. Although there was an obvious enthusiasm for the performance of models and methods, there were numerous statements indicating poor or only partially satisfactory results. Sometimes the reasons were given. In some cases, the results were uncertain;

TABLE 10
Number of Firms Using Specified Operations Research Techniques

Use				Results			
None	Some	Often	Technique	Poor	Fair	Good	Uncertain
194	113	53	Linear or other mathematical programming	8	46	86	26
134	163	63	Critical path scheduling (PERT)	10	68	122	26
279	68	13	Queueing (waiting line) models	3	28	34	16
173	115	72	Economic order-size or other inventory models	9	63	88	27
179	121	60	Simulations	5	44	112	20
305	44	11	Factor analysis	8	14	25	8
195	99	66	Regression analysis	7	46	93	19
159	127	74	Statistical sampling	2	41	136	22
313	25	21	Other	0	11	32	3

comments indicated that some applications and studies were still too new or too equivocal to be evaluated effectively. The reader may wish to speculate about some of the ratings in Table 10. The writer's impression is that the ratings reflected the respondents' reactions, rather than those of managers or operating personnel.

In this table there is reference to 46 uses of "other" techniques. These "other" techniques were sometimes extensions or combinations of the tools specified in the list, but they also included discriminant analysis, Markov chains, exponential smoothing, applications of probability theory, and heuristics.

An industry break-down of tool use is of some interest (Table 11). Obviously, the nature of an enterprise has considerable bearing on the use of particular

TABLE 11
Relative Use of Given Techniques in Industry Groups
(% of firms in industry group)

Industry	LP	CP	Q	I	S	F	R	X	
Heavy and light manufacturing	37%	56%	8%	52%	44%	10%	32%	43%	
Utilities and transportation	60	71	40	49	69	18	73	87	
Services	20	46	13	37	40	7	20	47	
"Scientific"	75	82	37	73	66	32	68	66	
Consumer goods	50	68	16	57	43	9	45	55	
Financial institutions	36	55	34	14	39	18	48	59	
Wholesale, retail (trading)	38	54	8	62	46	15	54	54	
Construction and materials	37	59	19	41	52	7	22	37	
									(Others)
All companies (360)	46%	63%	22%	52%	50%	15%	46%	56%	13%

LP = Linear Programming
CP = Critical Path Methods
Q = Queueing Models
I = Inventory Models
S = Simulations
F = Factor Analysis
R = Regression Analysis
X = Statistical Sampling

techniques, and some of the figures in this table are only what might be expected. Financial institutions would "obviously" have little or no use for inventory models, but some of them do use them! The most consistent and thorough user-industry would appear to be (as expected) the "scientific" group—drugs, chemicals and petroleum, electronics and aerospace firms. But as a group the utility companies are not far below the "scientifics." The rest do not show much difference, except that construction and materials and service operations show somewhat less use of OR tools than do other groups. Table 11 has taken into account all "sometimes" as well as "often" usages; it is expressed in percentages, to avoid awkward comparisons of dissimilar sets of numbers. But the reader is warned against a too literal interpretation of these figures, because of the wide range of factors that can be involved in the summaries. Obviously, the percentages are not additive, either horizontally or vertically; each number is an independent measure of the use of the specified tool in the given industry group.

Reasons for Not Using OR

A question was posed in the inquiry as to the reasons for not using OR. This was intended for those whose companies were listed as non-users. The figures in Table 12 show that some of the answers came from sources other than the 73

TABLE 12
Reasons Given for Non-Use of Operations Research

Inadequate access to appropriate equipment	31
Lack of sufficiently competent personnel	103
Lack of interest among operating managers	91
Not applicable to this business at all	8

non-users; the totals are reported here, because an adjustment to remove the users from the tabulation produced no significant differences. Lack of competent personnel vied with lack of interest among operating managers for the pole position in this array. It is significant that managerial apathy is almost as much of a stumbling block as the recruitment of properly trained personnel. Access to computer facilities is a reason for limited use of OR in a few cases. One can hardly restrain the observation that this is often true when a wide array of equipment is in use by the firm; further, it should be noted that availability of equipment is a hindrance, rather than a bar, to OR work. Only eight of the respondents thought that OR was inapplicable to their business. The comments on this question were largely extensions of the reasons given, or were observations about the trend of managerial and educational progress.

Special Data Requests

One frequently hears statements about the rigidity of accounting information—that accounting reports do not serve the uses they should, and that special purpose data cannot be provided by conventional systems. To get a little insight into this set of problems, there were two questions put into the inquiry. The first asked how often requests of this kind were received. Table 13 shows that special requests for information are not uncommon; 30% of the respondents said such requests were frequent, and 43% more said they occurred sometimes. Evidently the managers in these firms do not believe that accounting ends with the routine reports. However, the comments on the answers to this question indicated that many of the special requests were for supporting details or

TABLE 13
Requests for Special Data Not Ordinarily Supplied

Requests of this kind are seldom received	88
There are requests of this kind sometimes	154
Requests of this nature are made frequently	110
No answer	8
	360

breakdowns of reported information. The list of the most common of such requests included many different things which are difficult to classify. Subjects most often mentioned were: data for inventory and production control; cost estimates for special purposes such as increasing the production rate; meeting sales price concessions; the effects of price changes on product costs; profitability of different product lines; costs of starting or speeding up an operation; capital investment project analysis; "cost" of inability to deliver on time; measuring performance of administrative or technological units; projected or "what if" kinds of cost expectations; the effects of changes in selling price on the volume of sales. Evidently, the range of such questions can be quite wide—one respondent wrote, "it could be anything."

To discover what happens to such requests respondents were asked to estimate their disposition, in terms of the percentages reported in Table 14. Evidently, the bulk of all such requests are met, somehow; those that are not satisfied because of the cost of doing so are less than those for which extant systems cannot provide the information at all. Comments on this item did not indicate any other ways to dispose of requests, or any other reasons for not meeting them. However, it was clear that the respondents had difficulty in setting down these percentage replies; they were not sure that they had a good general measure of the fluctuating patterns of requests and dispositions. 118 of the respondents declined to answer, but the remaining 242 managed to have their answers add neatly to 100%. Although the range of answers on each part of the question ranged from 5 to 100%, they were fairly closely clustered about their weighted averages. These weighted averages are reported in Table 14.

TABLE 14
Responses to Requests for Unusual Information

Requests met completely without much delay	41%	
Requests met in part, or by substitution	33	
Total inquiries met in some fashion		74%
Requests not met because cost prohibitive	10%	
Requests not met because system cannot produce such information	16	
Total inquiries not met		26%
		100%

These are averages based on replies from 242 firms.

Probably these replies give no more than a very rough indication of the state of affairs. Further, there is no way to tell (even with some other set of questions) whether the requests for information are actually scaled down to the limitations of the system, or whether the meeting of requests for information actually satisfied the requester's needs. People will hardly ask for what they know is impossible to obtain; they may content themselves with inadequate information if they think there is no way to improve it. The problem is not one that can be readily solved.

The Future of Operations Research

A question that was aimed at expected future developments of OR in these firms asked for ratings of expected increase of OR activities in those firms within the next five years, between five and ten years, and after ten years. Table 15

TABLE 15
The Future of Operations Research
(How much do you think operations research techniques will increase from their present level in your company?)

	No Opinion	Not at All	A Little	Consider- ably	Very Much
(a) Within the next five years	7	19	120	180	34
(b) Between five and ten years	62	4	52	141	101
(c) After ten years	93	6	47	95	119

shows that the respondents were less willing to forecast over the longer terms; but those who did venture opinions seem to think that the short run shows less potential increase than the longer view; but even so, half the group expect considerable change within the next five years. This is in agreement with the patterns shown in Table 4 and with the number of firms that are just starting to apply OR in a serious way. The group as a whole does expect increasing emphasis on OR. Only a few say they expect no increase; a third of the group limit the increase to "a little" in the next five years; but more than half say "considerably" or "very much" within five years, and more than two thirds expect considerable or very much increase five to ten years hence. Despite the fact that a quarter of the group is unwilling to forecast beyond 10 years, only a handful (2%) saw no increase in OR for that period. The group as a whole appears confident of future expansion in OR activities.

Conclusion

The results of this inquiry do not form a basis for any set of sweeping generalizations. Most of what has been reported here is confirmation of that which many people have felt was true. There are not a great many companies doing very extensive OR work, but there is a considerable number that are doing interesting and useful things with the tools of OR, and in the context of that philosophy which characterizes the OR approach to problems. Perhaps the most pertinent overall observation is that there is a well established nucleus of interest and activity in which financial executives and accountants have a real stake; the results that are being sought (and obtained) are more than mere promise, and there is more than a dim glow in the Eastern sky.

20

Quantitative Decision Making*

WILLIAM A. RUCH

Every time you make a decision, you take a risk. If your objectives were completely clear and you knew all the ramifications of every course of action open to you, you wouldn't have to make a decision. The comparative consequences of various alternatives would dictate what should be done—and any sane supervisor would do it. Unfortunately, however, only in the most routine matters can the consequences of a decision be entirely predictable.

Knowing the risks you face, how can you make the best decision—in other words, choose the best alternative available to you? Not long ago, supervisors had to rely heavily on their intuition, feelings, and imagination in making decisions. It was their single most creative act. Management used to be more an art and less a science. Today—as a result of advances in quantitative decision making—the supervisor can reduce his intuitive judgment with mathematical formulations that help him make rational decisions. He still has to provide input and interpret answers—but the outcome involves far less risk.

Decisions that once took days in the minds of managers may now take nanoseconds in the core of a computer. But this shouldn't make *your* day any shorter. The hours saved by using quantitative decision-making techniques can now be spent on problems that are not readily quantifiable—problems such as worker satisfaction, increased productivity, ecology, and safety. The less time you spend on low-level problems, the more time you can spend on higher-level management problems. But before you can solve these higher-level problems, you should learn how to solve more quantifiable problems with mathematical techniques.

What Is Math?

Quantitative decision making is based on mathematical concepts. Before you can understand quantitative decision making, you should have a basic understanding of the mathematical processes involved. You don't, however, need to become a mathematician in order to give a systems analyst or a mathematician

*Source: Reprinted by permission of the publisher from *Supervisory Management* (January, 1974), 25-30. Copyright 1974 by AMACOM, a division of American Management Association.

enough information for them to help you solve a problem. You simply have to understand exactly how much information they need and in what form. To do this, you should understand the nature of the math involved—but not necessarily how to perform it.

Unlike chemistry and physics, mathematics is a language—not a science. Chemistry and physics are sciences because they deal with properties of the real world—and knowledge of these fields can be expanded through scientific investigation. Although mathematics is used in scientific investigation, the discipline itself exists only in symbolic representations and in the minds of those who practice it. It is based on a set number system and definitions of operations that this system can perform.

Thus, math is a system based on man-made premises. Think of it as the language that scientists use to quantify and test knowledge—and to communicate this knowledge to others.

When you were in school, did you learn that arithmetic, algebra, geometry, and calculus were all part of a single system called "mathematics"? Some people didn't get that message. Several years ago, for example, a state legislator (who shall remain nameless) proposed a bill to make *pi* (π) equal to exactly 3.0 in order to simplify calculations. Although he had apparently used *pi* at some point in his life, no one had ever told him that it was the ratio of the circumference of any circle to its diameter.

Educators today are trying to make more of an effort to teach mathematical *understanding* as well as knowledge. In the new math, for example, children are taught not only what to do but *why*. They develop a sound mathematical perspective. If you ask a youngster today, for example, whether one plus one equals two, he or she might tell you that one plus one does equal two—except in a binary system where one plus one equals ten. And this isn't blasphemy. The common decimal system (base ten) is only one of an infinite number of systems that can be used for calculating numbers. Although few people do calculations in a binary system, most computers work on a binary system and translate to a decimal system only for the convenience of those who read the output.

Most people are comfortable with the fact that two plus two equals four. They won't readily admit that this may not always be true—or that they don't know what this equation really means. Take the example of the father whose eight-year-old daughter asked him, "What's the difference between a number and a numeral, Daddy?" When he shrugged his head in ignorance, she explained that a number is a concept, like "twoness," and that the numeral is simply the symbol that represents that concept—like the Arabic "2" or the Roman numeral "II."

Children today are able to understand complicated mathematical processes that only a few years ago were reserved for graduate students—because they think of math as a second language, not a rigid set of magical and awesome laws. Don't despair if you're still stuck at the multiplication-tables or long-division school of mathematical understanding. Math is simply a set of symbols that almost anyone can understand. Try to think of it as a foreign language. When you read a mathematical section of a text book, journal article, or report, think of yourself as being bilingual.

Law students do not have to understand ancient Roman culture in order to understand the Latin phrases in their law books. Like a law student who must understand *some* Latin, accept the fact that you may have to read, write, and manage in two languages. If the meaning of a word or a symbol is not clear in either language, figure out the meaning from the context. If that fails, consult a reference book. Most dictionaries have sections explaining mathematical notations, and there are now many specialized books on mathematical symbols and formulae.

The Manager and the Mathematician

Once you can communicate and interpret some of the more basic mathematical concepts, you will be better able to work with mathematicians—who may include systems analysts, economists, or researchers working in your company. Why mathematicians? Because when you have a problem, they will be able to help you find a solution. If you can learn how to tap their knowledge, you will be able to make better decisions in half your usual time.

Let's look at the five steps in the decision-making process to see how a manager and a mathematician can work together to solve a problem. Here are the steps:

1. Identify and define the problem.
2. Develop a criterion measure.
3. Construct a model.
4. Derive a solution.
5. Implement the solution.

In certain problems, steps three and four may be: (3) Develop alternatives, and (4) choose one alternative.

You must perform steps one and two because (1) you are the only one who can recognize the problem and (2) you are responsible both for solving it and for choosing how the solution will be measured—whether in cost, time, man-hours, or some other criterion.

Then the mathematician comes into the picture. You will need his services for the third and fourth steps. Although you cannot give him carte blanche with the problem (you're still responsible for finding the solution), you should respect his expertise—as you would that of a corporate attorney or a family physician.

If you can define the problem well enough to communicate it to the mathematician, he will be able to develop a model from which he can derive a solution. Note that this is a solution to the *model,* and not to the problem. Only after the mathematician finds a solution to the model you can translate the model solution into organizational or departmental terms—temper the solution with judgment, implement it, and follow through.

Bedazzled

Some unfortunate supervisors cannot tell the difference between the solution to a model and the solution to a problem. Often the victim of this ailment, according to Herbert Simon in his book on the science of management decisions, is "so dazzled by the beauty of the mathematical results that he will not remember that his practical operating problem has not been solved."

Whenever you use the services of a technical expert in making a decision, don't lose sight of the importance of the interchanges between steps two and three and between steps four and five. You must be able to translate from one language to another and from one discipline to another. First you must be able to encode the problem so that the mathematician can understand it and, later, you must decode the model solution so that *you* can understand it. If you can't make the transition between steps four and five, you won't be able to use the mathematician's results to help you make a decision.

Both you and the mathematician should share the responsibility for communicating these transitional phases. A failure to communicate cannot be blamed on only one person. Doctors, for example, accept the responsibility for communicating their highly technical language so that their patients can understand it. Similarly, both the manager and the mathematician should make an effort to understand each other's language.

A Case in Point

Here's how one supervisor used the services of a mathematician to help him solve an important problem:

Production manager Fred Halloway had to make a production schedule for the coming week. He asked one of the operations-research people for some help. This is how he phrased the problem: "The B-26 turret lathe is down and the QC (quality-control) boys have frozen the last shipment of castings so that they can do some additional testing. Since we can't use those castings, we can switch over to the base plates for the McElwain contract, catch up on our housings production, or finish the X-101 gear covers. Should we try to do some of each to keep the sales department off our backs?"

The operations-research analyst didn't know what Fred was talking about. "Look, Fred," he said. "Let's sit down and try to work this thing out. Could you explain it in a different way?" After discussing the problem with the mathematician, Fred came up with this definition: "The company must allocate scarce resources (labor, materials, machines) to meet several competing needs (products) in a way that will maximize the total contribution—first to overhead and then, after overhead costs are met, to profit."

To Fred, it was a production problem; to the mathematician, a problem in linear programming. After receiving pertinent data from Fred, the operations-research analyst translated the problem into these symbols:

$$\text{Max } Z = 5.00A + 2.00B + 1.00C$$

Subject to:	Solution: Z = \$4600	
R: 3A + 5B + 4C ≤ 2700	A = 800	R = 0
S: 1A + 1B + 0C ≤ 1800	B = 300	S = 700
T: 3A + 2B + 0C ≤ 3000	C = 0	T = 0

Fred, of course, didn't understand the mathematician until he translated the symbols into Fred's language. The mathematician explained that A, B, and C were the real products, which contributed \$5.00, \$2.00, and \$1.00 per unit to overhead and profit. R, S, and T were the available resources, expressed as 2,700 hours of labor, 1,800 square feet of material #1, and 3,000 gallons of material #2.

The equations expressing the restraints imposed by the available resources also indicate how much of each resource is used in making each product. So, 3A + 5B + 4C ≤ 2700 means that each unit of Product A requires 3 units of labor; each unit of Product B, 5 units of labor; each unit of Product C, 4 units of labor; and that the total labor used must equal or be less than 2700 units. This is information that Fred gave the mathematician.

The solution to the *model*? Producing 800 units of Product A, 300 units of Product B, and none of Product C would yield the highest profit contribution: \$4600.00. All labor and all of material #2 would be used, but 700 square feet of material #1 would be left over.

Fred carefully considered this information. Then he decided to produce a minimum 100 units of Product C because of a special order that was coming in, adjusted the rest of the production schedule accordingly, and released it to the shop.

Neither Fred nor the operations-research analyst could have solved the problem alone. Each made a contribution to the problem-solving process—Fred at the beginning and end, the mathematician in the middle. The critical links in the process—where the operation came closest to failure—were the points at which the language of one discipline were translated into the language of the other.

Fred's approach to mathematics from the viewpoint that it was a specialized discipline, written in a foreign language, minimized much of his irrational—but natural—aversion to using math in solving managerial problems.

21

On the Need for Improvement in Implementation of O.R.*

DONALD G. MALCOLM

Several years ago George L. Parkhurst,[1] in addressing the Seventh National Meeting of ORSA, referred to operations research as "the scientific approach to the selection among alternatives under management control." He also referred to this same act of selecting among alternatives as the "essence of the executive function." Characteristically, little has been said or written about research on and participation in the implementation of O.R. results. Most operations researchers have tended to set up an operating pattern of either merely *presenting* alternatives to the manager for his decision concerning selection and implementation, or of concentrating on development of mathematics to support other staff planning groups. Indeed, in too many cases this latter pattern is the self-conscious limitation of the O.R. group's responsibility. This limitation poses a major problem to both the professional operations researcher and also to the continuing acceptance of operations research as a function in the management process. This paper is directed primarily to that class of O.R. studies aimed at the creation of new or improved systems of management information and/or control. Discussion will be directed to the following:

The Implementation Problem
The OR&D Process
An Approach in Developing an OR&D Program
Relation to the Computer

THE IMPLEMENTATION PROBLEM

Implementation Phase Not Properly Planned

The task of implementation is an important as well as time and cost consuming task that is often underestimated or even neglected in the operations

*Source: Reprinted by permission from *Management Science* (February, 1965), 48-58.
1/George L. Parkhurst, "A Challenge to Operations Research," *Operations Research*, vol. 3, no. 4 (November, 1955).

research analysis. The assumption too often is made that managing such implementation is a normal part of the management process and that the approval decision by management automatically sets the solution into operation. Such an approach to operations analysis presents the following problems to management. First, management itself must then evaluate whether the predicted gains to be made in the steady state are implementable and controllable, and secondly, *it* must make the determination of whether the transition costs—i.e., getting the solution implemented in the real world—can be amortized over the expected period of its effectivity. By "implementable and controllable," reference is made to a specific indication of the time-ordered steps and responsibilities required to make the proffered alternative an organic part of the decision-response pattern of the organization. Such an implementation plan and schedule is required in order for management to adequately assess the desirability of embarking on significant departures in its operating patterns for generally small and long-range gains in effectiveness.

In the last decade, operations researchers have learned on the one hand that dramatic short-range gains are generally not possible in well-managed companies and, on the other hand, that operations research is often too sophisticated for the problems of less than well-managed companies. So most operations research studies when implemented are directed toward achieving relatively small percentages in overall improvement which, in turn, require managerial control concepts to ensure the predicted gain in performance is actually achieved in practice. The cost of implementation of such control in all of its ramifications is often completely neglected or minimized in the O.R. report.

Growth of Diverging Interests in O.R. Practice

The operations researcher faced with this realization has two alternatives: he can either get involved in the implementation phase—*making his ideas work,* or he can direct his energies to the development and refinement of analytical tools—*getting a more comprehensive or more accurate model.* We have seen the profession move in these directions with little real communication between those interested in *theory* vs. those primarily interested in *application.* Too much concentration on the former leads to highly sophisticated models generally applicable only to lower levels of operation, which are not of real interest to nor understood by this level of management (where the problem exists). Too much concentration on application, on the other hand, can get the analyst overly involved in the particulars of a given problem generally without authority to resolve it. The analyst has only the opportunity to discuss, compromise and adapt the concept involved to the existing pattern of operation. This usually raises the cost of implementation and ensures that the predicted benefits are not realized. It is no wonder that many gifted analysts then turn more to the examination of the beauty of the analytic expression.

At this point it is worthwhile to reflect on the following conclusion:

Adaptation of the solution to meet practical considerations should have been made during the course of the O.R. study and *before* implementation was recommended. The method of implementation is a researchable subject and implementation costs are a part of a thorough O.R. study.

Measurement of Effectiveness of Operations Research Is Difficult

For the sake of discussion, we may compare operations research with physical research. At one point in the overall process of physical research, the results of the research are generally measured by a physical experiment in which the performance characteristics are determined and compared with predetermined criteria. In this, the physical world, we have learned to develop mensuration means which do not destroy the phenomenon we are attempting to measure. Or, as an alternative, the predicted effects of adding the measuring device can be used to correct the measurements taken.

However, in the world of operations research, we as yet have no good experimental method which permits real world measurements of determinable accuracy. Operations research problems usually involve people—the human factor—in one of two ways. First, the human is a "link" in the process and secondly, a human being is the manager or "controller" of the process at hand. The manager is also measured by the performance of the system under test. This added factor—indeed the central factor—makes it virtually impossible to measure results of an O.R. study in the real world environment, particularly where the desire for freedom from control is such an important factor. There is, of course, the approach of a pilot implementation to determine the bugs in the concept, but by that time full-scale implementation is either assumed or doomed.

Implementation Costs Are Generally Underestimated

Another problem in operations research studies has been the budget process. This has the impact of delaying studies until a new fiscal period, or requiring reprogramming of funds, which puts the proposed study into competition with other uses of the resource. All of this tends to force the proponents of a project to underestimate or understate the expected cost if the project is to be approved. One area that is often purposely minimized during this process is the cost of implementation of results. The costing of implementation generally neglects the fact that in reality parallel operation and redundancy more often than not occur.

Old approaches and old systems are seldom demised by plan; they die a slow and often agonizing death—if ever. This process drags out implementation and makes it costly and may even kill it by adding the cost of the redundant information system to the new system's operational cost. These costs need to be separated and controlled in the implementation plan. So we set up non-profit organizations if we're the military, or a staff O.R. group in industry, to avoid the budgetary constraints and then immediately set about to reduce the urgency of the project, letting the group virtually set its own goals and time frame for performance. "More time to think" often becomes the cry of the O.R. group which is more personally inquisitive than results- and action-oriented. Left alone and without a "development program" the group may well become completely disconnected with the organization's purpose and become more politically- or survival-oriented than desirous of creating needed change. Rationalization at this point often takes the form of recognizing the need for an "evolutionary approach" and a long-range point of view.

As a result, costs continue to rise for effecting marginal innovation. It would be useful to attempt to isolate these costs realistically for management for better control of desired managerial innovations.

The Need for an O.R. Development Plan

Faced with this situation, management loses interest, particularly if it isn't forced to take action by the power of the research and often the O.R. group itself is disappointed in a few years. Why? Largely because the research program is not fully planned and the projects within it are not connected with a requirement to implement the innovations involved. O.R. must of necessity be both research and development in outlook if its utility is to be recognized and desired by management.

Without this orientation, as Stillson[2] points out, management becomes disenchanted; the operating personnel become dubious and non-directed; the O.R. man becomes disinterested and the study will die in implementation. What is needed is a way around the budgetary constraints on project size and duration and a way to still provide the motivation necessary. This motivation will be provided if management insists on seeing a detailed, coordinated implementation plan as a part of the research project output. This plan should be realistic in terms of the required action of responsible parties affected, the steps, controls and measuring (or monitoring) points of progress that management should utilize in both evaluating the project's utility and in controlling the implementation. The plan should also include a series of milestones for phasing out redundant systems of management and obsolete organizational elements. Hitch pointed out[3] that an operations researcher should recommend policy, not merely understand and predict. To this it should be added that operations research recommendations should also include the costs and benefits of the policy as well as a plan for carrying it out. In physical R&D, for example, we

2/Paul Stillson, "Implementation of Problems in O.R.," *Operations Research*, vol. 11, no. 1 (January-February, 1963).

3/Charles Hitch, "An Appreciation of Systems Analysis," *Operations Research*, vol. 3, no. 4 (November, 1955).

have learned that we have to predict the cost and performance of development programs and to establish specific milestones or check-points for progress and outlook evaluations.

To carry this analogy to physical R&D forward, it appears that we should think professionally of our total field, not merely as Operations Research but more properly as *Operations Research and Development* (OR&D), where the concepts are carried to the point of proven operational capability. This would aid in placing proper emphasis on the totality of the process operations researchers are involved in. It would also aid in developing the proper criteria for evaluation of research results.

It is seen that the concept of OR&D includes the implementation phase. This can lead to discussion of just how far operations research goes. Aren't these last steps managerial responsibilities, or at least those of some other specialized function in the organization, like industrial engineering[4] or the controller, for example? The OR&D concept accepts responsibility for predicting the costs and benefits of the solutions, including implementation costs. To aid in communicating and/or implementing a solution, a given organization should be prepared to work in the implementation phase to the extent necessary. In some cases, this may include full responsibility, in others, merely participation in the implementation effort. We must learn to think of research and implementation as a connected process if we are to get results effectively implemented. There are a number of ways of accomplishing this.

Organizational Solutions

Since the implementation phase is becoming recognized as a major problem in managerial innovation, particularly where computers are involved, it seems that some discussion of the approach through organization is in order. Here it appears that three solutions are possible:

Add the implementation function to the O.R. group responsibility—perhaps the OR&D concept mentioned above.

Create a Management System Design and Implementation Function to take over and implement O.R. results. This should preferably report to the same head as the O.R. function and would involve mutual work efforts.

Rotate O.R. practitioners into line positions to implement their policy recommendations.

The last solution is often an effective one, particularly considering the complex nature and far-reaching effects of many O.R. recommendations. The professional opsearcher often will find it necessary to place himself in the position to implement his ideas, since they cannot be understood well enough

4/D. C. Malcolm, "The New Industrial Engineering," *The Journal of Industrial Engineering*, vol. 7, no. 6 (November-December, 1956).

nor is there enough motivation for anyone else to so dedicate himself. The case of Hitch[5] and other opsearchers who are reworking the planning, programming and budgetary practices of DOD is germane. Their activity heralds both the acceptance of the operations research approach and also the emergence of O.R. as a responsible profession interested in practical development of the research. The profession is enriched by its practitioners who are willing to guide their own ideas into effect. In this sense O.R. may be looked at as training ground for such implementation activity.

However, this function, implementation – or "organizational resynthesis," using Ellis Johnson's[6] excellent phrase for the activity–is generally not provided for in most organizations. Detailed, step-by-step plans are generally not developed, but rather a compromise, committee approach is used which results in piecemeal assignment of responsibilities for various tasks and changes required. There is generally no one project manager, as it were, responsible for seeing that the changes, the reorientation, or the new data–whatever the requirements may be that are involved in the O.R. solution–are actually achieved in a given period of time in accordance with stated criteria for acceptable compliance. The manager generally doesn't have the time or interest to do this job, and each functional group can hardly be expected to take the lead. As a result, many good ideas which are ordered into implementation just slowly get compromised into an unrecognizable confusion of committees and useless information.

The program planning, project manager approach to the design and implementation of operations research results is just as important and urgent as it is in the field of physical research.

The Lack of Proper Management Incentive for Innovation

Start-up costs for OR&D projects are generally heavy. Being system-oriented, they generally affect the requirement for facilities, equipment and manpower. In some cases the implementation can be done gradually and the cost and trauma spread out. In many cases, perhaps the more attractive ones from an overall savings point of view, the whole new system must be installed if the desired results are to be attained.

In several notable cases, the start-up costs have been so great that management profit sharing and bonus amounts are affected. This effect completely dampens the desire for the manager to spend his own personal money for future improvements. This has been the experience of several O.R. groups in profit-decentralized companies. We must find ways to reward managers on their ability to innovate and make it attractive to implement concepts which may

5/Charles J. Hitch, "Plans, Programs & Budgets in the Department of Defense," *Operations Research,* vol. 11, no. 1 (January-February, 1963).
6/Ellis A. Johnson, "The Crisis in Science and Technology and Its Effect on Military Development," *Operations Research,* vol. 6, no. 1 (January-February, 1958).

take two to three years in their pay off. Only in this way will overemphasis on short-range results be avoided. Perhaps if we could develop criteria for judging the state of managerial proficiency (which includes the quality of the management approaches, their acceptance and use) within an organization and measure managerial performance against the criteria, we could develop the incentive necessary to a better balance between short and long-range effects.

For example, decentralized management might be measured in part on the rate of installations and the use and acceptance of accepted management information systems and other practices. This would be done by a depth survey. Such an approach would be a compelling endorsement on the part of top management to the need for innovation successfully implemented.

THE OR&D PROCESS

We have discussed some of the many limiting factors in successful implementation of O.R. results. Since organizations are thought of by many as social processes and as being goal-seeking rather than controllable, certainly some argument will be offered that we cannot expect to "direct" innovation into being without major resistance. I would most emphatically agree with this point. Nevertheless, it is obvious that it *is* possible to predict the problems of implementation of desired innovations that are agreed upon and to plan for the education and controls necessary. Further, if such program planning *is* done, we may both reject nonimplementable concepts and reduce the costs of implementing acceptable concepts. This would be a positive benefit since planning is a relatively low cost operation compared to implementation.

With this in mind, let us list the steps which a successful OR&D project might be expected to take. This will be referred to as the OR&D process:

Problem Definition—stating the alternatives to be examined
Develop the Criteria for measuring effectiveness of alternatives
Select or Develop the Method of Analysis
Collection of Data for Analysis
Data Reduction and Analysis
Presentation of Alternatives, Decision
Preparations for Implementation of Chosen Alternative
    Design Information and Control Systems
    Develop System Description and Operating Manuals
    Develop System Training
    Develop Necessary Computer Program and Data Processing Capability
Pilot Implementation (full-scale if small enough system)
    Conduct System Training
    Set Up Information Flow
    Operate Data Processing
    Utilize Outputs

Measure Results of System against Established Criteria
Modify System and Establish New Cost Effectiveness Criteria
Develop Time-Phased Program for Full-Scale Implementation
Full-Scale Implementation according to Program
Periodic Management Progress Review
Update System as required

In stating the above, it is recognized that not all O.R. work requires extensive implementation effort; some supports a single decision made at a point in time; some is basic research, filling in the methodology or creating new. This portion of O.R. effort is needed and important. The remarks here, however, have been and continue to be directed toward the growing body of O.R. effort directed to helping recast the management process for more effective decision making and control. There are many indications that this will be the area of the profession that will grow as we cope with problems of communication and control.

Structuring a Program for OR&D

Enough experience in implementation has been generalized to estimate the tasks and costs involved and to relate them in proper sequence. It is obvious that this feedback to the earlier phases in the "process"—such as establishing criteria—will have an important impact on the decision to implement and on the ultimate support required and obtained. Facing up to these facts will lead to better support and less disillusionment. For example, a network plan of the implementation tasks made as part of the O.R. study will permit the O.R. group to develop a better cost estimate, a more realistic schedule for implementation and better statement of the technical objectives involved. If all the projects making up the OR&D program are then laid out with such time-phased goals, considering the tasks and cost of the development phase *before* implementation, O.R. will have a greater impact and utility.

In an established operations research and development program, one would expect then to see projects in various stages of the "process" described above. The projects will also be interrelated, and it is important to have good criteria for selecting projects in the OR&D program and to have a rationale for developing a balanced program of research, applied research and development whose progress can be periodically measured by management review. Implementation criteria should be included when selecting research projects for the OR&D program. Criteria for project selection will be discussed in a later section.

The Importance of an Adequate Training Approach

The installation of new approaches generally puts different elements of the organization in a position of needing to change their goals. For example, a well-balanced solution often will require that one part of the organization operate at less than total efficiency in order that the flow of work between functions is optimal at the total system level. Goals of this type, i.e., less than all-out performance, often are difficult to communicate. This, coupled with the fact that many of the reasons why a new solution is preferable over past operating patterns, is difficult to comprehend and leads to the need for effective training. This should be planned and provided for in the implementation plan. In this regard, the use of simulation exercises for portraying the action situation has been found helpful. It is expected that the use of simulation to aid in the understanding and acceptance of new procedures required in implementing operations research results will grow.

AN APPROACH IN DEVELOPING AN OR&D PROGRAM

In developing an OR&D program it is essential that projects be selected that represent a blending of long-range and short-range problems and of applied research and development problems. This mix is needed for the purpose of producing some results quickly enough to satisfy management and the group itself, and secondly, to work on problems of a more fundamental nature. The following procedure has been found useful in establishing a program for OR&D in both industry and government:

Establish criteria for evaluation and selection of O.R. projects
Survey problems amenable for OR&D from:
    Query of operating and staff groups
    Problems defined by management
    Potential application of techniques found successful in similar situations
Develop preliminary approach for each project
    Objectives of the study
    Type of model
    Uses of the model—How the model would be used
    Steps required in conduct of the study (typical)
        Complete development of the model
        Develop data required in operation of the model
        Use model to test effect of current policy and operational patterns
    Project economics
        Data collection requirement
        O.R. time
        Computing costs
        Savings—improved management service
    Other potential uses of concepts
    Functional organization interest in problem
    Implementation cost and schedule
Apply criteria for selection of projects
Rank projects in accordance with criteria, considering:

The capability of the operations research group
The investment deemed warranted in operations research
The proper mix of long- and short-range problems
Breadth of coverage of the organization
Select projects and lay out program consistent with desired investment.
Return-on-investment criteria may be applied
Establish review period for projects
Develop detailed implementation network for projects where implementation is recommended
Monitor implementation of approved projects
Review and modify program periodically with top management

It has been found important to spend a good amount of time in establishing the initial criteria referred to in step 1 above. The following criteria for evaluation and selection of O.R. projects have been found useful in this regard:

Potential benefits resulting from project
Savings in operating costs
Manpower
Equipment
Improvement in quality or quantity of service
Cost of the project, its implementation and operation
Cost of analysis
Availability of model to be used
Complexity of model to be used
Amount of calculation effort
Availability of computer programs
Travel requirements
Estimated cost for implementation of solution including training
Estimated operating costs of new methods of operation
Manpower
Equipment
Estimate of pay-off period
Time to achieve specified results
Service improvement
Requirements setting
Cost reduction
Ability to solve the problem
Data availability
Model state of the art
Technical know-how required
Training requirements
Extent of problem recognition
Recognized and defined problem
Current work on problem underway

Indoctrination and training requirements
Applicability to other areas of organization
Top management interest in problem
Effect on O.R. group's development
Variety of techniques, basic research
Short- long-range
Non-interference with other existing missions
Interrelatedness with other identified problems

Systematic application of these criteria to the rating of projects will permit the development of a balanced O.R. program meeting the mutual objectives of management and the O.R. specialists. In certain cases the organization must be changed to permit effective implementation. In such cases, the revised organization should be made concurrent with the start of implementation.

RELATION TO THE COMPUTER

It is worthwhile to comment that successful OR&D generally provides the logic for the necessary management information and control system to support its recommendations. As emphasis on centralization of decision making continues and the real-time control concept becomes more a reality, the relationship of OR&D to the computer programming and data processing capability will increase.

It seems desirable for these two functions to be managed from a common point of responsibility. The OR&D function should be responsible for an efficient, logical design of the system which formats the outputs for specific, not generalized, decisions. Development of such systems is truly a development process requiring easy access to computers. The data processing function is generally oriented toward efficient data processing, high computer utilization and a flexibility of outputs to meet any unexpected demands, with not as much interest in how the data is used or best used in the decision process. These necessarily different approaches can be put into proper harmony and balance through common management and joint planning for present as well as future data processing requirements.

22

The Process of Problem Finding*

WILLIAM F. POUNDS

INTRODUCTION

As a result of research efforts over the past twenty years, a number of extremely effective analytical techniques are currently available for the solution of management problems. Linear programming is used routinely in the specification of optimum cattle feeds and fertilizers. Decision rules based on inventory models form the basis for production and inventory control systems in a wide variety of manufacturing companies. Simulation is evolving from a means for doing research on complex managerial problems to a process which can provide useful information to managers on a real-time basis.

Like other technological changes, these methods raise a number of social and organizational issues within the organizations which use them, but their net contribution is no longer seriously in doubt. As a result, in most large organizations and in many smaller ones, operating managers either are aware of these methods or have ready access to help and advice in their application.

But the manager's job is not only to solve well-defined problems. He must also identify the problems to be solved. He must somehow assess the cost of analysis and its potential return. He must allocate resources to questions before he knows their answers. To many managers and students of management, the availability of formal problem solving procedures serves only to highlight those parts of the manager's job with which these procedures do *not* deal: problem identification, the assignment of problem priority, and the allocation of scarce resources to problems. These tasks, which must be performed without the benefit of a well-defined body of theory, may be among the most critical of the manager's decision making responsibilities.

This paper is concerned primarily with the first of these tasks—problem identification. It reviews some research relevant to understanding decisions of this type, presents a theoretical structure, and reports some results of an empirical study of the process by which managers in a successful industrial organization define their problems. Because this research was stimulated in part by an interest in the relationship between the so-called new techniques of

*Source: Reprinted by permission from *Industrial Management Review* (Fall, 1969), 1-19.

management and what might be called traditional managerial behavior, similarities between these two modes of management which are suggested both by the theory and the empirical evidence are briefly noted.

BACKGROUND

Prior to 1945, our understanding of most cognitive tasks within industrial organizations was not much better than our understanding of the process of problem finding is today. Inventory levels were maintained, production schedules were determined, and distribution systems were designed by individuals who, through years of experience, had learned ways to get these jobs done. With few exceptions these individuals were not explicit about how they performed these tasks and, as a result, training for these jobs was a slow process and the development and testing of new procedures was difficult indeed.

So it is with the process of problem finding today. All managers have discovered ways to maintain a list of problems that can occupy their working hours—and other hours as well. They frequently find it difficult, however, to be explicit about the process by which their problems are selected. Consequently, the development of improved problem finding procedures is difficult.

Since 1945, however, some progress has been made in understanding certain cognitive tasks in the areas of production and inventory control. Decisions rules have been derived from mathematical models of particular tasks, and in a number of cases these rules have performed as well as or better than the complex intuitive process they have replaced. The significant fact about these developments for this discussion is not, however, the economic impact of such rules, although it has been significant. Rather, it is the implication that the essential processes by which important decisions are made may be carried out satisfactorily by simple explicit decision rules which are easy to teach and execute and easy to improve through analysis, simulation, or experimentation.

Of course it is possible to discount these accomplishments by saying that inventory decisions were always rather simple ones to make. The validity of such arguments, however, seems suspiciously dependent on knowledge of what has been accomplished and on a lack of knowledge of inventory systems.

It is true, however, that mathematical analysis has been able only to suggest decision rules for a wide variety of managerial tasks. These tasks, including the definition of problems, seem to require symbols and analytical procedures not readily represented by standard mathematical forms. Some other means for discovering the decision rules by which such tasks are performed is clearly required.

Some progress in this direction has already been made. Encouraged both by the success of the analytical approach to decision problems, and by the availability of large digital computers, Newell, Simon, and others have been studying human decision behavior since the early 1950's. They have focused their attention primarily on tasks which would facilitate the development of a methodology for approaching decision situations not readily describable in mathematical terms. They have considered the decision processes involved in proving theorems in symbolic logic[1] and plane geometry.[2] They have considered decision processes involved in playing games like chess[3] and checkers.[4] They have worked on the assembly line balancing problem[5] and on trust investment.[6] The relevance of this research to problem finding can perhaps best be illustrated by considering the work on chess.

Research on Chess

Chess is a game with rules simple enough for almost anyone to learn and yet complex enough that even the largest computer cannot play it by working out the consequences of all possible moves. Chess is a game of strategy in which individual moves can not always be evaluated without considering future moves. Chess moves are inconvenient to describe in mathematical terms and few people can be explicit about how they play chess. For these reasons and several others, chess was an attractive medium in which to attempt to unravel human decision processes that could not be modeled mathematically.

Three aspects of the work on chess playing behavior are relevant to this discussion. First, simple explicit decision rules were discovered which make for very good chess play. This result has been tested by programming computers with such rules and observing the quality of play which resulted in response to the play of human experts. Second, the decision rules for chess playing were derived from observations, interviews, and the writings of chess masters. Thus, it is not necessary that simple, explicit decision rules be derived from mathematical or theoretical considerations. They can be abstracted from humans who have themselves never systematically considered the process of their own decision making. And, third, the decision rules by which humans play chess appear to be separable into three rather distinct classes: rules for defining alternative moves, rules for evaluating alternative moves, and rules for choosing a move from among evaluated alternatives. H. A. Simon has called these three classes of behavior intelligence, design, and choice, respectively,[7] and on the basis of his work both

1/A. Newell, J. C. Shaw, and H. A. Simon, "Empirical Explorations of the Logic Theory Machine," *Proceedings of the Western Joint Computer Conference* (February, 1957), pp. 218-30.

2/H. L. Gelernter, "Realization of a Geometry Theorem Proving Machine," *UNESCO Conference on Information Processing Proceedings* (1959).

3/A. Newell, J. C. Shaw, and H. A. Simon, "Chess-Playing Programs and the Problem of Complexity," *IBM Journal of Research and Development* (October, 1958), pp. 320-35.

4/A. L. Samuel, "Some Studies in Machine Learning, Using the Game of Checkers," *IBM Journal of Research and Development*, vol. 3, no. 3 (July, 1959), pp. 210-30.

5/F. M. Tonge, *A Heuristic Program for Assembly-Line Balancing* (Englewood Cliffs, N.J.: Prentice-Hall, 1962).

6/G. P. Clarkson, *Portfolio Selection: A Simulation of Trust Investment* (Englewood Cliffs, N.J.: Prentice-Hall, 1962).

7/H. A. Simon, *The New Science of Management Decision* (New York: Harper and Brothers, 1960).

on chess and other decision making situations has concluded that the process of intelligence or alternative definition is the key to effective behavior.

The work on chess and other complex tasks does not directly suggest how managers go about finding and defining the problems to which they devote their time. It does suggest, however, that tasks of this same order of complexity may be understood through careful observation of and abstraction from the behavior of human experts. It further suggests that, if useful insights into managerial problem finding can be gained, they may contribute significantly to managerial effectiveness.

AN EMPIRICAL STUDY OF MANAGERIAL PROBLEM FINDING

Since it was possible to gain useful insights into the process by which humans play chess by observing experts, it seemed likely that insights into the process of managerial problem finding might be derived from careful observation of successful managers. Arrangements were made therefore to interview, observe, and interrogate about 50 executives in a decentralized operating division of a large technically based corporation, which will be referred to as the Southern Company.

The study consisted of four relatively distinct activities. First, interviews were conducted during which executives were asked to describe the problems they faced and the processes by which they had become aware of these problems. Second, observations were made of meetings during which problems were identified, discussed, and sometimes solved. Third, investigations were made of the source and disposition of several specific problems. And, fourth, a questionnaire was devised and administered to each executive who participated in the study.

As data began to accumulate from each of these activities, it became clear that a major objective of the study would be to discover some level of abstraction which would preserve what seemed to be essential details of the managerial situations being observed and at the same time provide a structure which would convert isolated anecdotes into data from which some generalizations might be drawn. This structure will be described in the following pages together with some of the observations it explains. Observations made outside this particular study will also be reported.

Theoretical Structure

Like any number of other industrial tasks, the process of management can be viewed as the sequential execution of elementary activities. In describing their own work, executives find it easy to think and talk in terms of elementary activities like making out the production schedule, reading the quality control report, visiting a customer, etc. The attractive feature of this view of managerial work is that elementary tasks can be defined at almost any level of detail.

Clearly the task of preparing a production schedule is itself made up of more elementary tasks like collecting data on orders and labor availability, which are themselves made up of even more elementary activities. On the other hand, one can aggregate elements like production scheduling into larger units of analysis like managing production.

A choice of some level of abstraction cannot be avoided. For purposes of this study, the level chosen was that which the managers themselves used in describing their activities. Thus, even at the theoretical level, advantage was taken of the fact that the managers' language had evolved as a useful means for processing information about their jobs.

Elements of managerial activity will be referred to as *operators*. An operator transforms a set of input variables into a set of output variables according to some predetermined plan. For example, the operator "lay out a production schedule" takes machine capacities, labor productivities, product requirements, and other input variables and yields man, product, machine, and time associations covering some appropriate period of time. Since the action of an operator produces an effect which is more or less predictable, operators are frequently named for their effect on the environment. The operator "lay out production schedule" changes the production organization from one with no schedule to one with a schedule. The operator "hire qualified lathe operator" changes the size of the work force.[8]

The word "problem" is associated with the difference between some existing situation and some desired situation. The problem of reducing material cost, for example, indicates a difference between the existing material cost and some desired level of material cost. The problems of hiring qualified engineers and of reducing finished goods inventories similarly define differences to be reduced. Because problems are defined by differences and operators can be executed to reduce differences, strong associations are formed between problems and operators. The problem of devising a production schedule can ordinarily be "solved" by applying the operator "lay out production schedule." The problem of "increasing sales volume" can sometimes be "solved" by applying the operator "revise advertising budget." Since operator selection is triggered by the difference to be reduced, the process of problem finding is the process of defining differences. Problem solving, on the other hand, is the process of selecting operators which will reduce differences.

The manager defines differences by comparing what he perceives to the output of a *model* which predicts the same variables. A difference might be defined by comparing an idle machine to a production schedule which implies high machine utilization. In this case, the production schedule is the model used to define a difference. A difference might be defined by comparing a 10 percent reject rate in a department to a budgeted rate of 2 percent. In this case, the

8/Because this paper is concerned primarily with problem finding, the process of operator selection and execution will not be discussed. The definitions are included only to complete the description of the theoretical structure.

budget is the model. A difference might be defined by comparing available data to those required for a special report. The problem of understanding problem finding is therefore eventually reduced to the problem of understanding the models which managers use to define differences.

It should be noted that the theoretical framework proposed here has drawn on ideas discussed by Miller, Galanter, and Pribram,[9] who in turn refer to some basic work by Newell, Shaw, and Simon.[10] Figure 1 presents a flow chart of the process described in this section and, for comparison, the structures proposed by others.

FIGURE 1
Flow Chart of Managerial Behavior

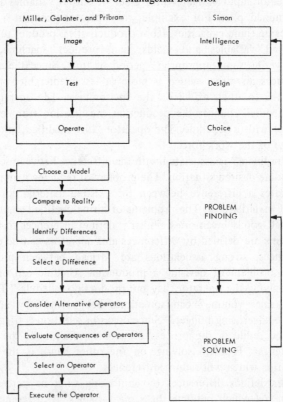

9/G. A. Miller, E. Galanter, and K. H. Pribram, *Plans and the Structure of Behavior* (New York: Henry Holt & Co., 1960).

10/A. Newell, J. C. Shaw, and H. A. Simon, "Report on a General Problem-Solving Program," *Proceedings of the ICIP* (June, 1960). Reprinted in: *Computers and Automation* (July, 1960), as "A General Problem-Solving Program for a Computer."

MANAGERIAL MODELS FOR PROBLEM FINDING

Historical Models

On the assumption that recent past experience is the best estimate of the short term future, managers maintain a wide variety of models based on the continuity of historical relationships: April sales exceed March sales by 10 percent; Department X runs 5 percent defective product; the cost of making item Y is $10.50 per thousand; the lead time on that raw material is three weeks, etc. Because the manager's world is complex and these models tend to be simple, discrepancies frequently arise between the models' predictions and what actually takes place. Such discrepancies are a major source of problems to which managers devote their time. Why is our inventory account drifting out of line? Why is our reject rate so high this week? What has happened to make so many deliveries late? What can be done to reverse this trend in absenteeism? Why is our safety record suddenly so good? All these problems and a host of others like them are triggered by discrepancies from historical models and can keep a manager and his organization busy all day every day.

For the most part these models are non-explicit. The manager "carries them in his head" or "just knows." In a number of cases, however, these models are strongly supported by routine reports. Pieces of paper on which are printed monthly P & L statements, weekly reports of sales totals, daily reports of orders behind schedule, semi-annual inventories, and many other items of interest flow across the manager's desk in a steady stream and, except in its historical context, each one has little meaning to the manager or anyone else.[11]

Recognizing this fact, most management reports in the Southern Company were prepared in such a way that current figures and recent reports of the same variables appeared side by side. Trends or sharp variations in any variable could be easily noted. The confidence placed in such analysis was clearly indicated by the fact that a large number of variables were added to routine reports following an unanticipated fluctuation in corporate profits. After several months, managers could review their history of "Return on Sales," "Return on Investment," and many other variables in addition to those previously reported.

The importance of routine reports as well as the use of an historical model to identify a problem were both illustrated when the rejection rate of one department moved past an historic high and thereby attracted attention to the Quality Assurance organization. A number of other examples could be cited. Out of 52 managers, 42 agreed with the statement that "most improvements come from correcting unsatisfactory situations," and, for the most part, unsatisfactory situations were defined by departures from historically established models of performance.

Departures of performance in a favorable direction—lower than historical cost

---

11/Budgets, which can also provide context for such data, are discussed in the next section.

or higher than historical sales, for example—were used to modify the historical model, not to define a problem *per se*. Several managers reported that better-than-average performance was frequently used as evidence of what could be accomplished when reduced cost allowances or increased profit expectations were being discussed. At the time of this study, the Southern Company was doing very well relative to its own past performance and a number of managers shared the sentiments of the one who reported, "This year is going too well." They were clearly concerned about their ability to continue to meet what would become a new historical standard. Several were already working on that problem-to-be.

Besides serving as triggers for corrective and innovative problem solving, historical models are used extensively in the process of devising plans for future operations. These plans are in turn converted into budget objectives, and the budget objectives can sometimes serve as models which trigger managerial problem solving. Because of the complex process by which they are devised, managerial planning models will be discussed separately from the more straight-forward historical ones.

Planning Models

Managers in the Southern Company devoted substantial amounts of time to planning future operations. Detailed projections of operating variables for the coming year and less detailed projections for the coming five years were presented annually to corporate officers by each product department manager. When approved, perhaps after some modification, these projections were used periodically to evaluate managerial performance, and for other purposes as well.

In view of the importance attributed to planning by the Southern Company, it might be expected that planning models would constitute an important part of the problem finding process. In fact they did not. Historical models were more influential on managerial behavior than planning models. To understand why, it is necessary to examine both the function of planning models and the process by which they were devised.

Among other things, plans are organizationally defined limits of managerial independence. So long as the manager is able to perform at least as well as his plan requires, he expects, and is normally granted, the right to define his problems as he sees fit. That is to say, as long as meeting his plan does not itself constitute a problem, the manager can use other criteria for defining his problems. If, however, he is unable to perform as well as he planned, he can expect to attract the attention of higher levels of management and to receive substantial assistance in problem identification. In other words, he will lose, perhaps only temporarily, the right to manage. One product manager put the matter this way: "The best way to remain in charge is to be successful." Other managers strongly supported this position. Success was defined relative to the predictions of the planning model.

In view of the fact that unfavorable deviations in performance were far more undesirable to managers than favorable deviations, it is not surprising that planning models were not simple descriptions of what the managers expected would happen. On the contrary, planning models represented the minimum performance the manager could reasonably expect if several of his plans failed or were based on the minimum organizational expectations of managerial performance, whichever was higher. Planning models were in general very conservatively biased historical models. For the most part these biases in plans were not injected surreptitiously. After approving a manager's plan, upper level managers always inquired about how he would deal with various contingencies. At this point the manager would reveal some but usually not all of his "hedges" against uncertainty. If he could report a number of conservative estimates and contingent plans to back up the plan being proposed, this was viewed as highly desirable.

In aggregating departmental plans, further "adjustments" were made which led the plan to depart from expectations. In some cases, these adjustments shifted expected profits from one department to another to "make the package look OK." In other cases, already conservative departmental estimates were "rounded down" to cover contingencies further. Some of these adjustments were made explicit at higher levels.

Even with all its conservative biases, the Division's plan still exceeded the Corporation's minimum profit and volume expectations. It is not surprising, therefore, that the planning model was a far less important source of management problems than historical models. Extrapolations of past performance simply implied much higher levels of performance than the planning model called for. Only in those cases (not observed) where the corporate expectations required improvements over historical trends would one expect planning models to be important in the process of problem finding.

Other People's Models

Some models which define problems for the manager are maintained by other people. A customer whose model of product quality is violated by the product he receives may notify the manager of the producing organization of this fact and thereby define a problem for him. A higher level manager may lack information to complete an analysis and this discrepancy can define a problem for a lower level manager. An employee may need a decision on vacation policy and his request will define a problem for his supervisor. A basic function of an organization structure is to channel problems which are identified by its various members to individuals especially qualified to solve them. Managers as well as other members of the organization do not always work on problems defined by their own models.

In the Southern Company, invitations to attend meetings, requests to prepare reports, and requests for projects of various kinds whether made by superiors, subordinates, or peers were rarely questioned by managers as appropriate ways to spend their time. While it was sometimes easy to get vehement testimony as to the uselessness of many of these activities, the behavior of managers clearly indicated the strong influence of other people's models. One reason for the influence of these models may be the cost to the manager of doubting them. Any attempt to validate each request made on him could easily imply a heavier workload on the manager than the simple execution of the work requested. In addition, by providing "good service" the manager builds (or at least many managers believe they build) a store of goodwill among other managers toward his own requests.

During the course of the company study, several clear examples of the influence of these models were observed. In a series of interviews, managers were asked to specify the problems currently faced by them and their organizations. Most of them mentioned from five to eight problems. Later in the same interview, each manager was asked to describe in broad terms his own activities for the previous week. In reviewing the data from these interviews as they were collected, it was noted that no manager had reported any activity which could be directly associated with the problems he had described.

In order to be sure that this result was not due to some semantic problem, this point was discussed with several managers—in some cases during the first interview with them and in other cases as a follow-up question. One manager found the point both accurate and amusing. He smiled as he replied, "That's right. I don't have time to work on *my* problems—I'm too busy." Another manager took a different tack in agreeing with the general conclusion. He replied rather confidentially, "I don't really make decisions. I just work here." In further discussion with a number of managers, the power of other people's models was repeatedly indicated. The influence of these models was also noted in the case of a rather involved project which was observed in some detail.

The Plant Engineering Department, using a quite different model, decided to look at the desirability of revising the management of the company's 21 fork trucks. Besides scheduling and other operating questions which were investigated by people within the Engineering Department, studies of the contract under which the trucks were leased and an economic evaluation of leasing versus buying trucks were also felt to be required. The Manager of Plant Engineering called representatives of the Comptroller's organization and the Legal Department to a meeting in which the project was discussed in some detail. This discussion clearly indicated that the project was risky both from the point of view of economic payoff and political considerations. The representatives accepted their tasks, however, and in due course their studies were completed. In neither case did the studies take much time, but the assumption that it was the job of the Accounting Department and the Legal Department to serve the Plant Engineering Department was clear. A problem found by someone in the organization carries with it substantial influence over the problems on which other parts of the organization will work.

Even clearer evidence of the power of other people's models was the time devoted by all the managers in the Southern Company to the preparation of reports "required" by higher management. These reports ranged in their demands on managerial time from a few minutes in the case of a request for routine information to several man months of work on the preparation of a plan for the coming year's operations. In reply to the question, "If you were responsible for the whole company's operations would you require more, the same, or less planning?" four managers responded that they would require more planning, 32 said the same amount of planning, and 16 replied less. For many managers the expectations of the organization were consistent with their own ideas of the time required for effective planning. For a number of others, however, the influence of other people was clear.

In discussing these models as a source of problems, it is difficult to avoid a negative connotation due to the widely held ethic which values individual problem definition. Two points are worth emphasizing. First, the study was conducted to find out how managers do define their problems—not how they should do so—although that, of course, may be a long-term objective of this work. Second, both the organization and the individuals described here would, by almost any standards, be judged to be highly successful and this fact should be included in any attempt to evaluate their behavior.

Because historical, planning, and other people's models require almost no generalization to make them relevant to particular events of interest to the manager, and because these three types of models can easily generate more problems than the manager can reasonably hope to deal with, it is not surprising, perhaps, that models requiring somewhat more generalization are less important elements of the process of problem finding. It is true, however, that on occasion managers draw on experiences other than their own to define problems for themselves and their organizations.

EXTRA-ORGANIZATIONAL MODELS

Trade journals which report new practices and their effects in other organizations can sometimes define useful areas for managerial analysis. Customers frequently serve the same function by reporting the accomplishments of competitors in the area of price, service, and/or product quality. General Motors is known for its practice of ranking the performance measures of a number of plants producing the same or similar products and making this information available to the managers of these facilities. The implication is strong in these comparisons that problems exist in plants where performance is poor relative to other plants.

In using all such extra-organizational models to define intra-organizational problems, the manager must resolve the difficult question of model validity. "Is the fact that our West Coast plant has lower maintenance costs relevant to our operations? After all, they have newer equipment." "Is the fact that our competitor is lowering its price relevant to our pricing policy? After all, our quality is better." There are enough attributes in any industrial situation to make it unlikely indeed that any extra-organizational model will fit the manager's situation perfectly. Judgments on the question of model validity must frequently be made by operating managers.

In the Southern Company one clear case was observed where two extra-organizational models were employed in an attempt to define a problem. A member of the Plant Engineering Department attended a meeting of an engineering society at which a technique called "work sampling" was discussed in the context of several successful applications in other plants. This model of a current engineering practice, which had not been employed by his department, led this man to consider the problem of finding an application for work sampling in the Southern Company. Clearly if this technique could be successfully applied, it would reduce the difference between his department and his extra-organizational model. A few days later this engineer noticed an idle, unattended fork truck in one of the manufacturing shops and he immediately thought that an analysis of fork truck operations might be the application he was looking for. He discussed this idea with his supervisors and they agreed that the project should be undertaken.

Because of the lack of direct responsibility for fork trucks, Plant Engineering was aware from the beginning of the project that its primary task would be to convince the product departments that their fork trucks indeed constituted a problem. To provide the department managers with evidence on this point, in addition to the internal work sampling study, a survey of fork truck operations was made in six nearby plants engaged in similar manufacturing operations. The explicit purpose of the survey was to define a basis (an extra-organizational model) on which internal fork truck operations could be evaluated.

The six company survey yielded in part the following results:

1. The number of trucks operated ranged from six to 50, with an average of 21—same as Southern Company;

2. Utilizations ranged from 50 percent to 71 percent, with an average of 63 percent—18.5 percent higher than Southern Company;

3. Responsibility for trucks was centralized in all six companies—contrary to Southern Company;

4. Trucks were controlled through dispatching or scheduling in five of the six companies (some used radio control)—contrary to Southern Company;

5. All companies owned rather than leased their trucks—contrary to Southern Company;

6. All companies performed their own maintenance of their trucks—contrary to Southern Company;

7. Three companies licensed their drivers, and assigned them full time to driving—contrary to Southern Company.

The fact that the surveyed companies on the average operated the same number of trucks as the Southern Company was clearly cited as evidence supporting the validity of this extra-organizational model.

Because the six company survey and the work sampling study had defined the problem in aggregate terms, the analysis and recommendations proceeded at this level. The Plant Engineering Department decided to make their recommendation on the basis of an overall utilization of 60 percent (the average utilization found in the six company survey) which implied a reduction of five trucks. They then looked at their work sampling data and re-allocated trucks among departments to bring individual truck utilization figures as close to 60 percent as possible. The recommended re-allocation in fact supplied a saving of five trucks. The recommendation went on to suggest that Product Departments "compensate [for this reduction in trucks] by establishing sharing arrangements between departments."

The recommendation also proposed "permanent [full time] licensed drivers" instead of production workers operating the trucks on an *ad hoc* basis as part of their regular duties. As a result of a study which had indicated that leasing was preferable to buying the fork trucks, no change in ownership or maintenance was proposed. The annual savings anticipated from the recommended changes amounted to $7,250.

It is interesting to note that the recommendations themselves constituted problems for the Product Department Managers. The task of "establishing sharing arrangements among departments" had not been resolved by the study and remained a thorny problem. The task of transferring qualified production workers to full-time truck driving duties involved not only complex problems of morale and labor relations but also economic trade-offs not evaluated by the study. The task of redefining departmental work procedures to relate to centrally controlled truck services was similarly unresolved. In return for these problems, the seven product department managers could expect to share in an annual saving of $7,250. Their response to the recommendation was less than enthusiastic. They agreed, after some bargaining, to return one truck to the leasing company but were not willing to pursue the matter any further.

Despite this rather negative conclusion, it is interesting to note that most managers considered the fork truck study a success. The validity of using the extra-organizational model derived from the survey as a means of defining the problem was never questioned and an evaluation of the existing policy on this basis was considered well-justified.

A more complicated use of extra-organizational models occurred in the case of several managers who had had personal experience in other organizations. In several situations they used this experience to define intra-organizational problems by emphasizing the personal element of this experience as evidence of its validity and by de-emphasizing (or not mentioning) where this experience was gained.

Extra-organizational models have a natural disadvantage as sources of problems because of the question of model validity which can always be raised against them. When extra-organizational experience agrees with local experience (historical model), it is seen as valid, but since it agrees with the local experience, it defines no problem. When extra-organizational experience disagrees with local experience and might therefore define a problem, the discrepancy itself raises the question of model validity. This attribute of extra-organizational models may serve to explain the fact that they were a relatively weak source of management problems in the Southern Company. Out of 52 managers, 47 agreed with the statement: "Most of our new ideas are generated within the company."

In the case of new organizations, of course, historical models are not available and extra-organizational models become more influential. One such situation was observed in the Southern Company. A promising new product was moving from the latter stages of development into the early stages of production and sales. A new product department was formed on an informal basis and the standard procedures of accounting data collection and reporting were instituted. No one expected the new department to be profitable immediately but after some months an executive at the product group level used a model not based on the history of the new department but one based on the performance of other departments to define a problem. He described the process this way:

> The numbers [on the monthly reports] were horrifying. I asked for a report and I got fuzzy answers that I didn't believe so I said, "Fellows, I'm taking over the right to ask questions."
>
> In asking questions I found I could pick holes in their analysis of the situation. Everything was loose.
>
> I analyzed their orders and found that with their overhead they couldn't make money.
>
> The department was reorganized.

In new organizations, extra-organizational models can be powerful sources of management problems.

SOME NORMATIVE QUESTIONS

The principal objective of this study was to find a relatively simple theoretical structure to explain the process of problem finding used by the managers at the Southern Company, and the set of four models just described represents that structure. These models, which range from ones maintained by other members of the organization, through simple historical and planning models, to those which apply the experience of other organizations to local situations, have been tested against the rather massive sample of data collected at the Southern Company and have been found sufficient to explain all these observations. That is to say, it is possible to trace all the observed behavior back to differences defined by one of these four classes of models. To this extent the study was successful.

But observations like these, even after abstraction into a theoretical structure, are only observations. They do not suggest the consequences of using other kinds of models or using these same models with different frequencies. They do not suggest how managers might behave more effectively than they do. Isolated observations cannot define differences. Observations must be compared to a model before normative questions can be answered.

One way to generate such comparisons would be to conduct comparative studies within and among a number of organizations. One could then answer such questions as: "Are these same models used by unsuccessful managers? If so, how can the difference in performance be explained? If not, what models are used? Do managers in other organizations use these models with different frequencies or under different circumstances? Are there systematic differences in the use of these models at different levels of the organization?" All such questions could be answered by careful study of several organizations or several levels of the same organization and these extra-organizational models might serve to suggest management improvements. Until such studies are completed, however, the only models which can be used to evaluate the behavior observed in the Southern Company are some which were not used there.

Scientific Models

When compared to models used in the physical and social sciences for quite similar purposes, the models used by the managers in the Southern Company (and elsewhere) are almost startling in their naivete. In the same company, electrical engineers explicitly used quite complex theoretical models to help them define problems associated with the design of a relatively simple electronic control system. Similarly, mechanical engineers employed a variety of quite general theories in the design of new high speed production equipment. In neither of these cases did the engineers base their predictions on their own experience except in a very general sense. They quite confidently applied theories derived from the observations of others and the equipment which resulted from their work required relatively little redesign after construction. Managers, on the other hand, based their expectations on relatively small samples of their own experience. Their rather simple theories, as has already been noted, yielded rather poor predictions, and managers therefore spent a substantial amount of time solving either their own problems or those defined by others.

The behavior of scientists (an extra-organizational model) suggests that there is an alternative to this rather frantic approach to a complex world. When discrepancies arise between a model and the environment, one can undertake to improve the model rather than change the environment. In fact, a scientist might even go so far as to suggest that, until one has a fairly reliable model of the environment, it is not only foolish but perhaps even dangerous to take action when its effect cannot be predicted.

If carried to an extreme, of course, the scientist's tendency to search for better models of the world as it is would leave no time for taking action to change it, and it seems unlikely that this allocation of time and talent would be an appropriate one for the operating manager. In the Southern Company, it must be remembered, those managers who based their actions on very simple models which took very little time to construct were judged to be quite successful by their organization.

On the other hand, the increasing use by managers of more sophisticated modeling techniques like those mentioned earlier in this paper may suggest that the balance between model building and action taking is shifting. A number of companies now base changes in distribution systems, production and inventory control systems, quality control systems, advertising allocation systems, etc., on the predictions of relatively complex models which are based on substantial bodies of theory and empirical evidence. To the extent that these models fail to describe events which take place, they, like the simpler models they replace, can serve to define problems. To the extent that these more complete models take into account events which the manager cannot, or prefers not to, control, these models can serve to protect the manager from problems on which he might otherwise waste his energy.

While it may be true that these more explicit scientific models will gradually replace simple intuitive models, several reasons suggest that the change will take some time. First, many operating managers today find the language of the new techniques foreign, despite increasing attempts to change this situation through training. Second, the new techniques often involve even more generalization than extra-organizational models, and honest questions of model validity will tend to delay their widespread use. And third, the process of problem finding currently used will perpetuate itself simply by keeping managers so busy that they will find little time to learn about and try these new methods of problem finding.

More important than any of these reasons, however, may be one which, curiously, has been created by the advocates of management science. In most, if not all, of the literature describing them, model building techniques are described as means for solving management problems. In their now classical book on operations research, Churchman, Ackoff and Arnoff, for example, suggest model building as a step which should follow "formulating the problem."[12] The process by which the problem should be formulated, however, is left totally unspecified—and this is where managers as well as students of management frequently report their greatest difficulty. They can see the process by which these techniques can solve problems but they cannot see how to define the problems.

The theory which has been proposed here suggests that problem definition

---

12/C. W. Churchman, R. L. Ackoff, and E. L. Arnoff, *Introduction to Operations Research* (New York: John Wiley & Sons, 1957).

cannot precede model construction. It is impossible to know, for example, that a cost is too high unless one has some basis (a model) which suggests it might be lower. This basis might be one's own experience, the experience of a competitor, or the output of a scientific model. Similarly, one cannot be sure that his distribution costs will be reduced by linear programming until a model is constructed and solved which suggests that rescheduling will lower costs. The imperfections of an inventory system are revealed only by comparing it to some theoretical model; they cannot be defined until after the model has been built. The logical inconsistency which suggests that problems must be clearly defined in order to justify model construction is very likely an important reason that scientific models will only slowly be recognized by operating managers as important aids in the definition of their problems.

Despite their current disadvantages, the so-called new techniques of model building are, as has already been noted, making significant contributions to management effectiveness. They represent, therefore, not only a means for evaluating current managerial behavior but also a new class of models which can be used by managers to define their problems.

THE PROBLEM OF MODEL SELECTION

The study of managers in the Southern Company indicates that concepts like image and intelligence which have been proposed to explain the process of problem finding can be made somewhat more operational. A rather small set of model classes has been defined which constitutes sufficient stimuli to trigger a fairly large sample of managerial behavior. This is not to say that future observations may not indicate the need for additional model classes or that future work is not required to make the process of managerial model building even more operational and testable. The study of the Southern Company represents perhaps only an encouraging start at understanding an important and little understood area of management.

Even with these initial insights, however, it is possible to see where major theoretical gaps still exist. Chief among these is the problem of model selection. As has already been noted, the requests of other people are sufficient to define a full time job for many managers. The problem of investigating and taking corrective action on discrepancies from historical trends can keep any manager busy all the time. The construction of extra-organizational and/or scientific models and the actions which they trigger are similarly time-consuming. Even after the manager has constructed the models he will use to define his problems, he must somehow select from among the differences which are simultaneously defined by these models. Personal requests, historical discrepancies, extra-organizational ideas, and the stimuli of scientific models do not in general define differences one at a time. The choice of the discrepancy to attend to next may be as important a process as the construction of the models which define them. It seems clear, however, that we must understand the process by which differences are defined before we can worry seriously about understanding the process of selecting from among them. The study in the Southern Company, therefore, largely ignored the priority problem and concentrated on difference definitions only.

It is impossible, however, to observe managers at work without getting some rough ideas about how they deal with the priority problem. Telephone calls for example are very high priority stimuli. A ringing telephone will interrupt work of virtually every kind. This priority rule is complicated sometimes by an intervening secretary but many managers pride themselves on always answering their own phone. One manager reported that he always worked on problems which would "get worse" before he worked on static problems. Thus, he dealt with a problem involving a conflict between a foreman and a troublesome employee before pressing forward on a cost reduction program.

Perhaps the most explicit priorities in the Southern Company were established by means of deadlines. Most problems defined by other members of the organization carried with them a time at which, or by which, the request should be satisfied. Certain reports were due monthly, a fixed number of working days after the end of the preceding month. Meetings were scheduled at stated times. Annual plans were required on a specified date. While a number of such requests might face a manager simultaneously, they almost never would have the same deadline and by this means the manager could decide which to do when. The fact that most problems triggered by other people's models carried deadlines may explain why these problems seemed to be given so much attention. When asked to indicate "Which problems do you usually get to first, time deadline, big payoff or personal interest?" 43 out of 52 managers indicated time deadline.

From a theoretical point of view, one could consider the flow of problems through an organization as analogous to the flow of jobs through a job shop and perhaps apply some of the theories which have been developed there to understand and perhaps prescribe the process of priority assignment. Managers, for example, must trade off relative lateness of their tasks with the duration of the tasks just as a foreman loading machines in a machine shop. Once the problem of problem definition is well understood it would appear that some theory is already available to structure the process of assigning problem priorities. The array of models used by and available to managers suggests that an understanding of the process by which problems are defined will not constitute a complete theory of problem finding. A process which assigns priorities to a set of simultaneously defined problems remains to be specified.

23

Do Managers Find Decision
Theory Useful?*

REX V. BROWN

For thousands of years, businessmen have been making decisions in the face
of uncertainty about the future. Such decisions have often served to separate
"the men from the boys" in business—and perhaps always will. In recent years,
however, the problem executives face has been altered by the introduction of a
set of techniques of quantitative analysis which I shall refer to here as Decision
Theory Analysis (DTA). These methods are familiar to HBR readers,[1] and they
have, in fact, stimulated widespread attention, both critical and laudatory, in the
business world.

As might be expected when a radically new approach is used, business
executives have often found DTA methods frustrating and unrewarding. Nevertheless, there is a steadily growing conviction in the management community
that DTA should and will occupy a very important place in an executive's
arsenal of problem-solving techniques. Only time can tell if, as some enthusiasts
claim, decision theory will be to the executive of tomorrow what the slide rule
is to the engineer of today. But clearly, in my opinion, the *potential* impact
of DTA is great.

The primary purpose of this article, which is based on a survey of 20 companies made in 1969, is to present some of the experiences of practitioners who
have been exploring various applications of DTA techniques to management decision making. These experiences should help would-be users to identify particu-

*Source: Reprinted by permission from *Harvard Business Review* (May-June, 1970),
78-89; Copyright 1970 by the President and Fellows of Harvard College.
Author's note: I wish to acknowledge the assistance of Paul Vatter, Howard Raiffa,
Stanley Buchin, and Robert Buzzell in arranging contacts for the survey discussed in this
article.
1/See, in particular, David B. Hertz, "Risk Analysis in Capital Investment" (January-
February, 1964), p. 95; John Magee, "Decision Trees for Decision Making" (July-August,
1964), p. 126; and "How to Use Decision Trees in Capital Investment" (September-
October, 1964), p. 79; Ralph O. Swalm, "Utility Theory—Insights into Risk Taking"
(November-December, 1966), p. 123; and John S. Hammond, III, "Better Decisions with
Preference Theory" (November-December, 1967), p. 123. Many other articles on other
methods of quantitative analysis are contained in HBR's Statistical Decision Series, Parts
I, II, and III.

lar situations in their own companies where the new technology might greatly benefit them, and to build on the lessons learned the hard way by earlier users.

Executives and staff specialists in the companies provided the bulk of the material. The companies included three organizations with several years of active experience with DTA (Du Pont, Pillsbury, and General Electric); a sampling of corporations that have taken up DTA in the past two or three years and are now quite active in employing it (e.g., General Mills and Inmont Corporation); one or two organizations whose experience with DTA has been disappointing; a few companies (such as Ford Motor and Time, Inc.) where there is a definite interest in DTA but—at least, as of 1969—little application; and a couple of consulting firms with well-known expertise in the area (notably Arthur D. Little, Inc. and McKinsey & Company).

During the course of the survey, particular attention was focused on such questions as the following, which will be discussed in this article:

What tangible impact does DTA have on how businesses are run and on how individual decisions are made?

What areas of decision making is DTA best suited for?

What practical benefits result?

What trends in usage are apparent?

What obstacles and pitfalls lie in the way of more effective usage?

What organization steps should management take to use DTA more effectively?

What remains to be done in developing and expanding the usefulness of DTA?

DTA IN REVIEW

Before turning to the findings of the survey, let us review some of the elements of DTA. (The theory does not, by the way, always go under this name. Sometimes it is called "Personalist Decision Theory" or "Bayesian Decision Theory.")

First, what information does DTA demand of the executive? It requires such inputs as executive judgment, experience, and attitudes, along with any "hard data," such as historical records. In particular, the executive is asked to:

1. Stipulate what decision alternatives are to be considered in the analysis of a problem.

2. Make a probabilistic statement of his assessment of critical uncertainties.

3. Quantify some possible consequences of various actions and his attitudes toward these consequences.

The logically preferred decision can then be derived routinely according to the highly developed statistical theory that underlies DTA, using decision trees, computer programs, and/or other computational devices.

The use of DTA is not restricted to investment, marketing, or other types of business decisions. Potential and actual applications are also to be found in the area of medical, military, engineering, and governmental decisions. The most ambitious application of decision theory yet reported apparently was employed in the hypothetical problem of whether to push the nuclear button if the President receives different kinds of ambiguous evidence of an impending Russian attack on the United States.

The analyst does not need to keep in his head all the considerations that are taken into account, and, indeed, all the considerations do not need to be evaluated by the same person (although whoever makes the decision must *accept* the evaluations). For instance:

> The company president might determine the company's attitude toward risk in new product planning.
>
> The vice president of marketing might choose the business decisions to be compared.
>
> The director of research might provide information on development times, likely success in solving technical problems, and so on.
>
> The probable costs might come from the controller's office.
>
> The probable sales might come from a sales manager or forecasting specialist.

Contentious elements in the analysis can be lifted out, and revised assessments substituted for them, without the analyst's having to reconsider every issue.

While, in principle, any decision problem *can* be analyzed by DTA methods, this is a very far cry from arguing that it always *should* be. In various instances, traditional decision making may be more economical, practical, and sound than modern methods of quantitative analysis.

(For a simplified illustration of problem solving by DTA, see Figure 1.)

Growing Use

Only a few U.S. companies appear to have used DTA in operations for any length of time. Two of these companies are Du Pont, which got started with the approach in the late 1950's, and Pillsbury, which got started in the early 1960's. However, there has been a dramatic increase in DTA activity since about 1964. That is when executive interest began to be stimulated, notably by articles in HBR, executive orientation seminars, and reports of successful applications on the part of pioneering companies, and, perhaps most important of all, a steady stream of DTA-trained MBAs who began to enter managerial ranks in substantial numbers. The principal intellectual thrust behind nearly all of these developments was the technical work and teaching of Robert O. Schlaifer and Howard Raiffa at the Harvard Business School.[2]

2/See, for example, Robert O. Schlaifer, *Analysis of Decisions under Uncertainty* (New York: McGraw-Hill Book Company, Inc., 1969) and Howard Raiffa, *Decision Analysis* (Reading, Massachusetts: Addison-Wesley Publishing Company, 1968).

FIGURE 1
An Example of Decision Tree Analysis

A. The Problem

B. The Solution

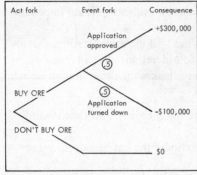

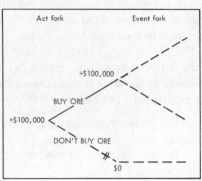

Key   ○ Probabilities —#— Rejected acts $ 000 Consequences or expected consequences

How DTA works

One version of DTA—the "decision tree" approach—lends itself readily to simple manual computations, and can be used to illustrate the general ideas involved in this subject.

All elements which an executive considers important to a decision, however subjective, can be represented on a decision tree. To show how the process of common-sense decision making can be expressed in the necessary manner, let us take an example involving a hypothetical, but realistic, business decision.

Suppose that a New York metal broker has an option to buy 100,000 tons of iron ore from a Far Eastern government at an advantageous price, of, say, $5 a ton. Other brokers have received the same offer, and so our man in New York feels that an immediate decision must be made. He knows he can get $8 a ton for this ore, but he believes there is a 50-50 chance that the U.S. government will refuse to grant an import license. In such an event, the contract would be annulled at a penalty of $1 a ton.

A decision tree, representing what I shall call the initial problem, is shown in Part A of Figure 1. Note that both the "act forks" (labeled in capitals) and the "event forks" (lower case) are represented by branches on the decision tree, and that at each fork there are as many branches as there are alternatives.

The choice between alternative acts (in this case, the decision whether or not to buy the ore) is under the control of the decision maker. On the other hand, the occurrence of a particular event (the approval or refusal of the import license) is beyond his control. He estimates a 50-50 chance of approval. The probabilities are noted in parentheses.

The uncertainty about the license makes it impossible to know in advance what the "best" decision would be. Every path through the tree corresponds to a possible sequence of acts and events, each with its own unique consequences. For example, if our broker decides to buy ore, but his license application is rejected, he stands to lose (assuming a penalty of $1 a ton) $100,000.

In order to reach a good decision, the broker clearly has to take into account the probabilities, as he sees them, of each of the two events, approval or refusal of the import license. Intuitively, it is easy to see that if the broker assesses a high probability of approval, he would be wise to go ahead and buy the ore; but since he actually thinks there is only a 50-50 chance of approval, he is faced with a 50% chance of obtaining $300,000 (his best estimate now of the potential profit) against an equal chance of losing $100,000. His estimates of the gains and losses are shown to the right of the decision tree, in Figure 1-A.

FIGURE 1–*Continued*

Which act should he prefer? His attitude toward possible consequences must be noted. Suppose he has a general policy of "playing the averages" and is not at all averse to taking risks. This can be restated formally as maximizing the "expected" monetary consequences. (By contrast, other people "play it safe" or, conversely, are "gamblers," indicating they like to deviate from the averages.)

Formal analysis begins by computing an "expected" consequence for all event forks at the right-hand edge of the decision tree. This value is treated as if it were the certain consequence of reaching the base of the event fork. Its value is then substituted for the actual event fork and its consequences, as shown in Figure 1-B. In this case, there is only one event fork (approval or rejection of the application) on the tree; it is therefore replaced by $100,000—that is, .5($300,000) + .5(−$100,000). If there were several event forks on the right, each would be replaced by an expected consequence.[a]

Since the event fork is now eliminated, only the act fork is left. The branch which has the highest expected consequence is now selected. That is the "Buy ore" branch with a consequence of $100,000. The analysis of this problem is now complete.

With such a simple problem, it may hardly seem worth going to the trouble of a formal analysis. The real pay-off is likely to occur when the problem has more separable elements than the decision maker can comfortably take account of in his head. Typically, in such cases, there will be more than two "echelons" of forks in a decision tree, and more than one fork at each echelon. By alternating the two methods described for eliminating event and act forks respectively, the origin at the left-hand side of the tree will eventually be reached, and both the optimum strategy and its expected consequence will be determined.

Although the analysis depicted in Figure 1 could be perfectly adequate in representing our New York broker's first thoughts about his problem, a little reflection may lead him to take into account new considerations whose action implications are less easy to think through informally. For instance, it may occur to him that the acts "Buy ore" and "Don't buy ore" are not the only ones immediately available for consideration. As in most business problems, he may have the option of delaying his decision while he gathers more information. If so, the additional options and the consequences of every set of act-event sequences could be shown on the decision tree, and an optimum strategy determined in essentially the same way. Similarly, he might want to take into account some aversion to risk that he may possess in certain circumstances, the possibility of nonmonetary side effects (like goodwill), or uncertainty about quantities he had previously treated as certain (such as the price he can get for the ore).

These considerations, too, can be handled in the same format and with very little in the way of additional technique.[b] However, more ambitious forms of DTA, such as computer simulations, often prove to be more convenient when there is a technical specialist available.

[a]See the examples discussed by John Magee in "Decision Trees for Decision Making," HBR (July-August, 1964), p. 126, and "How to Use Decision Trees in Capital Investment," HBR (September-October, 1964), p. 123; see also John S. Hammond, III, "Better Decisions with Preference Theory," HBR (November-December, 1967), p. 123.

[b]See Robert D. Buzzell, Donald F. Cox, and Rex V. Brown, *Marketing Research and Information Systems* (New York: McGraw-Hill Book Company, Inc., 1969), Chapters 9 and 10.

Stimulated by such developments, executives in a number of companies began to explore the potential applications of DTA to their own operations. For example:

General Electric set up an intensive study of DTA by a high-level committee that led to major changes in plant appropriation methods.

Ford Motor and other companies put literally hundreds of their middle and senior managers through training programs varying in length from a few days to several weeks.

Other companies, including General Mills, began to introduce DTA on a project-by-project basis.

IMPACT ON DECISION MAKING

Since the companies in the survey were selected on the basis of their actual or imputed use of DTA, no special significance can be attached to the fact that most of them do indeed use the tools. What is significant, in my opinion, is that even these companies, leaders though they are, do not show drastic changes in their general decision-making procedures as a result of DTA. However, *individual* decisions are often profoundly affected. Examples from the experience of the most active companies interviewed—Du Pont, Pillsbury, GE, and Inmont—give some measure of how DTA is being used by managers.

Application at Du Pont

Substantial DTA activity is going on throughout the Du Pont organization, stimulated by staff groups in the Development Department and elsewhere. Managers in the various departments have shown increasing interest in the staff groups' services (which are supplied for a fee) during the past ten years. Yet, even after all this time, Dr. Sig Andersen, manager of one of the consulting groups and perhaps the most prominent figure in the application of DTA, says he feels that DTA has not yet reached the point where it really has a major impact at the general manager level in Du Pont. J. T. Axon, Manager of the Management Sciences Division, says:

I think [Andersen and his colleagues] have indeed been pioneers and missionaries on behalf of DTA within Du Pont, and I share with them the conviction that their work has improved the quality of numerous decisions around the company. Their impact has been seriously limited, however, by the absence of appropriate educational efforts aimed at the decision makers. Even at this date, we have in Du Pont, in my judgment, very few key decision makers who are "alive" to the possibilities of DTA and comfortable in its use. It is this lack that has dragged down the Du Pont effort.

At Du Pont, middle and even senior managers increasingly will take action or submit recommendations that include DTA along with more conventional analyses, but the presentation to top management is likely to be supported by more informal reasoning, not DTA. Thus, in the case of a new product which had just reached the prototype stage at Du Pont, the question before management was: On what scale should initial pilot production be carried out?

Critical uncertainties involved the reliability of the military demand for which the prototype had been originally designed, and the amount of supplementary commercial business that would be generated.

DTA was performed on a computer to produce "risk profiles" of return on investment for various plant sizes and pricing strategies. The inputs included probability assessments of demand for each possible end-use of the product (based on market research), as well as assessments of cost and timing. The analysis indicated that, on the basis of the assessments used, a certain price was optimal, and a $3-million pilot plant would have the highest expected rate of return.

When this conclusion was transmitted to top management, it was couched in the language of informal reasoning, not of DTA. Management opted for a smaller, $1-million plant, but adopted—unchanged—the pricing recommendation of the study. It appears that top management, without explicitly disagreeing with the assumptions underlying the analysis, possessed an aversion to risk which was not assumed in the analysis.

Pillsbury's Approach

James R. Petersen, Vice President of The Pillsbury Company and General Manager of the Grocery Products Company, uses decision trees regularly in evaluating major recommendations submitted to him. More than a dozen marketing decisions a year are approved by him on the basis of the findings of detailed DTA. (Many more decisions in his divisions are rendered after first using a skeletal decision tree to clarify the key problem issues.)

Typically, a middle manager in the Grocery Products Company will spend a week or so developing a DTA approach, often with the help of a staff specialist. When the middle manager's recommendation comes to be considered by Petersen, this analysis is the vehicle for discussion. For instance, in one case, the issue before management was whether to switch from a box to a bag as a package for a certain grocery product. Petersen and his sales manager had been disposed to retain the box on the grounds of greater customer appeal. The brand manager, however, favored the bag on cost considerations. He supported his recommendation with a DTA based on his own best assessments of probable economic, marketing, and other consequences. Even when the sales manager's more pessimistic assessments of the market impact of a bag were substituted for the brand manager's, the bag still looked more profitable. Petersen adopted the recommendation, the bag was introduced, and the profits on the product climbed substantially.

During the course of discussions, some Pillsbury executives urged that the bag be test-marketed before management made a firm decision. The original DTA showed, however, only a one-in-ten chance that the bag would prove unprofitable—and if that occurred, it would probably be not too unprofitable. A simple, supplementary DTA showed that the value of making a market test could not remotely approach its cost. Accordingly, no test marketing was undertaken. Management's confidence in the analysis was later confirmed by the bag's success.

Uses at GE

At General Electric there has recently been a formal head office requirement that all investment requests of more than $500,000 be supported by a probabilistic assessment of rate of return and other key measures. In the wake of this requirement, and largely in the area of plant appropriations, more than 500 instances of computerized DTA have been recorded over the past four years.

Heavy use is made of a library of special DTA programs developed largely by Robert Newman, Manager of Planning Services, who works with managers in other GE operations on a consulting basis. The consulting relationship, no doubt enhanced by Newman's own experience in line management, often has an impact on issues beyond the scope of the originating inquiry, as the following example shows:

One GE division was faced with a shortage of manufacturing capacity for a mature industrial product. Using the information and assessments supplied by the division manager (including a suspicion that the product was obsolescent), Newman spent a few hours on a DTA which suggested that the division should not increase capacity, but raise prices. Both the consultant and the manager felt uneasy about this conclusion.

Further discussion yielded new but confidential information that the division was developing a product which promised to supplant the old one. This intelligence, plus various estimates of the probability of success and related matters, led to a new DTA (which employed GE's prepackaged computer programs). This study pointed to the conclusion that research and development expenditures on the new product should be increased by a factor of 20. The recommendation was adopted, the new product went into production two years later, and it achieved highly profitable sales of some $20 million a year.

Inmont's Programs

Although Inmont Corporation's usage of DTA is less extensive than that of the three companies just discussed, James T. Hill, President, comments that he often uses computer simulations in evaluating potential acquisition candidates. Preliminary information available on such candidates is programmed into a model by his assistant. This model is part of a prepackaged DTA simulation program which merges Inmont and the acquisition candidate according to the specific purchase strategy that Inmont is contemplating. The computer prints out detailed information as to the cost to Inmont and the return to the individual shareholders of the acquired company, including a pro forma balance sheet and income statement both before and after conversion of convertible securities.

Once the results are reviewed by Hill and his top executives, any alternative financing schemes that have been suggested can be explored in a matter of minutes in order to determine the best financial plan. Computer terminals are available at strategic decision-making locations in the head office, and the program is designed so as to enable any executive's secretary to put in data for different possible modes of acquisition. It is an easy matter, therefore, for alternative strategies to be evaluated quickly at any stage in the decision-making process.

When the most desirable financial approach has been determined, a second program can be utilized to run projected pro forma balance sheets and income statements for any period into the future. This program uses probability theory to arrive at the "best guess" as to the outcome of various operating strategies. It also enables executives to determine the factors most crucial to the future return on investment of a proposed merger. This "sensitivity analysis" thus focuses on the critical questions with which Inmont's management would have to deal if it were to undertake the acquisition.

This is what Hill says about Inmont's use of the procedure:

> The two programs, together, help ensure that the decision as to a potential acquisition is made after a comprehensive analysis of alternatives. It is not necessary to choose only one method of financing or one method of operation, for example. Rather, it is possible to explore, in a very short period of time, numerous strategies to discover that which will maximize the benefits to the merged companies. It is understood that the decision is no better than the reliability of the inputs, including the assigned probabilities.

Various other companies responding to my survey report that they are using DTA on a more-or-less systematic basis for marketing and allied decisions, most frequently in the area of new product selection and development, but also in promotion, pricing, test marketing, and other activities. In fact, about 50 specific applications of DTA to marketing problems are noted—and some of these will be mentioned subsequently in this article.

OBSTACLES & PITFALLS

Enthusiasm for DTA is very great in many quarters. For example, Robert Newman of General Electric predicts:

> Within 10 years, decision theory, conversational computers, and library programs should occupy the same role for the manager as calculus, slide rules, and mathematical tables do for the engineer today. The engineer

of Roman times had none of these, but he could make perfectly good bridges. However, he could not compete today, even in bridge-building, let alone astro-engineering. Management is today at the stage of Roman engineering. Needless to say, managers will still use specialists, just as engineers use heat transfer experts.

While Newman's time schedule may be optimistic, my survey findings in no way contradict the substance of his view. However, a number of more or less serious obstacles—many no doubt attributable to inexperience in using DTA—lie in the path of a major revolution such as Newman envisages.

Personal Competence

It is clear that companies will experience only limited success with a new analytical approach like DTA unless they have executives who are alive to its possibilities and use it effectively. While there is a substantial and rapidly expanding number of DTA-oriented executives in positions to influence management decisions, they represent a tiny fraction of the total managerial pool. The momentum of educational processes will remedy this problem in time—but it will take time.

Much the same can be said about the current scarcity of trained technical specialists needed to carry out or advise managers on DTA. After all, the first comprehensive handbook on applied DTA was published only recently.[3]

However, even if there were no manpower shortage, serious obstacles to successful and expanding use of DTA would still exist. Removing them may require more deliberate initiative and research on management's part than will correcting the lack of line and staff training.

Uncertainty over Return

For one thing, no substantial personal or corporate benefits of using the technique may be apparent to the potential user. Many effective managers have a "show me" attitude toward new decision-making techniques, and as yet there is little to show. Indeed, no firm evidence is available to prove that DTA *does* have widespread practical value. The evidence from my survey is encouraging, but far from conclusive; enough disappointments have been reported to sustain the doubts harbored by many businessmen. For example:

A central staff team for an international manufacturer of industrial components carried out a sophisticated and competent DTA designed to help a regional subsidiary choose which of several alternative markets to compete in. When the DTA part of the study was presented to the subsidiary's president, however, he perceived it as having little relevance to him in his decision making. He told me that the market forecast and other input data gathered for the

3/Robert O. Schlaifer, op. cit.

analysis were certainly of substantial value to him, but he could not see that the DTA itself added much that was useful. Indeed, while the market data provided a basis for much of the subsidiary's subsequent strategy, no specific action appeared to be traceable to the DTA part of the study (though some people in the company felt that the analysis had some diffuse influence on several decisions).

The managers of the subsidiary are seeking to adapt the DTA to meet their needs, and the prospects look encouraging. Moreover, the staff team from the head office has since introduced DTA to *other* subsidiaries with, it seems, substantial success.

Note that this experience was the first the company had had with DTA. Almost all of the most successful users of DTA have started out with one or more disappointing experiences. What accounts for such disappointments? Let us take the international manufacturer again as a case example. Its experience is typical of that of several other companies I know about:

1. The logic and language of DTA was unfamiliar to the president and his senior executives, and they could not readily and comfortably incorporate it into their normal mode of thinking. A more gradual introduction of the complex technology would surely have been more digestible.

2. The decision options addressed by the DTA turned out *not* to be the ones the president was concerned about. (For example, he was more interested in deciding *how* to develop a particular market sector than in whether to be in it at all.) Fuller and earlier communication between executive and staff analysts helps to counter this very common problem experienced in applying DTA.

3. The DTA was initiated and performed by "head office" people over whom the subsidiary had no direct control, and the subsidiary president may have felt some threat to his autonomy. Having such an analysis performed or commissioned by his own people would have removed the threat.

4. The subsidiary president told me that the way to make money in his business was to get good data and implement decisions effectively. He had little interest in improved ways of *processing* data to make decisions, which is, of course, the special province of DTA.

Diffused Decision Making

At Ford Motor Company, some 200 senior executives have passed through a brief DTA-oriented program during the past five years; the program has been followed up in some divisions by intensive workshops for junior executives. And yet, according to George H. Brown, former Director of Marketing Research at Ford headquarters, usage of DTA at Ford has been negligible in the marketing area, and the prospects unpromising, at least as of the time of this survey. In his opinion, large organizations with diffuse decision-making processes (like Ford) are not as well suited to the effective use of DTA as, say, the small or one-man organization is.

John J. Nevin, now Vice President of Marketing for Ford, adds the following observations:

I am not sure that there is any reason to be discouraged by the fact that, in many companies, DTA may be far more accepted and far more utilized by middle management. Maybe all analytical tools sneak into general usage through the back door. It does not seem to me to be improbable that the middle management people, who are more comfortable with these techniques and are using them on very specific technical problems today, will, as they grow to top management positions, feel as uncomfortable switching to some new decision-making process as many of today's managers feel in switching to a more disciplined analysis.

He also notes that the average executive has difficulty picking up all of the variables in a complex decision-making problem. He attributes this in large part to the executive's inability to discipline himself to use a new technique.

Nevertheless, several Ford divisions are now exploring DTA applications at their most senior executive levels. Since my survey began, early in 1969, there have been some cases of successful implementation. For instance, at Ford Tractor, a product policy decision was recently required. In a regional market suffering from competitive inroads, the main options were to reduce prices or to introduce one of several possible new models; a modest DTA was carried out on these choices. Several runs incorporating assessments and modifications advanced by the marketing manager, the assistant general manager, and the general manager were made. The somewhat controversial conclusion to introduce a certain model was presented in DTA form to the general manager, who adopted it and initiated the necessary engineering studies.

Organizational Obstacles

If there is one dominant feature that distinguishes the successful from the less successful applications of DTA, judging from the findings of this survey, it is the organizational arrangements for offering DTA. The most successful appears to be the "vest pocket" approach, where the analyst works intimately with the executive and typically reports directly to him (Pillsbury's Grocery Products Company and Inmont Corporation provide excellent examples of this approach).

At the other end of the spectrum is the arms'-length approach, which is characteristic of much operations research. In this approach the analysis is performed by a staff group which is organizationally distant from the executive being served. In such instances, the executive may feel threatened rather than supported by DTA, and critical weaknesses may thus develop in the communication of the problem and its analyses.

Relation with Consultants

The epitome of the arms'-length arrangement appears in the role of the outside consultant. The survey suggests that consulting firms are doing relatively little DTA work for their clients. (One exception is McKinsey & Company, which reports substantial DTA work in nonmarketing areas.) I find this significant, in view of the facts that potentially, at least, consulting firms are a major resource for companies that want to use DTA, and that leading consultants have done much to explain DTA to businessmen.[4]

It seems that clients often insist on holding some of their cards close to their chests—and effective DTA depends critically on incorporating in the analysis *all* of the elements that the decision maker sees as important. Many clients prefer to limit consultants to performing clearly specified technical or data-gathering tasks with a minimum of two-way communication; executives worry about jeopardizing company security and giving the consultant too much say in their business.

Dr. Harlan Meal, a departmental manager for Arthur D. Little, makes a telling observation concerning the role of consultants and general obstacles to the adoption of DTA:

> Many of the executives who hire consultants or who employ expert technical staff do so in order to reduce the uncertainty in their decision making, rather than to improve their ability to deal with uncertain situations. Many of the clients we have want to buy from us information which will make the outcome of a particular course of action more certain than it would otherwise have been. If all we can do for them is reduce the chance of making an incorrect decision or improve the expected performance of the decision they do make in the face of uncertainty, they are not very interested.
>
> It is on this point that I think the application of decision theory analysis gets stuck nearly every time. Very few executives think of themselves as gamblers or of making the best kind of decisions in a gambling situation. They want, instead, to think of themselves as individuals whose greater grasp of the available information and whose greater insight remove the uncertainty from the situation.
>
> When the information quality is so poor that the assignment of probabilities to outcomes seems an exercise in futility, decision theory analysis can be most useful. Yet most executives in such a situation say that the only thing which really can be useful is their own experienced intuition. The executive is going to behave as though he has information about the situation, whether he has it or not.

4/See, for example, John Magee and David B. Hertz, op. cit.

Technical Questions

A further obstacle to the widespread use of DTA has to do with the logical underpinnings of DTA. Some potential users, especially in staff positions, take the position that where information about an uncertain quantity is weak, there is no point in *attempting* to measure that uncertainty. This amounts to a rejection of a basic tenet of DTA, viz., that subjective judgment, however tenuous, must be taken into account *somehow* by the decision maker, and that a DTA approach may do the job more effectively than unaided intuition.

In addition, increase in the effectiveness of DTA is to some extent dependent on the state of the art. The development and propagation of economical and quick routines utilizing inputs and outputs that can be readily communicated will no doubt be a major factor. Such routines affect the practicality and appeal of DTA in a management setting. However, it seems clear that purely theoretical developments are not holding up further application of DTA; the frontiers of the technology are way ahead of the applications, in most cases.

REALIZING THE POTENTIALS

How beneficial is a DTA to a company? Does it lead to "better" decisions than other approaches to decision making? Logic alone cannot give us the answer. However, it seems clear that DTA may *not* be the best approach if:

1. The subjective inputs required for the analysis are inaccurately measured and recorded. (Executives, as Meal suggests in the comment quoted earlier in this article, may not explicitly admit to uncertainty about some critical variable, whereas they may take it into account in their informal reasoning.)

2. The DTA does not incorporate all the considerations which the executive would informally take into account—for example, some nonmonetary side effect like goodwill. (Where there is good communication between executive and analyst, the executive often can and does make "eyeball" adjustments for anything that has been left out of the analysis. Sometimes, though, such adjustments are so substantial that they swamp and thereby invalidate the entire DTA.)

Considering all the angles and factors that bear on a good DTA (or any other analysis) is time-consuming and sometimes quite frustrating. Clearly, though, it is one of the prerequisites of making this approach. The following experience should suffice to make the point:

A corporate staff team at General Mills evaluated an acquisition opportunity by means of a DTA computer program that took four months to develop and another two months to run with successively modified inputs corresponding to new assessments and assumptions made by the researchers and executives. In all, 140 computer runs were made before arriving at a recommendation to make the acquisition and to adopt a specific marketing and production strategy. The recommendation was rejected by top management, however, when the company's legal counsel advised against the acquisition on certain legal grounds. The lawyers discovered that a critical consideration had been omitted from the analysis which rendered it unusable for the purpose at hand.

It should be noted that this was the company's first major attempt at applying DTA, and the experience performed a valuable function in exposing line and staff to the scope and pitfalls of DTA. The company's record with DTA since then has been quite successful.

Cost vs. Benefits

The costs of applying DTA are by no means inconsequential. It is true that the out-of-pocket costs for technicians and computers, even for a large-scale analysis, may be relatively trivial. Moreover, these costs can be expected to decline as DTA technology becomes more streamlined. Other, less obvious costs, however, are not trivial and are unlikely to become so. For example, critical decisions may be unacceptably delayed while an analysis is being completed. (When General Mills does not use DTA for market planning decisions, this is cited as the most common reason.) A busy executive needs to devote some of his valuable time to making sure that all of the relevant judgments he can make have been fed into the analysis.

Even more serious a "cost" is the discomfort an executive feels as he forces his traditional way of thinking into an unfamiliar mold and lays bare to the discretion of a DTA specialist the most delicate considerations that enter into his decision making. These considerations sometimes include confidential information (as in the GE new product example previously noted), admissions of uncertainty (which often run counter to the prevailing managerial culture), and embarrassing motivations. In one instance of an elaborate analysis of possible locations for a European subsidiary, the actual decision was dominated by the fact that key personnel wanted to be near the International School in Geneva. Somehow, that consideration seemed too noneconomic and nonrational to be fed into the analysis.

However, such costs are by no means prohibitive if management's approach to DTA is sound and thorough. When that is the case, the advantages claimed by users of DTA are material and persuasive:

It focuses informal thinking on the critical elements of a decision.

It forces into the open hidden assumptions behind a decision and makes clear their logical implication.

It provides an effective vehicle for communicating the reasoning which underlies a recommendation.

Many of the executives most satisfied with DTA value it as a vehicle for communicating decision-making reasoning as well as for improving it. My own feeling is that DTA's contribution to the quality of decision making often seems to come more from forcing meaningful structure on informal reasoning than from supplementing it by formal analysis. For instance, in the Pillsbury Grocery Products Company, for every DTA pushed to its numerical conclusion, there are half a dozen cases where only a conceptual decision tree has been drawn. Such a tree is used to focus attention on the critical options and uncertainties, and is then dropped in favor of informal reasoning.

Suggestions for Starting

After reflecting on the experiences of successful and unsuccessful users of DTA, I want to offer some suggestions for the executive intent on trying out DTA in his organization:

Ensure the sympathetic involvement of the chief executive of the company (or operating unit).

Make sure that at least a few key executives have a minimal appreciation of what DTA can do for them and what it requires of them. (This might be done by means of one of the short DTA orientation courses currently available.)

Make at least one trial run on a decision problem—preferably a live one—with the help of a DTA specialist. Use the exercise as a training vehicle for your executives and staffers, without expecting immediate pay-offs.

Plan on recruiting or developing in-house staff specialists to do the detail on subsequent analyses. The specialists should report directly to you, not to part of an organizationally distant operations research group.

Wean yourself and your staff from outside specialists as soon as possible, using them only as residual technical resources.

On any particular DTA, follow the analysis closely enough to make sure that the problem which gets solved is the problem you have, and that you accept *all* of the underlying assumptions. This will probably mean a less sophisticated analysis than would gladden the heart of the typical technician. It will also probably mean you spend more time with the analysis than you think you can afford.

CONCLUSION

What efforts are needed to make DTA a more effective tool for the executive? It may be helpful to think of DTA as in some way analogous to an industrial product and to ask ourselves: What aspects of its "manufacture" or "marketing" stand most in need of attention?

The "fundamental research" and "product design" aspects (corresponding to statistical decision theory and the development of special analytical devices) appear to be in rather good shape. Rare are the instances in which successful use of DTA is held up through shortcomings in the purely technical state of the art. Of course, there are areas where improved DTA techniques need to be developed, such as the extraction of probability assessments, handling risk aversion and nonmonetary criteria for action, and accommodating group decision making. But, even so, it is clear that greater use of DTA does not depend on such refinements. The tools that exist are well in advance of the capacity of most companies to use them.

Improvements in "production technique"—i.e., in the ability to deliver competent DTA at an acceptable cost—appear to be somewhat harder to achieve. In one major analysis of a pricing problem, the only reason that subjective probabilities were not introduced explicitly was that the computer cost would have been too high. However, we can be confident that within a few years progress in computer technology will largely eliminate this deterrent.

The manpower costs and delays involved in performing a reasonably complete analysis are usually more intractable. With the emergence and propagation of generalized computer programs of the type developed independently by each of the leaders (notably General Electric) in the DTA field, such costs can also be expected to decline—but the improvement will be gradual during the next five to ten years.

The inadequacy of "production facilities"—that is, the ability of DTA analysts to use available methods and concepts—is another temporary obstacle. Solving this problem will take more formal education and increased awareness of the issues and techniques that others have learned. Certainly help to this end will come from university programs and professional publications. Need for access to physical facilities, such as computer services, does not seem to be a serious limiting factor.

"Promotion" and "packaging" are areas requiring serious attention because they have been more neglected. It is true that the "product awareness" needed to stimulate management demand has been created by publications and executive development programs. But willingness to *try* the product (DTA) requires communicating to a potential user the benefits he can expect. These benefits need to be ascertained and documented in a far more effective way than by incomplete testimonials from satisfied—and not so satisfied—users (as in a survey like the present one).

"Repeat buying" on the part of experimental users requires an attractive and convenient "package" so that an executive can contribute judgments and estimates with less pain and confusion, and also so that the conclusions of a DTA can be presented in a more effective, appealing manner. Confusing computer print-outs and technical reports account for many indifferent receptions to what are otherwise very adequate DTA's.

Somewhat allied to the packaging problem, and still more critical, is the question of how DTA should be *used* in the context of a company's operation. This raises the whole issue of how to organize the DTA function, how to implement recommendations, and how to identify suitable applications. Kent Quisel, a senior analyst at Du Pont, comments that he spends a third of his time on what he calls "user engineering," and that this amount is still not enough. At companies less experienced in DTA than Du Pont is, the proportion of time spent in this way is generally much less than a third, to the almost invariable detriment of DTA's effectiveness.

Possibly the most important area of all for study is "product evaluation." Just how good a product *is* DTA? How deserving is it of intensive development and promotion? The survey findings leave no doubt in my mind that many users are pleased with DTA, and with good cause. What is much less clear is just how important its impact can be on business as a whole. After all, only a very minute fraction of companies have so much as experimented with DTA. Can it really revolutionize management as mathematics has revolutionized engineering? Or will it forever be an occasionally helpful side calculation in a decision-making process that remains essentially unchanged?

The answers are clearly of major importance to businessmen and, indeed, depend in large measure on the businessmen themselves. How eager are they to improve the quality of their decision making? What scope for improvement is there? The answers to these questions are the key to many of the issues raised in this article.

24

Technological Forecasting in the Decision Process*

DANIEL D. ROMAN

INTRODUCTION

The New Technology

Companies in the United States are spending billions of dollars each year to research and develop new products. Technological expansion has vital economic, sociological and political implications.

The economic impact of technology is so great that some industries derive most of their current business from products which did not exist 20 years ago.[1] A study of 11 industries indicated that somewhere from 46 to 100 percent of anticipated short-term corporate growth could be attributed to new products.[2] It is now commonplace for major companies to derive 50 percent or more of current sales from products developed and introduced in the past 10 years.[3]

In a dynamic technology there must be recognition of potential human and capital obsolescence. Productive utilization of new knowledge will affect the demand and supply of present skills and new occupations not yet identifiable will emerge. Additionally, it is reasonably safe to assume that technological pressures will encourage increased interdisciplinary communication.

It is difficult to isolate the economic, sociological and political consequences of technology. It is obvious that economic and sociological factors could not be disassociated from political factors. It is also difficult to do justice to the full range of economic, sociological and political possibilities in a paper of this nature. However, recognition of the extent and direction of technological expansion can help provide the means to minimize disruption, lead to an orderly transition and assist in maximizing the positive aspects of technology.

*Source: Reprinted by permission from *Academy of Management Journal* (June, 1970), 127-38.

1/*Investing in Scientific Progress, 1961-1970,* Report NSF 61-27 (Washington, D.C.: National Science Foundation, 1961), p. 7.

2/*Management of New Products.* 4th ed. (New York: Booz, Allen and Hamilton, Inc., 1964), p. 6.

3/Ibid., p. 2, and *Report of the Joint Economic Committee,* U.S. Congress, 88th Congress, 2nd session (1964), p. 56.

The impact of technical developments such as lasers, jet aircraft, atomic energy and communication devices, to name a few, has been significant. On the horizon are such developments as new rapid transit systems, mechanical devices to replace human organs,[4] undersea farming and mining, economically useful desalinization of sea water, new synthetic materials for ultra-light construction, automatic language translators, and reliable weather forecasts. Other major technological breakthroughs are not so remote as to preclude planning for integration of these developments.[5]

As we move into a "post industrial society" phase, science and technology will be a compelling force for change.[6] In some environments managers must be alert and plan to compensate for change; in other situations a prime managerial function is to instigate technological change.[7]

In either case the manager must be aware of technological impact and be sensitive to the need for more precise planning for the future. Technological forecasting has been a response to this need.

TECHNOLOGICAL FORECASTING

Technological Forecasting—A Distinction

Technological forecasting, as distinct from general forecasting activity, has been described as "the probabilistic assessment, on a relatively high confidence level, of future technology transfer."[8] According to Jantsch, technology transfer is usually a complex process taking place at different technology transfer levels. These levels can be segregated into development and impact levels and are composed of vertical and horizontal technology transfer components. Vertical

4/In the November 1969 issue of *Industrial Research* there is an interesting discussion of the potential use of glassy materials in product design, specifically glass that won't clot blood which could be used for producing artificial organs.

5/Olaf Helmer, *Social Technology* (New York-London: Basic Books, Incorporated, 1966), pp. 56-57, and "New Products—Setting a Time Table," *Business Week* (May 27, 1967), pp. 52-61. Bright identifies seven technological trends: (1) increasing capability in transportation, (2) increased mastery of energy, (3) increased ability to control the life of animate and inanimate things, (4) increased ability to alter the characteristics of materials, (5) extension of man's sensory capabilities, (6) growing mechanization of physical activities, and (7) increasing mechanization of intellectual processes. James R. Bright, "Directions of Technological Change and Some Business Consequences," appearing in *Automation and Technological Change,* Report of the Assembly Jointly Sponsored by Battelle Memorial Institute and the American Assembly (May 9-11, 1963), pp. 9-22. Also, P. Michael Sinclair, "10 Years Ahead," *Industrial Research* (January 1969), pp. 68-72. Also, William O. Craig, "The Technology of Space—Earth," *Transportation & Distribution Management* (October 1969), pp. 22-26.

6/Editorial, "Managing Technology," *Science and Technology* (January 1969), pp. 72-73.

7/Marvin J. Cetron and Alan L. Weiser, "Technological Change, Technological Forecasting and Planning R&D—A View from the R&D Manager's Desk," *The George Washington Law Review,* vol. 36, no. 5 (July 1968), p. 1079.

8/E. Jantsch, *Technological Forecasting in Perspective* (Paris: Organization for Economic Cooperation and Development, 1967), p. 15.

transfer of technology progresses through a discovery phase, a creative phase, a substantiate phase, a development phase and an engineering phase. The engineering phase leads to a functional, technological system that could involve a hardware product, a process, or an intellectual concept. Jantsch feels that the extension of the vertical transfer by substantial subsequent horizontal technology transfer represents technological innovation.[9]

Cetron essentially supports Jantsch's definition. He cautions that a technological forecast is not a picture of what the future will bring; it is a prediction, based on confidence, that certain technical developments can occur within a specified time period with a given level of resource allocation. According to Cetron, "the foundation underlying technological forecasting is the level that individual R&D events are susceptible to influence." The periods where these events occur, if they are possible, can be significantly affected by the diversion of resources. Another fundamental of technological forecasting is that many futures can be achieved and the route to these occurrences can be determined.[10]

Exploratory and Normative Forecasting

It is important to recognize the two fundamental types of technological forecasts—exploratory and normative. The exploratory technological forecast starts from the existing base of knowledge and proceeds to the future on the assumption of logical technological progress. Exploratory technological forecasting is passive and primarily an analysis and reporting of anticipations. As a simple illustration, technological development in electronics can be cited. Starting with the post World War II period, transistors have evolved from an expensive and qualitatively unpredictable commodity to a modestly priced, reliable component. If exploratory forecasting were used in the 1940's to target in on this phase of technology, it would have been possible to predict increasing availability, lower price and more extensive use of transistors. The anticipations suggested would have been miniaturization of electronic systems and the potential for a vast number of new products resulting from application, such as portable radios, home appliances, etc.

It would seem that most industrial firms could effectively use exploratory forecasting. Reasonable identification of emerging technology and analysis of technological implications could provide clues for the firm as to competition, possible expansion of existing product lines, related product lines—which the firm should ease into, and new product areas where a foothold could provide a competitive edge. In short, a look into the future would enable better planning,

---

9/Ibid.
10/M. Cetron, "Prescription for the Military R&D Manager: Learn the Three Rx's," unpublished paper presented to The NATO Defense Research Group Seminar on Technological Forecasting and Its Application to Defense Research (Teddington, Middlesex, England), November 12, 1968, p. 2.

more effective use of resources and considerable avoidance of human and capital obsolescence.

Normative forecasting represents a different approach; it is mission- or goal-oriented. As distinct from exploratory forecasting, normative forecasting is an active or action-directed process.

In the normative method, future objectives are identified exclusive of the fact that technological gaps may currently exist that might act as constraints to attainment of these technological objectives. Normative technological forecasting can provide incentive to technological progress by focusing on the problems to be surmounted and solved. Perhaps the supersonic transport (SST) can be used to demonstrate normative forecasting. At a given time the state of the art for aircraft technology can be determined. It is decided that a need will exist five years from the base period for an aircraft incorporating the SST specifications. On a logical technological progression using exploratory forecasting some technical advancements can be predicted. However, technical gaps appear which indicate that the SST will not be an evolutionary development by the time the need or market will require the product. There are many problems beyond the technical expertise of this author which must be surmounted but some examples could be the development of materials necessary to make flying at supersonic speeds economical, safe and technically feasible.[11] Also, ways must be found to cope with sonic booms so the SST can be used over land routes.

In normative forecasting situations, the analyst works backward from the planned mission operational date and determines the technical obstacles. Normative forecasting could act as a directional force to channel effort and resources. In the example used, these resources would be diverted to solving such problems as the sonic boom or developing new materials. Since resources are limited, normative forecasting could be used in deciding priorities and decisions could be made in conjunction with cost effectiveness studies to determine whether the mission requirements are as critical as presented, are possible within the stipulated time and if the ultimate accomplishment of the mission is worth the resource expenditure.

Normative forecasting has been used primarily by the military, but industrial organizations could possibly use it. With the normative approach, the firm could examine the market potential, explore the technical feasibility, look at its expertise in the area, estimate the cost to accomplish product development and then decide whether the project should be undertaken.

Jantsch contends that presently the most difficult technological forecasting problem is establishing the correct time-frame in normative forecasting. In exploratory forecasting difficulty exists in conceiving an end-effect in the future

11/One such material emerging as a possibility is boron filament which has remarkable strength for its weight. See "Tough Featherweight Plays Hard to Get," *Business Week* (November 15, 1969), p. 38.

due to the time covered, but it is relatively simple to prognosticate compared to the normative forecast difficulties. In the normative method the forecast is predicated on objectives, requirements and sociological factors; the problem is the assumption that present requirements or anticipations are representative of the future.[12]

Methodologies of Technological Forecasting

Technological forecasting methods range from naive intuitive approaches to ultra sophisticated procedures.[13] Most of the methods are academic with limited practical adoption. Essentially, the methods can be refined to intuitive, extrapolative and correlative, and logical sequence or network type techniques.

Intuitive forecasting, the most common method employed, can be done individually by genius forecasting or by consensus. Generally this method represents an "educated guess" approach. It can vary from a very naive approach in a localized situation to a broad sampling and consensus of authoritative opinion. Delphi, the best known method under this classification, was developed by Olaf Helmer of the Rand Corporation.

A plethora of methods exist which are essentially variations of PERT. Relevance trees, graphic models, Planning-Programming-Budgeting Systems (PPBS), Mission networks, Decision Trees and Systems Analysis all use network construction to derive technological forecasts.

If numbers are any criteria it would seem that after some variation of Delphi, the network technique is the most popular avenue to technological forecasting. Networks help in identifying and establishing a logical pattern from an existing point to an anticipated goal. An intuitive method, regardless of individual technological perception, might ignore or minimize a significant obstacle to technological attainment. On the other hand, the network system is vulnerable in that all critical events might not be recognized, parallel technology might be ignored or unknown, information may be inaccurate, fragmentary, or misinterpreted (leading to wrong conclusions) and, finally, optimism or pessimism might permeate the forecast.

After examining the multitude of techniques available for technological forecasting, the author is of the opinion that while some methods appear quite scientific on the surface, minute examination almost invariably shows reliance on non-quantifiable and subjective factors before reaching conclusions. Additionally, the rationale of seemingly more sophisticated methods is often difficult to follow and the cost compared to ultimate value of the forecast could also be

12/Jantsch, op. cit., pp. 29-32.
13/Extensive treatment of technological forecasting methodologies can be found in M. J. Cetron, *Technological Forecasting* (New York: Gordon and Breach, 1969); Jantsch, op. cit.; and J. R. Bright, ed., *Technological Forecasting for Industry and Government* (Englewood Cliffs, N.J.: Prentice-Hall, Inc., 1968).

questioned, all of which might explain the popularity of the Delphi method or its derivatives.

TECHNOLOGICAL FORECASTING AS A MANAGEMENT TOOL

Some General Observations

Technological forecasting as an organized management concept is relatively new. The model depicted in Figure 1 shows how technological forecasting might be integrated into the management process. Objectives which represent the

FIGURE 1

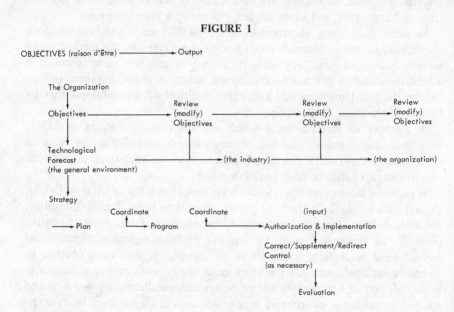

initial *raison d'etre* generally become fluid as the organization moves through its operational life cycle. The degree of modification of objectives and the extent of operational flexibility can be dictated by external and internal factors.

In the model, technological forecasting is shown as a prelude to operational activity. Technological forecasting, depending on the nature of the operation, can encompass the universe or it can be used to focus on a relatively small segment of the universe. It can be used by management in probing the general environment and then be refined to help in determining the implications for the industry and the specific organization. As each technological phase is explored, objectives should be reviewed and modified for compatibility with potential accomplishment. From this, procedure strategy can be derived to guide planning, programming, authorization, implementation, control and evaluation.

Advantages and Application

The incorporation of technological forecasting into the process of management is an extension of existing methodology. In the past it would appear that management has often intuitively drifted in this direction. Evidence can be advanced to support this contention from the information in Table 1 which shows a condensation of the time gap from innovation to application.

To be useful, technological forecasting does not have to be precise. If an innovation can be identified, and if the innovation can be translated into constructive action within a reasonable and discernible time frame, it can substantially contribute to the decision-making process.

Often, long-term commitments are undertaken on the basis of short-term technology. In many cases inability to anticipate technology leads to built-in obsolescence. Attendant to obsolescence are high modification costs to update facilities and operations, difficulty in selling change to entrenched interests and failure to exploit market potential.

An illustration of potential benefit from technological forecasting would be in product development. The technological forecasters have not yet developed the precise refinement of being able to localize specific innovations within a technological continuum. However, most technologies follow an "S" shaped curve and evaluation of existing and anticipated status of the technology can be meaningful in the decision to undergo or forego investment in product development. The technical scope, cost and time to develop a new product may be attractive or unattractive after technological forecasting information is assembled.

Generally, technological forecasting can assist management in several ways. It can represent an organized approach to a selective search for information. It can

TABLE 1*

Innovation	Year of Discovery	Year of Application
Electric motor	1821	1886
Vacuum tube	1882	1915
Radio broadcasting	1887	1922
X-ray tubes	1895	1913
Nuclear reactor	1932	1942
Radar	1935	1940
Atomic bomb	1938	1945
Transistor	1948	1951
Solar battery	1953	1955
Stereospecific rubbers & plastics	1955	1958

*Seymour L. Wolfbein, "The Pace of Technological Change and the Factors Affecting It," *Manpower Implications of Automation,* Papers presented by U.S. Department of Labor at the O.E.C.D. North American Regional Conference on Manpower Implications of Automation (Washington, D.C.: December 8-10, 1964), p. 19.

provoke thought by expanding horizons. It can help provide perspective and facilitate interdisciplinary communication. It can encourage operational sensitivity. It can assist management in determining the magnitude of anticipated change and provide a basis for estimating costs and requirements for people, facilities, equipment, etc. It can aid in giving direction to product development and market penetration. It can assist in recognizing competition and other possible restraints such as natural resources or technological limitations. It can be used to help determine sociological and economic trends.

Limitations

Several limitations to technological forecasting should be apparent to the discerning reader. The fact that limitations exist in technological forecasting just as there are limitations in other techniques should not discourage management; awareness should lead to more critical and productive application.

Information may be the greatest limitation to contributive technological forecasting. The information problem is extensive. For instance: What information is needed? How much information is required? Is the information accurate? Have related and unrelated disciplines been explored for possible information transfer or possible technological fallout?

Information interpretation is a vital ingredient in technological forecasting. No mechanical process presently exists which will evaluate the information in terms of available technical solutions, cost and value, product applicability and market potential. Human judgment is a factor in interpreting information and interpretation can be colored by optimism or pessimism and courage or conservatism. Information analysis can also differ due to the competence of the analyst and his functional orientation. Augmenting the difficulties cited is the fact that often pertinent information may not be available due to security restrictions and trade secrets. The unavailability of essential information may negate the entire process by establishing the technological forecast on incomplete or erroneous premises.

Forecasting is far from an exact science, so much so that standard methods and procedures have not been generally established. Although the literature abounds with methodology, in practice, it appears that variations of the Delphi technique and network construction are most commonly used. More exact and understandable techniques must be developed which are practical and provide management with reasonable confidence in their accuracy. However, a standard method may not be feasible since each organization based on its size and mission must develop forecasting techniques to suit its own operational environment.

Another limitation is that unanticipated discovery can lead to demand for a family of products which were previously inconceivable. Good examples are the transistor and the laser. A major discovery can instigate derived demand for related and supporting products and technology and give rise to satellite industries.[14]

Quinn points out that the interaction of many technological breakthroughs could lead to unforeseen prospects which would have a negating effect on all forecasts. He says,

Similarly, one cannot at present anticipate specifically how biological studies of cellular and molecular coding will interact with extremely high-polymer investigations which are beginning to produce synthetic molecules with many of the characteristics of living organisms. In such advanced areas one can only recognize that there is a strong probability of potential interactions which will increase the importance of both fields, and therefore do more extensive research or monitor such activities more closely.[15]

ORGANIZING FOR TECHNOLOGICAL FORECASTING

Many functions survive in organizations because of defensive management attitudes. Most managements desire a progressive image and as a consequence may install publicized new techniques without really embracing the concept. Utilization failures can often be attributed to management's unwillingness to get involved with things about which they are not familiar, and subsequently have misgivings about. Contributing to this attitude are the practitioners who lose themselves in technique and take little or no pains to translate their work into understandable terms and useful concepts which management would be willing to implement. This represents a very real threat to expanded management acceptance of technological forecasting.

A review of the literature leaves the impression of enamorment with technique. This can be disastrous if substance is sacrificed for method.

Some Organizational Considerations

There are several factors management must consider before commiting itself to technological forecasting. It must look at the type of operation in which it is involved. Is the organization in a technologically sensitive environment? Is the organization a leader or follower in its operational environment? Are operations large and diverse enough to justify commitment to a technological forecasting activity? How extensive a commitment should be made in terms of people, facilities and budget? Would management want sporadic technological forecasts on an informal basis or would there be formal reviews at set intervals? The answer to the last question could dictate the extent of commitment management

14/J. B. Quinn, "Technological Forecasting," *Harvard Business Review* (March-April 1967), pp. 101-103.
15/Ibid., p. 102.

is willing to make and the type of people it will have to train or recruit. In line with the aforementioned, management will have to select people with compatible skills to achieve technological forecasting objectives. Does management want a group of specialists in a range of technical areas? Does management want a group composed of multi-viewed individuals with broad perspective and minimal functional allegiance? Or is a combination of generalists and specialists more desirable? The range of possibilities is not exhausted because management can use in-house functional specialists in concert with management types to act as a technological forecasting advisory board. Finally, management may not want any internal commitment and may prefer to use outside specialists or consulting organizations to bring in fresh views to reconcile against internal prognostications.

Organizational Location

Technological forecasting can be a function or an activity within a function. Several organizational affiliations appear logical such as placement in long-range planning, marketing, materials management or in the research and development group. Technological forecasting can also be elevated to functional status with independent identity.

There are no clear cut answers or universal solutions to organizational location of technological forecasting. Strong arguments can be advanced for affiliation with each of the functions indicated or for independent status. The ultimate answer of placement might be dictated by factors such as functional utilization of the technological forecast or management's orientation. Functional affiliation may lead to high utilization but it can also mean that the technological forecasting activity is functionally captive and narrow in its perspective. A danger in this situation is that technological forecasting may be slanted to support the functional parent rather than provide general direction more compatible with the objectives of the total organization.

There are some compelling advantages to having technological forecasting as an independent operation and functional entity if the size and scope of the organization warrants technological forecasting. As a noncaptive operation it can be used by management for organizational checks and balances and as a directional force in assessing the validity of long-range planning and objectives. It can help in determining what emphasis to place in research and development and to give management insight into the reality of marketing goals. What must be guarded against if technological forecasting has functional independence is excessive cost generated by operational practice inconsistent with the organization's need and capacity.

CONCLUSIONS

Several significant theories and techniques have been incorporated into management practice in the past quarter of a century. Often these ideas have been accepted without critical examination. Adoption without adequate evaluation has, in many instances, initially led to disillusionment and obscured the true value. Uncritical acceptance and over commitment frequently can be attributed to the disciples of innovations who oversell a concept. The fact that all tools are not applicable in all situations, or, where applicable, have differing degrees of utility should not minimize the potential contribution. Management must recognize that no single panacea exists and must judiciously exploit ideas with consideration of the operational environment.

Technological forecasting as a formal concept can be traced back to the mid-1940's. Its present structure and direction took shape around 1960.[16] To date the greatest application and methodology development has been military-oriented. The military services have had encouraging success and indications are for intensification of effort in this area.

The idea of technological forecasting is relatively unknown in business circles. Professor Bright has probably been the most active disciple in promoting technological forecasting to industry. Indications are that inroads are being made. There has generally been enthusiastic reception from those industrial executives exposed to technological forecasting.

Technological forecasting in proper context should seriously be considered as an addition to the management process. As Jantsch so aptly stated: *Technological forecasting is not yet a science but an art, and is characterized today by attitudes, not tools; human judgment is enhanced, not substituted by it. The development of auxiliary techniques, gradually attaining higher degrees of sophistication (and complexity) since 1960, is oriented towards ultimate integration with evolving information technology.*[17]

16/Jantsch, p. 17.
17/Jantsch, p. 17.

part FIVE

Contemporary Management
in a Dynamic
Environment

A fundamental view of the editors is that despite a lack of any specifically organized body of knowledge or universally accepted school of management, a science of management is slowly emerging. In this text three overlapping schools—classical, behavioral, and management science—have been identified. Whether any of the three approaches are tenable and accurate is a moot question. The fact remains that an evolving science of management is forcing managers to evaluate and utilize concepts of each of the three schools.

The Complex Contemporary Environment

The manager in the 19th century concentrated primarily on producing a product. Major decision-making emphasis was placed on building factories, hiring able employees, and producing a salable product. Managing in such a way that production is the major focal point would not allow an organization to grow and remain stable in the contemporary environment. In modern organizations, many other factors are also apparent.

The *union* is a force that must be included in the development of managerial plans and controls. The *government* is playing an active role in such areas as collective bargaining, strike settlements, unemployment programs, and financing construction of plants in hard pressed urban areas. The *public* is more vociferous and concerned about the actions of business firms. This is especially evident in areas such as air pollution, conservation, and social responsibility. *International* competition is another factor complicating the environment of the contemporary manager.

293

The Importance of the Three Schools of Management

Meeting the increasing challenges offered by the union, government, public, and international competition will require special competence on the part of the contemporary manager. This type of competence will require the manager to use a number of different concepts, techniques, and models. Such specific concepts as unity of command, work groups, job enrichment programs, and linear programming may be used together to solve a problem. In addition, the social implications of the solution may also weigh heavily in the final outcome.

The manager of the future will be required to recognize that useful concepts exist in each of the three schools of management. Sole reliance on classical principles, functions or processes or behavioral suggestions such as participative management or management science models is as sterile and stagnant as relying solely on past experience. Instead, the need for a balance of classical, behavioral, and management science approaches coupled with experience is more realistic and contemporary.

In this final part of the book, the articles have been selected with this specific objective in mind. In addition, articles devoted to discussions of future developments in management are also included. The management literature abounds with predictions concerning the elements that are most likely to influence organizations and managers in the future. In some cases, the term future development is partially a misnomer since many of the future discussion points can actually be found in some of today's progressive organizations. While numerous areas could have been covered, the editors selected articles in the areas of organizational design, the multinational firm, the social environment, and women in management.

The first article in this section "Organization Patterns of the Future" by Robert T. Golembiewski is concerned with what the administrative world is likely to be in the future. The author distinguishes between two alternative sets of ideas; the managerial "push-theory" and "pull-theory." Each theory is carefully examined and the author indicates which approach he believes will be more appropriate for the future and why.

In "The Human Concept: New Philosophy for Business," Leslie M. Dawson believes that American business is entering a new era in which unprecedented human and social demands will be made upon it. According to the author, the perspectives of the traditional "marketing concept" are too limited to cope with the new pressures. Hence, a newer and broader philosophy has gradually evolved in many of the nation's more progressive firms. Dawson describes this as the "human concept," and he believes that widespread acceptance within the business community could have tremendous significance for human progress as well as for the future of business.

In the article "Toward a Concept of Managerial Control for a World Enterprise," M. Y. Yoshino examines the complex problems involved in managing a multinational firm. He notes that increasing competitive pressure, coupled with the inherent difficulties in managing a worldwide enterprise point to the need for insuring effective managerial arrangements. According to Yoshino, one of the most important tasks of managing a multinational firm is to design an effective management control system to enable top management to control the activities of a large number of foreign branches as a unified whole. He devotes his discussion to establishing meaningful standards of performance for the world enterprise.

There is little argument that the talents of women have been underutilized in our society. In the article "Full Utilization of Women in Employment: The Problem and an Action Program," the author, Dennis Slevin examines this very important problem. He cites the various laws that have been passed which indicate, according to him, that women's liberation is with us to stay. He notes that the problems of providing women with more opportunity will fall heaviest on administrators. To help overcome these problems which he identifies, the author presents an action program.

Many managers believe that the discontent expressed by young people today will not be able to be expressed in a corporate hierarchy. John S. Fielden the author of "Today the Campuses, Tomorrow the Corporations" believes otherwise. According to Fielden, in order to attract bright young people, corporations will have to become less autocratic in decision-making, and will have to become more responsive to social change. He believes that open, flexible, and socially responsible organizations will be able to attract the best young individuals for the top managerial positions of the future.

The final article in this section provides an actual example of business response to a community problem. The article "The Corporation and Community: Realities and Myths," by Frank H. Cassell also examines the entire issue of corporate involvement in the community presenting all sides of the issue. The example presents a dramatic departure from the traditional business method of dealing with community problems and the author discusses its real significance.

25

Organization Patterns of the Future: What They Mean to Personnel Administration*

ROBERT T. GOLEMBIEWSKI

Charting future organization patterns involves questions of what the administrative world is and how it should be. Two alternative sets of ideas may be distinguished. The first and dominant view amounts to a kind of managerial push-theory. In it, the employee scrambles and innovates and burns the midnight oil to avoid possible and perhaps inevitable harsh outcomes. In one version of this view, men work hard because it is morally bad to do otherwise. The properties of this view are like those of McGregor's Theory X or 9,1 on the Grid.

Whyte's *The Organization Man* illustrates the managerial push-theory, and laments its demise. Gone are the old stimuli to heroic effort such as survival-of-the-fittest "training programs" that tested a man's desire and skills, or broke him. In their place, Whyte saw manifold nicely-nicelies such as longish training programs that effectively closed the school of hard-knocks. In Whyte's view, organization men were whistling their way through the dark, hand-in-hand, neglecting harsh realities for which they were less and less prepared. Given the push-theory, no harshness, no progress.

In the managerial pull-theory, the focus is more on what you are reaching toward than on what you are seeking to avoid. In it, the employee also scrambles and innovates and burns the midnight oil. However, work is so need satisfying that it elicits massive employee efforts. The goal is dual: doing the job better, and doing it in ways that permit unprecedented personal freedom in organizations. Indeed, this view almost says that *it is only through greater personal freedom* that a better job can be accomplished. Organization life is demanding in this view, but it does promise fulfillment at work. Warren Bennis articulates both emphases clearly:[1]

> I think that the future I describe is not necessarily a "happy" one.

*Source: Reprinted from *Personnel Administration* (November-December, 1969), 9-24, by permission of the International Personnel Management Association.

1/Warren G. Bennis, "Beyond Bureaucracy," *Trans-Action,* vol. 2 (July-August, 1965), p. 35.

Coping with rapid change, living in temporary work systems—all augur social strains and psychological tensions . . .

In these new organizations of the future, participants will be called upon to use their minds more than at any other time in history. Fantasy, imagination, and creativity will be legitimate in ways that today seem strange. Social structures will no longer be instruments of psychic repression but will increasingly promote play and freedom on behalf of curiosity and thought.

The managerial pull-theory seeks to integrate personal needs and organizational demands.[2] In essence, the underlying rationale proposes that:

1. Many individuals find little satisfaction in their work, and this is a major deprivation for them personally and for their organization.
2. Many or all individuals will be more productive as they exercise greater control over their work, and as work permits satisfaction of a broadening range of needs.
3. Organizations increasingly need superior output from more and more of their employees; technological and skill requirements are such that these contributions must be elicited more than forced. Expenditures to redesign jobs and work relations, and to change managerial styles or techniques are reasonable; indeed, in the longer run they are probably necessary.

Concern with Managerial World-Views

It seems clear that personnel administration will have to be consciously concerned with both managerial theories. Thus, the pull-theory becomes increasingly appropriate as organizations move in the directions suggested in Table 1, and such movement seems very probable.

TABLE 1

From Basic Emphasis upon:	To Growing Emphasis upon:
regularity in operations ⟶	creativity in concept; adaptability in execution
programmed decisions ⟶	novel decisions
stable and simple competencies, technologies, and market ⟶	volatile and complex competencies, technologies, and markets
stop-and-go processing ⟶	continuous processing
stable product lines, programs ⟶	volatile product lines, programs
monolithic product lines, programs ⟶	variegated product lines, programs
demands of hierarchy ⟶	demands of task, technology, profession
departmental orientation ⟶	system orientation
expanding volume at central site ⟶	developing national and international field units

2/See especially Chris Argyris, *Integrating the Individual and the Organization* (New York: Wiley, 1964).

The reader can supply the full rationale for the relevance of the pull-theory under the conditions in the right column. To illustrate, you can order someone to obey when work or decisions are programmed. Ordering someone to be creative is quite another matter.

Personnel administration probably will also give significant attention to structure and policies consistent with the push-theory. Briefly, technological requirements influence which structure and managerial techniques are likely to be successful, and not all organizations will or even can move sharply rightward on the dimensions above. Certainly, at least different technologies and markets will move rightward at different times and paces. Thus today's plastics industry reflects the characteristics in the right column, but the cardboard industry does not. As compelling new evidence suggests, opposite managerial styles are effective in these two industries.[3] Roughly, the push-theory is more appropriate to the technology and market of the cardboard carton industry than to the plastics industry. To the degree that technologies and markets like the carton industry will continue to exist, then, so also will personnel administration have to give attention to structure and policies consistent with the push-theory.

The Managerial Pull-Theory

Since the managerial pull-theory seems congenial to the technology of the future, our focus narrows. We live in a transitional period, and the following analysis extends what is already happening into a reasonably coherent view of what the future implies for personnel administration.

Probable changes in organizational patterns consistent with the pull-theory can be described in terms of four polarities. Different times and technologies give different emphases to each. The four polarities are:

1. differentiation/integration;
2. repression/wriggle room (freedom to act);
3. stability/newness; and
4. function/flow of work.

Short of anarchy, there is no real choice of structure or no structure. The emphases placed on these four polarities, however, significantly influence the kind of structure that does develop in organizations. A wide range of alternative organization patterns are possible.

First, any organizing pattern reflects relative emphases on differentiation/integration. Following Lawrence and Lorsch, "differentiation" can be defined in terms of the development among the several units of an organization of "different formal reporting relationships, different criteria for rewards, and different control procedures." In sum, differentiation is defined in terms of "the

---

3/Paul R. Lawrence and Jay W. Lorsch, *Organization and Environment* (Boston: Harvard Graduate School of Business Administration, 1967).

difference in cognitive and emotional orientation among managers in different functional departments." Integration refers to "the quality of the state of collaboration that exists among departments that are required to achieve unity of effort by the demands of the environment."[4]

Organization patterns of the near-future will no doubt emphasize integration. Early organizational experience tended to reflect integration, as in the crafts. Over the first half of this century, however, the emphasis shifted to the differentiation of functions and skills. Thus "bureaucracy" dominated this phase of organization history, and that concept is rooted in differentiation. Bureaucracy includes:

1. a well-defined chain of command that vertically channels formal interaction;
2. a system of procedures and rules for dealing with all contingencies at work, which reinforces the reporting insularity of each bureau;
3. a division of labor based upon specialization by major function or process that vertically fragments a flow of work;
4. promotion and selection based on technical competence defined consistently with 1-3 above; and
5. impersonality in relations between organization members and between them and their clients.

More recently, integration has received increasing emphasis. The "system approach" and the computer are the major contemporary technical expressions of this integrative thrust. Behaviorally, integration implies meeting both human needs and technical demands at work.

Second, a basic foundation of any pattern for organizing deals with the relative emphasis on repression and "wriggle room." No technical definitions seem necessary here; and "surplus repression" is commonly seen as a major product of bureaucracy. Increasingly, an emerging integrative emphasis seeks an organizational climate having the minimal constraints consistent with quality performance. This is the essence of the contemporary stress on "management by objectives." Similarly, the popularity of sensitivity training reflects massive concern about such costs of repression as withheld effort or information.

There is no mistaking the root-cause of such de-emphasis on repression. Today's organizations reflect a growing need for an organic and evolving integration, as opposed to a mechanical structuring. Adherence to a mechanical system can be enforced; but commitment to an organic integration can only be elicited and encouraged. Put another way, the integrity of a stable and simple technology may be safeguarded by culling deviants. But changing and complex technologies require the careful husbanding of selected kinds of innovation or adaptability in a widening range of employees. Hence the growing importance of wriggle room, or freedom to act.

The change in emphasis on repression/wriggle room may be characterized

---

4/Lawrence and Lorsch, op. cit., pp. 10-11.

broadly, and with essential accuracy. The bureaucratic spirit is oriented toward developing a system to guard against man at his worst, to preclude error or venality. Hence flows of work are differentiated as functions or positions or motions, and surplus repression is the glue used to pull them together. The integrative spirit, on the other hand, is oriented toward creating an environment in which man can approach his productive best. Hence the emphasis on wriggle room, on learning how and when individuals can more often meet their own needs while contributing more effectively to a total flow of work with which they identify their interests.

Third, the relative emphasis on stability/newness also constitutes a major decision underlying any organizing pattern. The acceleration of newness has been described in many places, even if one cannot feel it in his bones. Hence the bare notice here that all-but-overwhelming newness is a trademark of our times, and that it is poorly served by bureaucratic properties.

Fourth, different emphases on the three polarities above imply different organization structures built around functions and flows of work, respectively. Take an easy case, to begin, the organization of three activities A, B, and C which when combined yield some product or service.[5] Figure 1 presents the skeletal structure consistent with these three emphases: differentiation, repression, and stability.

This characterization is easy to support. For example, Figure 1 essentially puts the same or similar activities together in its basic units of organization. That is, the model builds on departments *differentiated* by kinds of activities, usually called "functions" at high levels of organization and "processes" at lower levels. Relatedly, the narrow span of control is well designed to facilitate surplus *repression* in the details of operation. That is, the structure encourages centrali-

FIGURE 1
A Structure Consistent with the Values of Bureaucracy: Emphases on Differentiation, Repression, Stability, and Function

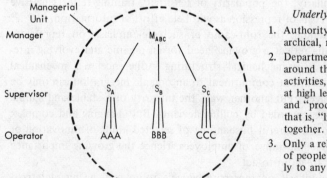

Underlying Properties

1. Authority is a vertical, or hierarchical, relation.
2. Departments are organized around the same or similar activities, called "functions" at high levels of organization and "processes" at low levels; that is, "like" activities are put together.
3. Only a relatively small number of people should report directly to any superior.

5/For a comparison of these models, see Robert T. Golembiewski, *Men, Management, and Morality* (New York: McGraw-Hill, 1965).

zation of decision-making at the level of MABC, who alone can make reasonable decisions about the flow of work A + B + C. Hence he alone controls a "managerial unit." Finally, the model presumes a *stable* state. The underlying model is that of a mechanical meshing of parts rather than of a dynamic flow of work.

Figure 2 presents an alternative structure that is consistent with the principal adaptive arrangements to the on-going organizational revolution. These adaptive arrangements include: decentralization; project management; matrix overlays; independent profit centers; management by objectives; autonomous teams; and numerous other variations on a theme. In common, as the Figure 2 model suggests, these adaptations stress integration, wriggle room, change, and flow of work.

Thus, the unorthodox model organizes around *integrative* departments, that is, it groups together activities that are related in a total flow of work. This integrative thrust can be extended to the operators, as through job rotation and job enlargement. In addition, the model seeks the *minimum control* that is consistent with end-item quality and quantity. The multiple opportunities for self-discipline and self-control built in the model, for example, reduce the need

FIGURE 2
An Alternative Structure: Emphasis on Integration, Wriggle
Room, Change, and Flow of Work

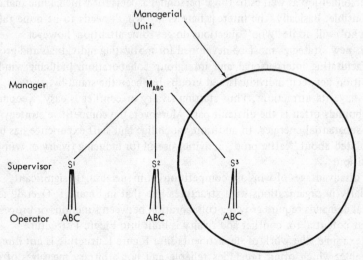

Underlying Properties

1. Authoritative relations occur up, down, and across the organization, and all these vectors should be directed to similar goals by an effective structure.
2. Departmentation reflects the "flow of work"; that is, related activities are put together whether they are "like" or "unlike."
3. A relatively large number of people may report to any superior, given a structure that facilitates measuring performance.

for external repression in tying individual needs to organizational goals. The key factors are teams which control a flow of work whose performance is easily and meaningfully comparable.

Moreover, Figure 2 variously facilitates adapting to *change* and to *growth*. For example, Figure 1 structures tend to grow "tall" very quickly, with consequent increases in reaction time, in communication costs, and so on. The limited span of control is the major culprit. Figure 2 structures are much less growth-sensitive and can remain relatively "flat" even with manifold increases in size.

Finally, Figure 2 structures departmentalize around *flows of work* as opposed to functions. Each S now controls a managerial unit.

The two structures are ideal types in that they are analytical extremes. In practice, they can be approached only in degree, often in complex mixtures. But approaches to one ideal model or the other will tend to generate significantly different consequences.

The Managerial Pull-Theory

1. *Differentiation/Integration.* At least three major challenges for personnel administration are involved in shifting emphasis from differentiation toward integration. As used here, "personnel administration" usually refers to both the staff personnel job as well as to those personnel aspects for which a line manager is responsible. Basically, the interest here is in "what" needs to be done rather than "who" will do it. "Who" questions do get some attention, however.

First, new strategies must be developed for motivating individuals and groups while facilitating interpersonal and intergroup collaboration. Inducing win-lose competition between individuals and groups has been the stand-by strategy, and it does have its attractions. Thus starting rivalry or conflict is easy. Keeping it within bounds often is the difficult part. Moreover, the competitive strategy can engage substantial energies. In addition, much line and staff experience has been accumulated about "cattle prod" activities useful for inducing rivalry or win-lose competition.

The disadvantages of win-lose competition loom increasingly significant,[6] and particularly in organizations with structures like that in Figure 1. Overall, technological demands require growing collaboration between functions or processes, but great potential for conflict and rivalry is built into Figure 1 structure.

For example, the work of departments in a Figure 1 structure is not directly comparable, which often precludes reliable and non-arbitrary measures of performance. Each department provides only a partial contribution to a variety of

6/To extend the argument, win-lose competition also is less useful at an inter-firm or inter-nation level. The magnitude of many projects requires exquisite coordination between "competing" firms, for example. And I have heard a major aerospace official say that, whatever the political issues between us, acute practical considerations require advanced cooperation on the SST between American firms and the French.

flows of work, which implies major problems in factoring-out departmental successes and failures. Because of this complexity, one department may "win" only as another department "loses," e.g., in a cost-accounting allocation.

Structures like that in Figure 2 require that S perform a managerially-integrative role, in contrast. The S takes a generalist role in fact as well as intent, in that he can make reasonable decisions about a total flow of work. These integrative features of Figure 2 structures have numerous advantages. Because the basic units of organization below MABC are autonomous and control an entire flow of work, for example, reliable and non-arbitrary measurement of performance is relatively simple. In addition, the basic unit of organization includes the full sequence of operations. Effort and performance are more likely to be congruent, as a consequence. Moreover, the "wins" of one department do not preclude "wins" by others. Even the competition in Figure 2 structures has integrative tendencies.

Since a Figure 2 structure may not exist, or cannot always be approached, the development of strategies for motivation that facilitate interpersonal and intergroup collaboration deserve high priority. For example, inter-departmental conflicts and rivalries encouraged by Figure 1 structures may be ameliorated by improving the processes of interpersonal and group interaction. Consider the chief executive of an organization patterned after Figure 1 who spotlighted the divisive forces induced by the traditional structure in these words: *The trouble with ABC is that nobody aside from me ever gives one damn about the overall goals of this place. They're all seeing the world through the lenses of their departmental biases. What we need around here are people who wear the ABC hat, not the engineering hat or the sales hat or the production hat.*[7] This complaint inspired the development of the ABC Hats, a group representing several functions and hierarchical levels that filled the integrative gaps resulting from a Figure 1 structure. Organizational applications of sensitivity training seek similar integration via improved interpersonal and group relations.[8]

Improving interpersonal and intergroup relations in a Figure 1 structure implies an uphill struggle all the way. Whatever improvement in communication processes results from sensitivity training or from a team-building experience, that is, the structure will tend to keep on generating conflict and rivalry. Consequently, "booster shots" are necessary. Indeed, some organizations have evolved a "change-agent" role to provide just such a stimulus to effective interaction between individuals and groups. Providing change-agent services, and particularly organizing for them, will generate major problems for personnel administration.

Second, personnel administration must give massive attention to developing

7/Warren G. Bennis, "Organizations of the Future," *Personnel Administration,* vol. 30 (September, 1967), p. 16.

8/For an analog of sensitivity training that shows promise, see Robert T. Golembiewski and Arthur Blumberg, "Confrontation as a Training Design in Complex Organizations," *Journal of Applied Behavioral Science,* vol. 3 (December, 1967), pp. 525-47.

a viable integrative function. Consider two possible approaches: some integrative role may be grafted to the basic functional structure, in Figure 1; or integrative teams may become the basic units of departmentation, as in Figure 2. Both cases present problems. The second case is more attractive in concept, but for most organizations it would mean a major and difficult organization development effort.

Consequently, integrative roles in organizations tend to be superimposed on a Figure 1 structure, as by establishing an interdepartmental coordinating committee or a "project manager." Both are integrative overlays designed to counteract the fragmenting tendencies of the traditional structure of departments organized by functions or processes. To illustrate, the project manager develops a temporary integrative team to do some specific job, making requests for personnel as necessary from the functional departments. Team members then respond to two authoritative sources: to their more-or-less temporary project manager; and to the head of the functional department to which they will return when the project is complete. The resulting multiple lines of authority are sometimes called a "matrix overlay."

Integrative arrangements superimposed on a traditional structure can help reduce the conflict and rivalry characteristic of a Figure 1 structure, but they are tricky.[9] Thus questions of multiple authority may vex personnel administration. Or power may remain in the permanent functional departments, and this can make life difficult for integrative agents such as project managers or interdepartmental coordinating committees. In both cases, in addition, what is to be done with a project manager when his project is terminated? The experience in the aero-space industry does not suggest any easy ways out. Making conscious arrangements for an integrative role, then, implies serious problems for personnel administration.

Third, shared-values that encourage organizational unity must be developed and broadly accepted. Otherwise, a significant shift of emphasis toward integration is unlikely. Prevailing organizational values—the "values of bureaucracy"—are hierarchy-serving in that they reinforce superior-subordinate relations, but they do so only at the expense of inhibiting the development of socio-emotional ties that can integrate individuals or groups performing different functions in different departments in a Figure 1 structure. Since today's organizations increasingly must be integrative, and since they increasingly must stress dynamic knowledge-gathering because they are truth-requiring, the values of bureaucracy will increasingly generate troublesome consequences.

The alternative to the values of bureaucracy is not yet clear. However, the following "climate of beliefs" seems adaptive to the knowledge-gathering and truth-requiring demands of today's technology:[10]

9/Richard M. Hodgetts, "Leadership Techniques in the Project Organization," *Academy of Management Journal,* vol. 11 (June, 1968), pp. 211-20.
10/Warren G. Bennis, *Changing Organizations* (New York: McGraw-Hill, 1966), pp. 15-16.

1. full and free communication, regardless of rank or power;
2. reliance on consensual processes in dealing with conflict, as opposed to coercion or compromise;
3. basing influence on technical competence and knowledge, as opposed to personal whim or hierarchical status;
4. an atmosphere that easily admits emotional expression as well as task-oriented behavior; and
5. acceptance of conflict between the individual and the organization, which conflict is to be coped with openly.

Getting acceptance of such values in principle and practice should constitute a major near-future challenge for personnel administration.

2. *Repression/Wriggle Room.* Two issues involved in the shift of emphasis toward wriggle room deserve special attention because they pose major problems for personnel administration. One issue involves tailoring both organization structure and interaction processes so as to meet human needs at work. The second issue deals with values and representational vehicles capable of supporting such changes in structure and interaction processes.

One major approach toward emphasizing wriggle room involves shaping organizations to fit people in the design of tasks and structure. Historically, people were fitted to the organization. Many observers have argued the merits of tailoring tasks to man,[11] as through job enlargement, so we note only two major derivative demands on personnel administration. In the federal government, "classification experts" still far outnumber "specialists in job design." A traditional personnel specialty, especially in the federal government, needs to be reoriented if more wriggle room is the goal. Moreover, job enlargement is easiest in a Figure 2 structure. Since a Figure 1 structure is what most organizations have, the implied challenge to public personnel administration is the development of a potent OD, or organization development, specialty. Experience in the federal government suggests the road will be arduous and long.

Relatedly, interaction processes can also usefully be tailored to man. Argyris has posited needs of man that are seen as typically frustrated in large organizations, and especially in organizations patterned after Figure 1.[12] Building satisfying interaction processes into organizations is a gargantuan task, and only scarcely begun. Thus some change-agents attempt to build sensitivity training groups directly into organizations, which raises major issues with traditional ways of organizing and managing. Others argue that building need-satisfying interaction into organizations is hopelessly utopian. Many variations exist between those anchor-positions.

However matters evolve, the face of personnel administration is certain to

11/David S. Brown, "Shaping the Organization to Fit People," *Management of Personnel Quarterly*, vol. 5 (Summer, 1966), pp. 12-16.
12/Chris Argyris, *Personality and Organization* (New York: Harper, 1957), especially pp. 49-53.

change substantially. That much is clear from these broad values of sensitivity training that imply what is often seen as lacking in organizations:[13]

1. an attitude of inquiry, reflecting a "hypothetical spirit" and an emphasis on experimentation;
2. an expanded awareness on the part of organization members, with a corresponding sense of a broader choice of alternatives for action;
3. an undergirding system of norms that stress collaboration and a problem-solving orientation to conflict; and
4. an emphasis on the helping relationship as a major way to concretely express man's interdependence with man.

Changes in tasks and interaction processes must be supported by appropriate values and representational vehicles. As an example, greater managerial concern for due process and sharing of influence seems necessary. Either the pull-theory or the push-theory can guide how the two are approached—since due process and influence-sharing will receive major attention, for good or ill—and the choice is a matter of real consequence. That is, influence-sharing or due process can be granted with top management support in sensitive dialog with employees whose needs and capabilities are diversely evolving; or at a polar extreme, they can be wrested away by employees after heated battle with a boulwareian management. The pull-theory recommends the former, of course.

No doubt much of the near-future resolution of issues involving due process and influence-sharing will be in familiar terms: employee unionization, more or less grudging management assent, and more or less successful efforts at rapprochement. Increasingly, however, the resolution will involve the breaking of new and uncertain ground. At least at managerial levels in many organizations, for example, determined efforts are underway to develop new and enhanced representational vehicles, encompassing "tell all" dinners, management councils, and God knows what. Only the brave fool would try to guess the product of this maelstrom, or even whether we can avoid a kind of organizational totalitarianism borne of ineptness or unwillingness in developing appropriate values and vehicles. That personnel administration vitally depends on the outcome of the search for viable approaches to power-sharing and to organizational due-process seems undeniable.

3. *Stability/Newness.* Any shift in emphasis toward newness implies at least two major issues.

First, the "change function" must be given greater priority, with such attendant challenges as better equipping people to tolerate ambiguity. We have only clues as to how to cope successfully with such an increased priority, both as to mechanics and organization.

As for mechanics, an increased priority for change implies an appropriate

13/Edgar H. Schein and Warren G. Bennis, editors, *Personal and Organizational Change through Group Methods* (New York: Wiley, 1965), pp. 30-35.

reward system. Existing reward systems usually are keyed to how much one produces, however, or how long one has been a producer. Neither bias facilitates change; both biases are at best irrelevant to change, if they are not inimical to it. Likely reinforcers of change imply a host of problems. I have in mind one labor agreement that rewards employees for their willingness to be continually retrained, as opposed to rewarding them for their productivity or for their seniority. Such arrangements imply very significant labor-management issues, with which we have precious little experience. One thing is clear, however. Much of the heart of traditional personnel administration—as in the classification and pay plans at the federal level—poorly suits arrangements designed to facilitate change. Nothing better could be expected of these products of our bureaucratic phase.

Organizationally, increased emphasis on change also poses real problems for personnel administration. The issues are most sharply joined in the evolving role of the "change-agent" which is devoted to facilitating change and inducing appropriate interpersonal and intergroup climates for change. Where is the change-agent to be located? Who is to be the change-agent?

Working answers to such questions have tended to be unsatisfactory. Relying on "external change-agents" such as consultants has some real advantages, but this places the change-agent outside the organization's authority-and-reward structure and may compromise his effectiveness. Relying on internal change agents ties them into the system, but this cuts both ways. If things got rough for them, change-agents might be motivated to become a kind of non-directive and even gentle but nonetheless efficient gestapo in the pursuit of their own interests.[14]

If the line manager becomes the change-agent, you avoid many ticklish authority problems but you run the risk of placing reliance for change in an individual who may be overbusy with day-to-day problems. Moreover, there is no guarantee that line officials will have the appropriate skills or training, or even the interest. Embody the change-agent role in a staff man or unit, and that implies all of the problems that have plagued line-staff relations. Managing the change-agent role, in sum, implies one grand job for personnel administration, conceived in its broad sense as an amalgam of line and staff responsibilities.

Second, the shifting emphasis to newness implies a growing need to quickly develop and disband both large and small work-units. The point clearly applies to the teams formed in project management, for example. Moreover, the need to revitalize today's organizations so as to prepare them for adapting to tomorrow's markets or programs also raises questions about managing temporary social systems.

Managing temporary social systems presents a formidable task in at least two

---

14/The temptation is great where such change-agents use sensitivity training sessions, for example, during which much data about individuals and groups may be divulged. A similar problem faces such professionals as psychiatrists employed by organizations.

major ways. Such management requires that people develop a kind of instant but still intense commitment. This is difficult, but seemingly unavoidable. Complex systems often permit no alternative to the technical and social compatibility of team members. In addition, organization members will need to learn how to experience the loss of one temporary social system in ways that do not inhibit their commitment to future systems.

We are gaining some experience with effective management of temporary social systems, as via "team-building." The approach uses learning analogs derived from the laboratory approach, whose purest form is the sensitivity-training group. For example, such team-building has proved useful in one multi-plant firm using periodic rotation of management teams.[15] Plant technology is based on continuous processing and delicate integration of activities, and rotation typically caused a variety of dislocation that registered as decreases in productivity and employee satisfaction. Roughly, the typical relearning dip in several plants of this firm approximated six months. Moreover, as the plant technology became more integrated, that break-in period seemed to lengthen. Now, three or four day team-building experiences are provided early in the life of each new team. The re-learning dip has been halved.

Less is known about disbanding a temporary social system in ways that do not inhibit the commitment of its members to future systems. Work with sensitivity training suggests that such "separation anxiety" can be effectively managed. However, socio-emotional de-briefing is still uncommon.

Experience with both creating and terminating temporary social systems seems worth developing. Consider aerospace firms, which typify what many organizations are increasingly becoming. One prominent feature of aerospace experience is the socio-emotional turmoil associated with developing, and more particularly with terminating, project teams. Members of teams gear themselves up to unflinching commitment, working long and hard. When the project is concluded, depression often sets in, marital difficulties seem unusually common and severe, and so on. Both research and popular news magazines have painted an alarming picture of this new problem, which we can expect to become increasingly common.[16]

Managing temporary social systems also implies two major technical issues. One of these concerns structural arrangements that encourage quick group identification and that also permit reinforcement by reward systems keyed to meaningful measures of performance. These dual goals are within reach. That is, both identification and the measurement of performance will be facilitated as organizations move toward Figure 2 structures. The point is of crucial signifi-

---

15/"Team-building" has also been utilized on a mass scale, by such firms as Alcan and TRW. See Alexander Winn, "The Laboratory Approach to Organization Development: A Tentative Model of Planned Change." Paper read at the Annual Conference, British Psychological Conference, Oxford, September 1968.

16/Warren G. Bennis and Philip E. Slater, The Temporary Society (New York: Harper and Row, 1968).

cance. Indeed, Figure 2 offers a way out of nagging organizational problems. Thus managing the change-agent role might be handled effectively through team effort by members of a small integrative managerial unit. A line manager and a staff personnel man could be assigned to each managerial unit, and be jointly responsible for the change-agent role. Team effort also could provide a basis for redefining line-staff relations, as is urged below. Consequently, such structural change must occupy much of the effort of personnel administrators over the near future.

Figure 2 structures also permit convenient changes in incentive systems and philosophy. In one Figure 1 structure, for example, a very complex system of different wage rates for specific jobs required an elaborate supervisory and clerical apparatus for wage administration. Under a Figure 2 structure, a simpler system was possible. Management negotiated a base-price tied to output with a producing team that controlled the entire flow of work, and the unit handled the internal distribution of its income.[17] That is, group incentives in a Figure 2 structure can help integrate a total flow of work and reinforce the allegiances encouraged by that structure. Supervision is consequently simplified. Compensation systems in Figure 1 structures, in contrast, tend to fragment flows of work and to complicate supervision.

A second major technical issue in managing temporary social systems concerns position classification. Figure 2 structures, and the temporary teams within them, encourage classification plans that place rank in the man rather than the job. On this score, the federal public service can expect special problems in managing temporary social systems. Although recent policies permit some recognition of the impact of the man on the job, the federal approach to classification emphasizes rank-in-position.

4. *Function/Flow of Work.* Basic structural change that shifts emphasis from particularistic to integrative departmentation, from functions to the flow of work, will make it easier to respond effectively to the challenges facing personnel administration; but that change will be difficult. The root-need is the development of a solid core of organization development (OD) specialists who can maintain real momentum in long-run programs of change. Ideally, perhaps, every manager should be his own OD specialist. Practically, the OD function often will become a staff personnel specialty.

Redefined line-staff relations are necessary if personnel officials are to operate effectively in an OD role, it is particularly important to note. Redefinition is necessary because OD means change, change in basic attitudes and values and ways of organizing work. Hence, the inappropriateness of the traditional concept of staff as outside the chain of command, as advisory, and as organizationally inferior to the line.

Structural arrangements for a suitable redefinition of line-staff relations also

17/P. G. Herbst, *Autonomous Group Functioning* (London: Tavistock Publications, 1962).

seem clear, in general. A Figure 2 structure, for example, could provide a common organizational home for both a line manager and a staff personnel man. Their shared responsibility for the success of a total managerial unit would encourage a team effort, rather than line vs. staff tension. The approach gets much support, both from experience[18] and from theoretical analysis.[19] In contrast, Figure 1 structures are organized around separate functions or processes. This encourages fragmentation of line from staff, and differentiation between line and staff.

Realistically, and especially in the public service, such a core of OD specialists can anticipate a formidable task. The difficulty is multidimensional. Unlike OD specialists in many business organizations, for example, such specialists in public agencies must not only convince their top management, but they must also reach powerful legislators or standing committees as well as multiple interest groups. This gives agency bureaus or groups such as Foreign Service Officers an opportunity to develop a resistance to top agency management (note Figure 3).

FIGURE 3

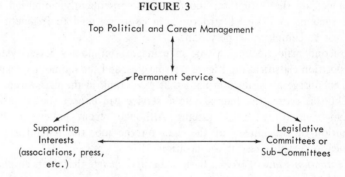

Top Political and Career Management

Permanent Service

Supporting
Interests
(associations, press,
etc.)

Legislative
Committees or
Sub-Committees

On this score, OD specialists will have their work cut out for them. In addition, the brief average tenure of political appointees adds to the problem. Finally, any protectionism induced by the civil service concept as it has evolved can serve to complicate any process of change. Perhaps the clearest reflections of the point are the complex "bumping arrangements" that apply to reductions-in-force.

Assuming the development of a core of OD specialists, three specific reorientations in outlook also seem necessary. They will only be sketched.

First, an emphasis on flow of work as opposed to functions will require a "bottom, up" approach to organizing work and to locating services. The first

18/Robert R. Blake and Jane Snygley Mouton, *Corporate Excellence Through Grid Organization Development* (Houston: Gulf Publishing, 1968), Appendix II.

19/Robert T. Golembiewski, *Organizing Men and Power: Patterns of Behavior and Line-Staff Models* (Chicago: Rand McNally, 1967).

point need not be emphasized, but the location of services has been given less attention. Given a "top, down" approach, services tend to drift upward in the typical hierarchy. For example, staff probably would report to MABC in Figure 1, even though many of their inputs might be made at the level of SA or below.

A "bottom, up" approach would generate a different pattern. The point may be illustrated briefly. Typically, an overhead staff unit would both design and monitor patterns of work motions. In one large electronics firm, however, "time and methods" has been handled differently. Employees are themselves instructed in the basics of motion analysis by overhead staff. These employees then design and monitor their own work-motion patterns.

Such "bottom-up" approaches as the example above imply multiple problems for personnel administration. Thus they may raise troublesome status questions for both MABC and the men who report to him. Moreover, suitable work environments for such approaches must have one or both of two characteristics: employee efforts must be measurable, easily and validly; or the employees must be motivated to apply the principles of motion analysis. These are major problems, but they are less troublesome than the problems of enforcement and evasion likely under a "top-down" approach to motion analysis. For example, Figure 2 structure can help significantly to reduce both mensural and motivational problems.[20]

Second, shifting emphasis to the flow of work requires a new "line-staff" concept. I have dealt with the matter at length elsewhere at the analytic level, and fragmentary research has proved very encouraging.[21] Note here only the multiple mischief of conceiving staff as a glorified prosthetic device, as a kind of enlargement of the senses of MABC in Figure 1. Such a notion does encourage centralized identification and location of staff. And such identification and location always will be necessary for some staff, at least some of the time. Often too much is made of a good thing, however, with obvious costs in increased managerial complexity, heightened line-staff conflict, long communication chains, and a general rigidifying of relations at work.

Third, greater emphasis on the flow of work will require basic value reorientations in wide segments of the population. This socialization of adults will require both defusing and infusing of values, as it were. As some intriguing research demonstrates, at least "middle-class" children seem to be acquainted with the essentials of a Figure 1 structure as early in life as the third or fourth grade.[22] This suggests the extent of the value-defusing that will be required, and

20/Golembiewski, *Organizing Men and Power,* pp. 90-110 and 154-73.
21/Robert T. Golembiewski, "Personality and Organization Structure: Staff Models and Behavioral Patterns," *Journal of the Academy of Management,* vol. 9 (September, 1966), pp. 211-30.
22/Herbert G. Wilcox has accumulated evidence of this socialization-effect with an interesting research design. "The Culture Trait of Hierarchy in Middle Class Children," *Public Administration Review,* vol. 28 (May, 1968), pp. 222-35.

implies a major training burden that extends far beyond the workplace into the value-generating processes of the socialization of children.

There seems a solid base on which to infuse values more appropriate for Figure 2 structures, however. Thus many observers explain the fascination with McGregor's Theory X/Theory Y formulation in terms of a broad managerial desire to increase the congruence between their personal values and the presently-legitimate organization values. The former values tend toward Theory Y; but the latter are Theory X-ish, decidedly. In addition, some evidence shows that managers in larger and technologically sophisticated firms are more likely to reflect Theory Y attitudes.[23] This suggests that contemporary technological demands will supply push/pull forces that will help change values such as those underlying a Figure 1 structure.

SUMMARY

Three generalizations may be drawn regarding the challenges facing the staff personnel man:

1. To the degree that the developmental trends sketched above do in fact become reality, so will personnel administration experience   profound challenges.
2. To the extent that specialists in personnel respond to those challenges, so will these specialists be able to ride the tiger of our on-going organizational revolution.
3. If personnel specialists do not make the required adaptations, someone else will try.

Five major themes will characterize successful approaches by specialists in personnel, none of which will come easy.

First, and most broadly, reorienting the basic concept of personnel administration is in order. Crudely, the reorientation must emphasize training and organization development more than orthodox approaches to position classification, compensation and incentives. Roughly, the reorientation is away from a punitive approach and toward a participative and hopefully a rewarding approach. Such a reorientation is fortunately underway in many areas, albeit in wildly diverse degrees.

Second, specialists in personnel administration must transcend the limitations of the traditional staff role as an appendage for human needs tacked on to an immutable technical structure for work, of staff conceived of as outside the lines of command. A basic redefinition of line-staff relations is in order. Basically, a training or OD role for personnel implies broad involvement in the go-go of the

23/Mason Haire, E. E. Ghiselli, and Lyman W. Porter, "Cultural Patterns in the Role of the Manager," *Industrial Relations,* vol. 2 (February, 1963), pp. 95-118.

organization. A Figure 2 structure aids in developing line-staff relations necessary to permit such involvement.

Third, specialists in personnel administration must gain support for their new effort, but in an interdependent mode. That is, personnel specialists must avoid the temptation of forcing OD programs down the line, after having gained top-level backing by subtly or grossly playing the informant's role. Such things do happen,[24] and they are the death of OD programs. This more or less standard staff strategy illustrates a dependent mode of promoting an OD program, much more consistent with the push-theory than the pull-theory.

Fourth, the processes within personnel departments will have to be analogs of the processes desired in the broader organization. If integrative teams are seen as the answer to the organization's ills, for example, personnel specialists must demonstrate their willingness and ability to develop such integrative teams and participate in them. At the very least, this means that other members of such teams will have trust, backed by experience, that their openness will not return to haunt them in the form of tales carried upward in the organization.

Fifth, personnel specialists will need fine skills in managing dependence-hostility as they broaden their role. It is a mature relation, indeed, in which "help" is given and accepted, period. When the issue is the change of long-standing patterns of behavior, both dependence on the "helper" and hostility toward him will become more prevalent. Both dependence and hostility will have to be confronted willingly and openly, which only means that everyone must be more heroic and emotionally healthy than sometimes is the case.

24/See Melville Dalton, *Men at Work* (New York: Wiley, 1959), esp. pp. 18-109.

26

The Human Concept: New Philosophy for Business*

LESLIE M. DAWSON

One of the more intriguing examples of graffiti reported in recent years is the scrawl on a New York City sidewalk, "Marvin Can't Relate to His Environment." While it is unlikely that Marvin was a business executive at the time of his immortalization in cement, a growing number of businessmen nonetheless share his problem. Certainly the business professional, in common with everyone else, has a vital need for *some* orientation to a world that daily grows more complex, convulsive, and confounding. To lack such a sense of relationship is to be "disoriented" or, according to *Webster's*, "to lose an appreciation of place and time or of one's own identity." Much of the literature of business since the end of World War II has harped on the idea that we live in a "marketing era" and that firms ought to adopt a marketing orientation or a marketing concept as the cornerstone of their corporate philosophy. A crucial question to be asked today, however, is whether a marketing orientation remains the correct orientation for the business executive.

Irwin Miller, chairman of Cummins Engine, observed recently that we are living in a remarkable and perplexing time; despite the long list of accomplishments of American business and the unprecedented prosperity of the nation, the businessman feels insecure and under attack from many groups: workers, customers, government, children, education, and even the church.[1] While the marketing concept may indeed have been ideally attuned to a marketing era, the evidence builds that we are well on the way into an era that must be described in some other way. The eminent sociologist, Pitirim A. Sorokin, has identified the decay of the sensate culture, with its emphasis upon materialism, and a movement toward an ideational, spiritually based form of culture as one of the basic trends of our time.

In the past several years, a number of institutions and foundations have undertaken serious research projects involving speculation as to the future. The Ford Foundation, the Rand Corporation, and the Hudson Institute have spon-

---

*Source: Reprinted by permission from *Business Horizons* (December, 1969), 29-38.
1/Irwin Miller, "Business Has a War to Win," *Harvard Business Review,* 47 (March-April, 1969), p. 4.

sored such studies, and the American Academy of Arts and Sciences has created the Committee on the Year 2000. A general theme of agreement in their published reports is that a strong accentuation of human values is likely to dominate the last third of this century. The committee makes this statement:

> Let it be added that in this "super-affluent" society of year 2000, it is not likely that efficiency (defined by the criteria of maximizing profit or income) will still be primary, though it will doubtless remain important.... We could think of this phenomenon as a shift to humanistic rather than vocational or advancement-oriented values, and conjecture that this tendency will increase over the next 33 years.[2]

This article suggests that, *first,* we are no longer living in a marketing era and are witnessing the start of what may ultimately be termed the human era; *second,* today's executive must cope with a variety of issues, many vaguely or directly threatening, which extend far beyond mere market considerations; *third,* a marketing concept is of little help in coping with such problems; and *fourth,* the actions of many leading corporations today do in fact testify to the gradual replacement of the marketing concept with a more embracing philosophy which, for want of a better term, may be called the human concept.

HISTORICAL-ECOLOGICAL PERSPECTIVE

At least one business scholar has suggested that cultural ecology, the study of the adaptation of a social system to its environment, provides a more meaningful perspective from which to study business activity than economics or any other social science.[3] Cultural ecology focuses upon the capacity of an organized behavior system to sustain itself by drawing upon the resources of its environment, in terms analogous to the capacity of a living creature to utilize life-sustaining resources. Survival and equilibrium are critical concepts in cultural ecology. Survival is the ultimate goal of the organized behavior system, but the system can exist only by adapting to environmental change and maintaining a dynamic ecological equilibrium.

It can be argued that the main thrust of business thought and action has always tended to reflect the basic orientation that top management believes to be most compatible with perceived contemporary environmental conditions. For example, three distinct phases of managerial orientation in twentieth century American business have been observed:[4]

*Production orientation (1900-30)—*An emphasis upon production volume and

2/Herman Kahn and Anthony J. Weiner, *The Year 2000: A Framework for Speculation on the Next Thirty-Three Years* (New York: The Macmillan Co., 1967), pp. 214-15.

3/Wroe Alderson, *Dynamic Marketing Behavior* (Homewood, Ill.: Richard D. Irwin, Inc., 1965), Ch. 13.

4/Robert J. Keith, "The Marketing Revolution," *Journal of Marketing,* 24 (January, 1960), pp. 35-38.

plant efficiency, in response to newly developed technology for mass production and expanded markets combined with a steady rise in consumer affluence and spending.

Sales orientation (1930-50)—An emphasis upon aggressive sales and distributive practices in response to mounting production saturation combined with new caution and moderation in consumer spending and business investment.

Marketing orientation (1950-?)—An emphasis upon consumer satisfaction, crystallized in the marketing concept, in response to new competitive interfaces among products and industries, an unprecedented level of consumer affluence, and a volatile mixture of other new postwar pressures.

Wroe Alderson has called attention to two crucial environmental levels in the cultural ecology of business: first, the proximate environment, the external domain with which a system is in direct and continuous contact (for a marketing firm, the markets in which it buys and sells and competes) and, second, the more embracing ultimate environment, composed of the technological, ideological, moral, and social dimensions of the culture. The figure illustrates this environmental perspective. In the long run the business enterprise must maintain dynamic ecological equilibrium with *both* environments. A system that fails to do so may fall into an "extinction mode."

None of the basic orientations described has been especially attuned to the relationship of the firm to its ultimate environment. Even the ubiquitous marketing concept, relevant and valuable as it has been in an era of marketing emphasis, has serious weaknesses as a management guide in an era reflecting deepened human concern. A fuller consideration of the marketing concept and the environmental conditions that spawned it may be helpful as a prelude to discussing these weaknesses.

THE MARKETING CONCEPT—
YESTERDAY AND TODAY

In the post-World War II years, the nation's economy not only recovered from the effects of the Depression, but swiftly advanced well beyond the highest prewar levels. Postwar prosperity ushered in the age of the affluent society in the United States. The postwar consumer not only was economically better off, better educated, and more sophisticated, but before long more saturated with goods as well. The notion of a limit to the "capacity to consume" became more than a mere theoretical concern, and the survival of the business enterprise depended largely upon its skill in determining, and flexibility in adjusting to, shifts in consumer tastes. An all-out commitment to market considerations—expressed as the "marketing concept"—became vital. A typical definition of this concept is the following: *A managerial philosophy concerned with the mobilization, utilization, and control of total corporate effort for the purpose of helping consumers solve selected problems, in ways compatible with planned enhancement of the profit position of the firm.*[5]

The implementation of a marketing concept often necessitates major organizational and operational changes for the firm. At the very least a new accentuation is placed upon interdepartmental consultation and synchronization (the "systems approach"). Reversal of the "normal" planning sequence is emphasized, so that plans and strategies are formulated first with a view to the marketplace and then translated "backwards" into the development of a profitable market offering. But in its essence the marketing concept represents a basic corporate philosophy, a rationale for the existence of the enterprise. The rationale is not the production of a particular product or service, but the fulfillment of a selected consumer need category, and thus the attention of management is redirected from precedent to potential.

The marketing concept has been one of the most plausible and useful concepts to emerge from business literature, and it has gained virtually universal acceptance in principle. In the context of the figure, the marketing concept represents an outward extension of environmental awareness and sensitivity in contrast to the more inward-looking production and sales orientations. Yet the perspective of the marketing concept remains essentially confined to the proximate environment. Preoccupied as it is with consumers and competitors, the concept is not especially attentive to the healthfulness of a firm's relationship to the various dimensions of the ultimate environment.

New Pressures on Business

It seems clear that the environmental forces which resulted in a greater focus on the marketplace will endure and intensify. Rapid technological progress, increased production efficiency, growing consumer affluence, a broader range of competitive interfaces among industries, the profit squeeze—these and similar pressures, which evoked the marketing orientation, are not likely to let up.

At the same time, the tumultuous events ushering in the last third of this century suggest that powerful new currents of change have begun to flow through the ultimate environment—currents that will profoundly affect the future of business in America. Consistent with the prediction of Sorokin and others, a great share of the pressures emanating from this environmental realm, ideological, moral, and social in nature, revolve around a deepening concern over the "human condition." The demand has been made for a far deeper commitment by business interests to the solution of the social problems which plague America, and for that matter, the entire world. Pressures are being brought upon business to exercise its vast power in such missions as the elimination of poverty,

5/Robert L. King, "The Marketing Concept," in George Schwartz, ed., *Science in Marketing* (New York: John Wiley & Sons, 1965), pp. 70-97.

An Environmental Perspective of the Firm

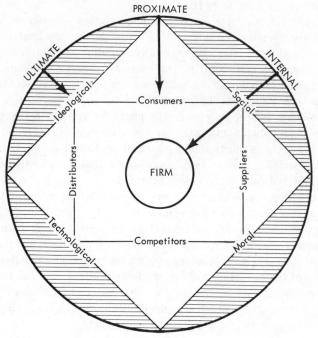

the cleansing of the atmosphere and waterways, and the eradication of social injustice in all its manifestations. Demands are made upon business to provide more genuine opportunities for individual development within the industrial organization. Business leaders are mandated to adopt roles of leadership in the advancement of our society to new levels of moral conduct.

It is significant that these pressures and demands are prominently associated with the brightest and best of the nation's youth. The business image among college students has ramifications for the future which extend far beyond the special (and worsening) problem of attracting a sufficient number of college graduates to business careers. The available evidence leaves room for disagreement as to the depth and breadth of student disenchantment with business, but it does show that the criticism of business is not limited to a vocal minority of young radicals whose value orientation is out of the mainstream of American life. *Fortune's* recent report on the present college generation indicates that fully 40 percent of the nation's college students can be included in a group characterized by a notable "lack of concern for making money" and "an extraordinary rejection of traditional American values."[6] Significantly, *Fortune* refers

6/Daniel Seligman, "A Special Kind of Rebellion," *Fortune,* 79 (January, 1969), p. 67.

to this group as the "forerunners," believing that as our society grows more affluent their percentage of the total college population will increase.

The Harris poll of the attitudes of the general public toward business, undertaken for *Newsweek* in 1966, covered 2,000 Americans in all age and income brackets.[7] The results led *Newsweek* to conclude that business faces a "clear and cogent mandate" to adopt a new and broader set of social goals.

The Marketing Concept Falters

In an environment that exerts upon the business enterprise a new milieu of pressures, predominantly oriented to humanistic values, the marketing concept appears unsuitable for providing the executive with a meaningful and viable sense of identity and direction. Several of its weaknesses become clear when thought is given to some new developments that are, or should be, of concern to several major industries.

1. The marketing concept stresses a *consumer* orientation. In one definition, the consumer is said to become "the absolute dead center of the universe" for the business firm. A consumer orientation directs the attention of the firm only to some fraction of the population of the society which supports it. Moreover, insofar as present or potential consumers are concerned, the consumer orientation generates concern only with the individual's role as a buyer or consumer of a particular product or service. Thus, the consumer orientation is limited in scope and one-dimensional in nature.

The tobacco industry has certainly been consumer oriented in postwar years. Playing a fine tune of market segmentation and product differentiation, the industry has adapted skillfully to changing consumer preferences as the major prewar brands have yielded to a proliferation of new shapes and styles. Industry sales and per capita cigarette consumption have gained steadily. Do we conclude that a consumer orientation is enabling this industry to adapt with perfect harmony to environmental change? Hardly. A powerful and growing array of forces are united in an effort to erase the industry altogether. These forces emanate from state and federal government, the medical profession, and concerned citizens at large. They are generated by persons whose most likely common bond is that they are *not* consumers of the product. These individuals have managed to create a steady stream of woe for the tobacco industry over the past five years.

It is irrelevant to speculate as to whether these forces will succeed (though it is worth noting that per capita cigarette consumption showed declines both in 1967 and 1968). The important point is that a consumer orientation can help not at all in eliminating what is unquestionably the major threat to the survival of this industry, because the threat specifically emanates from nonsmoking sectors of society. What has made the future of this industry in the coming

7/"Speak Now . . . a Newsweek Report," *Newsweek* (1966).

decades a question-mark is not its failure to provide consumers with a pleasant, satisfying product, but rather the product's vulnerability to society's deepening concern over human well-being.

Small firearms are another example of this vulnerability. Obviously, manufacturers are satisfying consumers with their product array of pistols, high-powered rifles, and shotguns; in fact, few industries can count upon a similar degree of consumer loyalty and dedication. The gun lobby, spearheaded by the National Rifle Association, has successfully fought off Presidents, senators, judges, public safety officials, and the FBI in their efforts to curb the sale and possession of guns. The cultural and constitutional aspects of gun ownership in a country with a revolutionary and pioneering heritage are complicated and fraught with emotion. But surely such vestiges of the frontier spirit are being wiped out by the slaughter of political leaders and by rising crime rates. The *Wall Street Journal* recently editorialized as follows:

> It seems predictable that in an urbanized and crowded America the gun lobby will in the end, for good or ill, find itself overwhelmed—much as the equally competent doctors' lobby eventually was in its fight against Medicare. Like civil rights legislation, domestic disarmament is likely to be voted in successive and increasing doses.[8]

Should the environmental clouds swirling about this industry continue to darken, a consumer orientation would be of little help to a member firm in clearing the way to a healthy long-run ecological balance.

2. The marketing concept emphasizes research and long-range planning, but with an almost exclusive stress on technological trends and product improvement. To be sure, a consumer orientation seeks to alert management to possible long-run shifts in tastes and preferences. But neither the technological nor the consumer perspective calls attention to a much broader form of "cultural obsolescence" which may occur in a world of rapidly changing values and priorities.

However naive and futile the peace demonstrator may appear amidst the violence and tensions which mark the international scene, industries that depend heavily upon military and defense contracts might do well to ponder their long-term prospects. From the M-1 rifle to the multimegaton neutron bomb the applied science of death and destruction represents a high degree of technological perfection. Yet throughout the world the clamor for arms control and ultimate disarmament grows louder. An expenditure in the billions is proposed in this nation for a thin antiballistic missile system, and yet the experts admit that it may well be obsolete before it is completed. Nations which cannot afford to feed their people adequately pour a steady stream of their national incomes into armaments.

Well-founded mistrust and caution certainly make genuine disarmament a

8/"Domestic Disarmament," *Wall Street Journal*, July 3, 1968.

long-range prospect at best. What is important here, however, is that the marketing concept is not very effective in alerting management of a firm heavily involved in armament production to the fact that the habitability of the environment may ultimately be in question, and that, indeed, society is trying to make the environment unsuitable for the continuation of such production.

The clamor against war and violence has even spilled over into the children's toy industry. In recent years the New York City toy fair has been picketed by mothers and children protesting the manufacture and sale of war-like toys. In a recent address to European toy manufacturers, Pope Paul VI added his voice to the outcry against toys that encourage antisocial behavior. This industry may find its future influenced far more by cultural acceptance than by mere consumer preferences or technical product improvements.

In fact, all manufacturers of consumer durable goods would be well-advised to raise their long-range planning sights above the levels of technology and taste to the more fundamental changes in life styles that may accompany the maturation of the next generation of young Americans. *Fortune* raises a crucial question in commenting upon the current "youthquake" in our culture:

> In its visible and audible impact on styles and tastes, the youthquake has been mostly fun so far. . . . Still, there is something a bit spooky, from a business point of view, about some implications that can be found in youth's widespread rejection of middle-class life styles ('Cheap is in'). Like so much else among the young that rejection may prove to be transient, but if it persists and becomes a dominant orientation, will these children of affluence grow up to be consumers on quite the economy-moving scale of their parents?[9]

3. Perhaps the most fundamental weakness of the marketing concept is that it satisfies selfish interest, thereby becoming incompatible with an age in which society demands a higher degree of selfless sacrifice on the part of its institutions and constituents. A marketing concept inevitably casts the industrial organization in the role of one of society's more predatory creatures, a giant corporation stealthily and eagerly stalking the marketplace, always at the ready to leap upon a new market opportunity or to devour a competitor. We can dust the cobwebs off models of pure competition and insist that the persistent search for commercial self-gain somehow, sometimes leads to ultimate good for all.

But indications mount that insofar as social and human progress is concerned, our society is becoming impatient and intolerant—unwilling to settle for the accidental by-products generated by businesses' self-centered pursuit of greater market opportunities and profit. Because of the market focus, the involvement of major corporations in social reform projects is more often than not met with skepticism and cynicism by the public. The young, in particular, are inclined to

9/Sheldon Zaleznick, "The Youthquake in Pop Culture," *Fortune,* 79 (January, 1969), p. 134.

dismiss such activities as conniving public relations gestures, financed by otherwise-taxable profits, and all aimed ultimately toward enhancing market position. Indeed, the marketing concept certainly does imply that the justification for social pursuits by business must ultimately rest upon market considerations.

Certainly it can be argued that it is a matter of self-interest, if not selfish interest, for business to lead in the fight against the grave weaknesses which beset our society, and thus such actions are not inconsistent with a marketing concept. But semantic confusion, if nothing else, renders the marketing concept less useful in a contemporary environmental context, simply because market considerations alone, even long run, can no longer determine what is good or bad, right or wrong, prudent or imprudent, urgent or nonurgent in the business community.

THE HUMAN CONCEPT

We have only to look at the actions of major business firms in recent years to recognize that many progressive organizations already are operating under some concept far more broad and meaningful for today's conditions than the marketing concept. These news stories have appeared during the last few years:

> Detroit's Big Three automakers take on tens of thousands of hard-core unemployables in massive retraining effort.

> Lockheed Space and Missile inaugurates new vocation improvement program with hiring limited to dropouts, welfare recipients, ex-convicts, and others with entirely unsatisfactory work records.

> Control Data opens new plants in black slums of Washington, D.C. and Minneapolis; AVCO opens new plant in Boston ghetto.

> SK & F Laboratories establishes information center to advise its black neighbors in Philadelphia ghetto on wide variety of employment, housing, health, education problems; Quaker Oats has similar program in Chicago slum area.

> U.S. Gypsum turns tenements into pleasant living units in pioneer private industry slum rehabilitation projects in New York, Cleveland, and Chicago ghetto areas.

> Life insurance industry pledges $1 billion investment in housing and industry in massive effort to reclaim slum areas.

Such actions are hardly more understandable under a marketing concept than under the economists' anachronism of profit maximization; therefore, the author suggests that they are manifestations of the gradual evolution of a new concept influencing the thoughts and actions of progressive business leaders. Far more responsive to human needs and values in their totality than the marketing concept, this is perhaps best described as the "human concept." An appraisal of the current range of concerns and activities of prominent business corporations indicates that a business enterprise, operating under a human concept, directs its attention, resources, and energies toward the fulfillment of human needs at three levels.

The *first* level is internal in nature, and pertains to the role of the enterprise as a developer of human resources within the organization. The benefits and security commonly provided for all levels of employees today testify to the gradual assumption by American business of a responsibility for employee welfare that transcends short-run profit goals. As indicated in the preceding examples, a number of corporations have now taken on the tremendous challenge of transforming the hard-core unemployables of our society into productive members of the work force.

This may be the beginning of an all-out commitment by private industry to a massive program of reclaiming the lost human resources of our society. But the interest of progressive management in human welfare has not been limited to the disadvantaged. All managerial levels are more interested in creating work opportunities that allow individuals to develop their full potentials and that genuinely meet the need of workers for occupational self-fulfillment. Private industry has become increasingly aware of the importance of recognition, esteem, and perceived contribution as complements to material rewards in producing job satisfaction.

Dr. Edwin H. Land, president of Polaroid, has said that the function of industry is the development of people. When Charles H. Percy headed Bell and Howell, he stated that "our basic objective is the development of individuals."[10] The fulfillment of such objectives thrusts upon management a vastly enlarged responsibility in the design and redesign of jobs and job relationships, refinements in selection and placement techniques, and advances in the provision of necessary education and training.

The *second* level of the human concept concerns the relationship of the enterprise to its consumers, competitors, suppliers, and distributors, that is, the proximate environment. It is primarily at this level where profit, the life-blood of the enterprise, is generated. The human concept implies no lessening in the need for the business organization to remain in dynamic ecological equilibrium with its proximate environment. The consumer orientation and need fulfillment imperatives, so well expounded and thoroughly developed under the doctrine of the marketing concept, remain vital to the firm under the human concept.

The *third* level concerns the relationship of the enterprise to society in general, that is, the ultimate environment. At this level the human concept commits the firm to involvement in a "market" far more significant and vast than the markets for toothpaste, television sets, or cars. This is the market for human fulfillment.

J. Wilson Newman, chairman of Dun & Bradstreet, argues that the purpose

10/Quoted by Henry G. Pearson, "A New Co-Aim for Business," *MSU Business Topics*, 16 (Spring, 1968), pp. 51-56.

of business has always been to answer human wants, and that the American market is now undergoing a transformation wherein the predominant wants are not material but psychological and social.[11] He foresees a total market averaging as much as $100 billion a year over the rest of the century to lift the smog, clean the rivers, rebuild the cities, unsnarl the traffic, and educate and reeducate the young and old. Marketing expert William Lazer has stated that "one of the next marketing frontiers may well be related to markets that extend beyond mere profit considerations to intrinsic values—to markets based on social concern, markets of the mind, and markets concerned with the development of people to the fullest extent of their capabilities."[12]

At the third level the human concept establishes an external social purpose for the business enterprise by linking its energies to the efforts of mankind to achieve a way of life that fulfills the human yearning not only for material comforts, but for security, dignity, and spiritual solace. Clearly the capacity of every business enterprise to contribute to this effort must be evaluated individually. By virtue of size, product category, or other unique attributes, some organizations have a far greater potential for such contributions than others. But the most important attributes undoubtedly are will and vision. A number of the corporate projects mentioned above are partially funded by public agencies. In some instances, modest profits have even been realized, though naturally less than could have been earned in alternative capital expenditures. The smaller enterprise should be able to participate too, whether on its own or in cooperation with state and local agencies and foundations.

The following is offered as a tentative attempt to summarize the meaning and scope of the human concept in definitional form:

> A managerial philosophy centered upon the continuous search for and evaluation of opportunities for the mobilization, utilization, and control of total corporate effort in: (1) achieving a genuine internal social purpose in the development of organization members to their fullest potential; (2) generating the necessary profit input within the proximate environment by devising solutions to selected consumer problems; (3) achieving a genuine external social purpose within the ultimate environment by contributing to the identification and fulfillment of the real human needs of our time.

Implementation of a human concept may involve organizational role and structure change, particularly in larger organizations, at least as fundamental as those called for under a marketing concept. For instance, the sales management position may have to be redefined to accentuate responsibility for the total development of the members of the selling force, constituting an important

---

11/J. Wilson Newman, "Does Business Have a Future?" *MSU Business Topics,* 15 (Autumn, 1967), pp. 16-20.

12/William Lazer, "Marketing's Changing Social Relationships," *Journal of Marketing,* 33 (January, 1969), p. 4.

share of the firm's human resources. Whereas this objective has traditionally been secondary to volume, or more recently profit, it is doubtful that such should be the case for an enterprise committed to a human concept. In a number of progressive firms the old-line public relations department has been supplanted, or at least supplemented, by such new departments as "community relations" and "college relations." These are surely reflections of increased awareness by business of the need for more links to the ultimate environment.

THE CONCEPT, PROFITS, THE FUTURE

Change in the ultimate environment is likely to assume special significance to the firm's destiny in the last third of the century. A marketing concept is not adequate to help business retain healthy ecological balance with an environment characterized by an increasing shift from sensate values to human, social, and moral values. A broader human concept can provide management with a sense of direction in an era of increased concern over the human condition by committing the business organization to the service of an internal and an external social purpose concurrent with the service of profit.

It is not suggested that the human concept offers, at last, an easy solution to the classic management conundrum of profit maximization versus social responsibility. At the one extreme, the private corporation clearly cannot be expected to become a philanthropic institution so long as its survival is in large measure determined in a competitive marketplace. At the other extreme, over several generations the will of the nation has been expressed, legally and otherwise, to restrain unbridled competition for maximum profits on the part of big business. Countless efforts have been made to apply a semantic crowbar to force a convergence of the two goals. For example, if profit is defined in sufficiently long-run and indirect terms, it can justifiably be argued that slum clearance maximizes profits by forestalling destructive riots, or that purification of the atmosphere maximizes profits by preventing customers (and everyone else) from being poisoned. What emerges from such arguments is a compromise goal of "enlightened profit maximization," wherein recognition is given to some socially determined limit on what the maximum can be.

The point is, simply, that the firm concerned only with profit performance may find its lack of other internal or external social purpose to be a growing threat to its survival in an increasingly humanistic world. To borrow from the lexicon of economics, profit may become the necessary, but not sufficient, condition for the survival of the firm. There is no need to remind the business executive of the sanctions imposed within the proximate environment for profit failure. But there *is* need to point out that the ultimate environment can impose very real sanctions too for a failure in social purpose. One of the more familiar of these is restrictive legislation. But such sanctions may take other forms as well: the drying up of the wellspring of new business recruits from the colleges; turmoil for the corporate headquarters not unlike contemporary campus disorders (Dow Chemical has already suffered through some relatively minor experiences); or work-interfering demonstrations such as those recently conducted by blacks against the construction unions and steel producers in Pittsburgh.

The contribution of the human concept lies in focus and commitment; it can extend the vision of management into those areas of corporate involvement where social purpose beyond profit can be found. Every business organization, regardless of size, can find genuine social purpose in its attitudes and actions concerning employees. Most firms, in alliance with local, state, and federal agencies and institutions, can find genuine external social purpose.

The human concept is not an easy cure for the managerial schizophrenia that may result from the attempt to reconcile profit with social responsibility. The human concept can no more supply the kind of executive judgment, sensitivity, creativity, and courage required for its successful implementation than could the marketing concept. It is for this very reason that business has an answer to the bright young people who turn away from a business career because they believe it offers no challenge and serves no lasting purpose. Challenge of the highest order is implicit in the human concept, and so is purpose of the utmost significance to human progress.

In considering the real value of the human concept as a basic corporate philosophy, one is reminded of the classic anecdote of the two bricklayers at a construction site. Each was asked what he was doing. The first replied, "I am laying bricks." The second answered, "I am building a cathedral." Business can answer its critics, revitalize its ranks, and provide itself with an unlimited future through acceptance of the spirit of the human concept. Such acceptance could be one of history's momentous turning points.

27

Toward a Concept of Managerial Control for a World Enterprise*

M. Y. YOSHINO

One of the most significant business trends today is the emergence of many American firms in the world market. The United States Department of Commerce reports that direct private investments overseas have almost tripled in the last decade, reaching $44 billion in 1964. In the same year, moreover, these investments earned $5.1 billion, of which $3.7 billion has been repatriated to the United States.[1] Over 3,300 American firms have some interest in overseas production either through licensing agreements or direct investments. For a substantial number of these firms, international business represents over 50 percent of earnings.

High profit potentials in the world market have also drawn a large number of firms from other industrially advanced nations into international business. As a result, competition in promising markets throughout the world is rapidly taking on a multinational character. Though international business continues to offer good profit potentials, there is mounting evidence that the return on foreign investment for many leading American firms, though still higher than on domestic investment, has been continuously declining over the last several years.[2] The increasing competitive pressure, coupled with the inherent difficulties in managing a worldwide enterprise, points to a need for ensuring effective managerial arrangements.

One of the critical tasks of managing multinational operations is to design an effective managerial control system to allow top management to coordinate and guide activities of a large number of far-flung foreign affiliates into a unified whole. Since entirely new variables enter into the calculus of decision-making in

*Source: Reprinted by permission from the March, 1966, issue of the *Michigan Business Review,* published by the Graduate School of Business Administration, The University of Michigan.

1/U.S. Department of Commerce, Office of Business Economics, *Survey of Current Business,* September 1965, p. 24.

2/For example, see Walter P. Stern, "U.S. Direct Investment Abroad," *Financial Analysts Journal,* January-February 1965, p. 98.

C. Wickham Skinner, "Management of International Production," *Harvard Business Review,* September-October 1964, p. 125.

international business, the mere extension of a domestic control system is inadequate in meeting the demands of multinational operations.

This article seeks to identify major problems faced by corporate management in exercising managerial control over foreign operations and to offer some basic suggestions toward development of a more meaningful way of viewing managerial control in multinational and cultural contexts.

Allocation of Decision-Making Authority

Though it is by no means unique to international business, one of the recurring issues raised by corporate management is the division of authority between headquarters and foreign affiliates. Some firms choose to centralize practically all decision-making at corporate headquarters and to require from foreign units extremely detailed operating plans and reports with great frequency. As one would expect, this arrangement tends to dampen the enthusiasm and initiative of the management overseas and to limit its flexibility and freedom in meeting local problems and opportunities.

Excessive demand for information and reports not only has a demoralizing effect upon local executives, but it also diverts them from more pressing operating problems. Frequently, the headquarters staff are paralyzed by the sheer volume of information coming from foreign affiliates and fail to make effective use of it. Decisions are likely to be delayed, leading to losses in operating effectiveness.

Interestingly, tight control does not necessarily guarantee that local management will adhere strictly to the policies of the home office. I have observed some local executives who ostensibly comply with the requirements of headquarters but in reality deviate substantially from the policy directives of the home office.

Some firms go to the other extreme by almost completely delegating decision-making authority to local management. My recent field research has revealed that corporate headquarters of some international firms exercise virtually no control over their foreign operations, as long as the foreign units somehow meet the minimum sales or profit goal established by the headquarters. This approach is observed to be particularly prevalent among manufacturers of consumer products with many years of international experience. Some do it out of a conviction that it is impossible to manage daily affairs of overseas units from a headquarters located several thousand miles away, while others follow this practice out of negligence.

Weaknesses of Laissez Faire Approach

Though the laissez faire approach gives maximum flexibility and freedom to local management, it suffers from two major weaknesses. Foreign affiliates which are virtually autonomous tend to generate subgoals not necessarily consistent with those of the headquarters. Also, extreme decentralization limits use of a wide variety of resources and experiences available at headquarters which are of potential value to foreign units. There seem to be nearly always some elements of a company's managerial competence that can be applied overseas. The latter point is particularly important inasmuch as the real strength of a world enterprise derives from its ability to integrate the activities of widely scattered affiliates.

Obviously, the optimum pattern lies somewhere between the two extremes described. Since the effectiveness of a particular pattern depends on such factors as nature of products, stage of organizational evolvement, size of the company, and availability of executive talents, it is impossible to prescribe a pattern that is equally suitable under any circumstances. However, it appears that distance, complexity, and instability in operating environments overseas tend to favor maximum decentralization of decision-making. Only the very critical decisions should be reserved for corporate management. These are likely to be decisions involving such elements as major capital investments, selection of top managerial personnel, important governmental negotiations, and introduction of new products. This approach tends to maximize contributions that both headquarters and local management are best qualified to make. It must be noted, however, that such an approach is effective only when the following conditions are satisfied: (1) The headquarters-foreign affiliates relationship must be examined in terms of the allocation of specific responsibilities. (2) Corporate headquarters must be properly informed by local units on major decisions that are made by the latter. (3) Finally, headquarters must design an effective system of control over those areas of responsibility that are delegated to the local units.

Establishing Meaningful Standards of Performance

A critical problem in planning managerial control for multinational operations is the determination of standards against which to evaluate the performance of foreign affiliates. In this regard, two points deserve careful consideration. They are (1) the appropriateness of reported profits as a measurement criterion, and (2) the need for multiple performance criteria. In multidivisional domestic operations, reported profit is generally accepted as the critical measure of managerial effectiveness. Each division is relatively self-contained, and interdivisional transactions can be adjusted through the mechanism of transfer pricing. Since general operating environments among various divisions are relatively homogeneous, top management can make some meaningful comparisons. In multinational operations, however, reported profit alone is quite inadequate as the measure of performance.

In the first place, the reported profit of a foreign operating unit is likely to be distorted by a number of external and internal variables that are absent in domestic operations. Because political and economic risks vary widely from country to country, what appears superficially to be high profit may, in fact, be quite unsatisfactory when risk factors are properly weighed. Foreign exchange regulations, legal restrictions, foreign tax structures, or unexpected political developments can have a decided impact upon the profit performance of a foreign affiliate. Yet the local management has virtually no control over these external factors.

Profit performance of a foreign affiliate can also be affected by intra-firm decisions that are beyond the control of local management. A worldwide enterprise has a wide range of alternatives in allocating its corporate resources. Hence, within the broad constraints of political and economic risk, a network of logistics can be developed on a global basis to maximize comparative advantages of each area. Obviously, company-wide logistics decisions can only be made at headquarters. Nevertheless, these decisions can affect profitability of foreign units rather markedly. Some financial decisions made centrally to expand worldwide profits may also lead to an increase of profits in one or more individual country affiliates and a decrease in others. These factors provide convincing evidence that the reported profit-and-loss data must be carefully scrutinized and adjusted by removing various extraneous influences on the operations of a local unit. In so doing the following guidelines are important.

Environmental Variables

The most serious problem is determining the degree of controllability of the environmental variables. It is evident that local management can exercise no control over such developments as galloping inflation in a foreign economy or a surge of nationalistic feelings. However, it is possible to minimize the impact of these developments on the particular firm through careful planning and judicious actions. Corporate management must somehow determine the degree to which local management should be held accountable for these environmental variables.

Obviously, there is no hard-and-fast rule that is applicable to every situation. It must be noted that there is an inherent tendency for management of most foreign affiliates to attribute poor performance mainly to hard-to-measure environmental variables or arbitrary decisions made by headquarters. Hence, each case must be reviewed carefully. Careless or arbitrary decisions in this respect contribute to poor morale among local management and relaxed control.

The next step involves technical adjustments of reported data. Here, two considerations are important. Since adjustments of profit-loss data of a host of foreign affiliates are highly complicated, time-consuming, and costly, they should be limited to major items large enough to make significant differences. Also, adjustments should be made only on a memorandum basis without entering into the formal accounting records.[3] Furthermore, it is important that the criteria and methods of adjustments be explicitly defined and understood by the management of foreign affiliates.

3/*International Enterprise: A New Dimension of American Business* (New York: McKinsey & Company, Inc., 1962), p. 30.

Evaluating Performance

Removing distortions from the reported profit is only one step. Performance of all foreign units must be evaluated on a comparative basis. This is essential not only for the purpose of managerial control but for future decisions on allocation of corporate resources on a global basis. Establishing a comparative criterion of profit performance is extremely difficult because of a wide diversity in operating environments overseas. It is obvious that an investment in a high-risk country should earn a greater return than one in a stable economy. But is it possible to quantify the rather elusive political and economic risks?

One solution has been suggested by Millard Pryor, Jr., in a recent article in the *Harvard Business Review*. Pryor proposes to establish "compensatory" financial goals for operations outside the United States. Such goals are constructed by adding to the basic financial goals established for domestic operations factors which quantify the long-range overseas political and monetary risks and the extra costs of absentee management.[4]

Another promising concept that needs further exploration is the development of a classification scheme to group various operations into a number of clusters on the basis of key environmental variables. Common performance criteria may then be set for these operations in the same classification. For example, an important variable for a particular type of business may be the level of economic development. The firm's operations throughout the world may be classified into several categories on this basis, regardless of their geographic locations; and common performance criteria may be set within each level. Relative homogeneity in operating environments would presumably allow more meaningful comparison.

Performance Criteria

Now let us turn to the second basic issue. This involves the question of the relative importance to be attached to profitability as a performance criterion. Though other standards are by no means insignificant, profitability is widely accepted as the final performance standard in multidivisional domestic operations. In view of added environmental dimensions, should the management of multinational operations rely predominantly or even exclusively on this single criterion in measuring managerial effectiveness of foreign affiliates? The answer is clearly negative when the following factors are considered. (1) Multinational operations are conducted in sovereign nations with diverse national goals and interests. (2) Foreign enterprise induces a potential conflict of interest between the American parent company, its local associates, and the governments of the host countries.

4/Millard Pryor, Jr., "Planning in a World Business," *Harvard Business Review*, January-February 1965, p. 134.

Any foreign enterprise that must rely heavily on local resources cannot expect to survive, let alone succeed, over the long run unless it is so structured and managed as to make the maximum contributions to the host country. This is particularly true in developing countries where productive resources are scarce and nationalistic feelings are rampant. Satisfaction on this requirement, however, may well conflict with the profitability criterion, at least in the short run. This conflict of interests must be recognized by top management in setting performance criteria for foreign affiliates.

Some may object to inclusion of such a consideration in performance criteria on the ground that it is beyond precise measurement. While very precise measurement is admittedly difficult, some imaginative approaches are being developed. For example, Professor Robinson has developed a conceptual framework to approximate the political and economic impact of a foreign enterprise on the host country.[5]

There is another area of potential conflict that must be recognized in establishing performance criteria. Many multinational operations involve joint ownership with local interests. Local investors can participate only in profits of the foreign enterprise, not those of the parent company located in the United States. Hence, performance criteria must be established in such a manner as to optimize the interests of different ownership groups. Otherwise, local management is likely to find itself subject to conflicting pressure groups in an atmosphere of indecision and confusion. Such a situation may lead to the ultimate emergence of one dominant group, which in turn enforces its own performance standards.

Designing an Effective Information System

The critical role of information in planning a managerial control system has been repeatedly emphasized in management literature. Distance, diversity, and instability in environments overseas place a premium on an effective information system in multinational operations. Information processing and analysis are much more complex and, correspondingly, more expensive in international business than in domestic operations. Top management, therefore, must balance comprehensiveness and speed on the one hand and the cost of information on the other.

Three basic considerations are important in designing an information system for a world enterprise. They are (1) the types of information sought, (2) the flow of information between headquarters and foreign affiliates, and (3) analysis of information for managerial planning and control.

The types of information sought must be determined by careful examination of the requirements of planning and control. The informational needs of a firm

---

5/Richard D. Robinson, *International Business Policy* (New York: Holt, Rinehart and Winston, 1964), pp. 99-145.

ultimately depend on corporate strategies and goals. This basic consideration, however, is often ignored. Though the exact requirements vary from company to company, basically three types of information are needed by the management of multinational operations. They are environmental data (political, social, and economic), competitive data (real and potential), and internal operating data (both quantitative and qualitative). In many multinational firms, the only type of data systematically and regularly gathered is that related to internal operations. Even those data are primarily designed for accounting purposes rather than for decision-making.

Since international operations are much more vulnerable to external variables than domestic operations, data on environmental and competitive conditions become all the more critical. Moreover, much internal data are meaningful only in the perspective of the general environment and in the light of competitive activity.

In view of their importance, it is dangerous to delegate overall intelligence functions solely to foreign affiliates. Though foreign affiliates are unquestionably an important source of vital information for management, local executives are usually preoccupied with daily operating problems, and they may overlook subtle developments with far-reaching implications. Furthermore, there are other equally important sources of environmental and competitive data available to headquarters. For example, United Nations, United States government agencies, and trade associations can provide useful information.

The Flow of Information

The second factor in designing a global information system is facilitating the flow of information between corporate headquarters and foreign affiliates. Two media of communication—written reports and personal visits—are available for this purpose. Though both serve useful functions, the balance between the two must be carefully considered. As noted earlier, excessive reliance on written reports tends to aggravate the already difficult and sometimes strained headquarters-foreign affiliates relationship. Action-oriented local executives find it time-consuming and difficult to prepare reports. Furthermore, foreign nationals are placed at a disadvantage because of language and cultural barriers. For these reasons, written communication should be kept to the minimum level. Headquarters must also standardize reporting procedures and methods to facilitate reporting and subsequent analysis.

Personal visits are used extensively by the management of most multinational corporations, though the character of personal visits varies widely as does their effectiveness. Too frequently, personal visits are used as a tool for trouble-shooting—to solve immediate problems occurring unexpectedly. Viewed in this fashion, personal visits have very limited educational value. Since face-to-face contacts can be useful in bridging the distance and cultural gaps that exist between headquarters and foreign affiliates, they must be well planned and made on a regular basis. Personal visits, if appropriately conducted, are useful in developing an insight into local problems, communicating policies of headquarters, discussing long-term plans, and sharing valuable experiences.

The most challenging area in designing an international intelligence system lies in analysis of data by headquarters staff for effective control and planning. Thus far, in many international firms relatively little has been done beyond the traditional accounting analysis. Comparative analysis of internal data is complicated by diverse environmental factors, as noted earlier; but this step is critical in identifying weak spots and unrealized opportunities. Some progressive firms have begun to make imaginative use of these ideas. For example, labor productivity, efficiency of logistics system, and effectiveness of a given marketing mix are analyzed and evaluated on a global basis.

Understanding Cultural Variables

Perhaps the most difficult and elusive aspect of managerial control in international operations is that control functions must be performed in a multicultural context. This is particularly significant when affiliates are managed by foreign nationals. Cultural variables affect managerial control in several ways.

First, culture may block effective communication between foreign affiliates and headquarters. Particularly serious from the viewpoint of managerial control are distortions introduced in reporting as a result of certain cultural values prevalent in some societies. Some cultures tend to emphasize politeness and agreeableness in superior-subordinate reporting relationships, even at the expense of accuracy and directness. Thus, local management may ignore or distort data deemed unpleasant to corporate headquarters.

Secondly, to a large degree culture prescribes the standard of achievement and dictates the concomitant system of rewards. Not every culture rewards what is considered to be productive achievement in advanced industrial societies, nor is the reward for similar achievements the same. For example, some traditional cultures place the ultimate reward upon loyalty, devotion, and contribution to the group rather than upon outstanding individual achievement. Thus, a system of motivations and incentives—an essential ingredient in managerial control— must be meaningful in terms of the local culture.

Culture also affects superior-subordinate relationships in an organization. As Professor Fayerweather concludes from his pioneering research, some cultures are prone to produce interpersonal relationships characterized by distance, distrust, and hostility; while others are more conducive to group-oriented, collaborative interpersonal relationships.[6] He further notes that the former type is relatively prevalent in more traditional societies, whereas the latter is predominant in Western societies, particularly in American culture. Though each

6/John Fayerweather, *The Executive Overseas* (Syracuse, New York: Syracuse University Press, 1959), pp. 15-40.

pattern is meaningful and effective in its own cultural environments, difficulties are likely to emerge when control functions must be performed among men of diverse cultural backgrounds and orientations.

Finally, there is the problem of sensitivity often manifested by national executives toward control exercised by American executives. This is particularly prevalent among those in underdeveloped and former colonial countries.

The only permanently effective way to overcome these cultural gaps is to view managerial control as an educational process rather than a superior-subordinate authority relationship. Continuous educational effort is the only feasible way to provide management of foreign affiliates with the necessary background to understand the headquarters' points of view. With this background, local management could intelligently interpret policy directives from the home office as well as effectively participate in the formation of such policies. Such an educational approach would also minimize the sensitivity problem mentioned above.

Conclusion

Managerial control in multinational operations is complicated by a number of external as well as internal variables unique to multinational operations. Clearly, it is impossible to rely solely on comfortable assumptions and generalizations developed out of domestic experience. A need is apparent for developing a conceptual framework for managerial control of multinational operations.

At the risk of oversimplification, this article has singled out four basic considerations as a step toward development of a useful way of viewing managerial control for a world enterprise. The task is by no means easy, but the undeniable facts of the tremendous potential of the expanding world market and increasing competition should provide sufficient incentive for American management to meet this challenge effectively.

28

Full Utilization of Women in Employment: The Problem and an Action Program*

DENNIS SLEVIN

The women's liberation movement is with us to stay. Signs of its permanence can be seen in the existence of state and federal laws that have already resulted in landmark cases, in the variety of private groups and public agencies whose missions are to remove sex discriminations from our society, and in the large literature the movement has inspired in both the popular and academic press. The movement toward women's liberation will be with us through the decade of the seventies and on through this century until the problem has been substantially solved.

The focus of the movement has been twofold: to eliminate early social-role stereotyping that results in nonaggressive, nonachieving roles for women; and to eliminate job discrimination. Administrators have discovered that eliminating job discrimination is a difficult problem. Organizations have found that no solution methodology or even a set of experiences exists to handle the problem. Each organization is feeling its way, responding to outside pressures and in some cases setting up progressive self-initiated programs. At this point we need a literature on the implementation of programs to fully utilize women in our social organizations.

The fact that discrimination against women exists in our organized society can be documented.

In 1968, median earnings for male year-round workers were $7664; while for the women who worked full time, median earnings were $4457, or 58% of the male rate.[1] Part of this discrepancy was due to the fact that, in some jobs, women were paid less than men; this, in fact, was the case in *many* jobs just a few years ago. However, the courts have begun to redress the problem and the major issue is no longer "equal pay for equal work"; it is "equal opportunity for

*Source: Reprinted by permission from *Human Resource Management* (Spring, 1973), 25-32.

1/ Juanita Kreps, *Sex in the Marketplace: American Women at Work,* Baltimore, The Johns Hopkins Press, 1971, p. 2.

equal work" and hence equal pay. There has been an historical tendency for women to concentrate in low-paying jobs. One fourth of all working women are presently employed in five occupations: secretary-stenographer, household worker, elementary school teacher, bookkeeper and waitress. It is not uncommon to find firms in which women represent 50 to 90% of the lower level jobs, but less than 10% of upper level positions. The problem, therefore, is one of shifting more women into more responsible positions. This is both an intra-organizational problem and a societal problem. Organizations must remove discrimination in selection, training and promotional policies; and society as a whole must reduce sex-role stereotyping and must encourage women to prepare themselves for responsible positions in job categories that will have strong needs for workers in the future. The solution therefore will be a combination of removing organizational constraints, and better career planning through the pursuit of more diverse educational opportunities by women.

However, this kind of career planning approach is a longer-term solution. The shorter term progress will come through action programs initiated by business firms, government agencies, and other organizations. Recent federal laws and enforcement agencies have placed added pressure on personnel managers to come up with innovative programs.

This is not an ephemeral problem—it is something that must be taken into serious account when one considers all the implications of the economic data, the law, and what the behavioral sciences are learning.

This paper proposes a solution strategy in the form of an action checklist which, if followed with care, will produce a comprehensive, total-systems approach to the problem.

AN ASIDE ON FEDERAL LAWS WHICH HAVE
BEEN A SOURCE OF PRESSURE FOR CHANGE

Since 1963, the following federal measures have been taken against sexual discrimination:

The Equal Pay Act of 1963 requires equal pay for equal work regardless of sex.

Title VII of the 1964 Civil Rights Act prohibits discrimination in private employment on the basis of race, color, religion, sex, or national origin.

Executive Order 11246 (as amended by Executive Order 11375 of October, 1967) bars discrimination by federal contractors on the basis of race, color, religion, sex, or national origin.

The Equal Rights Amendment (the 27th amendment to the constitution, passed by Congress, but not yet ratified by all the states) will make sex discrimination unconstitutional.

The Equal Pay Act

This act prohibits discrimination on the basis of sex in the payment of wages for equal work on jobs that require equal skill, effort, and responsibility and that are performed under similar working conditions. It also specifically prohibits employers from reducing the wage rates of any employee in order to equalize pay between the sexes. It applies to all employees subject to a minimum wage under the Fair Labor Standards Act. Executive, administrative, and professional employees who are exempt from the Fair Labor Standards Act are also exempt from the Equal Pay Act. In January, 1970, the U.S. Court of Appeals returned a landmark decision in the Schultz vs. Wheaton Glass Company case, holding that women performing the same general work as men should receive the same pay. The company had claimed that the jobs were not "identical." The Court asserted that they were "substantially equal."

Through April 1971, Wage and Hour compliance officers (the Wage and Hour Division of the Department of Labor is responsible for enforcement) have found close to $30 million owed in underpayment to nearly 80,000 employees, almost all of them women.[2]

Title VII of the 1964 Civil Rights Act

Title VII prohibits discrimination in private employment based on race, color, religion, sex, or national origin. Firms and labor organizations engaged in industries affecting commerce and having at least 25 employees or members are covered. The title exempts private membership clubs, educational, and religious organizations. Prohibited under the Act is discrimination in wages, terms or conditions of employment, hiring, or firing, assigning or promoting employees. Not prohibited under the Act is discrimination where sex is a bona fide occupational qualification (BFOQ) such as a washroom attendant. However, the courts have been quite reluctant to apply BFOQ to many job categories. Title VII is administered by the Equal Employment Opportunities Commission (EEOC) which investigates cases of discrimination and attempts to solve them by persuasion. If the complaint cannot be settled, the EEOC may initiate court action. If there exists a general pattern and practice of discrimination, the EEOC shares with the Justice Department the right to initiate a suit in U.S. District Court. As of 1974, the EEOC will have sole responsibility for pattern and practice suits. These new powers and a more aggressive stance by the EEOC imply that substantial additional pressures will be brought to bear on employers to remove sex discrimination in the near future.

2/Mary Hilton, "The Women's Bureau and Action Programs" in *Women: Action not Reaction, Proceedings of a Conference,* Editors, William C. Byham and Dennis P. Slevin, Graduate School of Business, University of Pittsburgh, Pittsburgh, Pa., 1971, p. 4.

Executive Orders

Executive Order 11246 (as amended by Executive Order 11375 on October 13, 1967) prohibits discrimination on the basis of sex by federal contractors and subcontractors. It specifically requires that government contractors and subcontractors institute affirmative action programs designed to insure hiring without regard to sex. This encompasses over 225,000 firms doing business with the government. The Executive Orders are administered by the Office of Federal Contract Compliance (OFCC) which is an agency within the Department of Labor. The OFCC has the strong enforcement option of cancelling contracts where sexual discrimination or lack of affirmative action has been found. In addition to private firms, the OFCC through the Department of Health, Education and Welfare, has authority over institutions of higher learning. Some traumatic confrontations have occurred between universities and HEW on affirmative action for women. Because of its strong enforcement option, the OFCC has probably exerted greater pressure than any other agency.[3]

Equal Rights Amendment

On March 24, 1972, Congress approved the Equal Rights Amendment by a two-thirds vote and submitted it to the states for ratification. The amendment states:

Section 1. Equality of rights under the law shall not be denied or abridged by the United States or by any State on account of sex.

Section 2. The Congress shall have the power to enforce, by appropriate legislation, the provisions of this Article.

If ratified by three-fourths (38) of the states, this amendment will become the 27th Amendment to the Constitution two years after final date of ratification. The states have seven years to complete the approval process and it appears that they are on their way to ratification. The purpose of the Amendment is to eliminate discrimination against both men and women on account of sex. Its effect will be to provide another, even stronger, basis for bringing suit because of sexual discrimination. With the ratification of this amendment, legal remedies for removing sexual discrimination will be more than adequate. The problem of finding "organizational" remedies will remain.

AN ACTION PROGRAM THAT LOOKS AT THE TOTAL PERSONNEL SYSTEM

The problems in providing women with more opportunity will fall heaviest on administrators. There will be some need to work with the attitudes of male

3/See Barbara Newell, "Action Programs" in Byham, Slevin, for an interesting case example at the University of Michigan.

managers (and we will come back to this shortly) but the immediate problems for administrators will best be answered by taking a "total systems" view of the problem. Look at the flow chart portrayed in Figure 1, and for the moment, ignore the words in parentheses. The recruitment, selection, training, and promotion process has a number of steps. The personnel department authenticates

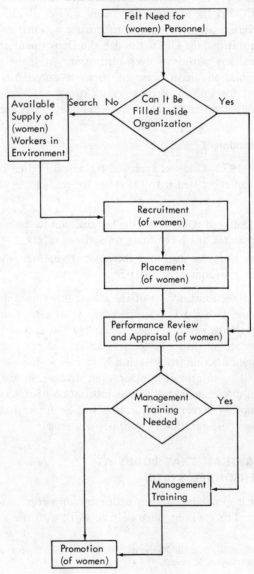

FIGURE 1
Staffing an Organization for
Full Utilization of Women

or determines the need for additional personnel as this need is felt by each department or division, and then asks "Can this need be filled from within the organization?" If the answer is *yes,* then performance review, management training, and promotion may be used for a relatively immediate solution to the problem. If the answer is *no,* the organization must search its environment and look through the available supply of workers for those who possess the characteristics required. The organization then recruits, by visiting college campuses, checking with placement firms, placing employment ads, etc. Once individuals have been recruited, they must be placed so that their characteristics match the requirements of the positions that need additional manpower. Maintaining these persons in the system necessitates providing adequate performance feedback and promotional opportunities; for this purpose, most organizations engage in some sort of annual performance review and appraisal. At this point, decisions are made about salary and any management training that seems, to the manager conducting the appraisal, necessary for promotion. If no training seems necessary, promotion may occur directly.

This flowchart is obviously an over-simplification of the complex problems that are experienced in attempting to plan, recruit, and staff so that an organization is maintained at a high level of efficiency; but this type of chart is a useful vehicle for examining how an organization would attempt to solve the problems of maximizing its investment in female employees. If we look again at this chart, this time including the words in parentheses, we see the types of problems that organizations must define and solve if they wish to employ women more fully.

First, there must be a felt need for women personnel if they are, in fact, not represented in sufficient numbers in the aggregate in the organization. This, clearly, will not be the simplest problem that will arise. Next, search activity must be conducted throughout the available supply of women workers in the environment for women of the caliber needed to assume managerial positions. This could include recruiting activities at predominantly female colleges and/or the use of innovative approaches to the recruitment problem which has, in the past, been a man's world.

In the past, the placement of women workers has not been much of a problem, even the placement of women with aspirations for higher-level positions, for the female college graduate has typically been asked if she can type at a reasonable speed and do shorthand (or if she would mind initially doing some speech writing, or manuscript editing or whatever else) before she's given any "decision-making responsibility." Because the problem of placing women has been ignored in the past, it will require special attention in the future. Similarly, the problems of performance review and appraisal have seldom been dealt with constructively as far as women are concerned. If women have been relegated to lower level jobs in the organizations, then their performance reviews and appraisals have likely been performed rather perfunctorily, with little worry as to their developmental needs and their future career paths.

When the organization decides whether its women workers do have certain developmental needs, it will also have to determine whether these needs will be different from the typical male workers because of the differences in background and experience and whether similar career paths can be promised them.

AN ACTION CHECKLIST

To create an effective action plan, an administrator must consider a host of problems, simultaneously and touch on all major issues. This action plan checklist highlights the necessary steps in any action plan and suggests what are, at least initially, the important priorities.

Top Management Commitment Audit

This is one of the most essential aspects of the action program. I have not talked to a single administrator who would disagree with the fact that top management commitment is essential to change the organization so that women's talents are more fully employed. The answers to questions one through five must be *yes* so that the necessary resources will be made available for a successful plan. In some cases, top management commitment may be already present or won by the simple expedients of providing information and persuasion. If top management commitment is *not* already firm, the checklist suggests three ways in which it may be achieved: a survey of the nature and magnitude of the problem as it exists, not in general, but at the immediate time in that specific organization; education about the benefits to the firm, and about the law of our country.

Top Management Commitment Audit

	yes	no
1. Does top management favor an affirmative action plan?	□	□
2. Is it willing to spend the resources necessary to develop and implement affirmative action?	□	□
3. Does it know what an action plan will cost?	□	□
4. Is it willing to provide the action plan administrator with the authority he or she needs?	□	□
5. Does it realize the benefits that will accrue from an action plan?	□	□

Action Steps

If all answers are yes, continue to administration audit. If one or more answers are "no," try educating top management in regard to:

the benefits of affirmative action
the magnitude of the problem in both the corporation and the nation
the law of the land

The end result of obtaining top management commitment should be a clear statement of policy that is signed by the chief executive officer and distributed throughout all levels of the organization. If top management commitment cannot be obtained, the plan has little chance of success.

Administration Audit

First, the "mission" and the objectives of the action plan must be clearly established; but it is also important that the administrator's position in the organizational framework be clearly defined so that he or she has the resources and authority needed to accomplish the task. Once these important preliminaries are settled, he or she must acquire the data that will be needed for decisions on future action as well as a working acquaintance with the law pertaining to the field if that is not already achieved. Many administrators find themselves being called on to interpret the law as it evolves and to make recommendations concerning the changing legal framework.

Administration Audit

	yes	no
1. Is a top-level administrator in charge of the action plan?	□	□
2. Does this administrator have clear lines of authority upward?	□	□
3. Does this administrator have clear lines of authority downward?	□	□
4. Have the mission and the objectives of the action plan been established?	□	□
5. Do the objectives have specific and reasonable time deadlines?	□	□
6. Does the administrator have sufficient support staff?	□	□
7. Does the administrator have accurate and accessible data concerning women at various levels in the organization?	□	□
8. Does the administrator have national statistics concerning the employment of women?	□	□
9. Have periodic reports been established (preferably monthly) on female employment by level so that progress (or lack of it) can be monitored continuously?	□	□
10. Does the administrator have a working knowledge of the law? (If not, write the Women's Bureau and talk to corporate legal counsel.)	□	□
11. Have targets been set for the percentage of women employees by job classification for the next five years?	□	□

Action Steps

If any of questions one through six are answered "no," return to top management for needed resources or direction.

If any of questions seven through eleven are answered "no," the administrator should be able to solve the problem by personal action.

Recruitment Audit

The administrator is now in a position to begin concrete action by studying the complex of recruiting policy and determining whether these policies guarantee that women will not be discriminated against. Effective recruiting is going to become more difficult in the future as more organizations begin to compete on the college recruiting scene for women with the talent to reach the top levels of the organization. The early bird is obviously going to have the advantage. In the June 1970 *Monthly Labor Review*, Janice Hedger notes that "reports from more than a hundred businesses and industrial firms surveyed in late 1969 ... indicated that they plan to hire one-fifth more women college graduates from the class of 1970 than from the previous class." Undoubtedly, with an economic upturn and increased government pressure, this recruitment activity will increase over what she notes.

Recruitment Audit

		yes	no
1.	Have recruitment goals for women been set?	☐	☐
2.	Are women being actively recruited now for jobs at all levels?	☐	☐
3.	Are you recruiting at any predominantly-female colleges?	☐	☐
4.	Are there any female recruiters?	☐	☐
5.	Are your recruiters aware of your action plan so that they can describe it to a potential recruit?	☐	☐
6.	Is the potential female recruit given a clear idea of her likely progress in your organization?	☐	☐
7.	Are you making any attempt to provide career guidance to sophomore and junior college women?	☐	☐
8.	Are you confident that your recruiters don't unconsciously or consciously discourage women applicants?	☐	☐
9.	Do you avoid any employment agencies that discriminate?	☐	☐
10.	Do you avoid any employment advertising in media that segregate ads according to sex?	☐	☐

Action Steps

If any of the questions are answered "no," the administrator should be in a position to change them immediately; if that is difficult, questionable or impossible, the administrator does not have clear lines of authority, and must return to the more basic questions of top management commitment. It is not unusual to find this kind of backtracking; it must receive first priority whenever it appears.

Selection Audit

Recruiting is only part of the answer. The EEOC has been very restrictive in its definitions of a bona fide occupational qualification, and there will be very few situations in which organizations will be permitted to routinely select males in preference to females for certain jobs (or vice versa). The administrator must check to see that no implicit discriminations exist in selection in the form of selection devices such as paper and pencil tests or interviewing and hiring practices of the various line managers. If there are any problems with selection procedures, the administrator should be in a position of sufficient power to change these problems by mandate.

Selection Audit

		yes	no
1.	Are you certain that your organization does not currently use any formal selection devices (such as mechanical aptitude tests) that might unfairly discriminate on the basis of sex?	☐	☐
2.	Have you eliminated all other selection practices that might be discriminatory (such as certain interview procedures)?	☐	☐

Selection Audit—*Continued*   yes   no

3. Do you have any jobs for which you have defined sex as a bona fide occupational qualification? . . . . □   □
4. Will these jobs stand up to the EEOC's rather restrictive definition of bona fide occupation qualification? . . . . □   □
5. Do you know the percentage of female applicants for each job category? □   □
6. Is the percentage of women hired in each category at least as great as the percentage of women in the qualified applicant pool? . . . . □   □
7. Have selection targets been set? . . . . □   □
8. If selection targets are not met, do you have a system of reporting that will explain why? . . . . □   □

Action Steps

If the answer to any question (except 3) is "no," you should have the power as action plan administrator to correct these conditions. If you have answered "yes" to all these questions, it means that you have reviewed all job classifications and eliminated all non-BFOQ sex requirements.

Promotion Policies Audit

This audit is an important step, for in order to keep talented female person-nel, upward mobility must be both possible and highly visible. One of the first things to do is to eliminate any inequities in pay—quickly and fairly straight-forwardly—to comply with the law. More important, however, is to test the value structure of the organization to determine whether management training and development is available to qualified women and whether promotion "policy" discourages the advancement of women. If informal policy does dis-courage their development and promotion, it will not be *easy* to change because value structures are highly resistant to change, but it is *essential* to the success of the program.

Promotion Policies Audit

                                                                yes   no

1. Are there instances of unequal pay for equal work? . . . . □   □
2. Are women afforded the same potential career paths as men in your organization? . . . . □   □
3. Have you developed targets for the proportion of women in each job category and done manpower planning for the next five years? . . . . □   □
4. Do you have a system (such as the assessment center) for identifying qualified women? . . . . □   □
5. Are your annual performance appraisals sexually unbiased? . . . . □   □
6. Does a woman who does not feel she is being promoted rapidly enough have an appeal procedure with her supervisor? . . . . □   □
7. Does a woman who does not feel she is being promoted rapidly enough have an appeal procedure with the action plan administrator? . . . . □   □
8. Are women participating sufficiently in attendance at management training and development seminars sponsored by your organization? . . . . □   □
9. Are women participating sufficiently in other management development efforts, such as job rotation, etc.? . . . . □   □

Action Steps

If question one is answered "yes," the situation can be changed by top management mandate. If questions two through nine are answered "no," substantial long-term effort in

Promotion Policies Audit—*Continued*

effecting the required organizational change will be required of the administrator. Much of this may be accomplished through the attitude change techniques described in the "attitude audit." However, in many cases, specific administrative action may be taken. Some examples are:

a. review of all job classifications in which either sex is not represented in reasonable numbers.
b. review of salary and promotion progress of men and women who were hired at the same time into similar jobs to see if their progress has been dissimilar.
c. review of each employee's record to make sure that he or she has reached the highest possible level given the employee's capabilities and the organization's needs.
d. institution of a method of job posting so that all employees are aware of vacancies as they occur and that promotion into these vacancies is based on qualifications, not sex.
e. review of layoff and rehiring procedures to ascertain that they do not discriminate on the basis of sex.
f. review of all union contracts. Make sure that there are no discriminatory clauses and that there is a policy statement that discrimination is a violation of the contract.

Attitude Audit

All the progressive programs I have discovered have some formalized approach to achieve change in male managers' attitudes. It is essential that the action-plan administrator know what the salient attitudes are and how strongly they are felt. Any attitude measurement must be done skillfully so *all* the important attitudes are tapped. The administrator must be willing to call in professionals to provide the necessary information for diagnosing the extent of the problem. Then he must initiate extensive efforts to change organizational attitudes.

Attitude Audit

	yes	no
1. Do you know the direction and strength of the attitudes held by male employees on the issue of sex discrimination?	☐	☐
2. Do you know the direction and strength of the attitudes held by female employees on the issue of sex discrimination?	☐	☐
3. Do you possess the behavioral science competence either in-house or via consulting arrangement to measure salient attitudes?	☐	☐
4. Are you engaged in a substantial attitude change effort through education, group discussion and other behavioral science methods?	☐	☐
5. Do you possess organization change and development capabilities and are you using them to reduce sex discrimination?	☐	☐

Action Steps

If the answer to any of these questions is "no," significant effort is required by the action plan administrator to find the resources and initiate a program of attitudinal and organizational change. The success of any action plan is contingent upon the success of the attitude change effort. The following attitude change devices should be considered:

a. sensitivity training (task oriented and directed toward the problems of women).
b. role playing (have male employees assume the role of having a female boss).
c. educational efforts through films, lectures, notes, etc., defining the managerial capabilities of women and exploding traditional sexual stereotypes.
d. small group discussions centering on constructive ways of getting women into top management.
e. team building with women as active members of the teams.

Periodic Program Review

Finally, the administrator must be ready to evaluate the program periodically in order to affirm whether it is continuing to operate. This is going to be particularly appropriate in the next five years because our environment will be changing at such a rate that any plan established now is going to have to undergo substantial changes to be effective over this period. For example, as recruitment pressures grow more severe with increasing competition, additional effort and significant change may be needed.

Periodic Program Review

	yes	no
1. Does the action plan administrator receive periodic reports (preferably monthly) on the status of recruitment, selection and promotional efforts?	☐	☐
2. Does the action plan administrator meet periodically with women who have recently been recruited or promoted to determine their feelings?	☐	☐
3. Does the action plan administrator meet frequently (biannually at least) with top management to brief them on the progress to date?	☐	☐

As legislative remedies and pressures from liberation groups increase, we will see a movement toward more complete use of women in our work organizations. The effectiveness with which organizations adopt and implement innovative programs will determine the time required to achieve employment equality. The payoffs for removing discrimination are many: an increased pool of managerial talent, increased ability for men and women to interact as emotional and intellectual peers, placement of additional emphasis on performance rather than sex, etc. The problems encountered in attempting to reach these payoffs will also be great and will be manifested by resistance to change—by organizations and by individuals, both male and female. Progress to this goal can be achieved by active and energetic administrators who look at the total system effects of their activities and who use some form of organized checklist for effective action.

29

Today the Campuses,
Tomorrow the Corporations*

JOHN S. FIELDEN

Top managers today are talking the way academic deans and university presidents talked ten years ago—it can't happen here. At that time, students were criticized for being apathetic; student activities were poorly attended, student governments were foundering, and student rallies were nonexistent. As we all know, things have changed, and the change took place quickly. Interviews with top executives of major companies, however, show that management feels safe from the problems of youth's upheaval: "You're crazy; it can't happen here. We in management aren't as soft as you in academic circles. We know how to deal with loud-mouthed kids!" My own feeling is that what has happened to us on the campuses is going to happen to the corporations tomorrow.

One of our interviews was with the publisher of a large number of magazines in the electronics field. About a week before the Oct. 15 Moratorium, his secretary told him that one of the editorial assistants way down the line had requested an interview with him. All smiles, especially since she was a curvaceous young lady, he ushered her in. She informed him that she felt his publishing company should take a stand against the war in Vietnam, and that the company ought to take a full-page ad in *The New York Times,* letting the world know that it strongly endorsed the Moratorium and calling for an immediate withdrawal of U.S. troops. He looked at her and said, "Do you realize this would cost approximately $15,000 to $16,000?" Her reply was, "Oh, that's a relief. I thought it would cost $25,000!"

That argument shot down, he tried another: "How can my publishing company take a single posture that speaks for all its members?" "Oh, I've taken care of that," she replied. "I have a petition here that I've put together." Naturally, he expected to find the petition had been signed by most of the lower level clerical help, eager for a day off. But, to his astonishment, he found that about 80 percent of his key editorial people had signed up!

Suddenly the fun went out of it. He then had to hold a mass meeting and decide on the proper posture for the company. Debate raged. Fortunately for

*Source: Reprinted by permission from *Business Horizons* (June, 1970), 13-20.

his budget, the idea of the *Times* advertisement was scuttled. Instead, the company managed to get by with time off during the day for those who wanted to march with the demonstrators in New York City. But even so, the publisher was deeply shaken.

Is this an isolated example? No, it is not! Can the traditional hierarchical organization of big business be seriously threatened in the years to come? Most definitely. We have only to look at what is happening in the world's oldest hierarchical organization, the Roman Catholic church, which for 2,000 years has managed to make authority and rank stick. As managers, we ought to keep our eyes on what is taking place within church management. Much of modern corporate organization—indeed, our whole management concept of line-and-staff —is patterned after the Roman Catholic church's organization chart. Hence, evidence of breakdowns in the authority of church management, which are becoming more and more frequent, should be of real concern to business managers.

Opposition to the Pope's authority has become more outspoken. The liberal wing of cardinals holds that modern times require decision making not with and under the Pope, but in a spirit of cooperation and coresponsibility. Large numbers of cardinals are urging a quick and broad implementation of collegiality or shared authority. And they are getting it. Early this year, the Pope hinted at the possibility of another Protestant Reformation, similar to the break 400 years ago, which could split the Christian world. For the first time he compared Catholic rebels to Protestants. The Pope, sounding much like a beleaguered university president, cried out that the present generation was on what he called an intoxicated quest for novelty. In the name of progress, he charged, the past was being forgotten, tradition disrupted, and habits abandoned:

> Innovation, innovation. Everything is being questioned, everything is in a state of crisis. Man is no longer calm. He is seized by a frenzy, a dizziness, and sometimes a madness which makes him want to turn everything upside down in a blind trust that a new order, a new world, a regeneration still not clearly foreseeable is about to emerge.[1]

That is a perfectly accurate statement. That, as I see it, is precisely what is happening in our society, and I predict that corporations will be drawn into it too. People have become distrustful of representative government and are reluctant to delegate decisions. This thrust of self-expression has been felt in the labor unions. Recently, in the case of a large company in Boston, the union's negotiating committee recommended a wage package to its membership, only to be voted down 7 to 1. The same happened in the New York mail strike, and similar examples are occurring all over the country.

Some business leaders are amused when an academic administrator, the Pope, or a labor leader has his troubles because everybody demands a personal part in

1/*The Boston Globe*, Jan. 16, 1969.

the decision-making process, but the businessmen we interviewed did not think it half so much fun when we implied that they are next on the list. But they are. Man is no longer calm. Man has lost his trust. A recent *Newsweek* survey entitled "The Troubled American" shows that 46 percent of the U.S. population feels that the nation is likely to change for the worse over the next decade, and 40 percent feel that we are less able to solve our problems than we were five years ago. Higher education and greater freedom has led more people to come to the conclusion that, since they trust no one else, they have the right to participate in decisions affecting their lives.

Is this all bad? Is our society so perfect that we want to preclude protest against that which is highly mechanistic and impersonal? We must be able to make a virtue out of this demand for greater participation. We must respect the desires of all those in the Western World who reject the benefits of the computerized society, those who demand that the human element be retrieved from the mechanistic, and that the benefits of this affluent nation be made available to everyone. If we overreact, we may undermine one of the most important constructs of the democratic system: the right and obligation of everyone to express his opinions, however outrageous.[2]

The dissidents of the sixties have performed a service by questioning the values, assumptions, and institutions of American society, and they should, difficult as it may be, be respected. After all, these dissidents have not "copped out." The real danger to our children is not that they will be young and idealistic and *care*, want to stop constant wars, and want to help the poor of our country and of the world. The real danger is that they will say, "The hell with it! The whole system is so fouled up, we might as well take drugs and drop out. Stop the world, I want to get off." The young people who care enough to put down their transistor radios, uncork their eyes from the TV, raise Cain about social ills, and hold whole universities hostage for war and the ills of our violence-ridden society—these are the young people who are going to build fires under corporate managers.

BUSINESS NEXT

Many of the top managers we interviewed rejected the possibility of challenge. Nevertheless, I see it as inescapable that American business organizations are going to be part of the world-wide breakdown of hierarchical authority that is taking place. Many managers I have talked with have wondered why university presidents and deans have not turned the hose on "loud-mouthed" demonstrators. They forget that these people are our "customers." They forget that, in the early part of this century, they too buckled under pressure when labor

2/Compare *The Annals of the American Academy of Political and Social Science* (March, 1969), pp. ix-x.

demanded a voice in management decisions. If they did not have the muscle to put down labor unions, which were made up of employees rather than customers, they are hardly in a position to criticize universities for reluctance to call the cops on their children. Because that is who they are—their children and mine.

Labor won its voice and its peace with management. Students are winning—and I think rightfully so—a voice in decisions affecting their academic lives. And I think that today's managers are going to experience in their lifetime a similarly greater demand for increased participation by lower managers.

It is already coming to pass. We found in our interviews that subordinates can no longer be pushed around the way they once were. Today when a valuable young man is told to pack up his family and move from Schenectady to Pasadena, then three years later back to Waltham, he objects and gets away with it. Today when a young man is told to drop whatever he is doing, say, in finance, and move to a staff job in marketing, he objects if he does not want to do it, and gets away with it. In the past the artument has been, if you do not like it, quit. That argument was used against rebelling preunion workers, and is used against today's rebelling student. It did not work then, and it does not work now. Valuable employees will not take it; poor ones will—and managers know it.

I think that for extremely complex reasons we are entering a period of increased corporate democracy with all that will be good and bad about it. But it will be coming. For example, I think that salary ranges will shrink, that in this corporate democracy it will be much more difficult to justify a salary for the president of a company that is infinitely greater than that received by the President of the United States. I think that we will find more meaningful boards of directors being truly responsive, not only to the wishes of the stockholders, but to the needs of the employees. I think that super-remunerative stock options will disappear or at least be made available to more than just a favored few.

Corporations, if they are to survive, will be dramatically more responsive to the needs of society. Like universities, they will be forced to examine more closely their relationships with the military and with political groups. Corporate presidents will have to face head-on the question of whether their corporations can afford a social conscience, and whether maximum returns to stockholders is the ultimate goal. Even now, for example, in the annual shareholders' meeting of the United Fruit Company last year, John Fox, chairman of the board, began his remarks by examining the role of business in social programs:

All business has a tremendous stake in the solution of urban problems. Furthermore, private enterprise, in my opinion, holds the keys to the problem. Jobs must be found for the hard-core, so-called unemployables of the ghetto. By jobs I mean productive, useful, self-confidence-building jobs, not WPA shovel-leaning, soul-destroying activities.

The corporations of this country are being called upon to use their

skills in training and their ingenuity in supervision to find a way of gain-
fully employing a half million of these people who, ordinarily, would not
qualify for employment under industry's rigid job standards.

It will be a difficult task and an expensive one. The cost will be borne
by the shareholders of our major corporations. . . . I can only say that we
must carry our share of this program. The price for *not* doing so is beyond
calculation.

Managers of the future will have to face, just as university administrations
have done, the challenge of coping with social change and a redefinition of the
decision-making processes. They will have to be less the autocrats and more the
politicians in the best sense. They will have to be more liberal in their thinking,
not clinging blindly to socially outmoded ways of arriving at decisions and
getting jobs done. I say that no generation of Babbitts today can hope to keep
our nation together in moving toward decency in standards of living and equality
of opportunity for all. I say that managers of the future are going to have to
participate vigorously and whole-heartedly in the task of making our nation in
actuality what it can be in its promise.

The New Breed

Most businessmen will not reject everything that has been said. But what they
do say is that they will not have any trouble in dealing with demands by lower-
level employees to participate in significant decisions because their hierarchical
systems are attractive only to those who like authority. SDS types will not
apply; those who do apply will be organizational types who will be quite
comfortable within the system because it has defined limits, because it has rules,
because it is law and order and rationality personified.

But there are some flaws in this argument. First, it is true, according to Daniel
Yankelovich who has done some first-rate research in this area, that radical
students make up only about 3 percent of our college population.[3] And probably at any time in our history we would find 3 percent of our population
wildly radical in one direction or another. But the important thing Yankelovich's
research indicates is that 41 percent of the current academic population falls
into what he called the forerunner group. This group, he feels, points out the
future direction for our society. They are young men and women who come
mainly from affluent middle-class families, the first depression-free generation.

Unlike past generations, they do not seek the traditional benefits of a college
education—earning more money, having a better career, and enjoying a higher
status in society. All this they take for granted and minimize. Rather, they are
searching for something far more intangible—they want to change society, rather
than make out well within the existing system. They believe in draft resistance

---

3/Daniel Yankelovich, "Karl Marx vs American Business: Round 2," *Bell Telephone
Magazine* (September-October, 1969).

and civil disobedience. They are against the Vietnam war, against the military, against the police, against restrictions on marijuana, against conventional sex morality, and against other forms of restraints. They believe that something fundamental is wrong with American society, and they enthusiastically support radical reform of our most cherished institutions.

The campus radicals are not traditional Marxists; many of them are truly anti-intellectual and pick up their notions secondhand. But they get Marxist theory, filtered down through pamphlets, articles, and speeches. Thus, as Yankelovich points out, the New Left has absorbed, as if by osmosis, a number of premises with a Marxian flavor. First of all, the New Left believes that economic motives dominate other people and institutions, but not themselves; the New Left underscores the importance of power and views society in terms of social class. It believes that our society concentrates its power and resources in profit-making institutions, and thus feels that large-scale social and economic inequities are inevitable in a capitalistic society, so much so that the average person is doomed to exploitation by the capitalistic system.

At this point, most managers will be hoping that Yankelovich is right, that only 44 percent of the college population is threatened with indoctrination in beliefs such as these. Such a hope is dimmed by another statistic from the same source: college students are not alone in their conviction that business is overly concerned with profits and not sufficiently concerned with public responsibilities. Ninety-four percent of all college students endorse this view strongly or partially, but so do 92 percent of the noncollege youths. Furthermore, 79 percent of the parents of college students and 84 percent of the parents of noncollege youths also believe that business is overly concerned with profits. In other words, the view that business is excessively profit-minded is spread throughout our society—and perhaps may even include businessmen.

If it is true that most Americans want decreased emphasis on profits and increased emphasis on social responsibility, then companies may not easily hire, as they claim, employees who readily accept the values and hierarchical organization of business. Admittedly, one is unable to prove that young people hired into management, even though more socially minded than their elders, will chafe at serving under them in the corporate hierarchies. It seems obvious, however, that this clash of values will be disruptive of the ongoing activities of the corporation—at least that is what has happened so far in the church and on the campuses.

Is It So Bad?

But why is the possibility of such challenging of values and authority by youth so bad? Does business really want to hire young people who are dependent personalities, who enjoy working within rigid, seniority-ridden, arbitrary, and hierarchical structures? Does business really want young people who do not question, who do not probe the system, who do not think up new ways of doing things? I do not think so. In the past, too many people like this have worked to the detriment of business, especially if they were in managerial positions. Government has no monopoly on bureaucrats. Top executives are always complaining about their company's need for managers with entrepreneurial drive. Without entrepreneurs the game will be over.

One of Harvard's great economists, Joseph Schumpeter, predicted that the fall of big-business oriented capitalism would come not from the challenge of any other ideology, but from the death of the entrepreneurial spirit.[4] Entrepreneurs are rebels, in a sense, against bureaucracy, bigness, and hierarchical structures. A viable free enterprise system needs challenges, and these challenges have usually come from youth.

Recently, many emotional accolades have been paid to our successful moon shot. Original plans, however, called for a direct flight to the moon. One man about five steps down in the hierarchical structure of NASA felt that a different plan was essential. This was to go into moon orbit and launch a ship from that position. To make his opinion heard, he went around to superiors and spoke to the head of the program. In many large companies, stubbornness of this kind is simply not tolerated, and the pride of senior executives can lead to the failure of the company or cause good people to leave. Some corporations would have fired an employee for such an action.

Many young people are becoming more aware of the fact that few innovations in business come from the senior people. For example, the modern supermarket as we know it was not developed by an established chain such as A&P or First National; A&P, in fact, has had a hard time maintaining its position. The modern supermarket has evolved through the efforts of small independents and younger men. The big, old organizations resisted this movement for years and were almost forced out of business because of their stubbornness. Similarly, the discount stores were developed by independents—Korvettes, Masters, and the rest—not by the established stores like Macy's, Gimbel's, or Filene's. In every case, young men were instrumental in beginning these ventures and in making them successful. Older organizations were threatened, were forced to change their practices, and to go along with the new trends.

The facts of life, the facts of business, and the facts of organizations are being taught at business schools today. Students are learning that major innovations are being made by young businessmen. They also learn that recognized institutions with senior executives often turn down exciting new ideas. For example, when Edwin Land was a sophomore at Harvard he went to Eastman Kodak with his now famous Polaroid camera. Kodak refused him on the grounds that, through their experience, the public would not be interested in such low-quality pictures. As every business school student knows, Land went out, started his own company, and became fabulously successful.

4/Joseph Schumpeter, *Capitalism, Socialism, and Democracy* (New York: Harper & Row, Publishers, 1942).

Another promising young man with a brilliant new idea was turned down by a large corporation. Joseph Wilson, believing in the Xerox technique as a new copying procedure, could not find anyone to support him. No established company would pick up his idea, so he developed it on his own and created a dazzlingly successful company without the financial backing of any large, reputable established organization. Another example is the development of the Cassette, a relatively new arrival on the corporate market. Companies such as RCA and CBS refused to touch the idea. As a result, it finally came out of a smaller, independent company in Europe and had to be exported to the United States.

Older people, if progressive, may go so far as to say to a young person with a new idea that, if the market research can support it, they will go along. Young people know, however, that one cannot market research a new idea. For example, who would have bought a Polaroid camera ten years ago before anyone knew anything about it? People cannot imagine new things.

To get ahead in business today certain qualities are required: courage and willingness to take a risk. But these are not qualities of the typical senior business executive. The outstanding business successes of the past few years have all been men who started their own organizations at a relatively early age, and who have acted in ways the Establishment considers unconventional and unacceptable. Some examples are Jim Ling of Ling-Temco-Vought; Saul Steinberg of Leasco; H. Ross Perot of Electronic Data Systems Corporation of Dallas who quit as a salesman for IBM when the company wouldn't listen to his ideas, formed his own company and now has an estimated net worth of over $300 million. In all these cases, each businessman was turned down by big corporations and well-known executives. Also worth noting is the fact that these newly formed companies have made more money and grown more phenomenally than have such corporate giants as Ford and General Motors.

Every argument has its rebuttal, of course. Cases like Land, Ling, and Steinberg and the rest still refer to people who accept the values of our capitalistic society. But many of the young people I am concerned with are rebelling against these values. And these youngsters may, indeed, be the brightest and most valuable people entering adult society today. Thus the vital question facing corporate managers is this: can you afford the risk of acquiring young people with a capacity for creative new thinking, who also carry with them the seeds of a challenge to, if not the destruction of, the traditional hierarchical structure of American business?

I think that business needs these bright, original people, and I think if they understood the potential for change within American business practices, they would want business. The situation resembles Freud's description of the two cold porcupines who wanted to huddle together for warmth. The closer they got, the more they stuck one another. This dilemma in human interrelations is going to trouble management ever more deeply in the future. What we need is to have the battle cry ring out and have everyone rush to the barricades—and, somehow, on some miraculous way, find that all of us are on the same side of the barbed wire. Making this miracle come to pass should be an important challenge to advertising executives who are used to solving problems of communication between groups of people who seemingly have nothing in common.

Research has proven that if senior executives want their employees to be innovative, creative, and responsible and to make contributions they must encourage participation in management decisions; otherwise, they only invite passive obedience and sycophancy. But if middle management allows lower management freedom, then top management must also allow middle management freedom. There is no evidence that age necessarily means better decisions, nor that more imposing titles mean better work.

We are now at the point where middle managers are managing lower managers, who know more than the middle managers. And top managers are managing people who know more than they do. This is due to the rapid advance of technology. As a result, top management people are twice removed from the young M.B.A. graduates, and the business pace is becoming more and more accelerated. Somehow these groups have to be brought together, but to do so deeply threatens seniority, which is the heart of all hierarchical organizations.

But to acquiesce to more participation in management decision making means that older executives in corporations must recognize the gap between their profit-oriented values and the ever-increasing social consciousness of our people. Senior executives must recognize the idealism of today's youth, their reluctance to simply "chase a buck." The Puritan ethic that motivated us is being rejected. When young people say that someone comes from a "good" family today, they do not necessarily mean he comes from a rich family. Our children's heroes are not Horatio Algers.

THE CORPORATE PLAN

If by this time a businessman remains convinced that it will be business as usual in the future, that the increasing social consciousness of the brightest young people today and its impact on corporations is a myth and a straw man, then he has nothing to worry about. If he thinks that even bright young M.B.A.s, whom he would have every reason to believe would be more tolerant of business values, will not increasingly chafe in the future over lack of participative opportunities, then full speed ahead. But if a businessman is willing to consider the possibility that corporations lead no charmed life in our society, if he suspects that they will be caught up in social change as much as—if not even more so—other institutions, then what should he do about it?

It seems to me that corporations are fortunate in not having to repeat the mistakes made in the past by other institutions, such as education and the church, which have borne the first brunt of questioning. First of all, top executives in corporations must, I feel, compromise on the position that their responsibility to return maximum profits to shareholders means that they must not divert significant corporate resources to the alleviation of social problems. They must recognize the fact that what is good for the nation is in the long run good for General Motors—that if our free enterprise system cannot divert resources to the have-nots of our population, the price may be constant turmoil in our streets.

Corporations must also reexamine their part in a world-wide social system that has led to constant warfare. I know of no executive who, as the SDS claims, wants warfare as a means of making profits. But we are all caught up on a mad merry-go-round offering no brass rings for mankind. If big business is truly influential in our country and throughout the world, surely we must learn how to force an outbreak of peace.

Corporations must face up to and eradicate racial and religious prejudice operative even implicitly in the organization's behavior. If we are a business-oriented society then business must intensify its already impressive beginnings.

Corporations must learn to seek commonly shared values through greater permissiveness and participation. As M.I.T. did last year, corporations may have to call a pause in ongoing operations and allow lengthy, fully participative meetings to occur among all segments and levels of persons in the organization, to allow all to ventilate feelings relative to the corporations' posture vis-a-vis self-interest and societal responsibility. Through greater participation, more shared values must result, and even those whose ideas are not adopted should at least feel they had a free voice prior to the decision.

Corporations therefore must have flatter organization charts, and a greater sense of community and dedication to achievement of mutually accepted goals should result. It is more than possible, I think, that if a corporation decided that it must both be fair in returning adequate dividends to stockholders and in contributing corporate resources toward the cure of society's problems, then it is reasonable for all members of that corporation to be willing to make the extra effort to generate the extra profits required.

From my talks with a wide range of young, bright people considering careers in business, I have come to the conclusion that it will be companies this open, this flexible, and this responsible, that will attract the best young people into tomorrow's top managerial roles. Age makes us cynical. Experience tells us that the world is gray, not black and white. But let us do the best we can for this country. By our actions, we must help America's youth recover some of the lost idealism we felt about our nation when we were young. Let us rebuild and emphasize social responsibility as *part of*—instead of *an alternative to*—the free enterprise system.

30

The Corporation and Community: Realities and Myths*

FRANK H. CASSELL

It is now twenty years since a board member of one of the largest Chicago banks proposed that the bank employ some Negroes. The board chairman, aghast at the suggestion, asked if the director didn't realize that then *they* would be sitting on the same toilet seats. The board turned down the proposal.

At the close of the decade of the 1960s the Chicago banks, including the one involved in that incident, passed the hat for $815,000 to finance a black "think tank," originated and headed by some of the most militant black leaders in Chicago.

That is change. It is change perhaps even broader in its implications than some of the contributing businessmen may yet realize, for it departs radically from the usual "safe" participations of business symbolized by Junior Chamber of Commerce man-of-the-year contests and the Community Fund charities administered by whites for blacks. It would be incorrect to interpret the support of the think tank as reflecting a trend in business in general. But its structure and support does imply that a number of businessmen, among them men considered leaders of the Chicago business community, have had their community stance affected by profound social changes in the city. And it is significant that it is in the historically conservative banking industry that such a change comes into focus.

Chicago, like other large American cities, is undergoing a painful metamorphosis. On the one hand, it is engaged in a vast effort to rebuild the central city. Billions of dollars worth of new steel and glass high-rise office and apartment buildings are going up. The banking and insurance industries have been in the forefront of this building boom.

Simultaneously, great changes are taking place in the character of life in the city. Chicago lost population during the 1960s and the rate was speeded in the last half of the decade; its population has decreased to pre-depression levels. A third of the remaining population is black; 56 percent of elementary school

*Source: Reprinted from *MSU Business Topics* (Autumn, 1970), 11-20, by permission of the publisher, Division of Research, Graduate School of Business Administration, Michigan State University.

pupils and 48 percent of the high school pupils are black, many of them increasingly angry at the system which they see as designed to keep them in second class roles. Black unemployment figures continue to be more than twice as high as white, and far higher than that among the young people. The jobs which the burgeoning black population might fill are fleeing to the suburbs; the metropolitan area outside the city gained 277,000 jobs from 1957 to 1966, but the city of Chicago lost 48,000 jobs. It is difficult or impossible for many blacks to follow the jobs because of housing discrimination in the suburbs and the great costs of commuting long distances.

These economic facts, plus a profound change in the feelings of the black community—growth in black consciousness, search for a black identity, regard for one's heritage, and reaction to white rejection in housing and school patterns—are making for a qualitative difference in the problems of the city. The Kerner Commission warning that we are drifting toward two separate societies, one white and one black, a sort of indigenous apartheid, has not altered the drift. Some say, including both white leaders and black militants, that it is only a matter of time.

Separateness may be much further advanced than many of us are willing to admit. Separateness has gone a long way when a militant black leader in Chicago attempts to roll down the curtain and not permit whites to enter black neighborhoods at night. The suggestion was made by the Rev. C. T. Vivian, Executive Director of "Think Tank," at a moment of deep fury in the black communities over a raid by district attorney's police on a Black Panther apartment, a raid in which two Panther leaders were killed. The Rev. Vivian withdrew his angry proposal for a curfew, but not before the whites got the message.

The political ferment is reflected in the high schools, too, where black students are increasingly strident—and sometimes threatening—about the lack of quality of their schools, about what they call irrelevancy of the traditional school program, and about the shortage of black teachers and administrators who, they believe, can understand the black perspective better than whites. In some areas this has led to demands for community control of schools, through little boards of education responsible to the people of an area rather than to a central hierarchy. In other areas, it has meant turmoil in the schools, particularly at times when community tension is high. In most areas, disillusion with school leads many black young people to drop out (or to be pushed out), which increases the unemployment problem, already a staggering one among poorly trained young blacks. White-managed industries in and near the ghettos feel the effects of this kind of unrest. If they fill their work forces from the area, they find the discontent transplanted into factories; some first line white supervisors leave because they fear for their own safety.

These forces add impetus to the flight of higher income whites from the city. Those who stay behind are more and more determined to preserve their turf and not let the blacks cross over from "the other side"—the other side of the city, or the neighborhood, or the street that has been a traditional dividing line between white homes and black. Where this has occurred in other smaller cities the remaining whites have sought to preserve their political power, giving only token appointments to blacks. This too has heightened political tension. The whites don't see the fact that the vital, pulsating new force of the cities is a rapid increase in determination by blacks to have a say in their own destiny. There is an increase in strong, savvy black leadership, including men of education and experience in coping with both the militants and with recalcitrant white leadership. They want a share of the power, and they are going to get it. The choice as to how they get it is pretty much up to the whites.

An Example of Business Response

It is in this context that Chicago's Strategy Center, the think tank, was born. Basically it provides business support for "the black communities to establish its own priorities," in the words of one of its supporters. At the Center, staff will be all black. It will use the funds for research and training, conducting surveys to establish needs, assisting with budgets, and taking packaged proposals to the city and federal government and to foundations for funding. There seem to be no grandiose ideas about training for the use of power; instead, the focus will be on the economic, educational, and health problems that plague the ghetto. Presumably the Center will not engage in politics, although some of the programs it devises will have to be promoted politically by someone.

The Center is being supported for a variety of motives—some lofty, some not. One of the motives is the hard-headed practical need to face reality. Planners think that by 1980 blacks will have the majority vote in Chicago and that a black mayor may be elected in that year.

Some of the most influential of the white contributors probably clearly perceive the need for an avenue for sharing power with the black community and would like it to be an avenue where they can erect some of the traffic signals. The Center, if it works well, can be a valuable training locale for black leaders. Leadership has been diffuse in the black community; it has been hard to know who to listen to. There is some feeling that the Center can be a black structure for the white power structure to deal with.

Others are perhaps more concerned with safeguarding their investment in the city and are thinking about the business climate of Chicago under a black administration. Business has no intention of abandoning its home base, and there are those new buildings to prove it. Some business supporters of the think tank see their contributions as sort of an insurance policy for all that plate glass.

Those are some of the white views of the Strategy Center, and they are a mixed bag, indeed. The black views may be just as mixed. There is no concensus that the people running the Center really are Chicago's black leaders. Some say the Center people are just being paid off by whites. There is much skepticism about the nature of business support. (One old-line black leader, not involved in the Strategy Center, wondered, for example, if the whites were "doing the right thing for the wrong reasons.") They wonder what will happen when the black-proposed solutions to problems don't coincide with white solutions.

There are, indeed, many pitfalls, and we don't know whether the Strategy Center will ever be able to change any of these facts the banker-supporter was talking about. Among the pitfalls are several financial ones: the Center still has not been given tax exempt status because it is not clear how it can avoid political action entirely, the businessmen have set up "fiscal safeguards for the disbursement of money" although they say they are not policing the programs, and there is no present provision for continued business support of the Center once the initial funds run out. There are other pitfalls, too; it seems inevitable that there will be considerable infighting, a good deal of rhetoric, and the destruction of some false hopes. One big question mark centers around Mayor Daley, without whom nothing much happens in Chicago, but who has taken a "hands off" approach to the Center.

Real Significance

But despite the conflicting views about the things that can go wrong, the establishment of the Center has real significance. It is a facing of the reality that blacks do have problems that concern us all and that blacks want a greater share in decision making to solve them. It is a recognition of the need for thinking and planning and understanding that you can't operate a society in change on an ad hoc basis. At the very least, the Center does give status to a point of view, a black perspective which black leaders have always insisted is simply not being heard. If the Center works, it can be a step toward an orderly transference of power to a soon-to-be-realized black majority in the city. If it doesn't work, the inevitable changes will be less orderly. Either way, it is a dramatic departure from the traditional business method of dealing with community problems, one very much out of character for conventional business organization and operation.

Traditional Business Response to Change

The mechanisms of business, like all authoritarian institutions, are not well suited for coping with basic change outside its product markets. Business has no strong internal mechanism for criticism of its performance in the community. Unlike an institution like Congress, it has no constituency that votes it in or out on the basis of its success in community life. Its organization is designed for stability, for continuity, not for change.

The conventional business policy has been to place the bets on those in power, people like Mayor Daley, because they seem to give the best promise of stability as against the more menacing leaders who want to change the status quo. Where the power structure has had to give way before powerful underlying forces, the strategy has usually consisted of participating in the least risky ventures, minimizing the risk with strings attached to the money contributed in order to control the speed and direction of the advance, and supporting politically only those dissidents who could be counted upon to merge with the establishment. (Martin Luther King was invited by business executives to talk in Winnetka, Illinois, not before Selma and Bull Conner's cattle prods, but after his "I have a dream" sermon at the March on Washington, a march the executives did not make.) However, the conventional business policy for action in the community has led to supporting the forces of reaction, the establishment, the entrenched political forces rather than the forces which accommodate change and prepare the way for new leadership. The Chicago Urban League is an interesting case in point. It is only a few years ago that business supporters of the League could have met in a telephone booth; the League was trying to cause the schools to change. But in 1970, 2,500 business leaders and others attended a luncheon to pay homage to the retiring Urban League director. A very safe event.

The interpretation of this by the underclass could hardly be that the establishment was in their favor. And when company policies began to change, it was to support organizations which, though useful, had themselves sometimes lost touch with the times and the realities and the people. The old line groups working for change got support only when newer, much more radical groups appeared and threatened.

Conventional corporate policy is based essentially upon a stable environment with change occurring only at a rate sufficient to be easily absorbed. Because business mistrusts unorthodoxy, it also mistrusts the "bubble up" theory of participative democracy, of community action programs which have been spawned in the cities under the sponsorship of the Office of Economic Opportunity. (This policy began to be abandoned in the closing months of the Johnson administration and has been buried by the Nixon administration.)

The businessman is a top-down person. That is how he is selected, how he is trained, and how he is developed in an environment which is essentially authoritarian and carefully structured. Important decision making is limited to the few at the top (despite the years of effort by Peter Drucker and Douglas MacGregor to change things); and those at the bottom are expected to comply. In some magical way hierarchical position seems to confer wisdom regardless of knowledge or experience; those down the line with less status have less wisdom and competence.

The Conventional Stand

The conventional business stand is in favor of strong top-down government as against grass roots neighborhood decision making because the former is perceived as the most "efficient" way to govern. This concept leads the businessman to work through established organizations which are essentially top-down, such as the charity and settlement house boards. The typical structure of a

Community Fund parallels the business organization; in fact, it is often designed by business consultants whose object is efficiency, not necessarily relevancy. Attempts of black people and poor people to participate in the fund allocation process are resisted bitterly, much as some school superintendents resent meddling by "outsiders" in the affairs of the schools. Most important, these money allocations are directed to preserving the structure and the underlying assumptions of those who control it; they are steered away from those in the black or Spanish-speaking community who would use the money to develop political power to challenge the establishment and change the system.

This is similar to the Community Action Organizations which were converted into nodules of political power and were opposed alike by northern big city mayors, southern governors, businessmen, and the established federal bureaucracies. The Community Action Program (CAP) was designed deliberately to skirt the established organizations because they had shown no particular talent or interest in solving the problems of hard core poverty or unemployment. It was thought that those experienced in the condition of poverty might contribute to its solution. No more upsetting measure could have been devised, and before the nodules could grow into power centers they were effectively squelched by the passage of the Green Amendment. And order has been restored with the new (or old) federalism so that poverty funds and other funds for relieving the condition of the poor are channeled through the offices of the governors, from there to the mayors, and from there to the neighborhoods—the trickle down theory.

The distaste of the businessmen for doing business with those outside the established organizations is represented by the virtual failure of the Concentrated Employment Program of the U.S. Department of Labor which began in the latter part of the 1960s. The object of this effort was to link up indigenous leadership of the ghetto with other organizations both public and private to provide a job delivery system including outreach, job readiness training, remedial health care, and job survival skills leading to a job in private enterprise.

It was believed that if those who needed jobs, those who operated the employment market, and those who had the jobs to give, were put under one administrative tent, the whole operation would be more efficient, duplication of functions would be reduced, and understandings would be developed among employers, government, and the poor which would lead to productive and cooperative relationships. Nothing of the kind happened. The Community Action Programs at the grass roots let the employers know in no uncertain terms that they were not liked in the slums; nor did they think private enterprise had much to offer in the line of social improvement. The employer reciprocated. He was not interested in revolutionaries and incompetents; furthermore, he didn't want to get mixed up with government bureaucracy—meaning the federal government.

About the same time the Labor Department developed the idea of contracting out to private enterprises the complete package of training and job development, with the expectation that the community action people would refer unemployed people to the job or training openings. And this didn't really work either. An example serves to illustrate this point. In a large city in Connecticut, a defense contractor received a contract under a Manpower Administration grant from the Labor Department to train ghetto people for employment in the various industries in the town. The defense contractor's office was located at one end of a large building in the slum area. At the other end of the building was the Community Action Program. A door between the two ends of the building was locked, having never been opened during the tenure of the tenants despite the fact that the CAP and the defense contractor were supposed to cooperate in putting people into the training program and to work.

In city after city this is the case. The employer prefers to do the job himself even if he does not have the expertise or the relationship with the slum. This he is doing under the National Alliance of Businessmen. No doubt he is more efficient in organizing to do the job of employment than the people at the bottom of the job scale. This reluctance of the businessman to share authority with others in the community represents a deep desire for order, the need to control his situation (as he has been taught in business schools), and the need to assure the continuity of the firm. It reflects also the public relations man's approach to things to make sure the numbers are counted and the credit goes where it belongs—to the company, as in the case of the National Alliance of Businessmen.

A Philosophical Gap

More importantly the inability of community action people, ghetto militants, and business to work together represents more than political differences, although this is a factor; more than the businessman's distaste for long hair and blue jeans, more than his resentment of having to share power with people he feels have not earned the honor by hard work. It represents a huge philosophical gulf. In the Connecticut situation the employer said that he did not cooperate with the CAP because the people whom the CAP sent for training did not fit the jobs and that they (the CAP) raised their expectations too high. The CAP people said that the employers did not have jobs which fit their people. Here is a conflict of tradition and of philosophy. The employer expects to reject people who are not qualified according to his standards. The individual, if not qualified, should adjust. This is the expectation of free private enterprise. The CAP people, however, expect the enterprise system to adjust to the people, that is, if they have no qualifications, make a job of some kind or redesign it and train the person to fill it. The enterprise system should help people realize their ambitions, even the lowliest of them. The company should serve people, not vice versa.

If one looks particularly closely at these arguments he will find that the CAP people are challenging the legitimacy of the private enterprise system. How can it be justified solely on the basis of profits? What about the welfare of people and the good of society? Does not business exist at the pleasure of the people? Should it not serve them? Would it not be better if business had a social purpose as its prime goal? Whether or not the businessman has sensed this, he has kept away from these people as much as possible.

A Corporate Dichotomy

The corporate ethos, regardless of the imperatives of community, is to make profits and not to produce social uplift. Social responsibility must always be an adjunct. Consequently, it is not reasonable to expect community relations to be the firm's specialization. It is equally unreasonable to expect the corporation to take the load of the community on its shoulders, or to expect it to be expert in solving such problems. Furthermore, if the corporation assumes this function it must then expect to live with the criticism which inevitably comes to all who would attempt to lead and influence social change, criticism which may affect it adversely in its product markets.

The realities are that the corporation faces two ways, inward and outward. Its inner core capitalizes upon the specialized skills of its managers and other employees to exploit markets. It is beyond the range of normal expectation that men expert in manufacturing and marketing will be equally expert in the political and social milieu of the outer environment. If the chairman of the firm is skilled in his ability to be persuasive with the commerce commission or relates well to black militants this is a bonus for the firm, but he is paid to make a profit. No matter how successful his community relations, he will not survive too many poor profit years.

Having to face both outward and inward leads to a dichotomizing of management. Over time individuals emerge who develop the characteristics which bring success in the outer environment, including interest in human beings, a capacity to understand political and social complexities, and above all the ability to exist in ambiguous situations. In contrast, those who live on the inside tend to work by plan, are often uneasy with politics, and are uncomfortable with ambiguity. In other words, specialization exerts itself to lead people either toward the inside of the corporation or toward the outside.

As time goes by a gap develops between the external and the internal people, much in the manner of the "growing apart" of the corporate labor relations people and the line operating people. In both cases there develop differences in viewpoint. The corporate labor relations people come to view the politics of elective leadership as they affect corporate collective bargaining strategy. This often places the labor relations people at odds with the internally oriented people whose lack of contact with the outside preserves a parochial view, often times a hard line which ignores the politics of power over which the firm has limited control.

In much the same way the corporation executives who face toward the community inevitably are confronted with the realities of a world which they cannot control. Employees can be fired, but not the community. Such executives often find themselves interpreting the outside to an unsympathetic internal management.

The people inside are often impatient with the tools of diplomacy and the complexities of social and political organization. The results of community activities cannot be chalked up neatly on the blackboard in the manner of so many automobiles produced per hour. The people operating on the inside, accustomed to operating within a structured and controlled environment, as contrasted to the uncontrolled community, have difficulty understanding why this outer world cannot be put in order.

Sufficient time has passed since business and industry have employed labor relations and community relations experts to suggest that these careers are not the roads to the top of the firm. When the promotion decisions are made, it is the person who has attended to the nitty gritty of selling, producing, or financing who gets the job. And this is entirely consistent with the object of the corporation, namely to make profits. As long as the goal of the firm is so perceived, the community relations function is likely to be secondary and correspondingly the level of skill and effort applied to it will lag behind the skill and effort devoted to the operation of the firm. In addition the evidence seems to be that men allocated by the corporation to handle the community relations of the corporation are not "main line" executives and consequently lack the prestige or power within the corporation to materially influence corporate policy. (In the case of companies which have taken on government contracts to train the hard core or to administer the Job Corps camps, the men assigned have not generally been main liners, and furthermore when cutbacks have occurred their reintegration into the main organization has either been accomplished with maximum difficulty or not at all. One large eastern firm which had held large government contracts to improve the skills of the poor was unable to effect the reintegration and tried to convert the government contracts division into an internal human-relations consulting division. It was not a success. The main divisions felt they could get along without internal human relations consultants.)

Calculating the Riskiness of Community Involvement

Although the financing of the black "think tank" may be a portent of things to come insofar as corporate policy toward the community is concerned, business today is not generally geared to engaging in such high risk community relations. The businessman is sophisticated in the things he does well, namely managing financial and entrepreneurial risk. Community risk, however, is another matter. Typically he ranks his risk from high to low in a sort of cost-benefits relationship. At the low risk end of the community activity scale (high prestige) is the Community Fund, the settlement house, or a liaison relationship between his suburban church and a community organization in the city. He has substantial control; the results, being based upon the past, are predictable; the assignment is not overly time consuming; and he is not likely to find his name in the newspaper because of some rash act of the staff. But in today's terms the organization is not likely to be particularly relevant either.

At the high risk end of the scale, he might find himself participating in a privately financed, slum based and led model city-type program which challenges the established political and economic institutions to which the company he represents is linked. This is a situation which exists in Chicago today. A number of firms are supporting a community based program called Towards Responsible Freedom. The program is located in the Kenwood-Oakland section of the city. It is a self-help effort to create community structure and machinery to cope with the problems left untouched by the established political structure and government programs—including preparation for better jobs, improvement of the local schools, elimination of garbage in the streets, better law and order—and justice for the residents, renovation and improvement of housing, and self-developed local businesses. No money was allocated to the area by the federal Model Cities program.

The community organization known as KOCO includes just about everybody in the area including the leaders of the Black P Stone Nation, a street gang. It does not, however, include the local alderman. It does not include the local school people. Many of its leaders have at one time or another been in jail or prison. A chief organizer of KOCO, who is also a leader of the Black P Stone Nation, was charged with murder but later acquitted. KOCO is financed through the Community Renewal Society from the contributions of foundations, individual givers, and a few corporations—referred to collectively by the Chicago police as soft-headed liberals who are financing revolution. The strings attached are minimal. During the past two years as KOCO has been getting under way, repeated police harassment of the organization generally has not frightened supporters into withholding their funds. But the police efforts have not helped to broaden the financial support either.

It is indeed significant that in the range of risk value, many Chicago corporations seem more willing to finance a "think tank" despite its often violent rhetoric than a community self development and self determination effort. Perhaps community action ranks higher on the risk scale than revolutionary speech, especially when the condition is that the speech must be non-political, in order to get tax deductible corporate contributions. After all, community self development effort may produce fundamental changes in the community.

The basic difference between the community fund and KOCO is that the businessman who supports KOCO does not have strings which he can pull if the neighborhood people get out of line. He has essentially given up his right to control as to how the money will be spent, and who will be employed. This is alien to the prudent businessman or the politician who needs to maintain control.

Whether it is the businessman or the established political structure, or old line unions, this kind of community activity is the ultimate in risk—though it may turn out that this is one of the few ways slum and ghetto people can be aided to enter the main stream of American society through self-government and breaking down of colonialist control.

The evidence so far is that businessmen in general are not yet ready for this kind of long range political planning. Support of rhetoric, yes, as long as it is apolitical—action no. And in this they are joined by practically everybody in the organized structure from the president of the United States on down. The burgeoning black and brown communities, however, will continue to militate for involvement in the action. The "think tank" and the Community Renewal Society efforts in Kenwood-Oakland are among the very few efforts remaining where the underclass can have a say and can develop community experience in leadership.

It seems to be that business efficiency can be brought to bear on solving unemployment, housing, and urban planning programs, as long as it is through the established structure. It can solve problems as long as the people of the slums have no effective say to change the plans, or to obstruct them. This is how the model cities program seems to be proceeding. Without the grass roots, business participation is easier to get. Without the CAP community action activities, the National Alliance of Businessmen is willing to exercise its talents in finding jobs for people.

Their efforts can be brought to bear best upon those things that cannot talk back—such as pollution. Maybe, as Tom Wicker observes rather cynically, Mr. Nixon's state of the Union message was a clever flank movement into the environment and away from the ghetto. Suddenly almost everyone rich and poor and in between is concerned about choking to death. These quite legitimate concerns represent finite challenges which can be met (unlike the ghetto) by energy, technology, and money without challenging the system.

That is the word: finite. Finite, certain, planned, order, continuity, those are the needs of business. And it attempts to shape the environment around it to fill those requirements. It can do that with the physical environment to some extent, it cannot do it with people.

This should be a troublesome concern for the educator, especially business school deans and faculties. How does one train a businessman to cope with a world in profound change where values are shifting, and the environment is quite uncertain? The business school training equips the individual with the tools to take the risk out of taking risks. It teaches him about controls so that he can operate with greater certainty that error will not creep in. He is given knowledge about systems planning so that he can account for every last item in his planning. He is taught supervisory skills which work when the work force is docile, or when it is organized and follows carefully designed procedures to settle differences. But he is not equipped or even selected because he has the capacity to cope with risk and uncertainty and revolutionary forces. There is nothing in the business school which lets him know that his tools will seldom if ever help him solve the problems of the community. It is a peculiar fact of life which also affects the business school that we believe we can manage the most difficult of all endeavors, namely, human affairs, by ear, without training, without knowledge, without experience. Perhaps that is why we do it so badly.

It is human qualities—generosity and selfishness, loving and hating, cooperativeness and perverseness—which make molasses out of the best designed procedures either inside or outside the organization. We teach people to delegate responsibility when they are not psychologically able to relinquish it. We skip over political concepts that have much to do with how people are governed and govern. We say very little about how authoritarian organizations such as business clash with the underlying notions of democracy.

We must ask whether business should be socially responsible. Can it have multiple and even contradictory objectives? Should it exist to serve the society or to make profits; what really is its ultimate objective? Does the man attracted to business have the special talents and the capacity to be a leader in a world of change and uncertainty which is characteristic of the community? Will businesses and businessmen respond constructively to increasingly harsh criticism, or will their response exacerbate the already wide gulf between the corporation and a large portion of the community?